8/24/07

PRISONS

LIBRARY IN A BOOK

————————————⬛━━━━━━━━━━————————————

PRISONS

Jeffrey Ferro

☑®
Facts On File, Inc.

PRISONS

Facts On File, Inc.
132 West 31st Street
New York NY 10001

Library of Congress Cataloging-in-Publication Data

Ferro, Jeffrey.
   Prisons / Jeffrey Ferro.
      p. cm.—(Library in a book)
   Includes bibliographical references and index.
   ISBN 0-8160-6035-5
   1. Prisons—United States. 2. Prisons—Research—United States. 3. Prisons—United States—Bibliography. I. Title. II. Series.
   HV9471. F465 2006
   365′.973—dc22   2005003370

Facts On File books are available at special discounts when purchased in bulk quantities for businesses, associations, institutions or sales promotions. Please call our Special Sales Department in New York at (212) 967-8800 or (800) 322-8755.

You can find Facts On File on the World Wide Web at http://www.factsonfile.com

Text design by Ron Monteleone
Graph by Sholto Ainslie

Printed in the United States of America

MP Hermitage 10 9 8 7 6 5 4 3 2 1

This book is printed on acid-free paper.

CONTENTS

PART III
APPENDICES

PART I

OVERVIEW OF THE TOPIC

CHAPTER 1

INTRODUCTION TO PRISONS

In a quote attributed to the 19th century Russian novelist and former prisoner Fyodor Dostoyevsky, "The degree of civilization in a society can be judged by entering its prisons." In American society, when measured against the total U.S. population, more Americans were incarcerated in state and federal prisons in the United States in 2003 than in any other country in the world. According to the Bureau of Justice Statistics, the rate of prison incarceration in the United States in 2003 was 482 per 100,000 residents, an increase from the 2002 rate of 411 per 100,000 U.S. residents.

Physical abuse of inmates occurred in American prisons nationwide, according to the *New York Times*,[1] and four correctional officers were killed in the line of duty in 2003. Indeed, U.S. prisons are highly dangerous places—for inmates and prison staff, alike. Housing a mix of criminal offenders, from drug abusers to murderers, while ensuring the safety of correctional staff and protecting the rights of inmates is a complex and daunting challenge undertaken each day in prisons nationwide.

Also troubling, in 2003, some nine out of 100 black males between the ages of 25 and 29 were incarcerated in prison or jail. Overall, nearly 13 percent of black males in the U.S. population were in prison, compared to less than 2 percent of white males. There is no sign that such racial disparities in the rate of incarceration are abating. For example, in New Jersey African Americans were 13 times more likely than whites to be incarcerated, although African Americans comprise only 14 percent of the state's total population.[2]

In the last two decades, the passage of tougher sentencing laws by many states and the federal government contributed to seriously overcrowded prisons nationwide. Conditions of prison overcrowding were exacerbated by the increasing reliance on prisons to house the mentally ill. For example, in 2001, more than 700,000 mentally ill persons were processed through U.S. prisons or jails, according to the American Psychiatric Association. In 2000, as many as one in five inmates was seriously mentally ill, according to a report by the American Psychiatric Association.

3

Prison overcrowding and the building of new prisons to ease over-crowded conditions has created budgetary problems for financially strapped states. As more new offenders enter the prison system, about two-thirds of those released are returned to prison within three years, further increasing the demands on state and federal correctional agencies.

HISTORICAL BACKGROUND

The use of incarceration as a form of punishment was not articulated in the earliest known codes of conduct. Instead, retaliation was the recommended redress for wrongdoing. The doctrine of "an eye for an eye, a tooth for a tooth," as articulated in the Bible (Exodus 21:24), was set forth in both the Sumerian codes, circa 1860 B.C., and in the code of King Hammurabi of Babylon, circa 1750 B.C. Punishment under both the Sumerian and Hammurabi codes of conduct was based on vengeance and included mutilation, flogging, and execution—often personally administered upon the wrong-doer by the victim.

Penal servitude, the enslavement of an individual to perform forced labor, was also used as punishment in ancient societies and served the dual purpose of helping to provide goods and services to society. Penal servitude was widely used in ancient Rome as a source of laborers to build and maintain public works. The idea of work as a form of punishment remained popular throughout history, including the modern era. For example, although penal servitude was illegal in the United States, chain gangs of prisoners shackled together to perform hard labor, often road work, was a common form of punishment in the early 20th century in state prisons in the South. Throughout the United States, offenders convicted of minor offenses are often required to perform community service, such as graffiti removal or picking up litter along public highways, sometimes as an alternative to incarceration.

In 621 B.C., Draco, ruler of Greece, implemented a harsh set of laws under which citizens and slaves received equal punishment. Under the Draconian code, any citizen could prosecute an offender in the name of the injured party for the protection of society. As the goal of punishment began to shift from personal vengeance to maintaining social order, the burden of punishment also shifted from the individual to the state. Because the line between church and state was often blurred, ancient codes of conduct included laws against both crime and sin. As such, the goal of punishment by the state was twofold: to deter crime and to inoculate the greater society from the wrath of God caused by the sins of a few. In effect, the state became an arm of God. Punishment in the name of God was often severe. For example, during the Salem witch hunts in colonial New England, beginning in 1692 in Salem, Massachusetts, those even suspected of witchcraft were tortured and sometimes burned alive by local authorities.

The concept of proportionality in punishment—that is, that the punishment should fit the crime—was established in the sixth century A.D. by the Byzantine emperor Justinian. Art from the Justinian period first depicted the scales of justice, a familiar symbol in modern-day jurisprudence. The dual concepts that punishment was to be administered by the state, as set forth in the Draconian code, and that the severity of punishment must be balanced with the gravity of the underlying crime, as established under the Justinian Code, helped to form the basis of Western law and its use of incarceration—the denial of liberty for a proscribed period of time—as a punishment for wrongdoing.

Although proportionality in punishment was established under Justinian, the practice of subjecting wrongdoers to severe physical abuse and agonizing forms of death persisted into the Middle Ages and beyond. In A.D. 1215, the church instituted the concept of trial by ordeal, in which individuals under the slightest suspicion of wrongdoing were tortured in the belief that the innocent would survive unharmed, while the guilty would suffer and die. Crimes prosecuted in this way included heresy, witchcraft, and "unnatural acts," which included what are today considered normal forms of sexual expression. Although barbaric, the medieval church's practice of punishment to determine guilt underscored the concept of free will—that individuals choose their actions and are responsible for their choices. Free will continues to be a cornerstone of modern justice systems worldwide, including in the United States.

Throughout history, the practice of punishing offenders in public was common. Public punishment was intended as a lesson in deterrence: Behave badly and this will happen to you. Executions by hanging, crucifixion, burning, and drowning were carried out in public squares and meeting places as a way of showing the ultimate price one could pay for violating the law. Nonlethal punishments such as flogging, branding, mutilation, or simple humiliation were also carried out in public as a means of deterring others in the community from engaging in crime or other transgressions as minor as gossiping. The spectacle of public punishment fueled a sense of social revenge. Punishment was expected to be brutal so as to deter others, repay society, and redeem the wrongdoer in the eyes of God. Incarceration was used to hold the wrongdoer until the actual punishment could be meted out.

The concept that incarceration was a form of punishment evolved slowly. The earliest known prison was the Mamertine, a series of underground dungeons built circa 64 B.C. in ancient Rome. It is not known if the Mamertine prison functioned in the manner of modern-day prisons by depriving inmates of their liberty as a form of punishment or if the dungeons at Mamertine were simply holding areas for lawbreakers awaiting punishment.

During the Middle Ages, following the fall of Rome around A.D. 476, fortresses and fortified town gates were constructed throughout Europe to defend against roving bands of outlaws. As gunpowder came into wider use in Europe during the 14th century, however, such barriers became increasingly useless against invaders armed with cannons and other artillery. The structures previously built for defensive purposes were often converted to places of confinement for prisoners. These fortified structures included walled monasteries, where during the Inquisition of the 13th and 14th centuries, prisons were built to confine those believed to have violated church law. In such prisons, solitary confinement was sometimes utilized to create an atmosphere of atonement and penitence for prisoners.

In 1557, the Bridewell workhouse was established in London to house undesirables, including the homeless, the unemployed, and sometimes juveniles who were orphaned or considered incorrigible. Residents were subjected to strict discipline and forced to work long hours in harsh conditions. Bridewell was deemed a success, at least in terms of public perception, for keeping undesirables out of sight and out of mind. In 1576, the English Parliament ordered the construction of a workhouse in every county in England. Soon the workhouse concept spread throughout Europe. Conditions inside workhouses were often deplorable. There was no attempt to segregate males and females or juvenile and adults. As a result, violence and abuse among inmates and exploitation by jailers was common, as the strong freely preyed upon the weak. Poor sanitation in workhouses resulted in outbreaks of typhus, also known as jail fever. The highly contagious disease often spread to the surrounding communities.

EUROPEAN REFORMERS

By the early 18th century, workhouses were in place throughout Europe. Although designed as places of training and care for the poor, in reality workhouses functioned as penal institutions. Their squalid conditions were similar to those found in local jails, which held inmates awaiting trial or execution. Jails also held inmates who owed fines but could not afford to pay them. In some cases, inmates were held indefinitely as a means of extorting payments from them. Corruption, violence, and unsafe living conditions were pervasive in workhouses and jails throughout Europe in the early 18th century. At the same time, the idea of the importance of the individual began to take hold in Europe. Many social reformers began to focus on the abuses in the criminal justice system. The French philosopher Voltaire was an outspoken opponent of torture and other inhumane practices carried out by the state against lawbreakers. Voltaire believed that an individual's fear of shame, not corporal punishment, was a deterrent to crime. Eventually Voltaire was imprisoned in the Bastille for his ideas, and in 1726, he was ordered to leave France in exchange for his freedom. In Italy, Cesare Beccaria was perhaps the most influential reformer of the era on issues of crime and punishment. Beccaria's most widely known work, *An Essay on Crimes and Punishment*, published in 1764, established the following principles:

- Every crime is an injury to society, and the seriousness of a crime must be determined by the extent of the injury caused by the crime.
- Prevention of crime is more important to society than punishing crime. Therefore, the main justification for punishment is to prevent crime.
- A person accused of a crime should be treated humanely and afforded the right to present evidence in his or her behalf in a public trial.
- When the purpose of punishment is to deter crime, and not to exact social revenge, then the certainty and swiftness of the punishment is more important than the severity of the punishment.
- Life imprisonment is a more effective deterrent to crime than capital punishment, which is irreparable and impossible to correct if mistakes are later discovered in the criminal justice process.
- Crimes of property should be punished by fines, or by imprisonment when the offender is unable to pay the fine.
- Imprisonment should replace corporal punishment as a mode of punishment.
- The conditions of imprisonment should be humane and include the segregation of prisoners by age, sex, and their degree of criminality.

Beccaria understood that his ideas were controversial for the time, so much so that his work was originally published anonymously because he feared retribution by the government. Instead, Beccaria's ideas were embraced by reformers throughout Europe, especially in France, where in 1810 the French penal code was revised to incorporate principles promoted by Beccaria. Among them:

- An accused is innocent until proved guilty.
- An accused has the right against self-incrimination, the right to legal counsel, and the right to cross-examine the state's witnesses.
- An accused has the right to a speedy public trial and, in most cases, to a trial by jury.

Prisons

An 18th century English reformer, Jeremy Bentham, promoted Beccaria's idea that punishment could act as a deterrent to crime, but only when the punishment was appropriate to the underlying crime. John Howard, Bentham's contemporary in England, advanced the concept that the rights of the accused extended to individuals who were convicted of crimes and incarcerated by the state. In 1773, Howard was appointed sheriff of Bedfordshire and witnessed firsthand the deplorable conditions in local jails. Howard observed inmates being starved because they could not afford food sold at inflated prices by their jailers. Prisoners were not segregated by sex or age and were crowded into cage-like cells with little or no sanitation. Appalled by what he saw, Howard began to tour prison facilities throughout Europe and found similar conditions almost everywhere, with some exceptions in Belgium, France, and Italy. In 1777, Howard published the *State of Prisons*, in which he described the best of the correctional facilities he had seen during his tours and suggested reforms. Some of Howard's reforms were enacted into law in 1779, when the English Parliament passed the Penitentiary Act, which contained the following principles:

- Construct and maintain secure and sanitary correctional facilities.
- Conduct regular inspections of correctional facilities.
- Abolish all fees charged to inmates by their jailers or the correctional institution.
- Implement a reformatory model designed to deter inmates from reoffending.

Following the passage of the Penitentiary Act, the first penitentiary was built at Wyndonham in Norfolk, England. The guidelines established by the Penitentiary Act proved difficult to implement, however, due to the strain placed on correctional facilities by the rising urban crime rate and the resulting influx of inmates. By the late 18th century, English authorities sought to ease prison overcrowding by deporting more criminals. The practice of deporting lawbreakers had begun in England in 1596 when convicts were shipped to the American colonies. In 1776, however, deportation abruptly ended as a consequence of the American Revolution. English authorities used Australia as an alternative, but transportation was limited and arduous. In what was intended as a quick fix to ease overcrowding in correctional facilities, some inmates were confined in hulks, old transport ships and obsolete war vessels abandoned in harbors and waterways throughout the British Isles. The conditions in hulks were worse than those in local jails. Hulks were unventilated and infested with vermin. Disease was rampant and sometimes wiped out entire populations of inmates. Males and females, adults and juveniles, were unsegregated and forced to perform labor. Offenders, from hardened felons to misdemeanants who could not afford to pay fines, were routinely flogged and physically abused. Some, including minors, were sexually abused by jailers and other inmates. Although intended as a temporary solution to alleviate prison overcrowding, the practice of using hulks as prisons persisted in England for 80 years, until 1858. Later in the 19th century, hulks were used in California to house inmates, and New York City converted a war barge into a floating jail.

After his tours of jails, John Howard documented the deplorable conditions of confinement throughout Europe. He also documented two notable exceptions: the Maison de Force in Ghent, Belgium, and the Hospice of San Michele in Rome. The Maison de Force was built in 1773 under the direction of Belgian administrator Jean-Jacques Vilain, who followed the basic pattern of European workhouses when designing the facility. At Maison de Force, however, Vilain segregated females and juveniles from serious offenders and housed inmates in individual cells. Although considered a strict disciplinarian who required prisoners to work in silence, Vilain opposed cruelty as a means of inmate control. The Hospice of San Michele, built in 1704 by Pope Clement XI, was one of the first correctional institutions designed exclusively for juvenile offenders. Those confined at San Michele were subjected to a regimen of hard work and Bible reading. The system of separate cells for sleeping quarters and a large central hall for working, modeled after monasteries, became the structural blueprint for penal institutions in the 19th century. The use of silence and prayer at both Maison de Force and the Hospice of San Michele was also patterned on monastic life.

EARLY AMERICAN CORRECTIONS

The reforms advocated by John Howard and Cesare Beccaria, among others in Europe, and the improved treatment of prisoners at facilities such as Belgium's Maison de Force and the Hospice of San Michele in Rome, were owed in part to the influence of William Penn, who in 1681 founded the Quaker settlement at Pennsylvania in colonial America. The American colonies were then governed under English codes, including the Hampshire code of 1664 and the codes established by the duke of York in 1676, which allowed for the use of executions and harsh corporal punishment for lawbreakers. Under the English codes, offenders were routinely branded, flogged, or subjected to public humiliation in devices such as the pillory, in which an offender's hands and head were immobilized between two boards that served as a backstop while the offender was pelted, or *pilloried*, with raw eggs, rotten fruit, and the like.

As a Quaker leader, Penn advocated a more humane treatment of law-breakers, as set forth in the Quaker code known as the Great Law. Under the Great Law, most offenses were punishable by hard labor in a house of correction, even some serious offenses punishable by execution under the English codes. The concept of confinement as a component of punishment, and not merely as the prelude to execution or corporal punishment, was unique in colonial America. Also unique under the Great Law was that punishable offenses were secular and did not include religious offenses like the English codes.

The Great Law was in force in colonial Pennsylvania from 1682 until 1718, when it was repealed one day after the death of William Penn. It was replaced by the English Anglican code, which was harsher in its treatment of lawbreakers than the earlier codes of the duke of York. The concept of punishment by confinement to a house of correction, or prison, however, remained part of the Quaker legacy.

In 1773, a state prison for felons was established in Simsbury, Connecticut, on the site of an abandoned copper mine. Inmates were confined in dank mine shafts. The facility was little more than a throwback to the underground dungeons of the Mamertine prison in ancient Rome. As a result of the poor conditions of confinement, in 1774, one year after it began operation, the prison was the site of one of America's earliest inmate riots.

THE PENNSYLVANIA SYSTEM

Not until 1790 was the prototype for the first correctional facility created in the United States, when the Pennsylvania legislature permitted the Quakers to operate a wing of the Walnut Street jail in Philadelphia as a penitentiary for convicted felons, except those sentenced to death. Reformers including Benjamin Franklin and Benjamin Rush, both signers of the U.S. Declaration of Independence, and Revolutionary War army hero William Bradford helped to develop a system of prison discipline at the Walnut Street jail that borrowed from the principles for the humane treatment of inmates advanced by Quaker William Penn and European reformers like Cesare Beccaria and John Howard. Eventually, the system developed at the Walnut Street jail became formally known as the Pennsylvania system.

Under the Pennsylvania system, inmates were isolated in solitary cells without work in order to reflect upon their crimes and repent their sins. As the prolonged effects of isolation and inactivity began to physically and psychologically debilitate inmates, work schedules of eight to 10 hours were introduced into the daily routine at the Walnut Street jail. Still, prisoners were required to work in isolation, usually on handicrafts and piecework. Eventually, the system broke down altogether due to overcrowding, which forced prison officials to house more than one felon per cell and compromised the segregation of male and female inmates.

Despite the failure of the Walnut Street jail, the Pennsylvania system continued to serve as the architectural and administrative model for other U.S. prisons in the early 19th century. The Pennsylvania system's emphasis on isolation and work was implemented to some degree at Newgate Prison in New York City, built in 1797, and state penitentiaries at Lamberton, New Jersey (1798); Frankfort, Kentucky, and Richmond, Virginia (1800); Charlestown, Massachusetts (1805); Windsor, Vermont (1809); Baltimore, Maryland, and Concord, New Hampshire (1812); Columbus, Ohio (1816); and Milledgeville, Georgia (1817). Like these prisons, the Western Penitentiary, built in 1826 in Pittsburgh, Pennsylvania, was designed with small, dark cells where prisoners were to live in near-total isolation. As at the Walnut Street jail, however, work was eventually added to the daily routine to alleviate some of the strain of solitary confinement. In 1833, the interior cells at the Western Penitentiary were demolished to alleviate the oppressive darkness in which inmates lived, and larger cells were built along the outside walls of the prison. This system of outside cells was quickly copied at the Eastern Penitentiary in Philadelphia, which was built in 1835 around a central hub from which rows of cell blocks extended like the spokes of a wheel. Still, the daily routine under the Pennsylvania system continued to be isolation, silence, and individual labor.

THE AUBURN SYSTEM

In 1816, a new prison at Auburn, New York, was built to ease overcrowding at Newgate prison. The design of the Auburn prison included communal areas where inmates could congregate for work and meals. Cells at Auburn, built vertically in tiers on five floors, were small and designed as individual sleeping quarters for inmates. Most prisoners at Auburn were allowed to work and eat in silence together during the day and separated only at night. Larger individual cells were added in 1819 to house prisoners placed in permanent solitary confinement as punishment for disobeying rules. Silence was used to foster an atmosphere of contemplation and repentance among inmates, but it also had the practical effect of minimizing escape plans. The philosophy behind the Auburn system, as it came to be known, was to give inmates the incentive to avoid permanent solitary confinement by obeying prison rules. The practice of permanent solitary confinement was eventually abandoned at Auburn in 1823 as the result of suicides, self-mutilations, and mental breakdowns that occurred because of

11

the unrelenting isolation. In place of isolation, prisoners who breached the rules were whipped.

Under the Auburn system, inmates were effectively managed after 1823 without the use of solitary confinement and its often debilitating consequences. On the other hand, the Pennsylvania system's reliance upon solitary confinement effectively eliminated the formation of criminal associations of inmates allowed to mingle in common areas. Eventually, the Auburn system prevailed, largely because of economics. Under the Auburn system, the building of prisons with smaller cells and centralized areas was more cost-effective. In addition, prison industries operated under Auburn's congregate system were more profitable for the state than piecework performed by solitary inmates. From 1825 to 1869, the Auburn system was implemented at some 35 U.S. prisons, including Ossining (Sing Sing) prison in New York, built in 1825, and San Quentin state prison in California, built in 1852. The Auburn system's structural design of tiers of cells, also known as cell blocks, became the model for most prisons built in the United States for the next 150 years.

Prison discipline under both the Auburn and Pennsylvania systems was built upon a monastic-like silence required of all inmates. Under the Auburn system, however, there was the challenge of controlling groups of inmates in common areas that outnumbered prison guards. Elam Lynds, warden at Auburn prison and later at Sing Sing, developed methods of inmate control and discipline that, although effective and modeled on other institutions, were also brutal and degrading to inmates. Lynds's methods of discipline were based on his belief that it was necessary to break an inmate's will or spirit before it was possible to control an inmate. Lynds punished even slight infractions with immediate whippings, either with a rawhide whip or a flogging device made from strands of wire. Silence was strictly enforced at all times. During meals, inmates were required to sit face-to-back and eat all of their food. The only permissible communication was to raise one hand for more food or to raise the other for less food.

At Auburn, Lynds developed a lockstep formation that required prisoners to line up with their hands placed on the shoulders or under the arms of the inmate in front, then move forward rapidly by shuffling, without lifting their feet off the ground. Prisoners who fell out of step risked being whipped or being trampled under the swiftly moving formation.

Clothing was also used as a means of inmate control. White uniforms with black stripes, also known as prison stripes, were introduced in 1815 in New York prisons. At Auburn and Sing Sing, Elam Lynds implemented color-coded clothing that signaled whether an inmate was a first-time or a repeat offender.

THE REFORMATORY ERA

In 1870, prison administrators met in Cincinnati, Ohio, at the American Prison Congress to discuss the future of corrections in the United States. They formed the National Prison Association, renamed the American Correctional Association in 1954, and elected as their first president the governor of Ohio, Rutherford B. Hayes, who in 1877 would become the 19th president of the United States. Many of the prison administrators in attendance were concerned about prison overcrowding and how to better design correctional facilities to alleviate it. Reform-minded corrections professionals advocated a new approach to the treatment of inmates, based in part upon the work of Captain Alexander Maconochie in England and Sir Walter Frederick Crofton in Ireland.

In 1840, Maconochie had been placed in charge of a British penal colony on Norfolk Island, some 800 miles east of Australia, which housed some of England's worst offenders. He implemented a series of reforms, including the elimination of so-called *flat* sentences under which an inmate was required to serve the full term of his sentence before there was any possibility of release. In its place Maconochie implemented a system of early release earned by good conduct and hard work. Under this system, a convict could earn points, called *marks*. With enough marks, it was possible for an inmate to purchase the right to perform the work of his choice and to gain other liberties, in preparation for the inmate's eventual release to society.

Building upon Maconochie's idea, in 1850 Sir Walter Crofton developed a system of indeterminate sentencing, which became know as the Irish system. Crofton reasoned that if penitentiaries were designed as places of repentance and personal reform, then there must be a mechanism in place for prisoners to benefit when they demonstrate their reform. Crofton's system had several stages. Completing each stage brought an inmate closer to release and shortened the length of the initial sentence. During the first stage, prisoners were placed in solitary confinement and required to perform monotonous work. In a series of intermediate stages, prisoners were awarded better work assignments and greater degrees of liberty within the prison. In the final stage, inmates were sent to an intermediate prison and allowed to work without supervision and to move freely in and out of the local community. Upon release, each prisoner was given a ticket-of-leave that could be revoked for any violation of law. The ticket-of-leave remained in force for the full length of the prisoner's original sentence. Crofton's plan of conditional liberty later evolved into the modern system of parole, under which an inmate is granted early release from prison by a parole board but remains under the supervision of a parole officer while living in the community. As under Crofton's ticket-of-leave plan, if a parolee violates any of the conditions of parole, he or she can be returned to prison.

At their meeting in Cincinnati, Ohio, in 1870, the members of the National Prison Association endorsed the ideas of Maconochie and Crofton that prisons should be places of reform, or reformatories, and issued a broad set of principles embodying that ideal. They included establishing a three-stage system of punishment, reform, and probation in all prisons and using indeterminate sentencing as a way to reward inmates for good behavior and hard work. The administrators also established the goals of providing education to inmates, treating inmates with respect, minimizing the use of physical force against inmates, and segregating juveniles, females, and males in separate facilities.

As a result of the National Prison Association's focus on reform over punishment, the first reformatory in the United States was built in 1876 in Elmira, New York. The Elmira reformatory was originally designed to house adult felons. Under the direction of Zebulon Brockway, the first superintendent at Elmira, however, the reformatory was used for first-time male offenders between the ages of 16 and 30, in the hope that they could be more effectively rehabilitated than hardened criminals. The programs at Elmira emphasized personal change through education and vocational training. A program of indeterminate sentencing was implemented, including a grading system that allowed inmates to earn points for early release through good conduct and hard work.

From 1876 to 1913, reformatories modeled after Elmira were built in 17 U.S. states. The reformatories were designed with the goal of providing educational and vocational training to both juvenile and adult offenders. Indeterminate sentencing and early-release plans were implemented to reward hard work and obedience. The reformatories were often staffed, however, with the same underpaid and poorly qualified personnel who worked in prisons. Harsh prison discipline quickly replaced the loftier ideal of reform, and conditions in many reformatories deteriorated to the point where there was little difference between reformatories and conventional prisons.

THE INDUSTRIAL PRISON

In addition to reformatories, some 16 state prisons were built in the 29 years from 1871 to 1900 after the National Prison Association established principles encouraging the humane treatment of inmates. Apart from plumbing and running water, these prisons were little changed from penitentiaries of the past that had been modeled on the Auburn system. The growing population of inmates in U.S. prisons represented a source of cheap labor to private industry. Increasingly, prisoners were put to work manufacturing goods that were sold on the open market.

At the end of the Civil War in 1865, able-bodied male inmates began to be exploited as laborers on a national scale. In the South, where the agrarian economy relied upon cheap farm labor, prisoners were used to replace the freed slaves. Because the prison population in the southern United States included many plantation blacks, the use of prison laborers became almost an extension of slavery. In the North, state prisons were commonly paid an annual fee by companies for the use of their inmate workers. In some cases, industry officials were allowed inside prisons to supervise inmates as they worked.

As prison industries grew, so did opposition from organized labor, which was hard-pressed to compete against a labor market of inmates working for a fraction of the cost of other workers. By 1900, some states placed restrictions on the sale of prison-made products. As a result of the high unemployment caused by the Great Depression, from 1929 to 1933, labor unions and industries that did not use inmate workers pressured state and federal legislatures to further restrict the availability of prison products to promote job growth in the private sector. With the passage of the Hawes-Cooper Act in 1929, interstate prison products became subject to the law of the state to which they were shipped. The Amhurst-Sumners Act, passed in 1935 and amended in 1940, permanently stopped the transport of all prison products shipped out-of-state. Most state prison industries were effectively eliminated, except for license plate manufacturing and some small state furniture shops. As a result, prisoners had little opportunity to earn work credits or acquire vocational training, and prisons reverted to being little more than warehouses for inmates, where order was maintained by punishment.

On June 23, 1934, the U.S. Congress established Federal Prison Industries (FPI) to provide vocational training and employment to federal inmates. The FPI is commonly referred to by its trade name, UNICOR. For fiscal year 2002, UNICOR operated 111 factories in 71 locations nationwide and employed nearly 22,000 federal inmates, who earned from 23 cents to $1.15 per hour, depending upon experience and skill.

In 2002, UNICOR generated $679 million in sales from a wide range of products, including furniture, electronics, and signs. UNICOR products are sold to various agencies of the federal government and are designed so as not to directly compete with products produced by private industry. About three-fourths of the revenue generated by UNICOR in fiscal year 2002 was used for the purchase of materials and supplies from vendors in the private sector. With a net income of $9 million in 2002, UNICOR was a self-sustaining operation.

MODERN CORRECTIONS

In 1934, Sanford Bates, the director of the U.S. Bureau of Prisons, introduced procedures in federal prisons for the diagnostic classification of inmates and for the use of mental health professionals in designing rehabilitation programs for prisoners. The procedures implemented under the leadership of Bates were credited with advancing the humane treatment of inmates and improving living conditions in the federal prison system. Despite these advances, however, long hours of idleness in locked and often forbidding institutions inevitably produced tensions among inmates and between inmates and staff.

As the result of rising inmate populations from 1930 to 1950, state and federal prison officials implemented restrictive measures to maintain order and security in overcrowded facilities. Women's reformatories began to adopt a more custodial and disciplinary atmosphere as the result of overcrowding, with less emphasis on education and job training.

In 1960, the modern era of corrections began during a period of social change in the United States. Prisoners demanded not only better conditions of confinement, but also the opportunity to exercise their basic rights under the U.S. Constitution. In 1969, in the case *Johnson v. Avery* the U.S. Supreme Court issued the first in a series of landmark rulings on prisoners' rights on issues including legal representation, cruel and unusual punishment, religious freedom, and medical care. In response to the Supreme Court's rulings, which are discussed in Chapter 2, corrections professionals implemented new prison policies that provided inmates with better access to medical care and legal representation, including access to legal materials in prison libraries. Also, prison officials were required to eliminate any use of force against inmates that was not necessary to maintain security and order in the institution.

As a result of the prison reform movement, women's prisons in the United States began to return to some of the principles of the women's reformatory movement. For example, in-prison maternity units were established in some prisons that permitted infants to remain with incarcerated mothers for a period of weeks or months, instead of being separated from their mothers at birth. Other parent-child services, including expanded visitation, were adopted, and female inmates began to receive the same educational and training opportunities as male inmates. However, some of these services were later curtailed as the population of female prisoners rose during the 1980s and 1990s, and many women's prisons adopted more custodial and punitive approaches to incarceration.

During the 25 years from 1970 to 1995, the rate of violent crime in the United States turned public sentiment away from prison reform toward punishment, including long periods of incarceration for the most serious offenders. According to the Bureau of Justice Statistics (BJS), between 1973 and 1995, victimizations from violent crimes for individuals 12 years of age and older occurred at a rate of between 47 and 52 victims for every 1,000 people in the U.S. population.[3] As a result, state and federal legislation was passed during the 1990s giving courts less discretion in sentencing repeat offenders. Advocates of these credited them with reducing almost by half the rate of violent crime in the United States, from 41.6 to 22.8 violent victimizations per 1,000 population between 1996 and 2002, according to the BJS. The impact of such laws on the inmate populations of federal and state prisons was dramatic. The total number of inmates confined to state and federal U.S. prisons nearly doubled, from 783,382 in 1990 to almost 1.4 million in 2002. With a rate of incarceration of 702 inmates per 100,000 population in 2002, the United States jailed and imprisoned more people per capita than any other country in the world.[4]

Modern developments in areas including prisoner classification, juvenile corrections, private prisons, and the shift in correctional philosophies from rehabilitation to punishment are discussed later in this chapter.

MODERN CORRECTIONAL PHILOSOPHIES

Historically the handling of lawbreakers evolved from simple retaliation in ancient societies to modern-day correctional approaches that include punishment, treatment, and prevention. These approaches sometimes overlap in correctional settings that must serve a variety of prisoners, from first-time offenders to habitual predators. Still, they represent distinct and competing ideologies on how society metes out the consequences of crime.

PUNISHMENT

Incarceration and execution are the most serious forms of punishment administered to criminal offenders in the United States. Probation, which places a convicted misdemeanant or felon under court supervision for a period of months or years, is imposed in combination with or in lieu of incarceration. Probation restricts an offender's liberty to an extent, such as where an offender is allowed to go or with whom an offender is allowed to associate. As such, probation constitutes a milder form of punishment than incarceration.

The three general rationales for punishment are retribution, deterrence, and incapacitation of the offender. From ancient times, the criminal was viewed as an enemy of society who purposely violated the rules of social order. Retribution satisfied the need to retaliate against those who caused such harm. From a theological perspective, retribution required wrongdoers, or sinners, to suffer for their sins. By suffering, the sinner's guilt was expiated, and the soul was cleansed through atonement. Under the Pennsylvania system, introduced in colonial America, the Quakers were among the first to promote the idea of incarceration as a form of retribution. The Quakers opposed corporal punishment and public humiliation, as was commonly practiced in the American colonies, and believed that retribution could be achieved by confining a criminal in total isolation in order to repent. Retribution also fulfilled the sociological function of restoring a sense of fairness, or justice, by holding lawbreakers accountable for their actions and imposing personal consequences upon them. Society expected criminal offenders to experience the same measure of suffering as their victims. Satisfying that social expectation helped to maintain social order.

Historically, deterrence was the lesson taught by punishment. That lesson was specific to the offender, who was discouraged by punishment from committing future offenses. Ultimately, the success of deterrence is in the hands of the offender. If an offender feels unjustly punished by society, negative behavior patterns are more likely to persist, and deterrence is ineffective. Conversely, deterrence has the best chance of success when an offender acknowledges wrongdoing and believes that the punishment was fair. In addition, successful deterrence gives the punished offender an opportunity to return to society and resume a normal life without stigma. Unfortunately, in the United States, the stigma of conviction often dogs ex-convicts for years after their release from prison, interfering with their ability to secure employment and, in many states, disqualifying them from voting and exercising other rights under felony disenfranchisement laws, as discussed later in this chapter.

By making an example of the offender, deterrence also served the general purpose of discouraging others from engaging in crime.

Incapacitation, also known as disablement, uses the punishment of incarceration as a crime-control strategy. In other words, keeping offenders locked up for many years eliminates any chance that they will reoffend, except in prison. Under incapacitation, there is little or no attempt at rehabilitation. Incapacitation is the rationale for three-strikes laws and determinate sentencing, which impose fixed prison terms on certain classes of offenders, such as violent or habitual felons. Similarly, truth-in-sentencing laws require imprisonment for no less than the stated term of the sentence. For example, as of 2003, all life sentences imposed in Illinois, Iowa, Louisiana, Maine, Pennsylvania, and South Dakota carried no possibility of parole, according to a report by the Sentencing Project.[5] Some states, including California, have implemented a blend of determinate and indeterminate sentencing. Under California's three-strikes law, offenders convicted of any felony with two prior convictions for violent felonies receive 25 years to life in state prison, with no possibility of release until completing the full determinate period of 25 years. After 25 years, three-strikes felons are periodically eligible for parole. However, there is no guarantee that parole will be granted, and felons may remain incarcerated for the rest of their lives. As a result of such laws, which give courts little or no discretion in sentencing, one out of every 11 prison inmates in the United States in 2003 was serving a life sentence, according to the Sentencing Project. Proponents of the incapacitation theory point to the reduction in the rate of violent crime in the United States by some 50 percent since the mid-1990s, when many such sentencing provisions became law.

TREATMENT

Under the punishment model, the offender is viewed as an enemy of society. By contrast, the treatment model in corrections views criminal behavior as a symptom of an underlying pathology, such as mental illness or drug addiction. Under the treatment model, the offender is incarcerated for placement in some type of correctional program, with the goal of reintegration in the community. There is also a component of punishment however, in removing an offender's liberty through incarceration.

Treatment in corrections consists of several stages, beginning with the diagnosis of an offender's underlying condition and needs. A program is then designed to meet the offender's needs, usually by placing the offender in an existing program where others with similar problems receive treatment. Periodic monitoring of the offender's progress and modification of the treatment plan are also essential for effective treatment. The rationale for treatment in modern-day corrections developed over time as the result of four main treatment doctrines: penitence, the educational doctrine, the medical model, and the reintegration model.

Beginning in colonial America, Quakers advocated for the use of penitence instead of the common practice of corporal punishment and public humiliation of offenders. Quakers believed that offenders were out of touch with God. Their treatment model was the isolation of an offender in solitary confinement under a strict regimen of Bible reading, reflection, and enforced silence. The goal was for the offender to reconnect with God. Quakers believed that once a reconnection with God was achieved, the offender's criminal behavior would cease, and the offender could safely return to the community.

Prison reformers in the late 19th century viewed offenders as disadvantaged and generally lacking in education and self-discipline. The first reformatory, opened in 1876 at Elmira, New York, and others that followed during the late 19th century operated according to the principles of the educational doctrine. Unlike traditional prisons at the time, where inmates were simply housed and punished, reformatories provided educational and vocational training under a regimen of strict discipline, with the goal of instilling in offenders the skills and internal behavioral controls necessary to function in society.

The medical model was developed by Sanford Bates during his tenure from 1930 to 1937 as the director of the U.S. Bureau of Prisons. Under the medical model, criminal behavior is viewed as the result of an underlying disease. Proponents of the medical model believe that, like a disease, the pathology of criminal behavior can respond to treatment, usually psychiatric, with the potential for a cure. Inmates under the medical model are viewed as patients. In theory, once the patient is made well, he or she is ready to return to the community under a system of aftercare managed by parole officers who function in a therapeutic role, in contrast to modern parole agents whose function is more closely aligned with law enforcement. Built into the medical model is the concept of early release, which occurs after successful treatment. As a result of the treatment model, by 1975, the federal courts and all state courts utilized a system of indeterminate sentencing, which allocated a minimum and maximum length of incarceration for every criminal offense. Offenders were sentenced to a span of time, instead of a fixed term, and could be released within that time frame by parole boards, which were given broad discretion in determining when an inmate was ready for release. Since 1976, the federal system and many state systems have either limited or abolished the sentencing discretion of parole boards.

The reintegration model originated in the late 1960s and remained popular for more than 20 years. Its premise was that criminality occurred as the result of factors in an offender's environment or community, such as poverty and unemployment. The goal of reintegration of the offender into society was accomplished through aftercare or alternatives to incarceration, such as diversion programs that provide rehabilitation or training opportunities.

PREVENTION

Under the prevention model, criminal behavior is viewed as a manifestation of emotional and social problems. In corrections settings, the prevention model operates with the dual objectives of reforming individual offenders and developing community-based programs designed to reduce the risk of reoffending. These programs may serve as alternatives to incarceration, or as adjuncts to incarceration, such as aftercare programs for parolees. Sometimes, the programs provide treatment to the offender. This combination of the prevention and treatment models is known as community corrections.

In community corrections, offenders are usually diverted from incarceration. For example, in 2000, by a margin of 2 to 1, California voters passed the Substance Abuse and Crime Prevention Act. Popularly known as Proposition 36, the legislation allowed first- and second-time nonviolent offenders convicted of drug possession to receive substance abuse treatment in lieu of incarceration. The goal was the prevention of reoffending through the treatment of the offender. In its first year of enforcement of Proposition 36, ending July 31, 2002, some 37,000 drug offenders were diverted from prisons and jails into treatment programs at an estimated savings to California taxpayers of $275 million.[6] As an ancillary benefit, offenders who successfully complete a program of treatment under Proposition 36 are eligible for the dismissal of the original charges against them. This judicial process, known as diversion, eliminates the stigma of a criminal conviction.

FACILITIES AND FUNCTIONS

Prisons and jails are the two main types of correctional facilities in the United States today. In general, jails house individuals whose criminal cases are proceeding through the court system, from arraignment to sentencing. Usually, jail inmates awaiting trial cannot afford to post bail for their release, although in serious cases, such as capital murder, jail inmates are often held without bail. Jails also house convicted offenders sentenced to short terms of incarceration, usually one year or less. Many convicted jail inmates are misdemeanants, although convicted felons are sometimes sentenced to jail for terms of incarceration of one year or less. Most jails are operated by local law enforcement agencies, such as a police department or the county sheriff.

Prisons house convicted felons serving sentences of one or more years and inmates awaiting execution under a sentence of death.

CLASSIFICATION AND HOUSING

In prison systems, incoming inmates customarily enter a reception or evaluation center, which is a prison where they are confined for a period of weeks or several months. During that time, new prisoners are assessed and classified as to their security risk and special needs, such as mental illness, pending permanent placement in an appropriate correctional facility. Classification of inmates was implemented on a national scale beginning in the late 1940s, after the end of World War II. At that time, there was concern among prison administrators over inmate idleness as a result of the severe curtailment of prison industries in the 1930s due to federal legislation. The National Prison Association, renamed the American Correctional Association in 1954, promoted the idea of assessing each incoming inmate's social, intellectual, and emotional capabilities and clinically identifying each inmate's deficiencies, with the goal of designing individualized rehabilitation and training programs for prisoners. In order to ensure that arriving prisoners were appropriately assessed, it was necessary to implement a standardized classification system.

In practice, classification systems fell short of one of their intended purposes, that of directing inmates into individualized treatment, in large part because of insufficient funding to administer programs to rehabilitate, educate, and train every inmate. There were other practical barriers as well. For example, most prisons depended upon inmate labor to operate essential prison services, including food preparation, laundry facilities, and janitorial duties, as they do today. Training and rehabilitation programs, if available, were not always the first priority in the day-to-day running of prisons. Inmates looking to earn credits for good behavior to gain early release or other privileges, such as selection of work assignments, were more inclined to please prison staff by placing institutional needs above their personal needs for education or counseling.

The primary objective of the classification system is determining the level of security necessary to safely manage each prisoner. The three basic levels of security are minimum, medium, and maximum. Of the more than 1.2 million prisoners in state and federal confinement facilities on June 30, 2000, over one-third (36 percent) were held in maximum security facilities, while medium security facilities housed 48 percent, and minimum security prisons held 16 percent of inmates.[7]

Minimum security prisons house the least violent and most trustworthy felons. Conditions of confinement are the least restrictive and may include guards who are unarmed and cyclone fences instead of walls around the facility. Work furloughs and educational release are commonly available to inmates, allowing them to leave the facility to go to jobs or attend classes in the community. While on prison grounds, inmates move to and from activities on their own instead of being escorted by guards. Minimum security prisons provide inmates with maximum freedom of movement and often rely on inmates' trustworthiness to maintain security. Inmates in minimum security prisons who violate the rules may be transferred to medium or even maximum security correctional facilities as a sanction for their infraction.

In the federal prison system, minimum security prisons are commonly referred to as camps. Typically, federal prisoners assigned to such facilities have less than 10 years remaining on their sentence and have earned the right to be housed in a minimum security setting as the result of their good behavior in maximum or medium security federal prisons. Typically, prisoners in federal camps with less than two years remaining on their sentence are eligible for furloughs away from the prison to spend time with their families, in order to begin the process of reintegration into the community. The quarters in federal camps are generally dormitory style, with beds separated in cubicles or simply aligned in rows. As in maximum and minimum security facilities, there is little personal privacy. Inmates at federal camps are usually required to work, sometimes outside the prison facility in nearby towns or military bases. Inmates at federal camps that are part of a complex with higher security facilities often provide services, such as food preparation and laundry services, to the higher security facilities. Staff members at federal minimum security facilities often enforce rules more strictly than at higher security facilities. For example, camp inmates with more than their allotted number of books or toiletry items are likely to receive sanctions, while such minor infractions might be overlooked in medium and maximum security institutions, where the concern of prison officials is largely focused on safety and security. Violence in minimum security prisons is generally low or even nonexistent, much like a workplace environment.

Medium security prisons generally house nonviolent offenders. Security is tighter than at minimum security facilities and generally includes armed guards and a walled perimeter. While there may be some regimentation of inmates during movement to and from activities, more personal freedom is permitted, which fosters an atmosphere more conducive to treatment and educational programs, although, unlike minimum security facilities, inmates are limited to on-site programs. In addition, visitor privileges are often fairly relaxed and may allow for personal contact. Many medium security prisons were designed with residential areas that are more akin to dormitories than cell blocks. Apart from outside fences, which often are topped with barbed wire or razor wire to discourage escapes, security is often maintained through electronic surveillance equipment.

Beginning in the 19th century, maximum security prisons in the United States were built as forbidding, fortresslike structures in the tradition of Gothic architecture. The intent was to overwhelm the prisoner with feelings of insignificance as a means of psychological control. By the early 20th century, the traditional Gothic design lost favor with penologists who wanted a less oppressive prison environment that was more conducive to treatment. As a result, modern maximum security facilities have abandoned the old design standards. Still, the function of maximum security prisons remains the same—to minimize inmate violence and the risk of escape by maximizing control over prisoners. Walls around the perimeter of maximum security facilities are continuously patrolled by armed guards and often reinforced with barbed wire. Some facilities utilize electrified fences that carry enough voltage to kill a human being on touch. Prisoner cells usually house one or two inmates and are often equipped with a toilet and sink to reduce the need to move inmates. Prisoners are locked inside their cells for 10 or 12 hours per day, generally from early evening until the next morning. Inmates are allowed out of their cells for meals, prison work assignments, physical exercise in the prison yard, and to attend training or

counseling, if available. Prisoner movement is regimented and strictly controlled by armed guards and video surveillance.

Despite layers of security measures, maximum security prisons are dangerous places for inmates and staff. They became more dangerous as the result of prison overcrowding. From the end of 1995 to June 30, 2003, the
number of prisoners in state custody increased by almost 3 percent annually,
and the number of inmates in federal prisons rose by 8 percent per year.[8]
Not only were there more prisoners, but they were serving longer sentences
as the result of determinate sentencing and three-strikes laws. In other
words, more felons were entering prisons and fewer were leaving. By 2003,
about one out of every 11 inmates, or 9.4 percent, was serving a life sentence
in state or federal prisons in the United States.[9] In effect, a growing sub-
population of prisoners with no hope of release had little to lose while in
prison.

THE SUPERMAX

The super maximum security prison, or supermax, was designed to control
inmates who are violent and disruptive in prison. Supermax prisons exist as
freestanding facilities or as specialized control units within maximum security prisons. From 1989 to 1993, 15 supermax facilities or control units were
opened in the United States, and from 1994 to 2000, another 10 went into
operation.[10] Since 1989, approximately one-half of the more than 50 supermax facilities and control units in the United States were put into operation.

Since 1989, the growth of supermax facilities has been unprecedented.
The concept of the super maximum security prison, however, is not new.
During the 1930s, with severe restrictions placed on prison industries,
prison administrators were hard-pressed to control the increasing numbers
of idled inmates in large prisons. The severe economic hardships caused by
the Great Depression left the public with little appetite for spending money
on rehabilitating convicted felons. J. Edgar Hoover, director of the Federal
Bureau of Investigation from 1924 to 1972, declared war on crime. It was in
this social climate in 1934 when a U.S. military prison built in 1909 was
converted to the first federal super maximum prison on Alcatraz Island in
the San Francisco Bay. Known as the Rock, Alcatraz prison was designed to
house the worst offenders, particularly those who were the least controllable
and the most disruptive in other prisons. In 1954, Mississippi became the
first state to open a supermax prison. Alcatraz prison closed in 1963 due to
high operating costs. During its 29 years of operation, Alcatraz gained a
reputation as the most repressive federal prison in the United States. In
1972, Alcatraz prison became part of the Golden Gate National Recreational Area.

Introduction to Prisons

In 1963, the same year Alcatraz closed, the U.S. prison at Marion, Illinois, went into operation, designed to hold 500 male felons who were difficult to control. In 1972, prisoners at Marion began a work stoppage to protest the beating of an inmate by prison guards. The work stoppage lasted for over a week until guards segregated 60 inmates identified as leaders and key participants in the work stoppage The 60 inmates were placed in the prison's H-unit and required to participate in a behavior modification program called the Control and Rehabilitation Effort, or CARE. Under the CARE program, the inmates were held in solitary confinement and subjected to intense psychological sessions designed to bring them under control. In 1973, Marion Prison's H-unit became known as a control unit.

The control unit was expanded throughout the Marion prison. Like Alcatraz, Marion prison became the end of the line for federal prisoners with serious disciplinary problems. In 1978, the U.S. Bureau of Prisons added a level 6 to its inmate classification system for the most violent and disruptive federal prisoners. In 1979, Marion prison was designated the only level 6 correctional facility in the federal prison system. As such, the U.S. prison at Marion effectively became a supermax facility.

In 1989, the Security Housing Unit, or SHU, was opened at the Pelican Bay state prison in Pelican Bay, California. The SHU at Pelican Bay became the model for supermax prisons and control units in both the state and federal prison systems. Designed for 1,056 inmates, prisoners at the SHU in Pelican Bay are confined in cells measuring 8 by 10 feet for all but 90 minutes each day, when they are allowed to go alone to a concrete exercise area that is about the size of three cells, with 20-foot walls and metal screens overhead. Cell doors are constructed of solid steel and are opened and closed by remote control. In 1993, the U.S. Bureau of Prisons opened a new supermax facility in Florence, Colorado, designed to house 480 of the most dangerous and aggressive inmates in the federal prison system.

In many supermax facilities, inmates are classified according to their level of controlled confinement. For example, the Mississippi Department of Corrections operates two supermax facilities in which inmates are assigned custody ratings. Inmates with the highest rating are considered dangerous to other inmates and the prison staff. They are segregated, not allowed visitors, and are placed in restraints during any movement within the prison. By comparison, prisoners assigned the lowest custody level are essentially housed in medium security conditions, even though they are still confined in a supermax facility. Generally, inmates must earn easement of their custody restrictions through good conduct. At the supermax facility at Ionia, Michigan, after six months of good behavior, inmates may earn the right to participate in limited activities outside the cell, including work. After one year of good conduct, restrictions can be further eased to allow participation in group activities and expanded visitation privileges.

Those critical of supermax prisons and control units contend that the long periods of isolation and severe restrictions of movement imposed upon inmates constitute cruel and unusual punishment, in violation of the Eighth Amendment of the U.S. Constitution. That argument has largely failed, primarily because the conditions of confinement within supermax facilities are considered to be within the legally permissible range of deprivations that correctional institutions may impose on noncompliant inmates to maintain discipline and order. Critics of supermax facilities also argue that, for those inmates who are not under a sentence of life imprisonment, it is difficult to justify how prolonged periods of isolation will prepare them for a successful return to society. However, proponents of the supermax system counter that by segregating extremely violent inmates, the majority of prisoners are made safer, as are prison staff members.

DEATH ROW

Prisons are responsible for the housing and execution of inmates under sentences of death in the United States. Prisoners awaiting the death penalty are typically confined in special housing units, or cell blocks, within prison facilities that are designated to administer capital punishment, which is execution by the government. Each of these special units is commonly referred to as a death row. The phrase *on death row* can refer to an individual inmate under sentence of death or collectively to all prisoners awaiting execution.

In 2003, the death penalty was legal in the federal system and in 38 states. Capital punishment was not permitted in the District of Columbia and the 12 states of Alaska, Hawaii, Iowa, Maine, Massachusetts, Michigan, Minnesota, North Dakota, Rhode Island, Vermont, West Virginia, and Wisconsin. From 1930 to 2002, some 4,679 persons were executed in the United States. On average, between 1977 and 2002, inmates were incarcerated in prisons for about 10 years until their executions. The length of time spent in correctional facilities between sentencing and execution more than doubled during that period, from about 51 months for inmates in 1977 to 127 months in 2002.

Historically, one of the earliest forms of the death penalty was banishment to the wilderness, where the offender usually died from starvation, dehydration, or animal attack. Over time, methods of execution have included burning alive, burying alive, boiling in oil, stoning, beheading, disemboweling, and smothering. Executions were usually administered in public, under the rationale that the spectacle of a gruesome death would deter those in attendance from committing similar crimes. Public executions are still carried out in some countries. Most modern nations, including the United States however, no longer permit the public viewing of executions. Nonetheless, limited viewing of executions is permitted in the United States, usually by selected media representatives, law enforcement officials, and family members of both the crime victim and the condemned individual. In addition, official witnesses are required in order to verify that the execution is carried out according the protocol.

The first execution by electrocution was carried out on William Kemmler for the crime of murder on August 6, 1890, at the Auburn penitentiary in New York. Thomas Edison, among others, opposed electrocution because it was extremely painful. As an alternative, opponents of electrocution proposed the use of lethal gas. On February 8, 1924, in Nevada, Gee Jon became the first person in the United States to be executed with cyanide gas in a gas chamber.

In 1972, executions were halted in the United States when the U.S. Supreme Court, in the case of *Furman v. Georgia*, ruled that Georgia's death penalty law violated the Eighth Amendment's ban against cruel and unusual punishment. However, in 1976, the Court held in *Gregg v. Georgia* that Georgia's newly revised guidelines for the application of the death penalty were constitutional, and executions resumed throughout the United States.

In 1977, Oklahoma became the first state to legalize execution by lethal injection, which was viewed as more humane, or at least less cruel. On December 6, 1982, in Texas, convicted murderer Charles Brooks became the first person in the United States to be executed by lethal injection. Lethal injection became the primary mode of execution in the United States in both the federal and state correctional systems. Of the 65 prisoners put to death in the United States in 2003, all were executed by lethal injection except for one Virginia inmate, who was executed by electrocution.[11]

In the federal prison system, on June 11, 2001, Timothy McVeigh became the first person executed by lethal injection for his part in killing 168 people in the 1995 bombing of the Alfred P. Murrah Federal Building in Oklahoma City, Oklahoma. Other federal executions by lethal injection included Juan Raul Garza, on June 19, 2001, for three murders in the continuance of a criminal enterprise (drug trafficking), and Louis Jones, Jr., on March 18, 2003, for kidnapping resulting in death.

Beginning with McVeigh, all federal executions were carried out at the federal prison in Terre Haute, Indiana, where the lethal injection facility, built in 1995 at a cost of $300,000, consists of an execution chamber surrounded by five viewing rooms. During federal executions, all procedures are monitored by the Justice Department in Washington, D. C., through an open telephone line with prison officials. Only the president of the United States has the power to grant clemency after the condemned has exhausted all legal appeals.

Although execution procedures in federal and state correctional systems vary in their specifics, all executions in the United States follow a general protocol. In the hours preceding the execution, the condemned inmate is served a meal of his or her choice, with certain restrictions, including no alcoholic beverages. In some states, inmates are allowed to shower and put on freshly laundered prison clothing before the execution. In other states, the inmate is required to remove all outer clothing prior to entering the death chamber. Generally, the prison's warden or chaplain visits the inmate and often remains with the inmate through the execution process.

Inside the chamber, the condemned is placed in restraints on a gurney and connected to an electrocardiogram (EKG) machine to determine when the inmate's heart stops and the time of death. Two intravenous tubes extending from an adjacent executioner's room are then inserted with catheters into the inmate's arms or legs. Once the tubes are in place, witnesses are allowed to observe through viewing windows. Individuals permitted to witness executions generally include relatives of the crime victim and the inmate, official witnesses selected by the state, representatives of the media, a spiritual adviser, prison guards, the prison's warden, and a prison employee designated as the executioner. Some jurisdictions use execution teams composed of two or three individuals. Each of the members simultaneously delivers liquid into the intravenous lines, but none of them knows which one is actually delivering the lethal drugs. The inmate may choose to make a final statement. The statement may be verbal or written and read aloud by the inmate or a prison representative, such as the warden or chaplain. The final statement is generally tape-recorded and later released to the media. The lethal drugs are then administered, in order. First, the anesthetic sodium thiopental induces sleep. Next a muscle relaxant, such as pancuronium bromide, is delivered in a dosage high enough to cause paralysis and stop the inmate's breathing. In 2003, concerns were raised by some U.S. medical experts, including anesthesiologist Edward Brunner, that the use of the paralyzing agent may induce suffocation, causing serious pain that cannot be communicated by the inmate. Despite the contentions of Dr. Brunner and others that death by lethal injections is not painless, paralyzing agents remain in use in all jurisdictions that perform such executions. In some jurisdictions, a third drug, potassium chloride, is administered to stop the heart. A physician or medical technician declares the inmate's death, which commonly takes five to 18 minutes from the administration of the first drug.

CORRECTIONAL SYSTEMS

In the United States, there are two main prison systems: state and federal. State prison systems include correctional facilities for males, females, and juvenile offenders. Every state and the District of Columbia operates a correctional system, and each functions in an autonomous manner under the authority of its particular jurisdiction. In the federal prison system, the Bureau of Prisons in the U.S. Department of Justice operates correctional institutions for males and females, and the U.S. Department of Defense operates military prisons for criminal offenders in the armed services. Private prisons are correctional facilities operated by companies in the private sector that are under contract with state or federal correctional agencies. As such, private prisons function under the umbrella of state and federal correctional systems.

STATE PRISON SYSTEMS

As a general rule, an individual who commits a felony in violation of state law is subject to imprisonment in the state where the crime occurred. Consequently, most prison inmates in the United States are confined in state prisons, because most felonies committed each year in the United States violate state laws. As of June 30, 2004, some 1.2 million inmates were incarcerated in state prisons nationwide, compared to nearly 170,000 inmates in U.S. federal prisons.[12]

All 50 states operate prisons, usually through state departments of correction. Most state departments of correction are administered by a director appointed by the state's governor and have cabinet-level status. As such, directors are able to exercise a high degree of autonomy in the allocation of fiscal resources and personnel within their departments. There is no central authority governing the state prison systems in the United States. Although there are similarities among state systems of corrections, each state system is essentially autonomous. The American Correction Association (ACA), founded in 1870 as the National Prison Association and renamed in 1954, serves as an umbrella organization for correctional agencies and professionals nationwide. In 1968, the ACA established an accreditation process for correctional institutions and created a standards committee composed of criminal justice professionals to administer the accreditation process. Through accreditation, the ACA established minimum standards on issues such as inmate health, institutional safety, and staff training. The ACA also publishes *Corrections Today* magazine and the peer-reviewed research journal *Corrections Compendium.*

In 2000, there were 1,023 state prisons in the United States that were classified as confinement facilities, according to the Bureau of Justice statistics,

Prisons

which conducts a census of U.S. correctional facilities every five years.[13] In addition, there were 297 community-based correctional facilities, for a total of 1,320 state correctional facilities, an increase of 204 facilities since 1995, the year of the previous census. Despite the overall increase in the number of state correctional facilities, state prisons in 2000 operated at 101 percent of rated capacity, meaning that, collectively, state correctional facilities nationwide housed more prisoners than they were designed to hold.

From 1995 to June 30, 2003, the incarceration rate for state prisoners rose by 14 percent, from 379 to 433 inmates per 100,000 U.S. residents.[14] As state prison populations rose, so did their operating costs. In fiscal year 2001, states spent a total of $29.5 billion on prison expenditures. When adjusted for inflation, that amounted to an increase of $5.5 billion since 1996, or almost $1 billion per year over the five-year period. On a per capita basis, from 1996 to 2001, state prison expenditures increased from $91 to $104 per U.S. resident. The average cost per state inmate in 2001 was $62.05 per day. By comparison, the cost per federal prisoner was nearly the same, at $62.01 per day. In 2001, California spent $4.2 billion on prison expenditures, the most of any state. The least spent by any state on prison expenditures was $26.8 million by North Dakota.[15]

One measure of these rising costs was the increase in employees at state prisons nationwide. From 1995 to 2000, the number of employees in confinement facilities increased by some 22 percent. Of those, about two-thirds of state prison staff in 2000 were correctional officers charged with maintaining security and control of inmates. Despite the overall increase in correctional staff, the ratio of the number of inmates to correctional officers remained the same between 1995 and 2000, at about 4.5 inmates per correctional employee at state confinement facilities.[16]

Beginning in the early 1980s, many states legislated determinate sentencing and truth-in-sentencing guidelines that lengthened prison terms for many crimes and for some offenses removed the possibility of parole. As a result, there was a significant increase in inmates serving life sentences. From 1984 to 1992, the violent crime rate nationwide rose by 40 percent, yet the number of inmates imprisoned for life doubled during that period. From 1992 to 2003, those serving life sentences increased by 83 percent, and those sentenced to life without the possibility of parole rose by 170 percent, despite an overall decline of 35 percent in the rate of violent crime.[17] As a result, from 1982 to 2001, state expenditures for corrections outpaced all other costs related to the administration of justice, rising by some 538 percent. By comparison, during the same time period, state expenditures for judicial and legal functions increased by about 425 percent, and by 270 percent for law enforcement.

Introduction to Prisons

Treatment in State Prison Systems

A wide range of prison programs operate under the umbrella of treatment in state prisons nationwide. They include counseling and educational programs, vocational training, and inmate self-help through organizations such as Alcoholics Anonymous.

Counseling is generally offered in group sessions, although individual psychological counseling is sometimes available. The general goals of both group and individual counseling in a correctional setting include:

- Coping with the frustrations of life in an institution and in society
- Recognizing the emotional roots of criminal behavior
- Understanding and accepting the consequences of inappropriate conduct
- Improving the overall emotional climate of the institution through interpersonal communication

Because correctional facilities are often underfunded, the hiring of clinically trained mental health professionals is not always possible. As an alternative, many institutions utilize group leaders, often correctional staff with some type of training in counseling. Fundamental personality changes are not the goal of group counseling. Rather, group meetings may help inmates to better understand how others perceive them and, in turn, stimulate a higher sense of self-awareness to more effectively deal with common problems.

State correctional institutions commonly offer educational programs that allow inmates to earn a high school diploma or an equivalent, usually the general educational development (GED) certificate. The GED program was developed as part of the GI Bill at the end of World War II to allow armed services personnel who were returning from the war to pursue educational opportunities. Some correctional institutions offer courses for college credits toward an associate or bachelor's degree. When available, educational programs beyond a high school diploma or its equivalency are often subject to limited enrollment due to lack of funding. In states such as Connecticut, Illinois, and Texas, statewide school districts were formed to meet the educational needs of inmates.

Participation in vocational training or a prison industry is often a key consideration for parole boards in determining when an inmate is suitable for release. A stable work record while incarcerated is often an inmate's only calling card when seeking employment after release. The following are among typical prison industries:

- Food services. Inmates prepare food for inmates and correctional staff. Duties include baking bread, cooking, cleaning, and the maintenance of kitchen facilities.

- Maintenance. Inmates tend to the buildings and grounds of the prison complex. Duties include skilled labor, including electrical work, masonry, plumbing, and painting, as well as unskilled work, such as cleaning and garbage collection.

- Laundry services. Inmates operate prison laundries that serve their institution and other smaller institutions that lack laundry facilities.

- Agriculture. Inmates work on prison farms that supply produce, dairy products, and poultry for use in their institution and other prisons.

Besides prison industry, vocational training is offered at many prisons. For example, New York State prisons offer over 40 trade and technical courses, including barber training, computer programming, auto mechanics, and radio and television repair. At many prisons, enrollment in vocational training classes is limited due to budgetary constraints, and equipment for training purposes is sometimes obsolete.

Work release or furlough programs allow inmates to leave the prison grounds during the day for a job in the community and return to the prison at night. Furlough programs are available to inmates who have demonstrated their trustworthiness over a period of time, often years. Work release programs allow inmates to gain valuable on-the-job experience. However, they also present a security risk, particularly with respect to contraband smuggled into the institution. In addition, because of the remote locations of many prisons, it is sometimes impractical for inmates to travel the distances required for a job in the community.

Inmate self-help groups are also available in many prisons, although they generally are not run by the correctional facility, but are offered by outside organizations. Such programs are called self-help in the sense that they are available to inmates with the initiative to join and attend meetings. Self-help groups are sometimes organized as chapters of national organizations, such as Alcoholics Anonymous, and are designed to address the emotional issues related to alcoholism or drug addiction. Other self-help groups are organized along racial or ethnic lines, such as the Afro-American Coalition and the Native American Brotherhood. These groups may be local, regional, or national in scope. Their goal is to establish a sense of community as a means of working for individual improvement in areas including literacy and legal education. Other types of self-help groups include national organizations such as the Fortune Society and Seventh Step, which attempt to raise the self-esteem of inmates to better prepare them for success after release from prison.

State Corrections for Juveniles

Juvenile correctional systems are administered by the 50 states and the District of Columbia. The federal prison system does not house juvenile offenders. Like state adult correctional systems, there is no central controlling authority for the administration of correctional institutions for juveniles. With the enactment of the Juvenile Justice and Delinquency Prevention Act in 1974, however, the U.S. Congress established federal core requirements for the treatment and handling of juvenile offenders. The act established the Coordinating Council on Juvenile Justice and Delinquency Prevention, an independent body within the executive branch of the federal government charged with monitoring juveniles in detention.

Historically, juvenile offenders were often mixed with male and female adults in correctional settings. By the early 19th century in the United States, shelters were developed for juvenile runaways and vagrants. In 1825, the House of Refuge was established in New York City and began accepting minors who were referred by the courts, usually for vagrancy or because they were victims of neglect or abuse. Within the House of Refuge, juveniles were segregated by sex. In 1826, the House of Reformation was established in Boston as a facility for juvenile offenders. More reformatories for juveniles were subsequently established in Maine, Massachusetts, Michigan, New York, and Ohio. These facilities housed both juvenile criminal offenders and minors known as status offenders, who had not violated any criminal laws but were deemed incorrigible as the result of truancy from school or running away from home. Still, many juvenile offenders continued to be incarcerated in adult prisons and jail in the United States.

In 1899, the Illinois Juvenile Court Act created a new judicial jurisdiction for juvenile delinquents that was separate from the adult criminal justice system. Among the most important provisions of the act was the strict segregation of juvenile and adult offenders in correctional settings. Using the Illinois Juvenile Court Act as a model, juvenile courts were established in 1901 in New York and Wisconsin and in 1902 in Maryland and Ohio. By 1912, some 22 states had established juvenile jurisdictions, and by 1928, only Maine and Wyoming did not have a juvenile court system in place. In 1945, Wyoming was the last state to establish a juvenile court system. Still, juvenile court systems were not uniform from state to state. For example, the segregation of juveniles and adults in correctional facilities was not mandated by North Dakota until 1969, and Maine did not do so until 1977.

Beginning in 1980, gun violence and homicides by juvenile offenders began to increase in the United States. The rising trend of criminal violence by juveniles peaked in 1993, but the public's perception that juvenile crime was out of control caused many states to enact tougher laws for juvenile offenders. Those measures sometimes included the lowering of the age of majority for certain crimes to allow the most serious juvenile offenders to be tried as adults and in some states to be committed to adult correctional facilities. As of June 30, 2004, some 2,477 inmates under the age of 18 were confined in state prisons nationwide.[18] In most states, criminal offenders who are 18 years of age and older are adults under the law. In Connecticut, New York, and North Carolina, the oldest age for original court jurisdiction in delinquency matters is 15, meaning that offenders who are 16 and older are treated as adults. Offenders 17 years of age and older are processed as adults in Georgia, Illinois, Louisiana, Massachusetts, Michigan, Missouri, New Hampshire, South Carolina, Texas, and Wisconsin.[19]

Jurisdictions differ in their administration and management of juveniles in correctional settings. In 16 states and the District of Columbia, state delinquency institutions are administered under the authority of a social or human services agency. In 16 other states, such facilities are under the authority of a state department of youth services, or youth authority. Juvenile detention facilities are administered under the umbrella of the adult corrections agency in 11 states, and in six states they are administered by agencies responsible for both child protection and delinquency functions.[20]

The Office of Juvenile Justice and Delinquency Prevention (OJJDP) was created under the Juvenile Justice and Delinquency Prevention Act of 1974 to monitor and study all facets of juvenile justice in the United States and to disseminate that information to the public. In October 2000, the OJJDP conducted its first census of residential facilities for juvenile offenders in the United States. The census counts as juveniles all offenders in residential placement who are under 21 years of age, which is over the age of juvenile jurisdiction in all states and the District of Columbia. In most states, however, offenders who are committed to residential placement when they were juveniles may be kept in that placement until they are 21 years old.

In 2000, there were 110,284 offenders under 21 years of age who were housed in some 3,061 juvenile facilities in the United States. About 70 percent of juveniles under 21 years of age were confined in publicly operated facilities, and the remainder were in privately run facilities, usually under state oversight. There was significant overcrowding in juvenile facilities in 2000, with about 39 percent of facilities reporting that they had fewer beds than residents.[21]

Overcrowding in juvenile correctional facilities placed minors at a higher risk of suffering injury as the result of violence. In 2000, about 45 percent of overcrowded facilities reported that they had transported juveniles in their custody to emergency rooms because of injuries suffered in fights. Only 38 percent of facilities operating at capacity or below capacity reported injuries that required hospital treatment. In 2000, there were 30 deaths reported of juveniles in custody. Of those, nine were ruled accidental, eight were due to illness, and seven were suicides. Four homicides were reported in 2000, but all of them occurred while the juveniles were temporarily outside of correctional custody for some reason, such as a weekend home visit.[22]

All states have laws that require minors to attend school. As a result, educational programs in juvenile correctional facilities are a requirement, not an option, as in adult corrections. Educational programs in juvenile corrections must be broad in scope to accommodate all offenders, including the developmentally challenged. Minors in custody are also entitled to healthcare services, recreational activities, and a safe physical environment. Unfortunately, in some states, juvenile correctional agencies have fallen short of delivering those minimal standards.

One of the most troubling examples of deficient standards in juvenile corrections occurred in California. In 2000, there were 285 juvenile correctional facilities operating in California, with a combined population of more than 19,000 juveniles under 21 years of age. As such, California had the largest number of juvenile facilities and housed the largest population of juvenile offenders of any U.S. state.[23] The most serious of those offenders were confined at the California Youth Authority (CYA), a division of the California Department of Corrections.

In 2003, CYA housed over 4,400 wards at 11 correctional facilities and four conservation camps. A report commissioned by the California Attorney General's Office in response to a lawsuit filed by the Prison Law Office found that nine of the CYA facilities were operated more like adult prisons, with emphasis placed on incapacitation instead of rehabilitation. According to the report, released in 2004, CYA facilities were deficient in 21 out of 22 minimal standards established by experts in juvenile corrections. Violations documented in the report included the use of locked cages to confine some wards during school classes. The cages measured four-feet square and were tall enough to allow wards to stand up. Larger cages measuring 12 feet by 15 feet were also used to confine some wards. Other violations included excessive use of psychotropic medications for behavior control, inadequate coordination of mental health professionals in treatment plans, and the overuse of chemical restraints, including pepper spray, by staff members with insufficient training in behavior management.[24] The report was presented to members of the California legislature and other state officials.

THE FEDERAL PRISON SYSTEM

Unlike state correctional systems, the federal prison system is centrally administered by the Federal Bureau of Prisons (BOP), an agency within the U.S. Department of Justice. The central office of the BOP is located in Washington, D.C. The federal prison system is divided into six regional offices, each administered by a regional director. The regional offices are located in Atlanta, Georgia; Dallas, Texas; Philadelphia, Pennsylvania; Burlingame, California; Annapolis, Maryland; and Kansas City, Kansas.

Prisons

Federal correctional facilities include prisons for men and women, military prisons, and privately operated correctional facilities that operate under federal oversight. Federal prisons house felons convicted in federal courts of criminal offenses against the United States. Some crimes are uniquely federal, such as treason or airline hijacking. Other crimes may overlap with state laws. For example, murder is a state crime. However, the killing of a federal employee during the course of his or her job is a federal crime, which is why Timothy McVeigh was charged and tried in federal court for his part in the 1995 bombing of the Alfred P. Murrah Federal Building that killed 168 people. Similarly, all states have drug laws, and most drug offenders are prosecuted in state courts. When individuals transport those same illegal drugs across state lines for sale, however, they commit the federal crime of interstate drug trafficking.

Historically, federal prisoners were housed in state and local institutions in the United States. In 1870, the Justice Department was established and placed in charge of the growing number of federal prisoners in state and local correctional facilities. As state prisons became increasingly overcrowded, some states only accepted federal prisoners who were residents of that state. From 1885 to 1895, the number of federal prisoners in state facilities more than doubled, from 1,027 to 2,516, and the number of federal prisoners in local jails increased from 10,000 to 15,000 during the same 10-year period.[25]

Under pressure from the states to establish federal correctional facilities to ease prison overcrowding, in 1891 the U.S. Congress authorized the construction of three penitentiaries. Until then the only federal penitentiary, at Fort Leavenworth, Kansas, was used to house military prisoners who were not confined in state or local facilities. In 1895, the U.S. War Department decided to transfer the military prisoners at Fort Leavenworth to alternate facilities at installations in the United States. As a result, space became available at the Leavenworth prison. For the first time in U.S. history, nonmilitary federal prisoners were transferred from state and local facilities for confinement in a federal prison.

On July 10, 1896, Congress appropriated funds for the construction of a federal prison for 1,200 inmates at a site approximately three miles from the Leavenworth prison. Built by convict labor, the prison was not completed until 1928. Meanwhile, a second federal penitentiary was completed in 1875 at McNeil Island, Washington, and a third in 1899 at Atlanta, Georgia. All three prisons were built in the Auburn style, with multitiered cell blocks in a fortresslike structure.

Between 1900 and 1935, federal criminal jurisdiction expanded significantly, in large measure due to the passage of the following legislation:

- The White Slave Act of 1910, outlawing interstate commerce in prostitution.
- The Harrison Narcotic Act of 1914, establishing controlled substances that were subject to taxation and strict government monitoring.
- The Volstead Act of 1918, prohibiting the sale and consumption of alcoholic beverages.
- The Dyer Act of 1919, criminalizing the interstate transportation of stolen vehicles.

The population of federal prisons swelled as the result of the increasing number of convictions in federal courts. In 1927, a 500-bed correctional facility for women was opened at Alderson, West Virginia, in response to the rising number of females in the federal correctional population. By 1929, overcrowding was so serious in New York City correctional facilities that a newly built three-story garage was converted to the Federal Detention Headquarters. Later that year, the U.S. House of Representatives Special Committee on Federal Penal Reformatory Institutions recommended the establishment of a centralized administration for federal prisons. On May 14, 1930, President Herbert Hoover signed into law the legislation that created the Federal Bureau of Prisons (BOP) and appointed Sanford Bates, then president of the American Correctional Association, as the first director of the BOP.

As constituted in 1930, the Bureau of Prisons operated three penitentiaries, as well as the U.S. Industrial Reformatory, the Alderson correctional facility for women, the Federal Detention Headquarters jail, and eight former army camps converted to makeshift correctional facilities to house the overflow of inmates entering the federal prison system. Still, the system was overtaxed, and the lack of space in federal facilities necessitated the housing of some prisoners in local jails. In response, the BOP moved quickly to establish new correctional facilities. In 1930, control of the U.S. Mint at New Orleans, Louisiana, was transferred from the U.S. Department of the Treasury to the Department of Justice for use as a jail. New regional jails went into operation in 1932 at La Tuna, Texas, and at Lewisburg, Pennsylvania, and in 1933 at Milan, Michigan. Also opened in 1933 was a men's reformatory at El Reno, Oklahoma, and a hospital for mentally ill inmates at Springfield, Missouri. In 1934, the military prison at Alcatraz Island, California, was converted to a maximum security facility for federal inmates. As the result of prison expansion, in 1940 the BOP was able to relocate narcotics violators confined at the military barracks at Fort Leavenworth and return the prison to the War Department. For the first time in U.S. history, all federal inmates were housed in federal correctional facilities.

Overcrowding in federal correctional facilities continued to be a problem. In 1954, at the request of the Bureau of Prisons, the U.S. Navy's military prison at Terminal Island, California, was converted to a federal prison. By 1955, the BOP operated some 28 correctional institutions. Still, there was insufficient space to house the nearly 21,000 federal inmates at that time. Forty years later, in 1995, there were 77 federal correctional facilities housing nearly 81,000 inmates. By June 30, 2000, the Bureau of Prisons had added seven additional facilities, for a total of 84 federal prisons, all of which were confinement facilities. Still, there were not enough prisons to keep up with the influx of federal inmates between 1995 and 2000, as shown by the increase in the rated capacity of federal facilities from 125 percent to 134 percent during those five years. In other words, in 2000, the 84 federal prisons in operation had space for about 83,000 inmates but housed nearly 111,000 prisoners.[26] By the end of 2003, overcrowding in federal prisons had eased only slightly, with federal correctional facilities operating at 39 percent above capacity.[27] As the result of overcrowding, the BOP resorted to placing some inmates in privately operated correctional facilities under federal oversight. As of June 30, 2004, of the 98,791 inmates housed in private facilities, some 24,506 were federal inmates. In other words, nearly one out of four inmates in private prisons in 2003 was a federal prisoner.[28]

Housing more inmates resulted in significantly higher operating costs for the federal prison system. From 1982 to 2001, federal expenditures for corrections rose from $541 million to nearly $5.2 billion, for a total increase of 861 percent and an annual rate of increase of almost 13 percent. During that period, federal corrections expenditures outpaced all other justice expenditures. For example, from 1982 to 2001, the costs of federal law enforcement rose by about 494 percent, while judicial and legal expenditures increased by 636 percent.[29]

Rehabilitation in the Federal Prison System

In 1934, under the direction of Sanford Bates, the Bureau of Prisons implemented a classification system that was unique in U.S. penology and did not exist in any of the state correctional systems at that time. Under the system, each federal correctional facility was classified as a penitentiary, reformatory, prison camp, or hospital. Also included were drug addiction treatment facilities operated by the U.S. Public Health Service. Within each facility, inmates were classified according to factors including age, sex, and type of offense, with the goal of developing individualized programs for rehabilitation. To meet that goal, the federal prison system expanded educational and vocational training departments and prison libraries. Specialists, including social workers, instructors, and chaplains, were recruited to run prison counseling and training programs. To encourage professional development, the BOP established five regional training centers for correctional staff, including corrections officers and other employees, and by 1937 all federal correctional personnel were placed under the jurisdiction of the Civil Service Commission. Federal parole was reorganized, and the supervision of parolees was transferred from the U.S. Marshall's Office to the probation offices of the federal courts in order to develop an aftercare system that was more treatment-oriented and less punitive in its approach to ex-convicts.

Over the next 40 years, inmate rehabilitation programs in the federal correctional system were expanded and refined. For example, the caseworker method of placing a large number of inmates housed throughout a prison under the supervision of one caseworker was replaced by the unit management concept in many federal institutions. Under the unit management system, inmates were housed in contained units and worked directly with case workers, correctional counselors, or educational professionals assigned to their unit. Both the caseworker and unit manager systems were built around the medical model of treatment developed by Sanford Bates during his tenure from 1930 to 1937 as the director of the Bureau of Prisons. Sanford and other proponents of the medical model believed that criminal behavior was the result of an underlying disorder that could be treated through medical or psychological methods.

The medical model eventually fell out of favor among correctional professionals. The demise of the medical model occurred at a time of increasing tensions in U.S. prisons. Beginning in the late 1960s, the U.S. Supreme Court issued a series of rulings expanding the rights of inmates in areas including legal representation, humane treatment, and medical care. The lawful exercise of constitutional rights by prisoners was often at odds with the increasingly punitive style of prison management and inmate control in U.S. corrections. The result was sometimes violent. In 1971, at the Attica prison in Attica, New York, a four-day protest over prison conditions turned violent, resulting in the deaths of 32 prisoners and 11 guards who were held hostage by the rioting inmates. In 1975 the BOP officially began to phase out the use of the medical model in favor of the correctional philosophies of deterrence and incapacitation, which were more in line with the aim of maintaining control over what was viewed as an increasingly vocal and sometimes violent prisoner population. Still, prison violence continued. In 1980, 33 people were killed as the result of an inmate riot at the New Mexico state prison. In the federal system, the prisons at Oakdale, Louisiana, and at Atlanta, Georgia, were held siege for 11 days in 1987 during an inmate uprising. Some 89 hostages were released unharmed. The Department of Justice ultimately chose to hold no one accountable for the uprising.

Military Prisons

Most federal prisoners in the United States are housed in facilities operated by the federal Bureau of Prisons, a branch of the U.S. Department of Justice. However, the federal government also operates military prisons for inmates who are under the jurisdiction of the U.S. armed services, including members of the army, air force, navy, marine corps, and coast guard. Military prisons are administered by the U.S. Department of Defense.

The oldest military prison in the United States is the U.S. Disciplinary Barracks at Fort Leavenworth, Kansas. Originally called the United States Military Prison, the facility has been in continuous operation since May 15, 1875. In 2002, a new 521-bed unit was opened at the facility. Beginning in 1897, military prisoners confined at the U.S. Disciplinary Barracks assisted in the construction of the U.S. Federal Penitentiary at Leavenworth, Kansas, which was not completed until 1928. In effect, this created two prisons that are commonly referred to by the same name—Leavenworth. They are distinct facilities, however, operated by different branches of the federal government. The U.S. Disciplinary Barracks is a maximum security facility for both commissioned officers and enlistees convicted by U.S. court martial.

Besides the military prison at Leavenworth, the U.S. Army operated five other correctional facilities at the end of 2003. In addition, there were six facilities operated by the marine corps, 11 by the navy, and 34 air force facilities, for a total of 57 military confinement facilities. In 2003, military prisons operated at 65 percent of capacity and housed some 2,377 prisoners, which was well below their design capacity of 3,249 inmates. Just over 40 percent of military prisoners in 2002 were confined at the Disciplinary Barracks at Leavenworth and the five other facilities operated by the U.S. Army. Correctional facilities operated by the navy held about 30 percent of military prisoners, and marine corps and air force facilities held 20 percent and 5 percent, respectively. Military prisons provided similar levels of educational and training programs as federal prisons for civilians.

PRISONERS OF WAR

During wartime, the U.S. military operates detainment facilities for prisoners of war. Commonly, these facilities are located abroad, in or around the area of conflict. In retaliation for the domestic terrorist attacks against the United States on September 11, 2001, the United States launched a war on terrorism. As a result, military forces led by the United States, with assistance from Great Britain and other countries, invaded Afghanistan, commencing with air attacks on October 7, 2001. On March 20, 2003, the

U.S. forces invaded Iraq, again with assistance from Great Britain and other countries, based on intelligence that Iraq possessed weapons of mass destruction. In early 2004, about one year after the invasion of Iraq, photographs were made public depicting the alleged abuse of prisoners of war by U.S. soldiers at the Abu Ghraib prison in Iraq. The photographs contained disturbing images of U.S. prisoners of war being subjected to alleged acts of physical brutality and sexual abuse. In the aftermath of the release of the photographs, the U.S. Congress and the Defense Department began investigations into alleged abuses of U.S. prisoners of war in Iraq and Afghanistan, including the deaths of some 40 prisoners of war. Chapter Two includes a discussion of the standards of international law governing the humane treatment of prisoners of war, as established under the Geneva Conventions.

Beginning in January 2002, additional military prisoners, or detainees, were held at the U.S. Naval Base at Guantánamo Bay, Cuba, as the result of the U.S. war on terrorism. On June 28, 2004, the U.S. Supreme Court ruled in two cases that detainees have limited rights to contest their detention in courts of law. Chapter Two includes analyses of those cases, *Hamdi v. Rumsfeld* and *Rasul v. Bush*. Because Guantánamo Bay, Cuba, is not within the jurisdiction of a federal court, the rulings were expected to necessitate the transfer of hundreds of detainees at Guantánamo Bay to U.S. military prisons within federal court jurisdictions, including the U.S. Disciplinary Barracks at Leavenworth.[30]

PRIVATE PRISONS

Prior to 1870, some states leased out prisoners to private companies to work as laborers. In exchange the companies paid the costs of feeding, clothing, and housing the prisoners, usually for a flat fee per year for each prisoner. In essence, prisoners were a source of revenue for states that participated in such arrangements with private companies. Inmates under this system were used much like slaves on a plantation to farm or harvest crops. Beginning in about 1870, with the growth of industrialization, private companies leased prisoners to build roads and railroads and to manufacture goods. To keep costs low, inmates were sometimes transported in rolling cages, where they were forced to live in unsanitary conditions, often without medical care or adequate food. When working outside of the cages, prisoners were shackled with ball and chain restraints, and groups of prisoners came to be known as chain gangs. Prisoners who attempted to escape from these brutal conditions were beaten and sometimes killed by heavily armed guards, or overseers. By 1930, many of these work programs were forced out of existence due to federal legislation that placed restrictions on prison labor. In the

1970s, a series of rulings by the U.S. Supreme Court on prisoners' rights, including medical care and basic standards for conditions of confinement, essentially eliminated any type of forced labor by prison inmates.

With the loss of prisoners as a source of revenue, correctional agencies shouldered all of the costs of housing prisoners. Rising inmate populations placed more financial pressure on the states. Increasingly, to save money, states turned to subcontractors in the private sector to deliver prison services, including educational and vocational training and transportation services. Prior to 1984, however, an entire correctional facility operated by a private company did not exist anywhere in the United States.[31]

In 1984, the first privately operated correctional facility was created when the Corrections Corporation of America (CCA) was awarded a contract to run a secure county correctional facility in Hamilton County, Tennessee. In 1985, CCA offered to take over the entire state prison system in Tennessee for $200 million. The bid by CCA was eventually rejected due to opposition from state employee unions and skepticism by state legislators; however, the era of private prisons had begun in the United States. In 1984, the U.S. government awarded a contract to CCA to run a federal detention center for illegal immigrants. The Texas Department of Corrections awarded contracts to run four 500-bed correctional facilities, two to CCA and two to the Wackenhut Corrections Corporation (WCC). By 1988, prisons and jails in 39 states and the District of Columbia were under court order to improve conditions of confinement and reduce prison overcrowding. As a result, the trend toward prison privatization gained momentum.

During the next decade, the contracted capacity of secure adult correctional facilities for state and federal prisoners increased by nearly 700 percent, from 15,300 in 1990 to 121,482 in 1999. By the end of 2002, nearly 94,000 inmates from 31 states and the federal prison system were confined in private prisons. Collectively, they comprised about 6 percent of all state prisoners and over 12 percent of all federal prisoners. As of June 30, 2003, in the United States, some 8.1 percent of all prisoners in the South were confined in private correctional facilities, followed by 6.1 percent in the West, 2.2 percent in the Midwest, and 1.8 percent of prisoners in the Northeast.

The cost of housing prisoners in private facilities varied by state. In fiscal year 2001, there were 11 states that reported no expenditures to house prisoners in private facilities or local jails. Those states were Alabama, Iowa, Kansas, Illinois, Maine, Massachusetts, Missouri, New Hampshire, North Carolina, Washington, and West Virginia. For the remaining states, the cost of contract housing for inmates averaged about 6 percent of their total prison expenditures. However, some states relied much more on alternative facilities to house state prisoners. For example, Montana and Louisiana each spent 37 percent of total prison expenditures on contract correctional housing. Similarly, the percentage of prison expenditures spent on contract housing was 36 percent in Tennessee, 30 percent in Oklahoma, 26 percent in Mississippi, 23 percent in Alaska, and 22 percent in New Mexico in the 2001 fiscal year.[32]

Reducing prison overcrowding was the primary objective identified by government agencies in deciding to enter into contracts with private correctional firms. Other reasons cited for prison privatization included operational flexibility, reducing administrative and construction costs, and improving the level of service. Generally, government agencies first identified a need, such as increasing prison capacity, before seeking bids from private correctional firms. In some cases, however, private correctional firms built facilities first, then solicited contracts from government agencies. These so-called *spec* prisons were popular in the late 1980s, when prison privatization was viewed as something of a panacea for expanding prison capacity and reducing costs.[33] A decade later, however, the building of spec prisons decreased significantly amid a declining trend in privatization, in part because of the mixed record of private prisons in savings costs. An audit conducted by the General Accounting Office (GAO) in 1996 concluded that it was unclear if privatization saved money. In 2001, the Bureau of Justice Statistics (BJS) reported an average savings of about 1 percent from prison privatization. In addition, the BJS report found no evidence of improvement of inmate services or the quality of confinement in privately operated correctional facilities. Since 2000, no states have negotiated contracts with private correctional firms, and some states have scaled back their use of private prisons. For example, in 2001, Arkansas took back control of two prisons operated under contract with the Wackenhut Corrections Corporation due to administrative problems.[34]

Proponents of private correctional facilities make some of the following claims:

- Private firms are less bureaucratic and more efficient in their delivery of goods and services.

- Private firms are less restricted than governmental agencies in the hiring and firing of employees and can better manage their workforce.

- Private firms must compete in the marketplace; they are more attentive than government agencies to controlling costs and delivering high-quality service.

- Marketplace competition, which is absent in public agencies, promotes a higher level of overall effectiveness.

- Government agencies spend their allocated budgets in order to receive more funding, while private firms strive to control costs.

Conversely, some of the arguments against prison privatization include:

- Private firms are more likely to hire low-paid and inexperienced employees in an effort to save money.
- Private firms are more susceptible to corruption in the form of kickbacks and collusive bidding for government contracts, thereby driving up the costs for providing services.
- Private contractors may go out of business.[35]

Perhaps of foremost concern is the ability of private prisons to manage serious crises. For example, on June 18, 1995, detainees at a privately operated facility for illegal immigrants rioted after making repeated allegations of inappropriate conditions of confinement. The contractor, ESMOR Inc., lost control of the 300-bed facility located in Elizabeth, New Jersey, and law enforcement officials were summoned to bring the situation in hand. The facility was closed but later reopened under new management by the Corrections Corporation of America. In 1997, violence at the Northeast Ohio Correctional Facility in Youngstown, Ohio, operated under contract with CCA, resulted in the deaths of two inmates and the escape of six dangerous offenders. The Ohio Department of Rehabilitation and Corrections was prevented from assisting CCA in restoring order at the facility because the state of Ohio lacked regulatory authority over private prisons. Legislation was passed in March 1998 that established state authority over private prisons in Ohio. A subsequent investigation by the U.S. Department of Justice cited a variety of reasons for the breakdown at the CCA facility, including a high rate of staff turnover and inadequate safety procedures. In August 1999, four inmates were murdered by prisoners at two private prisons in New Mexico operated by the Wackenhut Corrections Corporation. At one of the facilities, near Santa Rosa, New Mexico, prisoners rioted for three hours, during which they took control of two housing units and stabbed a guard to death. In response, over 100 of the most troublesome inmates at the Santa Rosa facility were transferred to a state prison in Virginia, raising concerns about the competence of private prisons in controlling violent inmates.

PRISON EXPANSION AND THE IMPACT ON COMMUNITIES

During the 20-year period from 1980 to 2000, the combined population of federal and state prisoners in the United States swelled from 315,974 to just over 1 million, an increase of 318 percent. With the rise in the prisoner population came the need for more correctional facilities. In 2000, there were 84 federal prisons in the United States, up from 77 facilities in 1995, and the number of private correctional facilities more than doubled during the same period, from 110 facilities in 1995 to 264 facilities in 2000.[36]

By far the largest increase in the growth of prisons occurred at the state level. In 1923, when many state correctional facilities still housed federal prisoners in addition to state offenders, there were 61 state prisons in the United States. By 1950, that number more than doubled, from 59 to 127 state prisons, and by 1974, there were 592 state correctional facilities nationwide. However, the greatest increase in the number of state facilities occurred in the last quarter of the 20th century, when the number of state prisons grew from 592 in 1974 to 1,023 in 2000, for an addition of 431 state facilities.

Ten states accounted for about two-thirds of the growth of state prisons nationwide between 1979 and 2000. Ranked from highest to lowest in prison growth, the 10 states were Texas, Florida, California, New York, Michigan, Georgia, Illinois, Ohio, Colorado, and Missouri. The number of state prisons more than doubled in all 10 states. The leader, Texas, added 120 state prisons between 1979 and 2000, for an increase of 706 percent in state correctional facilities. The lowest growth in state prisons from 1979 to 2000 occurred in Florida and New York, where the number of state prisons increased by 115 percent and 117 percent, respectively.[37]

The building of a new prison brings with it inherent challenges for the community where the facility is located. Concerns over safety and the influx of criminal offenders are sometimes seen as disincentives by communities that discourage the building of new correctional facilities. For some localities, however, especially small communities with high rates of poverty and unemployment, the addition of a state prison may be welcomed, even solicited, as a source of new jobs and a boost to the local economy. For example, in order to attract a state prison, in 1992, Abilene, Texas, offered an incentive package valued at $4 million that included more than 1,400 acres of land.

Whether economic benefits actually materialize from a new prison is another matter. A report by the Joint Center for Environmental and Urban Problems in Florida cast a positive light on the building of new prisons in communities, citing the creation of new jobs and little negative impact, such as an increase in crime or the lowering of property values. A study of the economic impact of a new prison in Potosi, Missouri, found that the prison eased unemployment somewhat by creating new jobs, despite the fact that many of the jobs went to individuals who resided outside of town. In a Colorado study, there was no difference in the rates of unemployment or per capita income in counties with prisons compared to those without prisons.[38] Another study conducted by Iowa State University concluded that the economic benefits of new prisons did not offset the investments, including free land, that were made by communities to attract and build new correctional facilities.[39]

Despite the mixed findings, new prisons were welcomed by many rural communities nationwide. From 1980 to 1991, some 213 adult correctional facilities were opened in rural communities, and another 83 prisons were opened in nonmetropolitan counties from 1992 to 1994. In New York State, the 38 prisons that opened from 1982 to 2000 were located in up-state counties that were largely rural. The new prisons were often sought after by county officials, and in some cases they were marketed by state officials. For example, the New York Department of Correctional Services estimated a windfall to Malone, New York, of $56 million in wages after the completion of a new prison there. After the prison's opening in 1999, more than 300 new jobs were created that generated estimated annual earnings of $13 million.[40]

A report by the Sentencing Project concluded that the 38 prisons built in nonmetropolitan communities in New York had little impact on the unemployment rates or per capita income of residents when compared to residents in counties without prisons. For example, from 1982 to 1988, unemployment rates declined by 42 percent in rural counties in New York with prisons, compared to a decline of 44 percent in counties without prisons. From 1988 to 1992, unemployment increased by 64 percent in counties with prisons, compared to an increase of only 55 percent in counties without prisons. Another decline in unemployment rates occurred from 1992 to 2001 in counties with and without prisons, but only by a difference of 3 percent. By comparison, from 1976 to 2000, per capita income rose by 141 percent in counties without a prison, and by 132 percent in counties with prisons. Overall in New York State, per capita income increased by 160 percent during that period.[41]

According to the report, the limited impact of new prisons on economic development in rural counties in New York may have been linked to the following factors:

• Prison employees, including correctional officers, do not always reside in the counties with prisons. Instead, they may live in nearby communities, and those communities would realize the economic benefit of new jobs created by the prison.

• Local residents of counties with prisons may not be qualified for constructions jobs while the prison is being built or for other skilled work needed to run the prison. Apart from lack of skills, restrictions on union membership may also be a factor in disqualifying some local residents from benefiting from job creation as a result of the new prison.

* Local businesses may not stock the necessary materials for the construction or running of the new prison, and contracts to purchase those supplies may be in place between the correctional agency and vendors outside the communities with prisons.

* Inmates often fill low-wage, unskilled jobs within the prison, such as custodial work. Because inmates are commonly paid wages below the legal minimum wage, residents from communities with prisons would be prevented from competing for those jobs.

Despite these findings, the economic advantages of a new prison to a community are not simply measured by new jobs and a strengthened local economy. For example, the U.S. Census, conducted every 10 years, counts prisoners as part of the population of the community where they are incarcerated. An increase in the population caused by a new prison entitles a community to additional funds from federal formula-based grants that may help pay for health services, road construction and repair, public housing, local law enforcement, and public libraries. Because most prisoners are not incarcerated in the communities where they resided, those communities, which now experience declines in their population due to the imprisonment of local citizens, stand to lose the same federal benefits. For example, based on the 2000 U.S. Census, Cook County in Illinois projected the loss of some $88 million in federal benefits due to declines in its population as the result of incarceration outside of the county. Similarly, in 2000, New York City accounted for about two-thirds of the prisoners in the state, but 91 percent of them were housed in other counties, resulting in a reduction of federal funds for the city.[42]

CHARACTERISTICS OF PRISONERS IN THE UNITED STATES

At the end of 2003, there were more than 1.4 million prisoners in the United States under the jurisdiction of state or federal correctional authorities, an increase of 2.1 percent from 2002, although less than the average annual growth since 1995 of 3.4 percent. Some 1.2 million inmates were state prisoners, and about 161,000 were confined in federal prisons. From 2002 to 2003, the number of federal prisoners increased by 6.6 percent, compared to a 1.4 percent increase in state prisoners. From 1995 to 2003, the average annual increase for federal prisoners was 7.7 percent, compared to an average annual increase of 2.7 percent for state prisoners.

When compared to similar statistics from other countries, the United States emerges as the worldwide leader in the incarceration of its citizens.

THE PRISON EXPERIENCE

Prisons in the United States are total institutions where inmates are locked behind walls, separated from the outside world, and required to abide by strict rules. Personal possessions are limited or forbidden, institutional attire is required, and normal human interactions are severely curtailed, including heterosexual relationships and contact with family and children.

Typically, when inmates arrive at prisons they are stripped, searched, and assigned living quarters, usually at a classification or reception center, where they are evaluated on the basis of their background and criminal history. Sometimes, psychological and educational testing is performed on incoming inmates. After completing the process, each inmate receives a classification and is assigned to a permanent correctional facility. For example, violent or repeat criminal offenders are likely to be assigned to a maximum security prison. Similarly, mentally ill inmates are commonly placed in facilities with psychiatric services.

Upon arrival at a permanent correctional facility, inmates are assigned to a cell, usually in the prison's general population. Inmates assigned to special population units are usually those who are at high risk of violence in prison, such as child molesters, or those with special needs, such as handicapped or mentally ill inmates. As the result of prison overcrowding, inmates in the general population are commonly required to share cells that were designed to hold fewer inmates. For example, two inmates may share a one-person cell, or three inmates may share a cell designed for two individuals. Inmates experience a loss of personal privacy and autonomy.

During the initial phase of imprisonment, inmates are commonly depressed at the prospect of the amount of time they must serve in prison. Inmates must learn who they can befriend, who they must avoid, and who will grant them favors, and for what price. Inmates must quickly learn to protect themselves from predatory inmates, including gang members who may attempt to sell them to other inmates as sex slaves in exchange for drugs and other favors. Prisoners develop various methods of coping with the stress of the prison environment, including keeping to themselves or involving in prison activities, such as educational or counseling programs. New inmates soon become aware of the underground prison economy, sometimes call the *hustle* or *hustling*, in contraband such as drugs, alcohol, weapons, and other commodities that are sold among inmates. Racial conflict also becomes a fact of life, and incoming inmates commonly segregate themselves along racial and ethnic lines to avoid conflicts. The process of adapting to the unique culture of prisons is commonly referred to as *prisonization*.

Women in Prison

Between 1930 and 1950 in the United States, only four correctional institutions for women were built in the United States. By comparison, from 1980 to 1990, some 34 women's prisons were built in the United States, and the number of imprisoned women increased proportionately. From 1995 to 2003, the total population of women in U.S. prisons increased by 48 percent, compared to a 29 percent increase for male prisoners. In other words, the number of female inmates increased at an annual rate of approximately 5.2 percent, compared to an annual growth rate of 3.5 percent for male prisoners. As a result of the increasing imprisonment of women in the United States, the likelihood that a woman born in 2001 will spend time in prison during her lifetime is six times higher than for a woman born in 1974, according to the Bureau of Justice Statistics.

The enactment of harsher sentencing laws beginning in the 1980s had a significant impact on the rise of females in state and federal prisons. As a result of such laws, judges had limited discretion in meting out sentences and were less likely to be lenient toward women offenders. In addition, more women offenders entered the criminal justice system in the United States. For example, according to the FBI's Uniform Crime Reports, of adult arrests for drug abuse violations in 2003, 18.3 percent were females, an increase of nearly 35 percent since 1994. By comparison, the increase in drug abuse arrests for males during the same 10-year period was only about 20 percent.

The underlying reasons for the increase in female criminality are complex. However, it is telling that over half the females in state prisons suffered physical or sexual abuse, or both, in their past. Some 47 percent of female inmates said they had been physically abused, and 39 percent reported being sexually abused. The psychological and emotional injury from such abuse may have factored into their criminal behavior, or at least contributed to a lifestyle that led them to offend. In addition, about one-fourth of all female prisoners had documented histories of mental illness, and over one-third earned less than $600 per month prior to their arrest.[43]

Like their male counterparts, about two-thirds of females incarcerated in U.S. prisons are under 35 years of age, and some 60 percent of women prisoners are either African American or Hispanic. The daily life of women in U.S. prisons differs from that of incarcerated males. For example, women's prisons tend be less violent, and inmates tend to pose less of a threat to each other and to correctional staff. Instead of directing their anger outward, like male inmates, female prisoners are more likely to engage in self-destructive acts, such as self-mutilation or attempted suicide. Also, the social code for female inmates tends to be less rigid than for male prisoners. So-called *make-believe families* are sometimes formed by female inmates to compensate for the separation from family and loved ones. In such make-believe families, females assume the masculine and feminine roles of mother and father, and some inmates take on the role of the child in the family.

THE CHILDREN AND FAMILIES OF PRISONERS

Over half of all adults incarcerated in state and federal prisons in the United States are the parents of minor children, including some 55 percent of male inmates and 65 percent of female prisoners. Some 58 percent of minor children of incarcerated parents are under 10 years of age, according to the Bureau of Justice Statistics. Commonly, long distances separate inmates from their children and families. On average, female inmates were housed in prisons that were 160 miles away from children and family members, while the average distance between male prisoners and their families was 100 miles, according to the Justice Policy Center of the Urban Institute. Such distances make regular visits difficult for family members. As a result, prisoners and their children are often forced into long-distance relationships that rely on telephone contact and written communications in lieu of personal contact. Despite these obstacles, some 60 percent of incarcerated mothers and about 40 percent of imprisoned fathers reported having weekly contact with their children.

The physical separation between parents and child caused by incarceration can give rise to serious issues, including a sense of abandonment and loss and weakened emotional attachment. The immediate effects of imprisonment on children of incarcerated parents include feelings of shame, social stigma, loss of financial support, and a decline in school performance. In addition, if the incarcerated parent was the primary caregiver prior to imprisonment, children are put at an increased risk of suffering abuse and neglect in their new custodial setting. Approximately two-thirds of incarcerated mothers in the United States were the sole custodial parent prior to imprisonment, according to the Bureau of Justice Statistics. By comparison, about 40 percent of incarcerated fathers reported living with their children prior to imprisonment, and most were not the primary caregiver.

In addition, imprisonment has a significant impact on the family of inmates. The forced separation of spouses and intimate partners is a source of great stress and places a strain on those relationships. Conjugal visits are often banned in prisons or are made available on an extremely limited basis, placing further strains on the relationships between spouses and intimate partners. As a result, divorce, relocation, and other changes in the family structure during an inmate's absence make it difficult or impossible for some inmates to return to the life they left prior to their incarceration. For example, when an inmate's spouse remarries, the introduction of a new parental figure in the lives of the inmate's children can alter their relationship with their incarcerated parent. Also, the social stigma of incarceration may alienate family members and cause estrangement.

The financial impact of incarceration can damage family relationships. About 71 percent of state prisoners were employed either full-time or part-time in the month preceding their arrest, according to the Bureau of Justice Statistics. Among imprisoned fathers, some 60 percent had full-time jobs prior to incarceration, compared to about 39 percent of incarcerated mothers. About 68 percent of incarcerated fathers reported that their wages were the primary source of family income. As a result, spouses of incarcerated fathers were forced to give up their role as full-time caregivers for their children, or seek public assistance. In addition, the loss of the family's primary income can result in relocation to less expensive housing, often requiring children to change schools.

The separation of inmates from their children and families presents challenges to correctional institutions to develop programs and policies to help inmates maintain supportive relationships with their children and families. About 78 percent of correctional institutions nationwide were either planning or implementing such programs, according to a survey in 2001 conducted by the National Institute of Corrections. Such programs include the placement of inmates in prisons near their families and visitation assistance, including transportation and assistance in finding nearby lodging for families and children of inmates. About 25 percent of correctional agencies reported planning or implementing parenting classes for inmates with children present, according to the National Institute of Corrections. Examples of other efforts to improve visitation with children included the opening in 2002 of a Child Visitation Unit at the Tennessee Prison for Women. The 16-bed unit was designed for weekend visits between inmates and children from three months to six years of age. The Florida Department of Corrections implemented a program offering weekly video conferences via the Internet between incarcerated mothers and their children. The McNeil Island Correction Center in Washington State developed a family and fatherhood program in which incarcerated fathers receive training in parenting and providing financial support to their families.

Prisons

Disproportionate Imprisonment of Minorities

In 2003, some 586,000 African-American males and 35,000 African-American females were incarcerated in U.S. prisons and jails, accounting for a total of 621,000 prisoners under state or federal jurisdiction. Since 1954, when about 98,000 African Americans were incarcerated, the number of African Americans in prison or jail increased by almost tenfold. If that trend continues, nearly one in three black males born in 2004 could expect to go to prison in his lifetime. Similarly, about one in 18 African-American females born in 2004 could expect to be incarcerated during her lifetime, a rate that is six times higher than for white females.

African Americans were more likely to be involved in certain crimes. For example, blacks accounted for almost 30 percent of arrests for violent crimes in 2002. One reason cited for the higher involvement of blacks in certain offenses is concentrated poverty, which appears to be prevalent in the housing patterns of low-income African Americans in the United States. In addition, African Americans were more likely to be convicted in U.S. courts than white or Hispanic criminal offenders. The rate of arrests of African Americans was also higher. For example, the U.S. Department of Health and Human Services estimated that blacks accounted for some 13 percent of monthly drug users, yet they comprised about 33 percent of all arrests for drug offenses in the United States in 2002. With regard to crack cocaine, in 2001, about two-thirds of all users of crack were white, yet 83 percent of defendants charged with offenses relating to crack cocaine were African American. As a result of the higher rate of arrests and convictions of African-American offenders, more African Americans were likely to have criminal records, which in turn made them more likely to receive sentencing enhancements in many states. For example, in California, blacks constituted about 29 percent of state prisoners in 2002, yet they comprised almost 45 percent of inmates serving sentences of 25 years to life under California's three-strikes law.[44]

According to the Sentencing Project, in 2001, a higher ratio of African-American inmates to white inmates occurred in all states and the District of Columbia, which had the highest ratio: 28.92 black inmates to every white inmate incarcerated in prison or jail. Following the District of Columbia, in 2001, the highest ratios of African-American inmates per one white inmate were 12.15 in New Jersey, 12.77 in Connecticut, 12.63 in Minnesota, 11.63 in Iowa, and 11.59 in Wisconsin. The lowest black-to-white ratios were 1.34 in Hawaii, 2.85 in Idaho, 4.02 in Alaska, 4.12 in Mississippi, and 4.14 in Georgia.[45]

Hispanics comprised about 17 percent of state prisoners in 2001 and some 32 percent of federal inmates. When combined, Hispanics comprised about 16 percent of all state and federal inmates in 2001, compared to about 11 percent in 1985, making them the fastest-growing segment of the prison population.

AGING PRISONERS

In the decade from 1992 to 2001, state and federal prisoners 50 years of age and older increased from about 42,000 to 113,358, for an increase of over 172 percent. In 1992, inmates 50 years of age and older represented 5.7 percent of the prison population in the United States. By 2001, they comprised almost 8 percent of the prison population. Demographic shifts, including the rise in the population known as the baby-boom generation, combined with tougher sentencing laws are largely responsible for the rise in older inmates. As a result of those tougher sentencing laws, older inmates are more likely to remain in prison than before, many for the rest of their lives.

Older inmates present special challenges in correctional settings. Among issues of concern regarding older inmates are:

• Vulnerability to abuse and predation as the result of physical infirmities or limitations.
• Difficulty establishing social relationships with younger inmates.
• The need for special accommodations in settings that are often rigid and inflexible.
• Disproportionate use of costly resources, such as health services.

According to a report by the National Institute of Corrections, there are three general types of inmates 50 years of age and older in U.S. prison populations: First-time offenders, recidivists, and long-term servers. About 50 percent of elderly prisoners nationwide are first-time offenders who were incarcerated after the age of 55, most commonly for aggravated assault or murder. Their crimes are often situational and spontaneous and sometimes manifest behaviors related to the aging process, including the loss of social inhibitions and inflexibility and paranoia that result in aggression. As such, first-time elderly offenders are commonly at higher risk for suicide or aggressiveness toward other inmates and correctional staff. Recidivists who are 50 years of age and older are commonly habitual offenders who have been in and out of prison all of their lives. They often have substance abuse issues and, as a result, are afflicted by chronic health problems, such as heart disease. Long-term servers are inmates who have grown old in prison. Of the three groups of elderly inmates, long-term servers tend to be better adjusted to prison life, in some case because they have known little else.[46]

Prisons

The average annual costs of incarceration for inmates 50 years of age and older is about $60,000 per inmate, compared to $27,000 for other inmates in the general population. Partly as a result of the increase in elderly inmates, health-care expenditures in U.S. prisons rose from about $2.7 billion in 1992 to nearly $3.5 billion in 2001, an increase of 27.1 percent.

MENTALLY ILL PRISONERS

Historically, the mentally ill received institutional care in the United States, primarily in mental hospitals or asylums. Beginning in the early 1960s, many states began to downsize their mental institutions. This occurred for several reasons, including the development of antipsychotic medication that made the severely mentally ill more manageable and allowed them to be treated in outpatient facilities at significantly lower costs to government agencies. In addition, changes to state and federal laws gave the mentally ill due process rights that included safeguards against involuntary commitments to mental institutions and reduced the length of time that patients could be involuntarily committed to mental hospitals. As a result, the rate of institutionalization of the mentally ill declined significantly, from 339 per 100,000 in the population in 1955 to only 29 per 100,000 in 1998.[47]

With deinstitutionalization came the promise of increased community services for the mentally ill. Many of those programs, however, never materialized due to lack of funding by the states and the federal government. The result was that mentally ill individuals were often cut off from publicly funded programs for treatment, either because the programs were limited or unavailable or because mentally ill patients did not have the ability or the support to avail themselves of the services. Without treatment, mentally ill persons sometimes resorted to self-medication through alcohol or drugs. Some became homeless, putting them at a higher risk of criminal victimization or arrest. In addition, the difficulty of obtaining court orders for involuntary commitments for the severely disturbed created a public safety issue. The consequence was that an increasing number of mentally ill individuals entered the U.S. criminal justice system, which was ill-equipped to care for them.

Mental health caseloads increased significantly in prisons nationwide. For example, from 1991 to 2002, the number of prisoners receiving mental health treatment in New York prisons rose by 73 percent. Colorado reported a fivefold increase in seriously mentally ill inmates in the decade between 1988 and 1998. Similarly, between 1993 and 1998, the number of mentally ill inmates doubled in Mississippi prisons and increased by 30 percent in the District of Columbia. This rising trend suggests an ongoing reliance on prisons to house the mentally ill. Indeed, in 2001, over 700,000 mentally ill persons were processed through U.S. prisons or jails, according to the American Psychiatric Association.[48]

In 2000, as many as one in five inmates was seriously mentally ill, according to a report by the American Psychiatric Association, which estimated that up to 5 percent of prisoners nationwide were psychotic at any given time. A report by the National Commission on Correctional Health Care, submitted to the U.S. Congress in March 2002, estimated that 2 to 4 percent of state prisoners were schizophrenic or psychotic. In addition, some 13 to 18 percent of prisoners suffered from major depression, and between 22 and 30 percent of prison inmates had an anxiety disorder. Statistics from individual prison systems supported those estimates. For example, in 2002, the California Department of Corrections reported that 14 percent of inmates statewide were on the prison mental health roster. The Pennsylvania Department of Corrections reported 16.5 percent of inmates on its mental health caseload in 2002, and about 11 percent of prisoners in New York State received mental health services.[49]

PRISONERS ON DEATH ROW

The number of prisoners under sentence of death in the United States increased from about 150 in 1953 to just over 500 in 1970. In 1972, the U.S. Supreme Court in *Furman v. Georgia* ruled that the death penalty violated the Eighth Amendment's ban against cruel and unusual punishment. However, beginning in 1976, when the Supreme Court reversed its ban on the death penalty in *Gregg v. Georgia*, the number of prisoners under sentence of death increased significantly, rising from nearly 500 to more than 3,500 individuals by 2002. Some 71 individuals were executed in 2002. In 2003, there were 65 executions in the United States, including 24 in Texas, 14 in Oklahoma, and seven in North Carolina, all by lethal injection.[50]

By the end of 2003, some 3,374 prisoners in 37 states and the federal prison system were under sentence of death, 188 fewer than in 2002, according to the Bureau of Justice Statistics. Of all prisoners under sentence of death in 2003, 56 percent were white and 42 percent African American. However, because African Americans comprised only about 12 percent of the U.S. population, there were proportionately more African Americans under sentence of death than any other ethnic group in the United States. Hispanics comprised 11.5 percent of persons under sentence of death in 2002. There were 47 women under sentence of death in 2003.

On March 1, 2005, the U.S. Supreme Court ruled in the case of *Roper v. Simmons* that the imposition of the death penalty for juveniles who were under 18 years of age at the time they committed a capital offense was a violation of the Eight Amendment's ban on cruel and unusual punishment and the Fourteenth Amendment's guarantee of due process. The Court's 5 to 4 decision in *Roper* abolished the death penalty for juvenile offenders in all state and federal jurisdictions.

At the time of the Court's ruling, some 20 states permitted the imposition of the death penalty for juveniles who were under the age of 18 at the time of their offenses. In 12 of those 20 states, there were some 72 individuals on death row who were juveniles at the time of their crimes, including 29 individuals in Texas and 14 in Alabama. Of the remaining states, Mississippi accounted for five death row inmates who were under the age of 18 at the time of their crimes; Arizona, Louisiana, and North Carolina accounted for four each; Florida and South Carolina accounted for three each; Georgia and Pennsylvania accounted for two each; and Nevada and Virginia each had one person on death row who was a juvenile at the time of his crime.

The Supreme Court's decision in *Roper v. Simmons* is discussed in detail in Chapter 2, in the *Cruel and Unusual Punishment* section of *U.S. Supreme Court Cases.*

PRISON VIOLENCE

The regimented daily routine of prison life gives inmates little individual responsibility. By not conforming to the order of prison life, inmates run the risk of being ostracized and becoming victims of violence. Even those who conform sometimes find it difficult to avoid conflict and violence in an oppressive and intolerant prison environment.

Prison violence is generally inflicted by one inmate against another inmate, although violence may also be directed against corrections staff. Inmate-on-inmate violence is most common in male prisons. Female prisoners are more likely to be victimized by staff members or to engage in self-inflicted violence, such as self-mutilation or attempted suicide.

There are myriad causes of prison violence, and the incidence of violence is usually a factor of the particular conditions and inmate population at a given institution. However, in general, one of the main causes of prison violence is overcrowding, which can make inmates more prone to commit acts of violence by creating elevated rates of depression, anxiety, and stress among inmates. Also, the shift from rehabilitation to punishment has exacerbated conditions that may lead to prison violence, such as harsh disciplinary action for even minor infractions.

In 2000, some 3,175 inmates died in state and federal prisons nationwide. Of those, some 2,402 inmates died of illness or natural causes, by far the most common causes of death. However, 56 inmate deaths were the result of homicides. In addition, there were over 34,000 documented assaults on prisoners in 2000, and nearly 18,000 assaults on correctional staff.[51]

PRISON GANGS

Affiliation with a prison gang was one of the most significant indicators of an inmate's potential for misconduct, including violence, according to a study by the Federal Bureau of Prisons.[52] Prison gang members were more likely to be involved in prison misconduct, including the use or selling of contraband and the destruction of property in correctional institutions. In particular, members of the Texas Syndicate and the Mexakanemi prison gangs were linked to a wide range of prison misconduct, including violence.

The Texas Syndicate originated in California in the mid-1970s and is composed largely of Hispanics from California whose families migrated to Texas. Cells of the gang are active in state prisons in California, Texas, New Mexico, Arizona, Florida, Illinois, and in federal prisons. With a reputation built on acts of violence in prison, the Texas Syndicate is suspected of involvement in some 50 homicides of staff and inmates within the Texas Department of Corrections since the gang's inception. Some of those homicides included members of the Texas Syndicate who ran afoul of the gang's strictly enforced code of conduct.

The Mexakanemi (MM) prison gang derives its name from the Aztec word meaning a free or liberated Mexican. Since its formation in Texas during the 1980s, MM has been the largest and fastest-growing prison gang within the Texas Department of Corrections, with members in other state and federal prisons as well. MM hierarchical structure includes a president, vice president, and generals who are responsible for specific prisons or groups of prisons. Generals appoint members of the gang to run certain activities in prison, including prostitution, the sale of drugs, and contract murders.

Large prison gangs, such as MM and the white supremacist Aryan Brotherhood, are commonly associated with street gangs and may utilize street gangs for access to drugs or to carry out assaults or killings ordered by the prison gang. As such, the power of a prison gang is measured, in part, by how much control it has over street-level gangs. Membership in a prison gang is often a way for inmates to seek protection from other predatory prisoners. Other inducements for membership include increased status, financial profit from gang activities, and peer acceptance. Prison gang members often utilize complex codes or arcane languages, such as Aztec, to communicate with associates both within and outside of correctional institutions. Longtime members of prison gangs, who have often spent much of their lives in prisons, can be keenly aware of nuances in correctional settings, including security breaches and staff shortages, through which they can gain access to other inmates or contraband.[53]

PRISONER RAPE AND SEXUAL ASSAULT

Inmate-on-inmate rape is perhaps the most pervasive yet underreported form of violence in prisons nationwide, according to a report by Human Rights Watch.[54] The underreporting of prison rape may occur for several reasons, including the reluctance of correctional officials to recognize the extent of the problem.

As many as 22 percent of male prisoners reported being the victims of rape or coercive sexual threats, according to a study by the Center for Effective Public Policy. In addition, each male prisoner who reported being sexually assaulted was victimized, on average, nine times by three different perpetrators. About half of those victimized did not report the incidents to anyone, including correctional staff. Those who disclosed the assault were more likely to confide in other inmates than they were to report the incident to correctional staff. Reasons cited by prisoners for nondisclosure included fear of retaliation and the reluctance of prison staff to believe them.[55]

Most perpetrators of rape on male prisoners were heterosexual males. Their victims tended to be inmates who were incarcerated for less serious offenses than those of their rapists. Most sexual abuse in prison was between individuals who knew each other. Generally, the sexual attack was preceded by a period of sexually aggressive comments and threats. The most serious concern of victims after being raped was the threat of contracting the human immunodeficiency virus (HIV), which was prevalent in about 2 percent of prisoners nationwide in 2001, a decrease of about 5 percent from 2000 despite an increase of 5 percent in the overall prison population.[56] The psychological impact of inmate rape included feelings of depression, shame, and attempted suicide. In 2000, some 198 prisoners in the United States committed suicide.

Although prisoner rape is prevalent in male prisons, some sexual activity between inmates is consensual. Heterosexual male inmates sometimes engage in consensual homosexual acts with other inmates. This so-called situational homosexuality is a result of the lack of any opportunity for intimacy with the opposite sex.

The incidence of sexual assaults on female prisoners by other prisoners varied from 6 to 27 percent, depending upon the correctional institution, according to the report by Human Rights Watch. Sexual assaults include rape or forced sexual acts. Female prisoners were also the victims of sexual misconduct by correctional staff. Sexual misconduct includes sexual harrassment and unwanted sexual advances that do not involve force. In 1998, some 36 state correctional agencies reported substantiated incidents of sexual misconduct between female inmates and correctional staff, according to a report by the National Institute of Corrections.[57] From 1990 to 1995, lawsuits were filed against 23 departments of correction by female inmates alleging sexual misconduct by prison staff. A 2001 survey by Amnesty International reported findings of sexual misconduct by staff against female prisoners in every correctional system in the United States except Minnesota.[58]

CORRECTIONAL STAFF

Prisons are 24-hour institutions. As such, there must be correctional staff members in place at all times for prisons to function. Among prison staff members, correctional officers are responsible for the control, security, and movement of inmates within correctional institutions. Correctional officers regularly interact with inmates, and individual officers often must control entire groups of prisoners in common areas of an institution, such as hallways and work areas. The job of correctional officer is stressful and can be dangerous. For example, in 2003, four correctional officers were killed by inmates in state prisons in Florida, Ohio, Tennessee, and Texas. In 2000, there were some 17,952 assaults by prisoners on correctional officers, five of which resulted in the death of a correctional officer.[59]

Correctional officers perform a variety of duties in prisons, including the following:

- Block Officers are responsible for supervising as many as 300 to 400 prisoners confined in a cell block. Their duties include watching for signs of self-destructive behavior, checking cells for fires or other hazards, and managing any behavioral or medical problem that may arise.

- Work Detail Supervisors oversee groups of inmates assigned to various work details within a prison, including the laundry room, kitchen, and industrial shop. They control access to supplies, including cutlery and work tools that can be used as weapons by prisoners against other inmates or correctional officers.

- Industrial Shop and School Officers are generally assigned in groups of two or three to supervise groups of inmates in vocational or educational settings. Generally, these officers work with civilian employees, such as teachers, and are therefore responsible for their security and safety, as well as that of inmates.

- Administrative Building Assignment Officers are responsible for the overall functioning of the correctional facility. Their duties include opening and closing security doors and staffing checkpoints where visitors enter and exit the prison. Generally, these officers have little direct contact with inmates.
- Wall Posts are correctional officers who are stationed on the wall towers located on the outer perimeter of most prisons. These officers generally work in small guard towers, where they are confined for most of their work shift.
- Relief Officers substitute for other correctional officers on their days off. Because relief officers are required to perform a variety of duties, their jobs offer some variety but are also stressful.

Job-related stress was widely reported by correctional officers, according to a report by the National Institute of Corrections. Sources of correctional officer stress include the need to work overtime and rotating shifts as the result of understaffing, threats and actual incidents of inmate violence against staff, poor public image, low pay, and the risk of job burnout. Another source of stress that was widely reported by correctional officers was inmates who attempt to manipulate correctional staff. For example, officers reported that some inmates repeatedly made demands for items such as cigarettes and extra food in exchange for their implicit promise to keep other inmates in line. In addition, about 22 percent of correctional officers reported that problems with coworkers created the most stressful aspect of their job. These problems included burned-out coworkers venting their frustrations on their colleagues, fear that certain coworkers would not assist in confrontations with inmates, and inappropriate behavior of coworkers toward inmates, such as helping prisoners smuggle contraband into the prison or using unnecessary force against inmates. Female correctional officers reported sexist attitudes by their colleagues and sexual harassment by their supervisors as a common source of stress on the job.[60]

PAROLE

There are three legal ways out of prison: death, pardon, and parole. Pardons are rare. Although state governors and the president of the United States have the power to pardon anyone, pardons are generally granted only in cases of false imprisonment due to egregious miscarriages of justice. Parole is the most common way that prisoners are released from prison. Parole is administered by federal and state correctional agencies.

Parole is sometimes confused with probation, which is a period of court supervision imposed on a criminal offender at the time of sentencing. Probation is imposed as an alternative to incarceration or as an adjunct to incarceration of one year or less in county jail. By contrast, parole occurs only after a period of imprisonment. Prisoners become eligible for parole after they have served the portion of their sentence required by law. For example, in California, individuals sentenced to prison for violent crimes, such as robbery, must serve 85 percent of their total sentence before becoming eligible for parole. If parole is granted, the term of parole is the amount of time remaining on the original sentence. For example, for an individual who is paroled after serving eight years of a 10-year sentence, the maximum term of parole is two years. Parole expires after that period of time, absent any violations of the law or of the conditions of parole.

The term *parole* originated in 1846, when it was first used by Boston philanthropist S. G. Howe in a letter to the Prison Association of New York. States began to adopt parole selection procedures, which were usually administered by a commissioner of parole appointed by the governor. As the result of abuses of power, however, many states replaced parole commissioners with parole boards, beginning around 1945. In some states, parole boards are part of the department of corrections, while in others they function independently. In both cases, members of a state's parole boards are usually appointed by the governor.

Federal parole began in 1910, when parole boards were established at each of the three federal prisons. In 1930, the U.S. Congress created the Board of Parole, which consisted of three members appointed by the U.S. attorney general. In 1950, membership was increased to eight. The Board of Parole was reorganized in 1972 into five regions, with one board member and five hearing examiners assigned to each region. The Comprehensive Crime Control Act of 1984 established the U.S. Sentencing Commission, which in 1987 promulgated determinate sentencing guidelines that significantly limited the power of the Board of Parole. The Comprehensive Crime Control Act of 1984 also contained a provision to phase out the Board of Parole by 1992 and to establish the U.S. Parole Commission to oversee defendants who committed offenses prior to adoption of federal sentencing guidelines on November 1, 1987. The Parole Commission Phaseout Act of 1996 required the attorney general to report annually to Congress whether it was more cost-effective to maintain the Parole Commission as a separate agency or to incorporate its functions into another government agency. As of 2003, the Parole Commission retains its authority as a separate agency of the federal government.

In both the state and federal parole systems, when an inmate is eligible for parole, he or she appears before the parole board at a hearing. Often, representatives of the prisoner's crime victims also have the right to be present if they wish to advocate against parole. If parole is granted based on an inmate's favorable behavior while incarcerated and the belief that the inmate is not likely to reoffend the parolee is required to report to a parole officer or agent in the community where the parolee plans to reside or is allowed to reside by the parole board. Often, paroled sex offenders are ordered to reside in localities other than their home communities in order to protect the sex offender from possible harassment or violence and to avoid inflaming the sex offender's home community. Parole is granted under certain conditions established by law and set forth by the parole board. Those conditions often include not associating with convicted felons, not owning or carrying a firearm, and reporting to a parole agent on a regular basis. Failure to comply with any of these conditions constitutes a technical violation of parole and may necessitate a parole revocation hearing. An arrest for a new felony also is grounds for revocation of parole. As a result of the 1971 ruling by the U.S. Supreme Court in *Morrissey v. Brewer* (408 U.S. 271), parolees are guaranteed certain rights at parole revocation hearings, including written notification of the pending charges or reasons for parole revocation and the right to hear evidence against them, refute testimony, and cross-examine witnesses.

In 2002, there were more than 750,000 individuals on parole in the United States, an increase of almost 3 percent from 2001 and almost twice the average increase of 1.5 percent since 1995. Mandatory releases accounted for 52 percent of those entering parole, compared to 45 percent in 1995. In other words, more prisoners were released on parole because it was required by law and not as the result of their good behavior or successful rehabilitation while in prison. Such mandatory releases are commonly part of the stricter sentencing laws implemented by many states and the federal government.

RECIDIVISM

Of those released from prison, about two-thirds were rearrested within three years, according to findings by the Bureau of Justice Statistics on the recidivism of inmates released in 1994. Most arrests occurred within the first year of release. Over 45 percent of rearrested ex-convicts were convicted of a new crime. About 52 percent of all inmates released in 1994 were re-incarcerated as the result of a new conviction or a technical violation of their parole.[61]

One reason for the high rate of recidivism was the decline of prison programs offering treatment, education, and vocational training prior to release, according to a report by the Sentencing Project. For example, in 1997, about 27 percent of inmates about to be released reported receiving some type of vocational training, compared to 31 percent of inmates who were about to be released in 1991. In addition, inmates with a higher number of previous arrests were more likely to be rearrested than those with fewer prior arrests. Among drug offenders, about 40 percent were rearrested on the same charges.[62]

FELONY DISENFRANCHISEMENT

In most states, convicted felons are not allowed to exercise certain rights, including the right to vote in elections. Laws prohibiting felons from voting and exercising other rights are known as felony disenfranchisement laws. For example, only in Vermont and Maine are convicted felons in prison allowed to vote in elections, according to a report by the Sentencing Project. All other states and the District of Columbia prohibit voting by prisoners. In addition, some 35 states do not allow convicted felons on parole to vote, and seven states deny voting rights to all convicted felons, including those who were released from prison and have successfully completed their parole. Those states are Arizona, Delaware, Maryland, Nevada, Tennessee, Virginia, and Wyoming.

As a result of felony disenfranchisement, an estimated 4.7 million Americans with felony convictions lost their right to vote, including 1.4 million African-American men. As many as 13 percent of all African-American males in the United States are not allowed to vote as the result of felony disenfranchisement laws. In addition, more than 500,000 women are prohibited from voting in U.S. elections because of felony convictions. In the states that permanently deny voting rights to individuals with felony convictions, about 25 percent of African-American males are prohibited from ever voting again.[63]

In 2001, there were over 5.6 million adults in the United States who at some period in their lives were incarcerated in prison. These individuals comprised about 2.7 percent of the U.S. population in 2001. By comparison, about 1.8 percent of adults in the U.S. population in 1991 were ever in prison and some 1.3 percent in 1974. If rates of the prevalence of imprisonment remain unchanged, more than 6 percent of all persons born in the United States in 2001 will go to state or federal prison during their lifetime.[64]

[1] Fox Butterfield. "Mistreatment of Prisoners Is Called Routine in U.S." *New York Times*, May 8, 2004, p. 1A.

[2] Kathy Barrett Carter. "New Jersey Leads States in Disparity of Blacks in Prison." *New Jersey Star-Ledger*, January 7, 2004, p. 1A.

[3] *National Crime Victimization Survey Violent Crime Trends, 1973–2002*. Bureau of Justice Statistics, Office of Justice Programs, U.S. Department of Justice, 2003, p. 1.

[4] "U.S. Prison Populations—Trends and Implications." Report, The Sentencing Project, 2003, p. 1.

[5] Marc Mauer, et al. "The Meaning of *Life:* Long Prison Sentences in Context." Report, The Sentencing Project May 2004, p. 3.

[6] "Prop. 36 Exceeds Expectations with Huge Savings." Press Release, Drug Policy Alliance, July 17, 2003, p. 1.

[7] James J. Stephan and Jennifer C. Karberg. *Census of State and Federal Correctional Facilities, 2000*. Bureau of Justice Statistics, August 2003, p. 7.

[8] Paige M. Harrison and Jennifer C. Karberg. "Prison and Jail Inmates at Midyear 2003." *Bulletin*, Bureau of Justice Statistics, May 2004, p. 2.

[9] Marc Mauer, et al. "The Meaning of *Life:* Long Prison Sentences in Context." Report, The Sentencing Project, May 2004, p. 3.

[10] Harry E. Allen and Clifford E. Simonsen. *Corrections in America: An Introduction, Ninth Edition*. Upper Saddle River, N.J.: Prentice Hall, 2000, p. 255.

[11] Thomas P. Bonczar and Tracy L. Snell. "Capital Punishment, 2002." *Bulletin*, Bureau of Justice Statistics, November 2003, p. 4.

[12] Paige M. Harrison and Allen J. Beck. "Prison and Jail Inmates at Midyear 2004." *Bulletin*, Bureau of Justice Statistics, April 2005, p. 2.

[13] James J. Stephan and Jennifer C. Karberg. *Census of State and Federal Correctional Facilities, 2000*. Bureau of Justice Statistics, August 2003, p. 1.

[14] Paige M. Harrison and Allen J. Beck. "Prison and Jail Inmates at Midyear 2004." *Bulletin*, Bureau of Justice Statistics, April 2005, p. 4.

[15] James J. Stephan. "State Prison Expenditures, 2001." Special Report, Bureau of Justice Statistics, June 2004, p. 2.

[16] James J. Stephan and Jennifer C. Karberg. *Census of State and Federal Correctional Facilities, 2000*. Bureau of Justice Statistics, August 2003, pp. 12–15.

[17] Marc Mauer, et al. "The Meaning of *Life:* Long Prison Sentences in Context." Report, The Sentencing Project, May 2004, p. 11.

[18] Paige M. Harrison and Allen J. Beck. "Prison and Jail Inmates at Midyear 2004." *Bulletin*, Bureau of Justice Statistics, April 2005, p. 5.

[19] Melissa Sickmund. "Juveniles in Court." *Juvenile Offenders and Victims National Report Series Bulletin*, Office of Juvenile Justice and Delinquency Prevention, June 2003, p. 5.

[20] "How Are State Delinquency Institutions Administered from State to State?" *State Juvenile Justice Profiles*, National Center for Juvenile Justice, March 31, 2003, p. 1.

[21] Melissa Sickmund. "Juvenile Residential Facility Census, 2000: Selected Findings." *Juvenile Offenders and Victims National Report Series Bulletin,* Office of Juvenile Justice and Delinquency Prevention, December 2002, pp. 2–3.

[22] Melissa Sickmund. "Juvenile Residential Facility Census, 2000: Selected Findings." *Juvenile Offenders and Victims National Report Series Bulletin,* Office of Juvenile Justice and Delinquency Prevention, December 2002, pp. 3–4.

[23] Melissa Sickmund. "Juvenile Residential Facility Census, 2000: Selected Findings." *Juvenile Offenders and Victims National Report Series Bulletin,* Office of Juvenile Justice and Delinquency Prevention, December 2002, p. 2.

[24] Karen de Sa. "Scathing Report on Youth Authority." *Mercury News,* January 8, 2004, p. 1A.

[25] Harry E. Allen and Clifford E. Simonsen. *Corrections in American: An Introduction, Ninth Edition.* Upper Saddle River, N.J.: Prentice Hall, 2000, p. 295.

[26] James J. Stephan and Jennifer C. Karberg. *Census of State and Federal Correctional Facilities, 2000.* Bureau of Justice Statistics, August 2003, pp. 4–5.

[27] Paige M. Harrison and Allen J. Beck. "Prisoners in 2003." *Bulletin,* Bureau of Justice Statistics, November 2004, p. 1.

[28] Paige M. Harrison and Allen J. Beck. "Prison and Jail Inmates at Midyear 2004." *Bulletin,* Bureau of Justice Statistics, April 2005, p. 4.

[29] Lynn Bauer and Steven D. Owens. "Justice Expenditures and Employment in the United States, 2001." *Bulletin,* Bureau of Justice Statistics, May 2004, p. 3.

[30] John Hendren. "Detainees May Be Moved Off Cuba Base." *L.A. Times,* June 30, 2004, p. 1A.

[31] Harry E. Allen and Clifford E. Simonsen. *Corrections in America: An Introduction, Ninth Edition.* Upper Saddle River, N.J.: Prentice Hall, 2000, p. 322.

[32] James J. Stephan. "State Prison Expenditures, 2001." Special Report, Bureau of Justice Statistics, June 2004, p. 7.

[33] Douglas McDonald and Carl Patten, Jr. "Governments' Management of Private Prisons." Report, Abt Associates, Inc., for the National Institute of Justice, September 15, 2003, p. 4.

[34] Amy Cheung. "Prison Privatization and the Use of Incarceration." Briefing Paper, The Sentencing Project, January 2002, pp. 2–3.

[35] Douglas McDonald and Carl Patten, Jr. "Governments' Management of Private Prisons." Report, Abt Associates, Inc., for the National Institute of Justice, September 15, 2003, p. 21.

[36] James J. Stephan and Jennifer C. Karberg. *Census of State and Federal Correctional Facilities, 2000.* Bureau of Justice Statistics, August 2003, p. 4.

[37] Sarah Lawrence and Jeremy Travis. "The New Landscape of Imprisonment: Mapping America's Prison Expansion." Research Report, Urban Institute Justice Policy Center, April 2004, pp. 8–9.

[38] Ryan S. King, et al. "Big Prisons, Small Towns: Prison Economics in Rural America." Report, The Sentencing Project, February 2003, p. 13.

[39] Terry Besser. "The Development of Last Resort." Paper, presented at the Rural Sociological Society, August 2003, p. 2.

[40] Ryan S. King, et al. "Big Prisons, Small Towns: Prison Economics in Rural America." Report, The Sentencing Project, February 2003, p. 5.

[41] Ryan S. King, et al. "Big Prisons, Small Towns: Prison Economics in Rural America." Report, The Sentencing Project, February 2003, pp. 8–11.

[42] Sarah Lawrence and Jeremy Travis. "The New Landscape of Imprisonment: Mapping America's Prison Expansion." Research Report, Urban Institute Justice Policy Center, April 2004, p. 3.

[43] "Women in Prison." Fact Sheet, The Sentencing Project, May 2003, p. 1.

[44] Marc Mauer and Ryan Scott King. "Schools and Prisons: Fifty Years after *Brown v. Board of Education*." Briefing Paper, The Sentencing Report, 2004, pp. 1–4.

[45] "State Rates of Incarceration by Race." Briefing Paper, The Sentencing Project, 2004, p. 3.

[46] B. Jaye Anno, et al. "Correctional Health Care: Addressing the Needs of Elderly, Chronically Ill, and Terminally Ill Inmates." Report, National Institute of Corrections, February 2004, pp. 10–11.

[47] Richard Lamb and Linda Weinberger. "Persons with Severe Mental Illness in Jails and Prisons: A Review." *Psychiatric Services* 49 (1998): 483.

[48] "Criminalization of the Mentally Ill." Report, National Alliance for the Mentally Ill, September 15, 2003, p. 1.

[49] "Ill-Equipped: U.S. Prisons and Offenders with Mental Illness." Report, Human Rights Watch, 2003, p. 17.

[50] Thomas P. Bonczar and Tracy L. Snell. "Capital Punishment, 2002," *Bulletin*, Bureau of Justice Statistics, November 2003, p. 11.

[51] James J. Stephan and Jennifer C. Karberg. *Census of State and Federal Correctional Facilities, 2000.* Bureau of Justice Statistics, August 2003, pp. 8–10.

[52] Gerald G. Gaes, et al. "The Influence of Prison Gang Affiliation on Violence and Other Prison Misconduct." Report, Federal Bureau of Prisons, March 9, 2001, p. 16.

[53] David M. Allender and Frank Marcell. "Career Criminals, Security Threat Groups, and Prison Gangs: An Interrelated Threat." *Law Enforcement Bulletin* 72, no. 6 (June 2003): 10–11.

[54] "No Escape: Male Rape in U.S. Prisons." Report, Human Rights Watch, 2001, p. 98.

[55] "The Prison Rape Elimination Act of 2003: Summary of Focus Group Discussion Points." Report, Center for Effective Public Policy, March 25, 2004, p. 4.

[56] Laura M. Maruschak. "HIV in Prisons, 2001." *Bulletin*, Bureau of Justice Statistics, January 2004, p. 1.

[57] "Sexual Misconduct in Prisons: Law, Remedies, and Incidence." *Special Issues in Corrections*, National Institute of Corrections, May 2000, p. 10.

[58] "Sexual Abuse of Prisoners." Fact Sheet, American Civil Liberties Union of Colorado, November 23, 2003, p. 1.

[59] James J. Stephan and Jennifer C. Karberg. *Census of State and Federal Correctional Facilities, 2000.* Bureau of Justice Statistics, August 2003, p. 10.

[60] Peter Finn. "Addressing Correctional Officer Stress: Programs and Strategies." *Issues and Practices in Criminal Justice*, National Institute of Justice, December 2000, pp. 11–14

[61] Patricia Langan and David Levin. "Recidivism of Prisoners Released in 1994." *Bulletin*, Bureau of Justice Statistics, June 2002, p. 1.

[62] *Recidivism of State Prisoners: Implications for Sentencing and Corrections Policy.* The Sentencing Project, August 2002, pp. 1–2.

[63] *Felony Disenfranchisement Laws in the United States.* The Sentencing Project, May 2004, pp. 1–2.

[64] Thomas P. Bonczar. "Prevalence of Imprisonment in the U.S. Population, 1974–2001." Special Report, Bureau of Justice Statistics, August 2003, p. 1.

CHAPTER 2

THE LAW OF PRISONS

The U.S. Constitution is the cornerstone of the legal system in the United States. The first 10 amendments to the Constitution comprise the Bill of Rights, which articulate the basic individual rights afforded to all Americans, including prisoners. They include the right of freedom of speech and religion under the First Amendment, the right of privacy and freedom from unreasonable searches under the Fourth Amendment, and the ban against cruel or unusual punishment under the Eighth Amendment. As originally articulated, the Bill of Rights applied only to actions by the federal government. However, under the due process clause of the Fourteenth Amendment, state and local governments are now held to the same standard. As a result, state and federal laws governing the administration of prisons and the treatment of prisoners in the United States must comply with constitutional protections. Otherwise, the laws may be challenged in state and federal courts, including the U.S. Supreme Court. A large body of rulings by the U.S. Supreme Court on the issues of prisons and prisoners' rights is presented later in this chapter, following a discussion of significant legislation on prisoners' rights and sentencing.

FEDERAL LEGISLATION

Section 1983 of Title 42 of the U.S. Code gives individuals the right to seek legal remedy in federal court if their constitutional rights are violated by state or local laws. Originally passed by the U.S. Congress as the Ku Klux Klan Act of 1871, section 1983 was enacted as a way to protect the newly acquired constitutional rights of African Americans after the end of the Civil War in 1865. Those rights included the prohibition of slavery under the Thirteenth Amendment, the right to due process of law and equal protection under the Fourteenth Amendment, and the right of every male citizen to vote under the Fifteenth Amendment. Because those rights were sometimes violated by state and local authorities, section 1983 gave victims the opportunity to bypass state courts and seek redress in the federal courts. The effect of section 1983 was largely muted, however, because of a tendency by federal judges to send cases back to the same state courts that had originally violated the victims' constitutional rights. Eventually, that practice helped to fuel the civil rights movement of the 1960s. As the cause of civil rights became national in scope, section 1983 began to be more effectively utilized by African Americans and others claiming violations of their civil rights, including prisoners.

Historically in the United States, prisoners were considered civilly dead. As such, state and federal courts adopted a *hands-off doctrine* toward prisoners who filed lawsuits, severely limiting the ability of prisoners to use the court system to seek redress for violations of their constitutional rights. The courts used the following rationales for their hands-off approach to prisoner litigation:

• Conditions of confinement in correctional facilities were an administrative matter that was best left to prison officials.

• Because society was largely unconcerned with conditions in prison, the courts had no public duty to interfere in the administration of prisons.

• Prisoners had fewer constitutional rights than other members of society. Therefore, prisoners' complaints were largely about their lack of privileges in prison and did not constitute a violation of their rights.

Beginning in the early 1960s, federal district courts began to move away from the hands-off doctrine, in part due to the efforts to advance prisoner litigation by organizations including the NAACP Legal Defense Fund and the American Civil Liberties Union's National Prison Project. In addition, the Black Muslims filed lawsuits on behalf of prisoners who were denied racial and religious equality. The legal avenue most widely used for prisoner litigation in federal courts was U.S. Code section 1983:

Every person who, under color of any statute, ordinance, regulation, custom, or usage of any State or Territory . . . subjects, or causes to be subjected, any citizen of the United States or other person within the jurisdiction thereof to the deprivation of any rights, privileges, or immunities secured by the Constitution and laws, shall be liable to the party innured in an action at law, suit in equity, or other proper proceeding for redress.

Prisoners began to organize around the idea of equal rights and to protest the conditions of their confinement. Such protests sometimes erupted into inmate uprisings in prisons nationwide, including the riot at the state prison at Attica in New York in 1971, which resulted in 39 deaths. Many prisoners, however, sought remedy through the court system, especially in federal courts under section 1983. As a result of such court actions, prisoners won court victories on a number of issues, including the following:

- Equal Protection. Prison officials were not allowed to discriminate against inmates on the basis of race, religion, nationality, sex, political beliefs, or for any other arbitrary reason.
- Due Process. Prison officials were not allowed to restrict inmates' access to attorneys or the courts and were required to implement fair administrative procedures governing the punishment of prisoners for infractions in prison.
- Free Speech. The right of prisoners to freedom of speech and expression was extended to access to certain reading materials, limits on the censorship of certain mail, telephone access, and freedom of religious activity.
- Conditions of Confinement. The Eighth Amendment's prohibition of cruel and unusual punishment was broadened in scope to include decent living conditions, medical care, and the opportunity for physical exercise.

Under section 1983, remedy is available in the form of monetary damages paid to the injured party by those responsible for the injury. Monetary damages may include compensatory damages to repay the costs suffered by the injured party and additional punitive damages that are intended to punish the party responsible for the injury and deter that behavior in the future. Remedy under section 1983 is also possible through injunctions and declaratory judgments. An injunction is a court order requiring a defendant to do or not to do something. For example, under an injunction, prison officials can be ordered to make changes in the prison conditions that caused injury to the victims who won the lawsuit. A declaratory judgment is a legal finding by a court that the defendant has certain legal obligations or duties that must be met. If those obligations are not met, then at a later date the court may issue an injunction ordering the changes necessary to meet the legal obligation.

THE PRISON LITIGATION REFORM ACT

As prisoners achieved court victories on issues of prisoners' rights, more lawsuits were filed, particularly by state prison inmates seeking redress in the federal court system. For example, in 1966, some 218 cases were filed in federal courts by state prisoners. In 1992, there were 26,824 such filings by state inmates, and in 1996, there were more than 42,000 petitions filed in U.S. district courts by both federal and state inmates.[1]

As early as 1980, the U.S. Congress attempted to reduce the rising number of federal court actions brought by prison inmates by passing the Civil Rights of Institutionalized Persons Act (CRIPA). One provision of CRIPA required state prisoners to exhaust their state prison grievance procedures before filing any action in federal court under section 1983. Because state participation in CRIPA was voluntary, however, the act had minimal effect on the increasing number of federal actions brought by prisoners. Federal courts exercised judicial discretion as another means of eliminating claims without merit that were brought by prisoners. For example, courts may dismiss actions that lack any arguable basis in fact or law. In some cases, federal courts dismissed claims by prisoners attempting to re-litigate previous actions. However, these efforts also failed to abate the rising number of federal lawsuits by prisoners. In part, the limited impact of CRIPA and judicial discretion was due to the rising number of prisoners in the United States as the result of sentencing reforms. For example, between 1980 and 1996, the rate at which prisoners filed actions in federal courts actually declined by some 17 percent.[2] In other words, decrease in the rate of filings was offset by the increase in prisoners nationwide, resulting in a net increase in filings in federal courts. In addition, news reports of frivolous filings by prisoners over issues such as being deprived of shampoo or deodorant helped to fuel the public's impression that lawsuits brought by prisoners were often without merit.

On April 26, 1996, the U.S. Congress passed the Prison Litigation Reform Act of 1995 (PLRA), which placed significant restrictions on the ability of prisoners to file civil rights claims in federal court under U.S. Code section 1983. The controlling authority for the PRLA is contained in U.S. Code, Title VIII, sections 801 and 802.

The PLRA was divided into two parts. The first part contained provisions originally included in the Stop Turning Out Prisoners Act of 1995, which was incorporated into the PLRA. Those provisions limited the ability of federal courts to enter injunctions against certain types of prison conditions, including overcrowding, in order to discourage courts from attempting to manage prisons. In that sense, the provisions in part one of the PRLA were a throwback to the *hands-off doctrine* of courts prior to 1960. The second part of the PRLA established a procedural framework for the filing of civil suits in federal court by prisoners. The procedures, which attempted to limit the number of actions in federal courts by making it more difficult to file lawsuits, included the following:

- Indigent litigants must pay a filing fee, although the fee may be paid in installments.
- Courts may dismiss lawsuits brought by prisoners if the action is "frivolous, malicious, or fails to state a claim" or if the named defendant is immune from such litigation.
- Prisoners are disqualified from filing lawsuits if they have three prior lawsuits that were dismissed as frivolous, malicious, or failing to state a claim. The only exception is if the prisoner is in imminent danger of serious harm.
- Prisoners must exhaust all administrative remedies before filing a lawsuit over prison conditions.
- Courts must dismiss all lawsuits by prisoners for "mental or emotional injury suffered while in custody" unless there is also a showing that there was physical injury.
- Attorneys are limited in the amount of fees they may collect for representing prisoner litigants.

By limiting federal actions available to prisoners, proponents of the PRLA hoped to reduce the caseload in federal courts and to encourage state and local correctional agencies to develop alternatives to litigation in the federal courts. Four common alternatives to litigation are the grievance board, the inmate grievance committee, the ombudsman, and mediation.

The grievance board is typically composed of correctional staff and may include lay members from the jurisdiction of the correctional facility. Grievance boards are charged with hearing and investigating complaints from inmates. After such an investigation, the board may issue recommendations, although the recommendations are not usually binding on staff members. If the recommendations are ignored by correctional staff, however, additional grievances may be filed with the grievance board. On the other hand, if the inmate's complaint is investigated but shown to have no merit, the grievance board has a record of the investigation, which may be used to demonstrate their good faith effort to resolve the issue if it is pursued in court.

Inmate grievance committees operate much like grievance boards. The main difference is that inmate grievance committees include inmates among their members. Allowing inmates to sit on such committees is an attempt to bring some legitimacy to the process of investigating grievances, both to the inmates who filed complaints and to officials who oversee the board's actions. The use of inmates on grievance committees can be problematic, however. For example, inmates who sit on such committees might attempt to use their influence to control or intimidate other prisoners. Conversely, inmate committee members could be subjected to intimidation by inmates with grievances before the committee.

Ombudsman programs utilize an individual to represent the interests of the inmate filing a grievance. The ombudsman may be a correctional employee or someone from outside the correctional facility who is appointed or hired to fulfill that role. The role of the ombudsman is to ensure that the inmate has a fair hearing. To that end, the ombudsman is commonly allowed access to all parts of the correctional institution, including its records. An ombudsman is often free to expand an investigation if there is evidence of a more widespread problem than the inmate's initial complaint.

In most mediations, a professional mediator with no connections to the correctional institution or its controlling agency intervenes to reach a resolution that is binding on the parties to a dispute. Both parties enter into mediation with the understanding that the decision by the mediator is binding. In some jurisdictions, however, the prison's warden is given final authority over the mediator's decision. If the mediator's decision is overruled, the warden is generally required to do so in writing, and the warden's decision is commonly reviewed by officials within the correctional agency.

Appendix B contains the full text of the Prison Litigation Reform Act.

THE PRISON RAPE ELIMINATION ACT

In 2001, the report *No Escape: Male Rape in U.S. Prisons* by Human Rights Watch reported what many prison inmates and penologists already knew: Despite widespread anecdotal evidence of prison rape and sexual assault, there was no conclusive national data on the prevalence of inmate-on-inmate rape and sexual abuse in U.S. prisons. The paucity of data was due to a number of factors, including:

• Widespread underreporting of rapes and sexual abuse by inmate victims due to shame and fear of retaliation from predatory inmates.

• A failure among prison administrators to recognize the serious nature of sexual victimization in correctional settings and to implement meaningful prevention programs.

• A lack of specialized training for correctional staff charged with investigating reported incidents of prison rape and sexual abuse, resulting in a failure to preserve crime scene evidence and inadequate forensic interviewing of victims and perpetrators.

In response to reports of widespread prison rape and sexual assault by former inmates, activist organizations such as Human Rights Watch, and others, the Prison Rape Elimination Act (PREA) was passed by the 108th

Prisons

Congress of the United States and enacted into law on January 7, 2003. The PREA contained the following findings:

> *Insufficient research has been conducted and insufficient data reported on the extent of prison rape. However, experts have conservatively estimated that at least 13 percent of the inmates in the United States have been sexually assaulted in prison. Many inmates have suffered repeated assaults . . . The total number of inmates who have been sexually assaulted in the past 20 years likely exceeds 1,000,000. (section 2, paragraph 2).*

The PREA established a zero-tolerance for prison rape in state and federal prisons nationwide, with the goal of implementing national standards for the reporting, punishment, and prevention of prison rape. Under the PREA, the Bureau of Justice Statistics (BJS) was mandated to conduct an annual statistic review of the incidence and effects of prison rape in correctional institutions nationwide. The PREA appropriated $15 million annually from fiscal years 2004 to 2010 to conduct the mandated research. On March 25, 2004, the BJS set forth a summary of focus groups' discussion points in order to assist researchers in defining the nature and prevalence of prison rape and sexual assault.

Appendix C contains the full text of the Prison Rape Elimination Act.

FEDERAL SENTENCING GUIDELINES

In 1984, amid public concern over prison unrest and rising crime rates nationwide, Congress established the U.S. Sentencing Commission as an independent agency within the judicial branch of the federal government. In 1985, the commission called for strict federal sentencing guidelines and issued the following recommendations for federal courts:

- Reducing the use of probation, especially for crimes against persons and serious drug offenses.
- Eliminating straight probation without incarceration in favor of probation with conditions of confinement, which requires imprisonment for a fixed period of time for any violation of probation or new offense.
- Increasing the length of prison terms for violent crimes.

The Comprehensive Crime Control Act of 1984 included provisions for lengthy sentences for repeat offenders. The Anti-Drug Abuse Act of 1986 contained similar provisions for serious drug offenders. Those laws combined with the implementation of the guidelines recommended by the U.S.

Sentencing Commission effectively eliminated the use in federal courts of indeterminate sentencing, which was an outgrowth of the medical model in corrections and gave broad discretion to parole boards in granting early release to inmates. As a result, many more criminal offenders in federal courts received fixed and often lengthy determinate sentences for their offenses. For federal prisons, that meant housing more prisoners for longer periods of incarceration and a shift in correctional philosophy from rehabilitation to incapacitation.

STATE LEGISLATION

State prisons house nearly 90 percent of all prisoners nationwide. During the 1980s, in reaction to rising rates of violent crimes, many states passed legislation aimed at keeping criminal offenders in prison for longer periods of time. As a direct result of sentencing reforms, state prison populations increased significantly, as did expenditures for state correctional agencies nationwide. Sentencing reform at the state level included three general types of legislation: habitual offenders statutes, determinate sentencing, and sentencing enhancements.

Habitual offender statutes provide for the mandatory long-term sentences for repeat criminal offenders and commonly do not give courts any discretion in sentencing. In other words, under habitual offender statutes, judges are forced to ignore any mitigating factors that may be associated with a crime and, instead, must focus solely on the prior criminal history of repeat offenders. For example, under California's habitual offender statute, commonly known as the three-strikes law, any criminal offender with two prior convictions for violent felonies who commits a third felony must be sentenced to a term of 25 years to life in prison. The third felony need not be violent under California's three-strikes law. In addition, there is no possibility for parole until after serving 25 years of the sentence.

Under determinate sentencing laws, also known as truth-in-sentencing laws, a crime is assigned a fixed term of imprisonment that must be served by an offender convicted of that crime. As with habitual offender statutes, courts are commonly afforded no discretion at sentencing. Determinate sentences take a one-size-fits-all approach to crime and ignore both mitigating and aggravating factors of a criminal offense.

Sentencing enhancement laws are used to increase the penalties for crimes under certain circumstances. For example, in each state, the crime of robbery is assigned a term or range of imprisonment. With sentencing enhancements, however, the use of a gun during the commission of a robbery will add prison time. In other words, the use of a firearm enhances the sentence for robbery, which is the underlying crime. Such enhancements are usually proscribed by law and do not give discretion to courts as to whether or not to add the sentencing enhancement.

State sentencing reforms utilizing habitual offender statutes, determinate sentencing, and sentencing enhancements have significantly increased the number of prisoners with no possibility of parole. For example, in 1992, about 18 percent of prisoners in the United States who were serving a life sentence had no possibility for parole. By 2003, over 26 percent of prisoners serving a life sentence had no chance for parole.

In 2003, states nationwide were collectively facing a $200 billion budget shortfall for state government functions. Faced with rising budget deficits and increasing expenditures for corrections, some states began to reevaluate their harsh sentencing laws and to consider some of the following reforms:

• Eliminate mandatory minimum sentencing laws

• Return some discretion in sentencing to courts

• Divert nonviolent drug offenders into community treatment programs that are far less costly than incarceration

• Expand parole opportunities for certain offenders and eliminate automatic re-imprisonment for minor technical violations of parole

At the end of 2002, some 18 states had rolled back some mandatory minimum sentencing requirements, especially for nonviolent drug offenders and other low-level offenders. For example, in Texas, mandatory minimum sentences were eliminated for first-time felony drug possession offenses involving less than a gram of narcotics and such offenders were diverted into treatment programs. Washington State legislators amended sentencing guidelines to give courts more discretion and to allow the diversion of nonviolent drug offenders into treatment programs. In Kansas, mandatory sentencing enhancements for repeat drug offenders were eliminated in favor of diversion into treatment programs. Under Michigan's so-called 650 Lifer Law, the requirement of life in prison without parole for anyone convicted of delivering 650 or more grams of heroin or cocaine was significantly eased for first-time offenders. In addition, some 1,200 offenders sentenced under the old mandatory minimums requirements became eligible for parole consideration.

Mississippi's truth-in-sentencing laws were amended to allow for earlier parole of nonviolent first offenders. Texas, Washington, Colorado, and Kentucky also implemented reforms in their state parole systems to allow for earlier release and enhanced community supervision of nonviolent offenders.[3]

INTERNATIONAL LAW AND PRISONERS' RIGHTS

When U.S. armed forces are engaged in conflict with a foreign enemy, it is often necessary to detain prisoners of war for interrogation or pending further legal action, including criminal prosecution. The standards of confinement and treatment of prisoners of war detained by U.S. military personnel is controlled under international law, primarily by the Geneva Conventions.

There are four Geneva Conventions, signed on August 12, 1949, by the United States and other countries that are parties to the conventions. Convention I establishes the protections for members of the armed forces who become wounded or sick. Convention II expands those protections to wounded, sick, and shipwrecked members of naval forces. Convention III lists the rights of prisoners of war. Convention IV outlines the protections afforded to civilians during times of war. On June 8, 1977, two protocols were added to the Geneva Conventions that deal with the protections given to victims of international armed conflict, including victims of wars against racist regimes, wars of self-determination, and wars against invading forces.

The Geneva Conventions include the following key provisions:

• Prisoners of war must be humanely treated at all times. Any unlawful act which causes death or seriously endangers the health of a prisoner of war is a grave breach of the Geneva Conventions. In particular, prisoners must not be subject to physical mutilation, biological experiments, violence, intimidation, insults, and public curiosity. *Convention III, Article 13.*

• Prisoners of war must be interred on land and only in clean and healthy areas. *Convention III, Article 22.*

• Prisoners of war are entitled to the same treatment given to a country's own forces, including total surface and cubic space of dormitories, fire protection, adequate heating and lighting, and separate dormitories for women. *Convention III, Article 25.*

• Prisoners of war must receive enough food to maintain weight and to prevent nutritional deficiencies. Food must be similar to the prisoners regular diet, if possible. Food must not be used for disciplinary purposes. *Convention III, Article 26.*

• Prisoners of war must receive adequate clothing, including underwear and footwear. The clothing must be kept in good repair and prisoners who work must receive clothing appropriate to their tasks. *Convention III, Article 27.*

77

Prisons

- Prisoners of war must have adequate sanitary facilities, with separate facilities for women prisoners. *Convention III, Article 29.*
- Prisoners of war must receive adequate medical attention. *Convention III, Article 30.*
- Collective punishment for individual acts, corporal punishment, imprisonment without daylight, and all forms of torture and cruelty are forbidden. *Convention III, Article 87.*
- Imprisonment in premises without daylight is forbidden. *Convention III, Article 87.*
- Immediately upon capture or within a week after arrival at a prisoner-of-war camp, transit camp, or hospital, prisoners have the right to write directly to their families. *Convention III, Article 70.*
- Prisoners of war must receive adequate medical attention. Each camp must have an adequate infirmary, with isolation wards if needed for cases of contagious or mental disease. *Convention III, Article 30.*
- Those seriously ill or requiring special treatment must be admitted to any military or civilian medical unit where such treatment can be given. *Convention III, Article 30.*
- Prisoners may not be prevented from seeing medical personnel. Any costs of treatment, including dentures, eyeglasses, and other artificial appliances, will be borne by the detaining power. *Convention III, Article 30.*
- Medical inspections, which must include the recording of the weight of each prisoner, must be held at least once a month for the purpose of supervising the general state of health, nutrition and cleanliness and to detect contagious diseases. *Convention III, Article 31.*

In addition, the Geneva Conventions stipulate that prisoners of war must receive due process and fair trials, that any time spent in confinement waiting for trial will count toward time served, and that all prisoners have the right of appeal and must be informed of these rights and of any time limits on them. *(Convention III, Article 106.)* Appendix D contains an abridged version of Convention III, which governs the treatment of prisoners of war.

After the terrorist attacks on the United States that occurred on September 11, 2001, the federal government began to detain individuals suspected of possible involvement in terrorist activities against the United States at the U.S. detention facility in Guantánamo Bay, Cuba. In 2004, the U.S. Supreme Court ruled in *Rasul v. Bush* that detainees held at Guantánamo Bay had the right to challenge their detention in a hearing before a judge. The case is presented later in this chapter.

U.S. SUPREME COURT CASES

Beginning in 1964, with its decision in *Cooper v. Pate* (378 U.S. 546), the U.S. Supreme Court departed from the *hands-off doctrine* historically used by U.S. courts to dismiss actions brought by prison inmates. The court ruled that prisoners had the same right as other U.S. citizens to seek remedy for grievances brought under the Civil Rights Act of 1871. In the wake of *Cooper v. Pate*, the U.S. Supreme Court ruled in dozens of cases brought by prisoners nationwide, including the landmark cases presented in this chapter that addressed the rights of inmates in the following areas:

- **Access to the Courts** *Cooper v. Pate (1964), Johnson v. Avery (1969), Bounds v. Smith (1977), Lewis v. Casey (1996), Rasul v. Bush (2004)*
- **Free Speech and Religious Expression** *Procunier v. Martinez (1974), Pell v. Procunier (1974), Jones v. North Carolina Prisoners' Labor Union, Inc. (1977), Turner v. Safley (1987), O'Lone v. Estate of Shabazz (1987), Thornburgh v. Abbott (1989)*
- **Due Process** *Wolff v. McDonnell (1974), Superintendant v. Hill (1985), Sandin v. Conner (1995)*
- **Cruel and Unusual Punishment** *Rhodes v. Chapman (1981), Whitley v. Albers (1986), Wilson v. Seiter (1991), Hudson v. McMillian (1992), Roper v. Simmons (2005)*
- **Medical Care** *Estelle v. Gamble (1976), Washington v. Harper (1990)*
- **Parole** *Morrissey v. Brewer (1972), Johnson v. United States (2000)*
- **Sentencing** *Apprendi v. New Jersey (2000), Blakely v. Washington (2004)*
- **Capital Sentencing** *Ring v. Arizona (2002)*

Access to the Courts

COOPER V. PATE, 378 U.S. 546 (1964)

Background

In 1963, Thomas Cooper was an inmate at the Illinois State Penitentiary. Cooper requested copies of the Koran (Qur'an) and other books dealing with Islam and the Muslim faith but was denied access to books. The prison's warden, Frank J. Pate, forbade the dissemination of any materials associated with the Black Muslims, which prison officials considered to be a revolutionary movement that advocated black supremacy and had the potential of disrupting security in the prison. Cooper denied that he was an organizer for the Black Muslims or that he had any other ulterior motive for requesting the reading materials. Cooper's insistence on receiving the books he requested resulted in Cooper being placed in solitary confinement as a disciplinary measure.

Legal Issues

In 1963, Thomas Cooper was an inmate at the Illinois State Penitentiary. Cooper requested copies of the Koran (Qur'an) and other books dealing with Islam and the Muslim faith but was denied access to books. The prison's warden, Frank J. Pate, forbade the dissemination of any materials associated with the Black Muslims, which prison officials considered to be a revolutionary movement that advocated black supremacy and had the potential of disrupting security in the prison. Cooper denied that he was an organizer for the Black Muslims or that he had any other ulterior motive for requesting the reading materials. Cooper's insistence on receiving the books he requested resulted in Cooper being placed in solitary confinement as a disciplinary measure.tain religious groups, including the Black Muslims, constituted a "threat to maintaining order in a crowded prison environment."

Decision

The U.S. Supreme Court reversed the decision on the grounds that Cooper's complaint contained a legitimate cause of action—that Cooper was the victim of discrimination when he was denied access to Muslim publications while other prisoners were allowed to have reading materials from other religious faiths. The Court held that the lower courts were in error to dismiss the cause of action stated in Cooper's complaint without a hearing as to its merits, regardless of Cooper's status as an inmate in a state prison.

Impact

The *Cooper* ruling did not address the issue of Cooper's civil rights. Rather, the Supreme Court simply held that Cooper had a legitimate cause of action and therefore had legitimate standing to be heard. Still, with its ruling, the Supreme Court moved away from the *hands-off doctrine* that previous courts had used to deny prisoners the right to litigate their grievances. The *hands-off doctrine* was articulated in 1866 by the U.S. Supreme Court in the case of *Pervear v. Massachusetts* (72 U.S. 678), in which the plaintiff, a state prisoner in Massachusetts, argued that poor prison conditions constituted a violation of the Eighth Amendment's ban on cruel or unusual punishment. In its ruling the *Pervear* court declared that because the federal government lacked a legitimate interest in the administration of state institutions, state prison inmates could not invoke the protections afforded under the Eighth Amendment. Similarly, in 1871, the Virginia Supreme Court in *Ruffin v. Common-wealth* (62 Va. 790) ruled that inmates were effectively "slaves of the state" who lacked standing in a court of law to seek remedy for violations of their civil rights because they forfeited those rights when sentenced to prison.

In 1941, in the case *Ex parte Hull* (312 U.S. 546), the U.S. Supreme Court acknowledged that prisoners had a right to judicial review. However, the court's finding that relief was not merited based on the facts of the *Hull* case effectively reinforced the use of the *hands-off doctrine*. As late as 1958, in the case of *Gore v. United States* (357 U.S. 386), the U.S. Supreme Court maintained its noninterventionist policy with regard to prisoners seeking redress for violations of their civil rights. The *Cooper* case effectively opened the courthouse doors to thousands of U.S. prisoners to be heard in federal courts.

JOHNSON V. AVERY, 393 U.S. 483 (1969)

Background

In 1965, while serving a life sentence at the Tennessee state penitentiary, William Joe Johnson was moved to a maximum security prison as a disciplinary action for assisting other prisoners in preparing legal documents, which was a violation of the prison's regulations. Johnson sought remedy in federal district court, claiming that he had been unfairly disciplined and asking the court for access to law books and a typewriter in order to continue preparing legal documents for other inmates.

Legal Issues

The district court ruled in Johnson's favor, holding that the prison regulation preventing Johnson from assisting other inmates was in conflict with federal law because the rule effectively barred illiterate prisoners from access to the courts. The circuit court reversed the ruling, however, on the grounds that maintaining prison discipline by limiting the practice of law to attorneys justified the potential burden on illiterate prisoners in filing court documents without the assistance of legal counsel.

Decision

In reversing the circuit court the Supreme Court ruled that, absent "reasonable alternatives" by the state of Tennessee to assist illiterate or poorly educated inmates in preparing post-conviction petitions, the state's regulation against allowing prisoners to help other inmates prepare court documents was unconstitutional. The Court recognized that inmates who provided legal assistance were placed in a position of power that could be used to exploit disadvantaged prisoners and potentially disrupt prison order. The Court ruled, however, that the right of legal assistance in a correctional setting was more important.

Impact

The *Johnson* ruling went a step further in giving prisoners access to relief in federal court by allowing them to assist each other in the preparation of post-conviction petitions, as well as other court documents. However, the Court left open the possibility of closing that opportunity for inmates in the interest of institutional security if the state provided "reasonable alternatives" for disadvantaged inmates to obtain legal assistance in prison. The precise meaning of "reasonable alternatives" was not articulated by the Court until its later ruling in *Lewis v. Casey*, which is presented later in this section.

BOUNDS V. SMITH, 430 U.S. 817 (1977)

Background

In 1976, three lawsuits against the Division of Prisons of the North Carolina Department of Corrections were brought by several inmates. Their cases were consolidated by the U.S. Supreme Court. The inmates initially sought relief in district court under Title 42 of the U.S. Code, section 1983, for the failure of the state of North Carolina to provide them with access to legal research materials, in violation of their due process rights under the Fourteenth Amendment.

Legal Issues

The district court ruled in favor of the inmates, declaring that North Carolina's sole prison library was inadequate to meet the needs of state inmates with no other legal assistance available to them. The state proposed to open seven libraries in correctional institutions throughout North Carolina. Under the state's plan, inmates were required to make appointments to use the prison library. Inmates in institutions without a library would be provided with transportation and housing. Still, given North Carolina's inmate population at the time, there was a waiting time of three or four weeks to use a library. The parties to the lawsuit returned to district court and claimed that the state's plan was inadequate. The district court rejected their claim and ruled that the state's plan afforded the inmates reasonable access to legal research materials in order to effectively pursue actions in court. On appeal, the Court of Appeals for the Fourth Circuit affirmed the district court's ruling and approved the state's plan for new libraries, with one exception. The circuit court held that North Carolina's library plan failed to provide female prisoners with the same library access as male prisoners. Absent any legal justification by the state for this oversight, the court held that female prisoners were unconstitutionally discriminated against under the state's plan.

Decision

The U.S. Supreme Court ruled in favor of the inmates who objected to the state's library plan. The Court held that prisoners were entitled to the fundamental constitutional right of access to the courts. As such, correctional authorities were required to provide inmates with access to legal resources, including assistance from persons trained in matters of law. In other words, by denying inmates the ability to prepare and file documents with the courts, the state was effectively denying them access to the courts, which was an unconstitutional violation of their Fourteenth Amendment rights.

Impact

The ruling in *Bounds* built upon the 1971 decision by the U.S. Supreme Court in *Young v. Gilmore* (404 U.S. 15) that the rights of access to the courts and equal protection under the law were violated when prisoners did not have access to assistance in the initial preparation of post-conviction petitions filed in federal court. In *Bounds*, the Court broadened the scope of its ruling in *Young* by declaring that inmates must have *meaningful* access to the courts and, therefore, to legal research materials and other supplies in order to competently prepare petitions and other court documents. As such, correctional agencies were obligated to afford such access to prisoners under their authority.

LEWIS V. CASEY, 518 U.S. 343 (1996)

Background

Twenty-three inmates from several state prisons in Arizona filed a class action lawsuit in district court claiming the Arizona Department of Corrections (ADOC) failed to provide them with adequate legal research facilities, thereby depriving them of their constitutional right of access to the courts as established in the 1977 ruling by the U.S. Supreme Court in *Bounds v. Smith*.

Legal Issues

The district court ruled in favor of the prisoners and issued an injunction against the ADOC to make sweeping improvements in its system of law libraries and legal assistance programs for inmates. On appeal by the ADOC, the U.S. Court of Appeals, Ninth Circuit, affirmed the district court's ruling and agreed in large part with the terms of the injunction against the ADOC, which included detailed instructions, including the hours of operation of prison libraries.

Decision

The U.S. Supreme Court reversed both the district and circuit courts, citing the failure of the prisoners to show a systemic failure by the ADOC to provide inmates with access to legal research facilities and legal assistance. Instead, the Court found that the prisoners had only identified isolated instances of the ADOC's failure to provide such access and services. Citing the decision in *Bounds*, the Court held, in part, that *"Bounds* did not create an abstract, free-standing right to a law library or legal assistance; rather, the right that *Bounds* acknowledged was the right of access to the courts . . . Moreover, *Bounds* does not guarantee inmates the wherewithal to file any and every type of legal claim, but requires only that they be provided with the tools to attack their sentences . . . and to challenge the conditions of their confinement." The Court held that any remedy provided by a court must be limited to the actual injury to the plaintiff and, therefore, the injunction against the ADOC issued by the district court and upheld by the circuit court was "inordinately intrusive" and improper.

Impact

The Court clarified the right of access to the courts by inmates and limited the remedy imposed by a court upon a correctional agency to address only the actual injury to the plaintiff. The Court held that the widespread systemic failure of a correctional agency to provide inmates with access to the courts requires proof by the plaintiffs showing a widespread pattern of injury. The ruling decried the use of courts to micromanage correctional institutions and in that respect was somewhat reminiscent of the *hand-off doctrine* of the Court prior to its 1964 decision in *Cooper v. Pate*. Further, the Court made clear that while *Bounds* held that correctional institutions bear a duty to provide inmates with legal resources to assist them in post-conviction actions, that duty does not extend to assisting inmates in discovering new grievances.

RASUL V. BUSH, 124 S. CT. 2686 (2004)

Background

In 2002, during hostilities between the United States and the Taliban as a result of the terrorist attack on the United States on September 11, 2001, two Australian citizens and 12 Kuwait; citizens were captured in Afghanistan by U.S. forces. The detainees were subsequently transported to the U.S. Naval Base at Guantánamo Bay, Cuba, where they were held along with some 640 other enemy combatants captured abroad by U.S. forces during the war on terrorism.

Legal Issues

The two Australians, Mamdouh Habib and David Hicks, each filed petitions in the U.S. Court for the District of Columbia challenging the legality of their detention and seeking release from custody, access to legal counsel, and freedom from interrogations. Shafiq Rasul and the other 11 detainees from Kuwait filed a complaint in federal court seeking to be informed of the charges against them, access to legal counsel, and the right to be heard in a U.S. court of law or some other impartial tribunal. The district court dismissed all of the actions on the grounds that the court lacked jurisdiction because the U.S. Naval Base at Guantánamo Bay, Cuba, was not within the jurisdiction of any federal court. The court held, in part, that "the privilege of litigation does not extend to aliens in military custody who have no presence in any territory over which the United States is sovereign." As such, the detainees at Guantánamo Bay, Cuba, lacked standing to bring an action in federal court. In affirming the ruling, the Court of Appeals agreed that the district court correctly interpreted the 1973 U.S. Supreme Court's decision in *Johnson v. Eisentrager* (339 U.S. 763) to mean that aliens detained outside the sovereign territory of the United States did not have the right to bring actions in federal court.

Decision

The U.S. Supreme Court reversed the decision and ruled that U.S. courts had at least limited jurisdiction to consider challenges to the legality of the detention of foreign nationals captured abroad and held at Guantánamo Bay, Cuba. The court based its ruling, in part, on Title 28 of the U.S. Code, section 2241, which authorized federal district courts to consider actions brought by individuals claiming to be held "in custody in violation of the laws of the United States." The Court interpreted the language of the statute to include "aliens held in a territory over which the United States exercises . . . jurisdiction, but not sovereignty." Because the United States exercised jurisdiction over the Naval Base at Guantánamo Bay, Cuba, detainees there had standing to at least challenge their detention in federal district courts.

The Court rejected the district court's interpretation of the *Eisentrager* case on the grounds that the detainees at Guantánamo Bay, Cuba, were not nationals of countries at war with the United States, as the German prisoners were in *Eisentrager*. The court noted that the detainees at Guantánamo Bay, Cuba, denied that they engaged in terrorist plots against the United States and were never charged or convicted of any wrongdoing, yet they were detained for over two years without access to any court or impartial tribunal.

Impact

The Court's ruling clarified that detainees held by authorities have at least the limited right of access to courts to challenge their detention, whether they are held in the sovereign United States or in territorial areas over which the United States exercised some jurisdiction. The Court echoed its finding in the case of *Hamdi v. Rumsfeld* (Case No. 03-6696), which was decided on June 28, 2004, the same date as the decision in the *Rasul* case. Yaser Esam Hamdi was born an American citizen in Louisiana in 1980 and later moved with his family to Saudi Arabia. In 2002, Hamdi was captured in Afghanistan by coalition forces and turned over to the custody of the United States, in part because of his status as a U.S. citizen. Hamdi was interrogated and detained by the United States and classified as an enemy combatant for allegedly taking up arms with the Taliban in Afghanistan. Hamdi was transferred to the U.S. Naval Base at Guantánamo Bay, Cuba, and later to the naval brig at Norfolk, Virginia, and held without formal charges or court proceedings. Hamdi's capture and detention was challenged on the basis of his rights to due process under the Fifth and Fourteenth Amendments to the U.S. Constitution. In *Hamdi*, the U.S. Supreme Court ruled that Hamdi had the right to "a limited judicial inquiry into his detention's legality . . . but not a search reviewing of the factual determinations underlying his seizure." In both *Hamdi* and *Rasul*, the Court made clear that detainees have an absolute right to challenge their detentions and be heard in a court of law, even if that hearing is limited to the narrow issue of the legality of their detention.

Free Speech and Religious Expression

PROCUNIER V. MARTINEZ, 416 U.S. 396 (APRIL 29, 1974)

Background

In 1973, the California Department of Corrections authorized the censorship of prisoner's mail. Prison regulations prohibited inmates from mailing correspondence in which they "unduly complained, magnified grievances, or expressed inflammatory political, racial, religious, or other views or beliefs," or in which inmates expressed any views deemed by prison officials to be "defamatory" or "otherwise inappropriate." Under the same rationale, California prison regulations permitted inmates to meet with their attorneys but not with their attorney's law clerks or paralegals, who were sometimes dispatched to conduct interviews with inmates or to provide legal information or assistance under the direction of the inmates' attorneys.

Legal Issues

California state prison inmates brought a class action lawsuit against the California Department of Corrections in which they challenged the prison regulations. The central justification for the challenge was that by censoring the inmates' mail, prison officials violated the prisoners' right of free speech, as guaranteed under the First Amendment to the U.S. Constitution. The district court agreed with the prisoners, holding that the prison regulations violated their right of free speech under the First Amendment and that the regulations were vague, in violation of the due process clause of the Fourteenth Amendment. The district court also held that banning inmates from meeting with law clerks and paralegals violated the inmates' right of access to the courts.

Decision

The U.S. Supreme Court affirmed the lower court's ruling on the issue of the First Amendment. The Court held that "censorship of direct personal correspondence involves incidental restrictions on the right to free speech of both prisoners and their correspondents." However, the Court held that censorship of mail by prison officials was justifiable under certain conditions. First, the censorship "must further one or more of the important and substantial governmental interests of security, order, and the rehabilitation of inmates." Secondly, the censorship "must be no greater than is necessary to further the legitimate governmental interest involved." Using this two-pronged standard, known as the "strict scrutiny" standard, the Court held that the regulations concerning prisoners' mail by the California Department of Corrections were "far broader than any legitimate interest of penal administration demands . . ."

The Court also agreed with the district court on the issue of prohibiting inmates from meeting with law clerks and paralegals. The Court held that such a ban constituted an unjustifiable restriction on inmates' access to the courts because the ban "created an arbitrary distinction between law students employed by attorneys and those associated with law school programs," who were not banned from meeting with inmates under the same California prison regulations.

Impact

The *Procunier v. Martinez* ruling was significant in two ways. First, the Court clearly upheld the right of free speech for prisoners. Second, the Court established a two-pronged standard to guide penal institutions in the regulation of inmates' mail. As such, the Court attempted to strike a balance between the constitutional rights of prisoners as citizens and the duty of correctional institutions to maintain order and control for the safety of their prisoners and the protection of society. Significantly, the Court's ruling only addressed the censorship of mail between prisoners and individuals outside the prison. The court did not take up the issue of inmate-to-inmate mail until 1987 in its ruling in *Turner v. Safley*, which is presented later in this section.

PELL V. PROCUNIER, 417 U.S. 817 (JUNE 24, 1974)

Background

In 1973, a regulation contained in the California Department of Corrections Manual prohibited "press and other media interviews with specific inmates." Under the regulation, the press was generally allowed to interview inmates but prohibited from conducting individual face-to-face interviews or giving special media coverage to a particular inmate. The California Department of Corrections instituted the regulation after certain inmates gained notoriety as a result of such interviews with the press. Because of their notoriety, the department claimed, those inmates gained influence over other prisoners and threatened to undermine the control and discipline of the institution.

Legal Issues

Four California state prison inmates and three journalists challenged the regulation in a federal district court. With regard to the inmates, the court declared that the regulation was an unconstitutional violation of free speech under the First Amendment. The court also held that the regulation was vague and, therefore, violated the Fourteenth Amendment's due process clause. However, the court dismissed the claims brought by the journalists that the regulation was unfair to them by limiting their access to prisoners. The court held that the regulation did not infringe upon the rights of the journalists because they were allowed to enter correctional institutions for the purpose of conducting general interviews with inmates.

The Law of Prisons

Decision

On an appeal brought by the journalists and prison officials, the U.S. Supreme Court affirmed the lower court's ruling with regard to the journalists and reversed it with regard to the prisoners' rights, ruling that the regulations by the California Department of Corrections violated neither the journalists' nor the prisoners' free speech. According to the Court, the ban on face-to-face media interviews with inmates was reasonable because it did not prevent the press communicating with inmates by other means, including the mail. The Court held that "the First Amendment does not guarantee the press a constitutional right of special access to information not available to the public generally." As for the inmates, the Court ruled that they had many avenues of communication, including the mail and visits from family members, attorneys, and clergy. As such, the ban against face-to-face media interviews did not constitute an unconstitutional restriction on prisoners' free speech. The Court reasoned that constitutional rights, including freedom of speech, must be balanced against the needs of a correctional institution to maintain order and discipline for the protection of inmates and the public. As the Court stated, "such considerations are peculiarly within the province and professional expertise of corrections officials, and . . . courts should ordinarily defer to their expert judgment in such matters."

Impact

Following its ruling in *Procunier v. Martinez*, the Court declared that prisoners do not have an unlimited right of free speech and that communication between inmates and others outside of prison, including the press, must be balanced against institutional needs for security and safety. In combination, the *Martinez* and *Pell* decisions gave prison officials the authority to limit prisoners' expression of certain constitutional rights and provided a two-pronged standard by which to formulate prison regulations limiting free speech and other rights.

JONES V. NORTH CAROLINA PRISONERS' LABOR UNION, INC., 433 U.S. 119 (1977)

Background

In 1974, a group of prisoners under the authority of the North Carolina Department of Corrections formed the North Carolina Prisoners' Labor Union. The union was incorporated with the stated goal of installing a

Prisons

chapter of the union at every prison and jail in North Carolina and of working through collective bargaining to improve prison conditions. By early 1975, some 2,000 inmates in 40 different prisons throughout the state had joined the union. The North Carolina Department of Corrections was unhappy with this development and, on March 26, 1975, passed a regulation prohibiting inmates from soliciting other prisoners to join the union. The regulation also banned union meetings and mass mailings concerning union activities.

Legal Issues

Under Title 42 of the U.S. Code, section 1983, the union filed action in federal court claiming that the regulation violated their rights of free speech and association guaranteed by the First Amendment. The union members also claimed that their rights were violated under the equal protection clause of the Fourteenth Amendment because other organizations, including the Jaycees and Alcoholics Anonymous, were permitted to conduct meetings, recruit members, and distribute bulk mailing materials within prisons in North Carolina. The district court ruled that if inmates were allowed to join the union, then the North Carolina Department of Corrections could not prohibit them from soliciting new members or holding meetings. The district court also agreed with the union on the issue of bulk mailings, holding that the North Carolina Department of Corrections could not "pick and choose" which groups could engage in such mailings and which groups could not utilize bulk mailings to promote their activities.

Decision

The U.S. Supreme Court reversed the lower court and ruled that the regulation by the North Carolina Department of Corrections did not violate the rights of the prisoners under either the First or Fourteenth Amendments to the U.S. Constitution. Citing its previous decision in *Martinez* and *Pell*, the Court criticized the district court for not deferring to the needs of prison officials to maintain order and security in correctional settings. The Court held that the North Carolina Department of Corrections' regulation limiting union activity "was no broader than necessary to meet the perceived threat of group meetings and organizational activity to [prison] order and security." The Court faulted the district court's reasoning that mass mailings must be permitted for the prisoners' union if they are permitted for other groups, including the Jaycees and Alcoholics Anonymous. The court reasoned that a prison was not a public forum and, as such, prison officials were only obligated to demonstrate a "rational basis" for distinguishing between various organizations. As such, organizations like the Jaycees and Alcoholics Anonymous conducted rehabilitative work in accord with the goals of the prison, whereas the prisoners' union constituted "an adversarial organization at odds with institutional goals."

Impact

Unionization by prisoners reached its peak during the 1970s, and union activities by prisoners have significantly diminished since that time. Nonetheless, while the *Jones* case placed limits on the rights of prisoners to conduct union activities in correctional settings, the Court did not establish clear guidelines for correctional officials in formulating rules governing prisoners' unions. In the 1987 case of *Turner v. Safley*, however, the Court established guidelines regarding inmate-to-inmate communications that may be applicable in other cases involving prisoners' unions.

TURNER V. SAFLEY, 482 U.S. 78 (JUNE 1, 1987)

Background

In 1986, the Missouri Division of Corrections allowed written correspondence between two prisoners if they were immediate family members housed at different institutions in Missouri or if the correspondence dealt with legal matters. Otherwise, Missouri state prisoners were allowed to write to each other only if prison officials deemed that the correspondence was in the best interest of both parties. Another prison regulation permitted a Missouri state prisoner to marry only with the prison superintendent's permission, which was usually granted only in cases of pregnancy where there was an impending birth of an illegitimate child. Missouri state inmates filed a class action lawsuit in district court challenging the constitutionality of both regulations.

Legal Issues

The federal district court ruled that both regulations were unconstitutional, and the court of appeals affirmed the ruling. Both courts found that the Missouri Division of Correction's regulations on inmate-to-inmate correspondence restricted the free speech of prisoners. The courts also agreed that prisoners had a constitutional right to marry.

Decision

The U.S. Supreme Court then reversed on the issue of intra-institutional correspondence between inmates, holding that the prison's regulation was reasonable based on the following four relevant factors:

• The regulation was reasonably related to a legitimate or neutral government interest. In other words, banning most inmate-to-inmate communications reduced the risk of a breach in control or security. Allowing such communication increased that risk. Therefore, the regulation was reasonably related to the correctional agency's interest of maintaining security and control in prisons under its authority.
• The regulation did not preclude all alternative means of expressing the same constitutional right. For example, Missouri inmates could still communicate by mail with relatives or friends outside prison to convey information to immediate family members at other institutions.
• The potential impact of modifying or abolishing the regulation placed an unreasonable burden on Missouri prison officials whose primary responsibility was for the security and control of correctional institutions.
• There was no valid alternative to the regulation that did not compromise the safety and security of the institution.

On the issue of a prisoner's right to marry, the Court agreed with the lower courts, holding that "prisoners have a constitutionally protected right to marry [even if] such a marriage is subject to substantial restrictions as a result of incarceration . . ."

Impact

The Court established a new precedent for balancing the constitutional rights of prisoners with the duty of prison officials to maintain institutional order and security. The Court held that the district and circuit courts incorrectly applied the previous standard of "strict scrutiny" that was established in *Procunier v. Martinez*. Under the two-pronged "strict scrutiny" standard, prison officials were required to make a showing that any violation of a prisoner's constitutional rights was justified by "the important and substantial governmental interests of security, order, and the rehabilitation of inmates" and that the infringement upon a prisoner's constitutional rights "must be no greater than is necessary to further the legitimate governmental interest involved." In *Turner*, the Court introduced a less rigorous "rational basis" test to determine if a prison regulation violated prisoners' constitutional rights. According to the Court, the "rational basis" for determining the constitutionality of prison regulations and policy was determining the reasonableness of those polices, based upon a four-pronged test devised by the Court.

O'LONE V. ESTATE OF SHABAZZ, 482 U.S. 342 (JUNE 9, 1987)

Background

In 1983, New Jersey state prisoners confined at the Leesburg prison were placed in one of three security classifications. The highest security classification was "maximum status," followed by "gang minimum status." The lowest security classification was "full minimum status." Under a new prison regulation, prisoners classified as gang minimum status or full minimum status were assigned to work crews outside of the main building. The new regulation, known as Standard 853, was implemented gradually. During the initial phase, some Muslim inmates assigned to outside work crews were allowed to remain in the main building on Fridays in order to attend Jumu'ah, a weekly Islamic religious service. In March 1984, however, inmates on minimum gang status or full minimum status were no longer allowed in the main building while assigned to outside work crews, except in cases of emergency. As a result, some Muslim inmates were prevented from attending Jumu'ah on Fridays.

Legal Issues

Muslim inmates filed suit in federal court alleging a violation of the First Amendment right of freedom of religious expression. The district court ruled that work detail procedure at Leesburg State Prison did not violate the rights of the Muslim inmates and that prison officials had authority to regulate work details in order to maintain a secure and orderly prison environment. However, the U.S. Court of Appeals for the Third Circuit reversed the ruling and held that New Jersey prison officials failed to demonstrate that they explored every reasonable method to accommodate the Muslim inmates. Absent that showing, the court of appeals ruled that the Muslim inmates were correct in claiming their rights were violated under the First Amendment.

Decision

In a 5 to 4 opinion written by Chief Justice William Rehnquist, the U.S. Supreme Court reversed the Third Circuit and rejected the idea that prison administrators must explore every possible means of avoiding infringements on prisoners' constitutional rights. Deferring to the authority of prison administrators, Chief Justice Rehnquist wrote, "This court will not substitute its judgment on difficult and sensitive matters of institutional administration for the determinations of those charged with the formidable task of running a prison." Although the Court recognized that the prison's policies prevented some Muslim inmates from attending Jumu'ah, the Court held that the "reasonableness [of the prison policies] is supported by the fact that they do no deprive respondents of all forms of religious exercise, but instead allow participation in a number of Muslim religious ceremonies." The Court also noted that prison officials accommodated Muslim inmates in other ways. For example, Muslim inmates were offered different meals whenever pork was served at the prison. In addition, Muslim inmates were allowed to have early breakfasts and late dinners to accommodate the observance of Ramadan, a monthlong period of fasting and prayer during daylight hours.

Impact

This was the first case in which the Supreme Court applied the *Turner v. Safley* test for the impact of prison regulations on inmates' First Amendment right of freedom of religious expression. In applying the "rational basis" test, the Court moved away from the previous "strict scrutiny" test that required courts to more rigorously examine the impact of prison regulations on the exercise of constitutional rights.

THORNBURGH V. ABBOTT, 490 U.S. 401 (1989)

Background

In 1989, the Federal Bureau of Prisons permitted federal prisoners to subscribe to or receive periodicals or other publications without prior approval by their prison's warden. However, each warden was authorized to reject any publication considered to be "detrimental to the security, good order, or discipline of the institution, or if [the publication] might facilitate criminal activity." Publications could not be rejected solely because a publication's content was "religious, philosophical, political, or sexual, or because its content [was] unpopular or repugnant."

Legal Issues

Certain inmates and some of the publishers of the 46 publications rejected in federal prisons filed suit in federal district court claiming that their First Amendment right of free speech was violated according to the "strict scrutiny" standards established in *Procunier v. Martinez*. The district court analyzed the plaintiff's claim by applying the "rational basis" test set forth in *Turner v. Safely* and upheld the federal prison regulations. The Court of Appeals, however, followed *Martinez* and reversed the district court, holding that the federal prison regulations on publications were unconstitutional and invalid.

Decision

The U.S. Supreme Court reversed the Court of Appeals and upheld the district court's ruling using the "rational basis" test articulated in *Turner v. Safley*. The Court found that, under the standard of reasonableness articulated in *Turner*, the Bureau of Prison's regulations concerning publications were constitutionally valid. However, the Court agreed in part with the appellate court that the plaintiffs were entitled to a case-by-case review of all 46 publications.

Impact

The court reestablished its reliance on the *Turner v. Safley* test of reasonableness and not the *Martinez* test of "strict scrutiny" in balancing the civil right of prisoners with the duty of prison officials to maintain order and control in institutions. This effectively shifted the burden to plaintiffs to not only demonstrate that their constitutional rights were violated, but also that the prison's regulation or policy abridging that right was unreasonable in its intent to maintain order and control.

Due Process

WOLFF V. MCDONNELL, 418 U.S. 539 (1974)

Background

In 1974, Nebraska state prisoners were subjected to disciplinary procedures, including confinement in a disciplinary cell and forfeiture or withholding of good-time credits, which inmates could accumulate in order to move up their date of release. Nebraska state prisons used the following procedure in cases of alleged misconduct: (1) the inmate was orally informed of the charges, and the merits of the allegations were discussed in a preliminary conference with the chief corrections supervisor and the charging party; (2) a conduct report was prepared; (3) a hearing was held before the prison's disciplinary board at which the accused inmate was able to question the charging party.

Prisons

Legal Issues

Inmate Robert O. Mcdonnell, on behalf of himself and other Nebraska state prisoners, filed an action in federal district court alleging that his due process rights were violated and seeking damages and injunctive relief under Title 42 of the U.S. Code, section 1983. The district court rejected Mc-Donnell's claim. However, the Court of Appeals reversed and held that Mc-Donnell's due process claim should be evaluated under the U.S. Supreme Court 1972 decision in *Morrissey v. Brewer* (408 U.S. 471) and the Court's 1973 decision in *Gagnon v. Scarpelli* (411 U.S. 778), which set forth a series of procedures for parole and probation revocation hearings.

Decision

The U.S. Supreme Court affirmed the appellate court and held that inmates have constitutionally guaranteed due process rights in prison disciplinary proceedings. According to the Court, while prisoners did not enjoy the full range of due process rights, those rights must be accommodated in disciplinary proceedings to the extent that institutional needs allowed. The Court held that inmates were entitled to advance written notice of disciplinary actions no less than 24 hours prior to their appearance before the disciplinary board and that the disciplinary board must be impartial. In addition, the inmate must be provided with a written statement by the fact finders stating what evidence they relied upon and their reasons for recommending disciplinary action. In balancing the due process rights of inmates with institutional safety, the Court held that inmates have the right to call witnesses and present evidence in their defense, as long as doing so does not endanger other inmates or otherwise jeopardize institutional control. The Court concluded that inmates' constitutional rights in disciplinary hearings do not include the right to confront and cross-examine witnesses or the right to an attorney.

Impact

In its ruling, the Court was specific in defining the minimal due process rights for inmates at disciplinary hearings. The effect of the ruling, however, was to discourage the use of arbitrary decision making in such hearings, which remain tightly controlled by prison officials. The Court still allowed prison officials significant leeway in leveraging the due process rights of inmates against the interests of institutional security and control.

Superintendant v. Hill, 472 U.S. 445 (1985)

Background

In 1982, at the state prison in Walpole, Massachusetts, a correctional officer heard commotion in a prison corridor. When the officer went to the lo-

96

cation to investigate the source of the noise, he observed an injured inmate and three other inmates fleeing down the corridor, including Gerald Hill and Joseph Crawford. Hill, Crawford, and the third inmate observed fleeing the scene of the assault received disciplinary reports alleging that they had assaulted the injured inmate discovered by the correctional officer. At a hearing, the prison's disciplinary board heard testimony from the correctional officer and received the officer's written report. Based on the officer's testimony and written report, the board held the inmates responsible for the assault and revoked their good-time credits. Hill and Crawford unsuccessfully appealed the board's decision to the prison superintendent.

Legal Issues

Hill and Crawford filed suit in the Massachusetts Superior Court claiming that their due process rights were violated because there was no evidence, other than the correctional officer's testimony and report, that supported the prison board's ruling. The Superior Court ruled in favor of the inmates and held that the evidence supporting the board's finding of guilt was constitutionally inadequate. On appeal by the prison administration, the Massachusetts Supreme Judicial Court affirmed the superior court's ruling in favor of the inmates Hill and Crawford.

Decision

The U.S. Supreme Court reversed the decisions of the Massachusetts courts. The Court held that good-time credits constituted a protected liberty interest and, as such, the minimum requirements of due process were required in order to revoke them. The Court ruled that the minimum requirement of due process in prison disciplinary hearings was necessary in order to prevent "arbitrary deprivation" of the constitutional rights of inmates. However, in balancing the due process requirements against the imposition of "undue administrative burdens" on the prison, the Court held that, as long as there is "some evidence" of guilt, the standard of due process is satisfied in prison disciplinary hearings. The Court noted that prison officials were not required to weigh the entire record of evidence or to conduct independent assessments of the credibility of witnesses. Rather, "the relevant question is whether there is any evidence in the record to support the disciplinary board's conclusion." The Court found that there was enough evidence to support a finding of guilt against Hill and Crawford based on the correctional officer's testimony and written statement presented before the prison disciplinary board at the Walpole State Prison. As such, Hill and Crawford were afforded a minimal standard of due process sufficient to protect their constitutional rights.

Prisons

Impact

The Court acknowledged the rights of due process in prison disciplinary hearings but only insofar as the standard of due process does not interfere with the administration of the prison. As in its rulings on First Amendment issues, the Court stressed the need for a balance between protecting inmates' rights and managing a prison. The Court articulated a minimal standard for prison officials to use in disciplinary hearings, without intruding on the ability of prison officials to maintain institutional safety and control.

SANDIN V. CONNER, 515 U.S. 472 (1995)

Background

DeMont Conner was serving a sentence of 30 years to life for the crimes of murder, kidnapping, robbery, and burglary. In August 1987, while a prisoner at the Halawa Correctional Facility, a maximum security prison at Oahu, Hawaii, Conner was strip-searched by a correctional officer. Conner was angered by the search and uttered profanities at the correctional officer. Conner was later notified that he was being charged with disciplinary infractions, including the use of physical interference to impair a correctional function and harassment of a correctional officer with abusive language. Conner appeared before the prison disciplinary committee, which denied Conner's request to present witnesses at his hearing because the witnesses were unavailable. The board found Conner guilty of misconduct and placed him in disciplinary segregation for 30 days. Conner requested an administrative review. Nine months later, Conner was advised by the prison's deputy administrator that the disciplinary charges against him were unsupported. By that time, however, Conner had filed a lawsuit against prison officials in federal district court.

Legal Issues

Conner alleged that he was deprived of his due process rights at the prison disciplinary hearing when he was not permitted to present witnesses. The district court disagreed and ruled in favor of the prison officials. The Court of Appeals for the Ninth Circuit reversed the judgment, however, and held that Conner had a liberty interest in remaining free from disciplinary segregation. The Ninth Circuit questioned whether Conner received all of the due process protections articulated in the 1974 Supreme Court case *Wolff v. McDonnell* (418 U.S. 539), in light of a Hawaii state prison regulation that a finding of misconduct in disciplinary hearings must be supported by "substantial evidence."

98

Decision

The U.S. Supreme Court reversed the Ninth Circuit. The Court held that Conner did not have a protected liberty interest under the due process clause of the Fourteenth Amendment or the Hawaii prison regulation. As such, the Court ruled that Conner was not entitled to the procedural due process protections set forth in *Wolff*, in which the Court held that Nebraska state law, not the U.S. Constitution, created a liberty interest in good-time credits. Because the liberty interest was created under state law in *Wolff*, state prisoners were entitled to due process protections before their good-time credits were taken away as a form of disciplinary punishment. The Court held that while states may create such liberty interests for prisoners, they generally apply only when significant deprivations are placed on inmates, such as a longer term of imprisonment by losing good-time credits. The Court found that Conner's 30-day segregation in a disciplinary housing unit did not constitute a significant hardship or deprivation because Conner was already serving a sentence of 30 years to life. As the Court noted, "Conner's situation . . . does not present a case where the State's action will inevitably affect the duration of his sentence." Therefore, Conner's procedural due process rights were not violated under Constitution nor under Hawaii state law.

Impact

In the 1983 case *Hewitt v. Helmes* (459 U.S. 460), the Supreme Court expanded the ability of prisoners to claim a violation of due process rights under a state-created liberty interest. In *Hewitt*, the Court held that the language of state laws and prison regulations was critical and that the words "shall" or "will" in reference to a particular action automatically triggered the due process clause. In *Sandin*, however, the Court backed away from its strict interpretation of language as set forth in *Hewitt*, saying that mandatory language in a law or regulation was not the test for triggering a liberty interest. The Court held that liberty interests are limited, regardless of statutory language, and that the due process clause is only triggered when the disciplinary action imposed upon a prisoner creates a significant hardship.

Cruel and Unusual Punishment

RHODES V. CHAPMAN, 452 U.S. 337 (1981)

Background

In 1975, the Southern Ohio Correctional Facility, a maximum security state prison in Lucasville, Ohio, began assigning two inmates to cells that were designed for single inmate occupancy. This practice, called double-celling, was deemed necessary due to overcrowding in prisons throughout Ohio. Inmates Kelly Chapman and Richard Jaworski were among the prisoners at the Southern Ohio Correctional Facility who were required to share a single-occupancy cell.

Legal Issues

Chapman and Jaworski filed suit in federal district court on behalf of themselves and all inmates who were double-celled at the Southern Ohio Correctional Facility. Under Title 42 of the U.S. Code, section 1983, Chapman and Jaworski claimed that the practice of double-celling was an unconstitutional violation of the ban against cruel and unusual punishment in the Eighth Amendment, made applicable to states under the due process clause of the Fourteenth Amendment. The district court agreed with Chapman and Jaworski that their conditions of confinement constituted cruel and unusual punishment. The court based its ruling on the following five criteria: (1) double-celled inmates at the prison were serving long sentences; (2) the prison was seriously overcrowded and operating at 138 percent of design capacity; (3) double-celled inmates were forced to share a space of 63 square feet, despite several studies that recommended at least 55 square feet of living space for each inmate; (4) double-celled inmates were forced to spend most of their day confined to their cells; (5) double-celling was not a temporary measure but a permanent condition of confinement at the prison. The court granted the injunction sought by Chapman and Jaworski that barred officials at the Southern Ohio Correctional Facility from housing more than one inmate in a cell, except as a temporary measure. The Court of Appeals for the Sixth Circuit affirmed the district court's ruling.

Decision

The U.S. Supreme Court reversed the lower courts and held that the practice of double-celling at the Southern Ohio Correctional Facility did not rise to the level of cruel and unusual punishment prohibited by the Eighth Amendment. According to the Court, conditions of confinement could be deemed cruel and unusual only if they involved "the wanton and unnecessary infliction of pain [or were] grossly disproportionate to the severity of the crime warranting imprisonment." The Court ruled that simply because conditions of confinement are restrictive, or even harsh, "they are part of the penalty that criminals pay for their offenses against society." As such, they do not rise to the level of cruel and unusual punishment. The Court noted that the five criteria used by the district court to support a finding of cruel and unusual punishment at the prison were "insufficient to support its constitutional conclusion." As such, the Court found no violation of the constitutional rights of Chapman or Jaworski absent evidence that double-celling "either inflicts unnecessary or wanton pain, or is grossly disproportionate to the severity of the crime warranting imprisonment." The Court deferred to the judgment of prison officials regarding conditions of confinement, stating that "courts cannot assume that state legislatures and prison officials are insensitive to the requirements of the Constitution or to the sociological problems of how best to achieve the goals of the penal function in the criminal justice system."

Impact

As with issues concerning first amendment rights and due process, the Court allowed leeway for prison officials in doing the best they can to safely operate penal institutions. Furthermore, the Court made clear that, in its view, criminals must pay a penalty for their crimes, and that penalty may include confinement in unpleasant and even harsh conditions. The Court clarified that the standard of cruel and unusual punishment is not that prisoners suffer, but that they suffer the wanton infliction of pain or equally severe measures that are grossly disproportionate to their crime.

WHITLEY V. ALBERS, 475 U.S. 312 (1986)

Background

On June 27, 1980, Gerald Albers was a prisoner at the Oregon state penitentiary. Prison guards attempted to move several intoxicated prisoners from an annex. The intoxicated prisoners resisted the guards, in full view of Albers and some 200 other inmates confined in Albers's cellblock. Some of the onlookers became agitated, thinking the guards were using unnecessary force on the drunken inmates. Correctional officers ordered Albers and the other prisoners in the cellblock to return to their cells, but some inmates refused to obey the order. A fight erupted between the guards and some of the inmates, and one of the correctional officers was taken hostage. The uprising escalated, and Harold Whitley, the prison security manager, organized an assault squad. Whitley ordered the members of the squad to arm themselves with shotguns and to take control of the cellblock by force. Shooting erupted, and Albers was wounded in his left knee as he was running up a flight of stairs during the confusion. As a result, Albers sustained a severe leg injury and mental and emotional distress.

101

Prisons

Legal Issues

Albers filed suit in federal district court under Title 42 of the U.S. Code, section 1983, alleging that his shooting constituted cruel and unusual punishment and, as such, his constitutional rights were violated under the Eighth Amendment. The district court ruled against Albers. The Court of Appeals for the Ninth Circuit however, reversed on the issue of Albers's claims that he was subjected to cruel and unusual punishment in violation of his constitutional rights. The Ninth Circuit held that an Eighth Amendment violation would be established if Albers was deliberately shot by a prison official who knew or should have known that shooting Albers was unnecessary or if the retaking of the cellblock by prison guards was carried out with deliberate indifference to the right of Albers to be free of cruel unusual punishment. In its ruling, the Ninth Circuit noted that there was evidence that the uprising in the cellblock was subsiding when Albers was shot and that the use of deadly force by the prison guard was excessive and should have been preceded by a verbal warning to Albers to stop running.

Decision

The U.S. Supreme Court reversed the appellate court and ruled that the shooting of Albers by a prison guard during an inmate uprising did not constitute cruel and unusual punishment under the Eighth Amendment. The Court held that in a correctional setting neither inadvertence nor an error made in good faith by corrections officials "characterizes the conduct prohibited by the cruel and unusual punishments clause, whether that conduct occurs in connection with establishing conditions of confinement, supplying medical needs, or restoring control over a tumultuous cellblock." As to the appellate court's finding that the deadly force used against Albers by the prison guard was excessive and should have been preceded by a warning, The court noted that "the infliction of pain in the course of a prison security measure . . . does not amount to cruel and unusual punishment simply because it may appear in retrospect that the degree of force authorized or applied for security purposes was unreasonable and . . . unnecessary in the strict sense." The Court held that, in evaluating the totality of circumstances at the time of Albers's injury, the shooting must be viewed as "part and parcel of a good-faith effort to restore prison security."

Impact

In ruling that prison officials could not be held liable for the use of deadly force without showing that they acted in a wanton manner, the Court set a high standard for inmates to meet on constitutional claims of cruel and unusual punishment as the result of deadly force. However, the Court's ruling left unclear if that standard applied only in situations involving deadly force or in all situations involving any degree of force. That issue was later addressed by the Court in its 1992 ruling in *Hudson v. McMillian* (503 U.S. 1), which is presented later in this section.

WILSON V. SEITER, 501 U.S. 294 (1991)

Background

In 1990, Pearly L. Wilson was a state prisoner incarcerated at the Hocking Correctional Facility in Nelsonville, Ohio. Wilson objected to numerous conditions of his confinement, including overcrowding, excessive noise, insufficient locker storage space, inadequate heating and cooling, improper ventilation, unclean restrooms, unsanitary dining facilities and food preparation, and being housed with mentally and physically ill inmates. Wilson had complained to prison officials about the conditions but claimed that no action was taken to improve them.

Legal Issues

Wilson filed suit in federal district court seeking declaratory and injunctive relief and $900,000 in compensatory and punitive damages under Title 42 of the U.S. Code, section 1983. In his action, brought against Carl Humphreys, the prison's warden, and Richard P. Seiter, director of the Ohio Department of Corrections, Wilson alleged that the conditions of his confinement constituted cruel and unusual punishment in violation of the Eighth Amendment. The district court ruled in favor of prison officials. The court of appeals affirmed, ruling that Wilson failed to establish a culpable state of mind on the part of prison officials who had taken no action to improve the conditions in the prison. The appellate court held that it was necessary to establish the standard of "behavior marked by persistent malicious cruelty" in order to make a showing of a culpable state of mind.

Decision

The U.S. Supreme Court held that the appellate court applied the incorrect standard in establishing that a culpable state of mind by prison officials was necessary to establish that the prison's conditions of confinement constituted cruel and unusual punishment in violation of the Eighth Amendment. The Court ruled that the appropriate standard was the "deliberate indifference" standard applied in *Estelle v. Gamble* (429 U.S. 97) , a case involving the medical care of prisoners, which is presented later in this chapter. The Court held that the application of the wrong standard to establish a culpable state of mind may have constituted harmless error. Nonetheless, the Court remanded the case to the lower courts.

Impact

The significance of *Wilson v. Seiter* is that courts must use the standard of deliberate indifference to prove a culpable state of mind by prison officials when considering whether conditions of confinement rise to the level of cruel and unusual punishment. The Court cited the case of *Estelle v. Gamble* as establishing the deliberate indifference standard. The standard, however, was not clearly defined in either *Estelle* or *Seiter.* The Court provided some clarification on the issue in its 1994 ruling in *Farmer v. Brennan* (511 U.S. 825), in which a subjective standard was applied to determine deliberate indifference by prison officials to a substantial risk of serious harm to an inmate, in violation of the Eighth Amendment. Under the subjective standard, "prison officials may not be held liable if they prove that they were unaware of even an obvious risk, or if they responded reasonably to a known risk, even if the harm ultimately was not averted." As such, the Court set a very high bar for plaintiffs claiming a violation of their rights under the Eighth Amendment as the result of inaction by third parties, such as prison administrators, to inmates whose conditions of confinement place them at substantial risk of harm or injury.

HUDSON V. MCMILLIAN, 503 U.S. 1 (1992)

Background

On October 30, 1983, Keith Hudson was an inmate at the state penitentiary in Angola, Louisiana. Hudson had an argument with Jack McMillian, a corrections officer at the prison. With the assistance of another officer, McMillian placed Hudson in handcuffs and shackles and escorted him to the lockdown area of the prison. En route, Hudson claimed he was punched by McMillian "in the mouth, eyes, chest, and stomach," while the other corrections officer held Hudson from behind while kicking and punching Hudson. A supervisor witnessed the beating. Instead of intervening, the supervisor told the officers "not to have too much fun." As a result of this incident, Hudson suffered loose teeth, minor bruises, and swelling of his face, mouth, and lip. Hudson's partial dental plate was cracked, and Hudson was unable to use it for several months.

The Law of Prisons

Legal Issues

Hudson filed suit against the two corrections officer and the supervisor in federal district court under Title 42 of the U.S. Code, section 1983, alleging a violation of the Eighth Amendment's ban on cruel and unusual punishments. The parties consented to disposition of the case before a magistrate, who found in favor of Hudson and awarded him $800 in compensatory damages. The Court of Appeals for the Fifth Circuit reversed on the grounds that inmates who allege the use of excessive force in violation of the Eighth Amendment must prove significant injury resulting directly from the use of excessive force that was objectively unreasonable and constituted an "unnecessary and wanton infliction of pain." However, the appellate court held that the use of force against Hudson was objectively unreasonable because no force was required, since Hudson was in handcuffs and shackles. The court also found that the conduct of the correctional officers constituted excessive force through "an unnecessary and wanton infliction of pain." However, the appellate court ruled Hudson fell short of his claim that his mistreatment constituted cruel and unusual punishment under the Eighth Amendment because Hudson's injuries were "minor" and required no medical attention.

Decision

The U.S. Supreme Court reversed the appellate court and ruled that the use of excessive physical force against a prisoner may constitute cruel and unusual punishment under the Eighth Amendment regardless of the degree of the injury to the prisoner. The Court began by applying the standard set forth in *Whitley v. Albers* (475 U.S. 312) to determine "whether force was applied in a good faith effort to maintain or restore discipline, or maliciously and sadistically to cause harm." The Court found that the force against Hudson was applied maliciously and sadistically to cause harm and, by extension, constituted an "unnecessary and wanton infliction of pain" that rises to the level of cruel and unusual punishment. The Court ruled that the absence of serious injury is relevant to an Eighth Amendment inquiry but not essential to establish a constitutional violation.

Impact

The Court reiterated the standard set forth in *Whitley* that force applied "maliciously and sadistically to cause harm" violates the Eighth Amendment. The Court reasoned that once that standard is met, the use of force passes the test for the "unnecessary and wanton infliction of pain," regardless of the extent of injury to the prisoner. In 2002, in the case *Hope v. Pelzer*

(536 U.S. 730), the Court returned to the issue of the unnecessary and wanton infliction of pain as a benchmark for a violation of a prisoner's rights under the Eighth Amendment. In *Hope* the Court found clear evidence that an Alabama state prison's disciplinary procedure of handcuffing an inmate to a hitching post and subjecting him to exposure from the elements, thirst, and injury violated the Eighth Amendment's prohibition of cruel and unusual punishment. The question in *Hope* was whether correctional officers who subjected the inmate to such disciplinary action were shielded from liability because their conduct did not violate "clearly established statutory or constitutional rights of which a reasonable person would have known." In other words, did the correctional officers know that their conduct was unlawful before they engaged in the conduct at question. The Court ruled in favor of Hope, the Alabama inmate who brought suit, holding that correctional officers who "reasonably" should have known that their conduct was unlawful are not shielded from liability.

ROPER, SUPERINTENDENT, POTOSI CORRECTIONAL CENTER, V. SIMMONS, NO. 03-633 (2005)

Background

On September 8, 1993, Christopher Simmons was 17 years of age and still in junior high school when he and his 15-year-old friend, Charles Benjamin, entered the home of Shirley Crook at approximately 2 A.M. by reaching through an open window and unlocking the back door. Simmons and Benjamin bound Crook with duct tape, drove her to a Missouri state park, and threw her from a railroad trestle into the Meramec River, where her body was recovered the next afternoon by fishermen. The day after Crook's body was found, Simmons was arrested at school on suspicion of murder. After nearly two hours of interrogation, Simmons not only confessed to Crook's murder but admitted that he had proposed the crime to Benjamin because Simmons thought they could get away with it because they were minors. Simmons told police that he resolved to kill Crook after entering her home and recognizing her from a previous auto accident that had involved both of them. In addition, Simmons allowed police to videotape him as he performed a reenactment of the crime.

Legal Issues

Although Simmons was 17 at the time of Crook's murder, he was tried as an adult and eligible for the death penalty under Missouri state law, which permitted the imposition of the death penalty for capital crimes committed at

The Law of Prisons

the age of 16 or older. At trial, Simmons's videotaped reenactment of the crime was played to the jury, who also heard testimony from Simmons's friends that he bragged to them about the killing. Simmons was convicted and the trial proceeded to the penalty phase, at which the defense argued for leniency based on Simmons's age and his lack of a criminal history. However, the jury returned with a recommendation for the death penalty.

Simmons obtained a new attorney, who moved to set aside the conviction based on ineffective assistance of counsel, contending in part that Simmons's former attorney failed to present testimony that Simmons had a difficult home life which contributed to his poor grades and his abuse of alcohol and drugs. After reviewing the case, the court denied Simmons's motion for a new trial based on ineffective assistance of counsel. The decision was ultimately affirmed by the Missouri Supreme Court.

Simmons then filed a new appeal in state court based on the U.S. Supreme Court's ruling in 2002 in *Atkins v. Virginia* (536 U.S. 304) that the execution of mentally retarded persons was unconstitutional. Using the Court's reasoning in *Atkins*, Simmons argued that the execution of juveniles who were under 18 years of age at the time of their crimes violated the Eighth Amendment's ban against cruel and unusual punishment and the Fourteenth Amendment's right of due process. The Missouri Supreme Court agreed and set aside Simmons's death sentence in favor of life imprisonment without the possibility of parole.

Decision

In a 5 to 4 decision, the U.S. Supreme Court affirmed the ruling of the state court. In the majority opinion for the Court, Justice Anthony M. Kennedy wrote that "from a moral standpoint, it would be misguided to equate the failings of a minor with those of an adult, for a greater possibility exists that a minor's character deficiencies will be reformed." The Court noted three general differences between juveniles under 18 years of age and adult offenders. First, because juveniles are susceptible to immature behavior, "their irresponsible conduct is not as morally reprehensible as an adult." Second, when compared to adults, juveniles lack control over their immediate surroundings and, therefore, "have a greater claim than adults to be forgiven for failing to escape negative influences in their whole environment." Finally, the fact that juveniles are struggling to define their identity "means it is less supportable to conclude that even a heinous crime committed by a juvenile is evidence of irretrievably depraved character."

In rejecting the imposition of the death penalty on juveniles as a violation of the Eighth Amendment's ban against cruel and unusual punishment, the Court held that capital punishment must be limited to those offenders who commit "a narrow category of the most serious crimes," and whose "extreme culpability makes them the most deserving of execution." Justice Kennedy, who was joined by Justices John Paul Stevens, David H. Souter, Ruth Bader Ginsburg, and Stephen G. Breyer, noted that the United States was the only country in the world that continued to sanction the juvenile death penalty. Representatives of the European Union and attorneys from the United Kingdom were among those in the international community who filed briefs as friends of the court urging the Supreme Court to strike down the death penalty for juveniles in the United States.

In a show of strong disagreement, Justice Antonin Scalia read the dissenting opinion from the bench and criticized the majority for concluding "that juries cannot be trusted with the delicate task of weighing a defendant's youth along with other mitigating and aggravating factors of his crime. This startling conclusion undermines the very foundations of our capital sentencing system, which entrusts juries with making the difficult and uniquely human judgments that defy codification and that build discretion, equity, and flexibility into a legal system." Justice Scalia was joined in the dissent by Chief Justice William H. Rehnquist and Justices Sandra Day O'Connor and Clarence Thomas.

Impact

In its ruling of *Atkins* in 2002, the Court reasoned that current standards of decency—not the standards in place at the time the Eighth Amendment was adopted—must be considered in determining when punishment is cruel and excessive. The Court recognized state and federal legislation as the best objective evidence of evolving standards of decency. It noted that in 1989, when the U.S. Supreme Court ruled in *Penry v. Lynaugh* (492 U.S. 302) that the Eighth Amendment did not bar the execution of mentally retarded individuals, only Georgia and Maryland prohibited executing mentally retarded capital offenders. In the intervening years from the Court's decision in *Penry* in 1989 until the *Atkins* decision in 2002, an additional 15 states and the federal government enacted legislation barring the execution of mentally retarded individuals. The Court reasoned that the increasing number of jurisdictions since 1989 that banned such executions was evidence of a trend in evolving standards of decency that viewed the death penalty as cruel and excessive when applied to persons with mental retardation. In response, the Court ruled in *Atkins* that the execution of mentally retarded individuals was unconstitutional under the Eighth Amendment's ban against cruel and unusual punishment, as measured by modern standards of decency.

Applying similar reasoning in *Roper*, the Court held that evolving standards of decency in the United States and among the international community did not support the idea of holding juvenile offenders to the same degree of culpability as adults, even in the most repugnant cases of violent crimes. As such, the Court determined that executing juvenile offenders was morally and socially unacceptable by modern standards of decency. As in *Atkins*, the Court's decision in *Roper* was far-reaching by saying that the right of a jury to recommend capital punishment in the most egregious cases was trumped by an evolving sense of social justice that placed juveniles, like the mentally retarded, beyond the reach of the executioner.

Medical Care

ESTELLE V. GAMBLE, 429 U.S. 97 (1976)

Background

On November 9, 1973, J. W. Gamble, an inmate of the Texas Department of Corrections, was injured when a bale of cotton fell on him while he was unloading a truck. When Gamble complained of stiffness, he was sent to the prison's hospital, where he was checked for a hernia by a medical assistant and sent back to his cell. Later that day, Gamble's pain became so intense that he returned to the hospital, where he received pain pills from an inmate nurse and was subsequently examined by a physician. Gamble was diagnosed with a lower back strain and was prescribed medication. Over the next several weeks, Gamble was reexamined and received refills of his medication. In early December, Gamble was certified for light work by the prison's physician, despite Gamble's complaint that his back pain had not abated since the date of his injury. Two days later, Gamble was taken before the prison disciplinary committee for refusing to work. When the committee heard Gamble's complaint of continuing back pain and that he suffered from hypertension, Gamble was referred to another doctor, who prescribed new medication for Gamble's back pain and hypertension. On January 31, 1974, Gamble again was brought before the prison disciplinary committee for refusing to work, and he once again advised the committee that he was unable to work due to severe back pain and hypertension. The disciplinary committee placed Gamble in solitary confinement as punishment for refusing to work. Four days later, Gamble complained of chest pains and blackouts and asked to see a doctor. Gamble was hospitalized and medicated for irregular cardiac rhythm, then placed in administrative segregation. Three days later, Gamble complained of pain in his chest, back, and left arm. Gamble's ongoing requests to see a doctor were refused by prison guards. Finally, after two days, Gamble was allowed to see the prison physician.

109

Prisons

Legal Issues

Gamble brought action in federal district court under Title 42 of the U.S. Code, section 1983, alleging that his mistreatment and poor medical care in prison constituted cruel and unusual punishment in violation of his constitutional rights under the Eighth Amendment. Gamble's complaint was dismissed by the district court for failure to state a cause of action for which relief could be granted. The ruling was reversed on appeal on the grounds that the insufficiency of Gamble's medical treatment in prison constituted a legitimate complaint.

Decision

The U.S. Supreme Court reversed the appellate court. The Court held that, while "deliberate indifference by prison personnel to a prisoner's serious illness or injury constitutes cruel and unusual punishment contravening the Eighth Amendment," the medical care received by Gamble in prison "did not suggest such indifference." The Court noted that Gamble was allowed to see medical staff, including physicians, on 17 occasions during a three-month period and that Gamble received treatment by medical staff for his injury and other medical problems. According to the Court, the failure to perform an X-ray or other diagnostic tests constituted medical malpractice, at worst, but did not rise to the level of cruel and unusual punishment.

Impact

In *Estelle v. Gamble*, the Court established "deliberate indifference" as the standard in evaluating the medical care of prisoners in the context of the Eighth Amendment's prohibition of cruel and unusual punishment. Under the deliberate indifference standard, inmates have the burden of showing that proper medical treatment was not provided because of deliberate indifference by prison officials to inmates' medical needs. In this context, behavior that constitutes deliberate indifference may include poor medical treatment, a refusal to treat, or interference with proper treatment. The action or inaction by prison officials must be intentional, however, in order to rise to the level of a violation of constitutional rights. For example, as demonstrated in *Estelle*, medical malpractice, in and of itself, does not qualify as deliberate indifference. Similarly, simple negligence by prison officials does not rise to the level of deliberate indifference. Following *Estelle v. Gamble*, more prisons privatized their medical services, primarily to reduce costs. Because privatized medical services, even within correctional settings, are not directly provided by correctional officials, however, they also at least partially insulate prisons from liability. Privatized services commonly follow well-defined medical protocols and practices, which further reduce the risk of legal exposure.

WASHINGTON V. HARPER, 494 U.S. 210 (1990)

Background

Walter Harper was sentenced to prison in 1976 for robbery and was incarcerated at the Washington state penitentiary. Harper was housed primarily in the prison's mental health unit, where he consented to psychiatric treatment and received antipsychotic medication. In 1980 Harper was paroled on the condition that he continue receiving psychiatric treatment. Harper complied, but in December 1981, his parole was revoked after he assaulted two nurses at a mental hospital where he was confined by civil commitment. Harper was returned to prison and housed in the Special Offender Center, a correctional facility for the diagnosis and treatment of convicted felons with serious mental disorders. Harper was diagnosed with a manic-depressive disorder and gave voluntary consent to mental health treatment at the center, including the administration of antipsychotic medications. However, in November 1982, Harper refused to continue taking the medications. His treating psychiatrist decided to medicate Harper over Harper's objections. Under the terms of a policy at the center, psychiatrists were permitted to subject inmates to involuntary treatment with medication if the inmate suffered from a mental disorder and was gravely disabled or posed a "likelihood of serious harm" to self, others, or their property. According to the policy, an inmate subjected to involuntary medication was entitled to an administrative hearing by a special committee composed of a psychiatrist, a psychologist, and a prison official, none of whom could be involved in the inmate's treatment. If the committee's psychiatrist and at least one other committee member determined that the inmate suffered from a mental disorder and was gravely disabled or dangerous, the inmate could be medicated involuntarily.

Legal Issues

In February 1985, Harper filed suit under Title 42 of the U.S. Code, section 1983. Harper claimed that a judicial hearing, and not merely an administrative hearing, was required to involuntarily administer medication to a mentally ill inmate. Harper alleged that the failure to provide him with a judicial hearing before being involuntarily medicated was a violation of his due process rights guaranteed under the Fourteenth Amendment of the U.S. Constitution. The trial court ruled against Harper. The Washington Supreme Court reversed, however, holding that under the due process clause of the Fourteenth Amendment, the state could administer medication to a competent, non-consenting inmate only if the inmate was afforded the full protections of a judicial hearing, which included the requirement for the state to prove by "clear, cogent, and convincing evidence" that the medication was necessary to further a compelling interest of the state.

Decision

The U.S. Supreme Court reversed the state supreme court, ruling that the involuntary administration of antipsychotic medication does not violate an inmate's due process rights if the state has first established that the inmate is dangerous to self or others or is "seriously disruptive to the environment, and that such treatment is in his 'medical interest.'" The Court held that although Harper had a liberty interest under the due process clause in being free from the arbitrary administration of medication, the prison's policy comported with substantive due process requirements in furtherance of the state's legitimate interest in averting the danger posed by a violent, mentally ill inmate. The Court found that the prison's policy was rational because it applied only to mentally ill inmates who were gravely disabled or were a significant danger to themselves or others and because of the requirement that a licensed psychiatrist administer the medication. The Court rejected Harper's contention that prior to the involuntary administration of medication the state was first required to find him incompetent and then obtain court approval. The Court held that such a requirement would impede the state's legitimate interest in treating Harper for the purpose of reducing the danger that he posed to himself and others.

Impact

In its ruling the Court gave the state authority to administer medication against an inmate's will without first being required to put the matter before a judicial hearing. The Court made clear however, that such forced medication was only permitted when certain procedural safeguards were in place, as they were in the center where Harper received medication without his consent. In *Estelle v. Gamble*, the Court insulated prison officials from liability absent their deliberate indifference. In *Harper*, the Court further protected the state's interest in controlling inmates who present a danger to self or others.

Parole

MORRISSEY V. BREWER, 408 U.S. 471 (1972)

Background

In 1967, John J. Morrissey pleaded guilty and was convicted of false drawing or uttering of checks and was sentenced to not more than seven years in prison. After his parole from the Iowa state penitentiary in June 1968, Morrissey purchased a car under an assumed name and gave false statements about his address and insurance after a minor auto accident. Morrissey also obtained a credit card using a false name, and he failed to report his place of residence to his parole officer. As a result of his violations of state law and the conditions of his parole, Morrissey was arrested at the direction of his parole officer and incarcerated in county jail. After reviewing the parole officer's written report in the matter, the Iowa Board of Parole revoked Morrissey's parole, and he was returned to prison.

Another individual, G. Donald Booher, was convicted of forgery in 1966 and sentenced to a maximum term of 10 years in an Iowa state prison. Booher was paroled November 14, 1968. In August 1969, at his parole officer's direction, Booher was arrested for a violation of his parole and confined in county jail. A report prepared by Booher's parole officer cited numerous violations of law and parole, including that Booher obtained a driver's license under an assumed name, operated a motor vehicle without permission, and failed to remain gainfully employed, as required under his conditions of parole. The report included admissions to the parole officer by Booher to many of the violations. On September 13, 1969, based on the parole officer's written report, the Iowa Board of Parole revoked Booher's parole, and Booher was returned to state prison.

Legal Issues

After Morrissey and Booher exhausted remedies in state court, both filed petitions in federal district court alleging violations of their due process rights under the Fourteenth Amendment because each was denied a parole revocation hearing prior to the revocation of parole. The district court, ruling separately on each matter, held that the due process rights of Morrissey and Booher were not violated for lack of a parole revocation hearing. Morrissey and Booher filed appeals in federal circuit court, where their cases were consolidated. In a divided ruling of 4 to 3, the court of appeals agreed with the district court that due process does not require a hearing. The majority expressed the traditional view of parole as a privilege, not a right, and held that prison officials should have broad discretion in revoking parole. As such, the court expressed reluctance to interfere in matters that were properly under the control of state prison officials.

Decision

The U.S. Supreme Court reversed the lower courts. The Court recognized that parole revocation does not afford a defendant the same full range of rights as a criminal proceeding. However, "because a parolee's liberty involves significant values within the protection of the due process clause of the Fourteenth Amendment," an informal hearing is required in order to terminate a parolee's liberty. The Court held that "verified facts to support the revocation" of parole must be presented at the informal hearing. The Court also held that, in order to satisfy due process requirements, parolees should receive prior notice of the hearing containing the alleged violation of parole and the purpose of the hearing. At the hearing, a parolee should be allowed to present information relevant to the allegations and to question adverse informants. On the other hand, the Court held that any revocation of parole must be based on probable cause, a far less rigorous standard than beyond reasonable doubt, which is the standard in criminal trials.

Impact

Morrissey v. Brewer was a landmark case because the U.S. Supreme Court established that certain due process requirements apply to the parole process and that those minimal requirements cannot be abrogated by prison officials. Prior to *Morrissey*, states were free to revoke parole according to their own standards. While some states provided for some type of parole revocation hearing prior to *Morrissey*, the rights afforded to alleged parole violators at these hearings varied from state to state. In some states, including California, parole revocation hearings were confidential, without a written record of the proceedings. While *Morrissey* addressed due process rights in parole revocation, the issue of probation revocation itself was not addressed until 1973 in *Gagnon v. Scarpelli* (411 U.S. 778), when the U.S. Supreme Court held that the same due process standards established in *Morrissey* applied in preliminary and final probation revocation hearings.

Johnson v. United States, 529 U.S. 694 (2000)

Background

Under the Sentencing Reform Act of 1984, most forms of federal parole were replaced with supervised release overseen by the sentencing court.

If the conditions of supervised release were violated, the court could revoke the release and require the person to serve a prison term for all or part of the term of supervised release that was originally determined by the court, without credit for any time previously served on supervised release.

In March 1994, the United States District Court for the Eastern District of Tennessee sentenced Cornell Johnson to 25 months in federal prison, to be followed by three years of supervised release, which was the maximum term available under federal law at that time. Johnson received good-conduct credits while incarcerated that allowed him to be released on August 14, 1995, at which time he began serving his three-year term of supervised release. Seven months after his release from prison, Johnson was arrested, and he was later convicted of four state forgery offenses in Virginia. As a result, Johnson was found to be in violation of two of the conditions of his supervised release; namely, that he not commit another crime during his term of supervised release and that he remain in the judicial district where he was sentenced unless given permission to leave. The federal district court revoked Johnson's supervised release and imposed a prison term of 18 months. In addition, the court ordered Johnson placed on supervised release for 12 months following imprisonment, although the court failed to cite the source of its authority to do so.

Legal Issues

Johnson filed an appeal claiming that the district court had no authority to impose the additional term of 12 months of supervised release and that by doing so the court violated the ex post facto clause of the Constitution, which forbids punishment to be applied retroactively. The Court of Appeals for the Sixth Circuit affirmed the ruling of the district court, reasoning that the addition of 12 months of supervised release was not retroactive punishment for a previous offense but, rather, constituted punishment for Johnson's current offense of violating the conditions of his supervised release. Thus, because the punishment was not retroactive, there was no violation of the ex post facto clause.

Decision

The U.S. Supreme Court affirmed the ruling. The Court held that to prevail on an ex post facto claim, Johnson must show that the penalties are attributable to the original conviction, not to the defendant's new offenses for violating his conditions of supervised release. The Court held that the district court had statutory authority to impose a new term of supervised release.

Prisons

Impact

The Court's ruling strengthened the power of the Court under the Sentencing Reform Act of 1984. As a result of the act, many more criminal offenders in federal courts received fixed and often lengthy determinate sentences for their offenses. The Court added to that the possibility for offenders to be compelled to serve additional terms of supervised release for a violation of a previously imposed term of supervised release.

Sentencing

APPRENDI V. NEW JERSEY, 530 U.S. 466 (2000)

Background

In the predawn hours of December 22, 1994, in Vineland, New Jersey, Charles C. Apprendi, Jr., fired several gunshots into the home of a family of African Americans who had recently moved into the previously all-white neighborhood. Apprendi was arrested and admitted that he was the shooter. Apprendi made a statement to police, which he later recanted, that he did not personally know the occupants of the house but he did not want them in the neighborhood because they were "black in color." Apprendi was charged in a 23-count indictment with various shooting offenses and the unlawful possession of weapons. None of the counts referred to New Jersey's hate-crime statute or alleged that Apprendi acted with a racially biased purpose. Apprendi pleaded guilty to two counts of second-degree possession of a firearm for an unlawful purpose and one count of unlawful possession of an antipersonnel bomb. The state dismissed the other 20 counts. As part of the plea agreement, the state reserved the right to ask the court to impose a higher "enhanced" sentence for one of the counts on the grounds that the offense was committed with a biased purpose. After the plea hearing, which established evidence of Apprendi's guilt, the trial judge accepted three guilty pleas from Apprendi and held an evidentiary hearing to determine if Apprendi's sentence was subject to enhancement under New Jersey's hate-crime statute. The trial judge held that the hate-crime enhancement applied to one of the counts and sentenced Apprendi to 12 years in state prison on that count and to shorter concurrent sentences on the remaining two counts.

Legal Issues

Apprendi appealed the enhancement of his sentence under New Jersey's hate-crime law as a violation of his due process rights under the Fourteenth

116

Amendment to the U.S. Constitution. Following the 1970 ruling by the U.S. Supreme Court in *In re Winship* (397 U.S. 358), Apprendi argued that the hate-crime sentence enhancement was based on a finding of bias, which must be proved to a jury beyond a reasonable doubt. The appeals court relied, however, on the U.S. Supreme Court's 1986 decision in *McMillan v. Pennsylvania* and held that the intent of the New Jersey state legislature was to make the state's hate-crime enhancement a "sentencing factor," not an element of an underlying offense. As such, the trial court had judicial authority to impose the enhancement based on Apprendi's "motive" in the commission of the offense and not the underlying elements of the offense. The New Jersey Supreme Court affirmed.

Decision

In reversing the lower courts, the U.S. Supreme Court held that, in order to satisfy the due process clause under the Fourteenth Amendment, "any fact that increases the penalty for a crime beyond the prescribed statutory maximum, other than the fact of a prior conviction, must be submitted to a jury and proved beyond a reasonable doubt." The Court's ruling was foreshadowed by its 1999 ruling in *Jones v. United States* (526 U.S. 227) that the due process guarantee of a jury trial under the Fifth and Sixth Amendments require that any fact which increases the maximum penalty for a crime must be charged in an indictment or complaint, submitted to a jury, and proved beyond a reasonable doubt. Thus, the Court held that the same protections must apply to due process rights under the Fourteenth Amendment. As such, a state cannot circumvent those protections by substituting the elements of crimes with factors that only increase the punishment for those crimes. In other words, the New Jersey legislature could not disguise an element of the offense by simply placing it in the state's sentencing laws and calling it an enhancement provision. The Court distinguished its ruling in *Apprendi* from its 1986 holding in *McMillan v. Pennsylvania* (477 U.S. 79), in which the Court introduced the term "sentencing factor" to mean a fact that was not part of a jury's finding but could nonetheless affect the sentence imposed by a judge. In *McMillan*, the Court upheld as constitutional the Pennsylvania Mandatory Minimum Sentencing Act. Under that law, Pennsylvania judges were permitted to impose a mandatory minimum sentence of five years in prison for certain felonies in which the offender used a firearm, as determined by the judge using the stand of a preponderance of evidence. In contrast to the situation in *Apprendi*, under the set of facts in *McMillan*, judges were prohibited from imposing any sentence greater than the statutory maximum for the crime of which the defendant was convicted.

Prisons

Impact

In the Supreme Court's 2002 ruling in *Ring v. Arizona* (536 US 584), the Court overturned its 1990 ruling in *Walton v. Arizona* (530 US. 466) and held that any finding of aggravated circumstances to impose the death penalty must be made by a jury, not a judge, in order to satisfy the Sixth Amendment. The Court explained that it was required to overturn *Walton* in light of *Apprendi* because the two decisions were irreconcilable. The Supreme Court addressed the impact of *Apprendi* on U.S. Sentencing Guidelines in its 2002 ruling in *Harris v. United States* (538 U.S. 1052). In *Harris*, the Court examined Title 18 of the U.S. Code, section 924(c)(1)(A), which provides that a person who uses or carries a firearm in relation to a drug-trafficking crime "shall, in addition to the punishment for the crime" receive a sentencing enhancement of five, seven, or 10 years, depending upon circumstances defined in the statute. In a 5 to 4 decision, the Court held that the statute defines sentencing factors as elements to be determined by a judge, not elements of a crime to be found by a jury. The ruling was significant because the brandishing and firing of a weapon are factors that have an impact on sentencing in many crimes under the U.S. Sentencing Guidelines.

BLAKELY V. WASHINGTON, NO. 02-1632 (2004)

Background

Yolanda and Ralph Howard Blakely, Jr., were married in 1973. During their marriage, Ralph Blakely was diagnosed at various times with psychological and personality disorders, including paranoid schizophrenia. Yolanda Blakely eventually filed for divorce. In 1998, Ralph Blakely abducted Yolanda from their home in Grant County, Washington. He bound her with duct tape and forced her at knifepoint into a wooden box in the bed of his pickup truck. Blakely implored her to dismiss the divorce suit. When Ralphy Blakely, the couple's 13-year-old son, returned home from school, Blakely ordered him to follow in another car, threatening to harm Yolanda if he did not comply. Ralphy followed the couple, then escaped and sought help when they stopped at a gas station. Blakely continued to hold Yolanda captive and drove to a friend's house in Montana, where Blakely was arrested. Blakely was charged by the state with first-degree kidnapping. In a plea agreement, the charge was reduced to second-degree kidnapping involving domestic violence and the use of a firearm. When entering his plea of guilty, Blakely admitted the elements of second-degree kidnapping and the allegations of domestic violence and use of a firearm.

The Law of Prisons

Legal Issues

At Blakely's sentencing hearing, the state recommended imprisonment within the statutory range of 49 to 53 months. After hearing Yolanda's description of the kidnapping, however, the trial judge imposed a sentence of 90 months in prison, which was 37 months beyond the standard maximum. The judge justified the sentence on the grounds that Blakely had acted with "deliberate cruelty," as defined in a Washington statute that allowed courts to depart from standard sentences in domestic violence cases. Blakely objected to the increase in his sentence, and the judge conducted a bench hearing, at which additional testimony was provided by Yolanda Blakely, Ralphy Blakely, a police officer, and medical experts. After the hearing, the judge justified the extended sentence of 90 months with 32 findings of fact, including that Blakely "used stealth and surprise, and took advantage of the victim's isolation . . . employed physical violence . . . threatened [Yolanda] with injury and death . . . and violated a restraining order [that prohibited him from having contact with Yolanda]." Blakely filed an appeal, arguing that he had a federal constitutional right to have a jury determine beyond a reasonable doubt all facts that were legally essential to impose the 90-month sentence. The Washington Court of Appeals affirmed the trial courts sentence.

Decision

The U.S. Supreme Court reversed the lower courts. The Court held that Blakely's sentencing constituted a violation of his constitutional right under the Sixth Amendment to a jury trial "because the facts supporting Blakely's exceptional sentence were neither admitted by him nor found by a jury." The Court applied the rule in its decision in *Apprendi v. New Jersey* (530 U.S. 466), that "other than the fact of a prior conviction, any fact that increases the penalty for a crime beyond the prescribed statutory maximum must be submitted to a jury, and proved beyond a reasonable doubt." Under *Apprendi* the maximum sentence imposed by a judge must be based "solely on the facts reflected in the jury verdict or admitted by the defendant." The Court held that the Washington state sentencing statute that the trial judge followed was unconstitutional because the enhanced sentencing allowed by the statute was not based on the facts admitted in Blakely's guilty plea or on facts determined by a jury. The Court noted that *Blakely* was not analogous to its ruling in *McMillan v. Pennsylvania* (477 U. S. 79). In *McMillan*, the length of the enhanced sentence was not greater than the maximum term allowable based on the verdict alone. Importantly, as the Court also noted, *Blakely* "is not about the constitutionality of determinate sentencing, but only about how it can be implemented in a way that respects the Sixth

119

Amendment. The Framers' paradigm for criminal justice is the common-law ideal of limited state power accomplished by strict division of authority between judge and jury."

Impact

The significance of *Blakely* is its potential impact on state sentencing statutes, particularly sentencing enhancement statutes that allow courts to increase maximum terms of imprisonment on facts not admitted by a defendant or elements not found by a jury. Under *Blakely* such sentencing schemes appear to be unconstitutional. The Court was clear, however, that its ruling in *Blakely* did not constitutionally undermine determinate sentencing laws but only those sentencing laws that depart from the guarantees of the Sixth Amendment.

Capital Sentencing

RING V. ARIZONA, 536 U.S. 584 (2002)

Background

Timothy Stuart Ring was placed on trial in Arizona for murder, armed robbery, and other charges. During the guilt phase of the trial, the trial judge gave the jury instructions that it could convict Ring of premeditated murder or felony murder, which is a murder that occurs during the commission of another felony. The jury deadlocked on premeditated murder but convicted Ring of felony murder occurring during the commission of an armed robbery.

Legal Issues

Based on the jury's conviction on felony murder, Ring could not be sentenced to death under Arizona law unless the judge found at least one aggravating circumstance and no mitigating circumstance compelling enough for the court to grant leniency. At Ring's sentencing hearing, the judge found two aggravating factors among those enumerated in the Arizona death penalty statute that qualified Ring to receive the death penalty. The two aggravating factors were that Ring committed the offense for monetary gain and that the offense was heinous, cruel, or depraved. The judge found Ring's minimal criminal history to be a mitigating factor, but not sufficiently compelling to call for leniency. Ring was sentenced to death. On appeal to the Arizona Supreme Court, Ring argued that the state's death penalty statute was unconstitutional under the Sixth Amendment because it permitted a judge to impose the death penalty after a jury verdict that did not qualify for the death penalty under Arizona law. However, the Arizona Supreme Court upheld Ring's death sentence.

Decision

The U.S. Supreme Court reversed the ruling. The Court held that the Sixth Amendment requires a jury to determine all of the facts, including aggravating circumstances, in order to impose the death penalty. In 1990, the U.S. Supreme Court had ruled in *Walton v. Arizona* (497 U.S. 639) that the Sixth Amendment did not require a jury to specify the aggravating factors that trigger the death penalty. Those aggravating factors were not elements of the offense that were decided by the *Ring* jury. Rather, the aggravating factors were among the sentencing considerations enumerated under the Arizona law that allowed the trial judges to decide if the death penalty was merited in certain cases. In 2000, the U.S. Supreme Court had appeared to contradict its ruling in *Walton*, however, by holding in *Apprendi v. New Jersey* (530 U.S. 466) that if a defendant's punishment is increased based on a finding of fact, that fact must be established by a jury or by a defendant's free and voluntary admission of the fact. As such, in *Apprendi* the Court held that the defendant's rights under the Sixth Amendment were violated when a New Jersey trial judge increased the defendant's maximum sentence absent any finding by a jury or any such admission by the defendant. In *Apprendi*, the Court attempted to reconcile its decision with the *Walton* ruling and held that both rulings remained valid. In *Ring*, however, the Court concluded that *Walton* was irreconcilable with *Apprendi*, and *Walton* was overruled by the Court. *Ring* established that the same constitutional protections under the Sixth Amendment must be afforded to all defendants, regardless of whether their crimes qualify for the death penalty.

Impact

Historically, challenges to the death penalty had focused on the constitutionality of the method of execution until the U.S. Supreme Court's 1972 ruling in *Furman v. Georgia* (408 U.S. 238), in which the Court considered the constitutionality of the death penalty itself. In *Furman*, the Court struck down Georgia's death penalty law because it did not give juries proper standards and guidelines for imposing the death penalty, thereby allowing the death penalty to be applied in an arbitrary manner, in violation of the Eighth Amendment's ban on cruel and unusual punishment. In 1976, just four years after *Furman*, the Court in *Gregg v. Georgia* (428 U.S. 153) upheld Georgia's rewritten death penalty law because the law provided the guidelines and standards that were lacking under *Furman*. *Gregg* established that the death penalty itself was not unconstitutional, effectively ending *Furman's* moratorium on the death penalty in the United States. Like *Furman* and *Gregg*, *Ring* addressed state laws on the death penalty. *Ring* dealt specifically with sentencing laws and guidelines, however, some of which had been enacted during the 1980s and 1990s in an attempt to get tough on crime. Under *Ring*, the Court held that a state's sentencing guidelines cannot undermine the Sixth Amendment and that a sentence in criminal court cannot be increased to death based solely on the determination of a judge, without a finding of fact by a jury.

In 2004, the U.S. Supreme Court held in *Schriro v. Summerlin* (124 S. Ct. 2519) that the *Ring* ruling did not apply retroactively to death penalty cases that were under review by appellate courts before the *Ring* decision in 2002. *Schriro* concerned the 1981 case of Warren Wesley Summerlin, who was convicted of first-degree murder and sexual assault. As in the *Ring* case, under Arizona law, the crimes of which Summerlin was convicted were not punishable by death without a finding of aggravating factors by the trial judge, not a jury. The trial judge in the case identified two aggravating factors enumerated in Arizona's death penalty law. The factors in aggravation were a prior felony conviction involving the use or threatened use of violence and commission of the offense in an especially heinous, cruel, or depraved manner. The trial judge found no mitigating factors for leniency and sentenced Summerlin to death. A series of state and federal appeals worked their way through the courts over the next 20 years. From 2000 to 2003, Summerlin's federal appeal was pending in the U.S. Court of Appeals, Ninth Circuit. During that time period, the U.S. Supreme Court issued rulings in *Apprendi v. Arizona* in 2000, and *Ring v. Arizona* in 2002. The Ninth Circuit, relying on *Ring*, invalidated Summerlin's death sentence, and rejected the argument that *Ring* did not apply because Summerlin's conviction and sentencing were on review before *Ring* was decided. In *Schriro v. Summerlin*, the U.S. Supreme Court reversed the Ninth Circuit. The Court held that, although new substantive rules established under rulings by the U.S. Supreme Court "generally apply retroactively . . . new procedural rules generally do not." The one exception cited by the Court was "watershed rules of criminal procedure implicating the fundamental fairness and accuracy of the criminal proceeding, [which] are given retroactive effect." The Court defined such a rule as "one without which the likelihood of an accurate conviction is seriously diminished." Technically, the Ring ruling did not apply to Summerlin's conviction but only to his sentencing. On that point, as stated in *Schriro*, "this Court cannot confidently say that judicial fact-finding seriously diminishes [the] accuracy [of Summerlin's death sentence]." The Court held that its ruling in *Ring* was procedural because the ruling "did not alter the range of conduct or the class of persons subject to the death penalty in Arizona but only the method of determining whether the defendant engaged in that conduct."

Writing for the majority in the Court's 5 to 4 ruling in *Schriro v. Summerlin*, Justice Antonin Scalia cited the Court's 1968 decision in *DeStefano v. Woods* (392 U. S. 631). In *DeStefano*, the Court refused to give retroactive effect to its ruling earlier in 1968 in *Duncan v. Louisiana* (391 U. S. 145), "which applied the Sixth Amendment's jury-trial guarantee to the States." As Justice Scalia wrote, joined by Justices Sandra Day O'Connor, Clarence Thomas, Anthony Kennedy, and Chief Justice William H. Rehnquist, "We noted that, although the right to jury trial generally tends to prevent arbitrariness and repression . . . we would not assert . . . that every criminal trial—or any particular trial—held before a judge alone is unfair, or that a defendant may never be as fairly treated by a judge as he would be by a jury. We concluded that 'the values implemented by the right to jury trial would not measurably be served by requiring retrial of all persons convicted in the past by procedures not consistent with the Sixth Amendment right to jury trial.' If, under *DeStefano*, a trial held entirely without a jury was not impermissibly inaccurate, it is hard to see how a trial in which a judge finds only aggravating factors could be."

In dissenting, Justice Steven Breyer, joined by Justices John Paul Stevens III, David Souter, and Justice Ruth Bader Ginsburg, wrote, "In my view, [the *Ring*] holding amounts to a 'watershed' procedural ruling that a federal habeas court must apply when considering a constitutional challenge to a 'final' death sentence—i.e., a sentence that was already final on direct review when *Ring* was decided . . . *Ring's* requirement that a jury, and not a judge, must apply the death sentence aggravators announces a watershed rule of criminal procedure that should be applied retroactively in habeas proceedings."

---

[1] Ann H. Matthews. "The Inapplicability of the Prison Litigation Reform Act to Prisoner Claims of Excessive Force." *New York University Law Review* 77:536 (May 2002): 542.

[2] Ann H. Matthews. "The Inapplicability of the Prison Litigation Reform Act to Prisoner Claims of Excessive Force." *New York University Law Review* 77:536 (May 2002): 551.

[3] Judith A. Greene. *Positive Trends in State-Level Sentencing and Corrections Policy.* Families Against Mandatory Minimums, November 2003, pp. 6–11.

CHAPTER 3

CHRONOLOGY

This chapter presents a chronology of significant developments in the history of prisons, with emphasis on developments in corrections in the United States.

circa 1750 B.C.

- The Code of Hammurabi is established by King Hammurabi of Babylon. Like the earlier Sumerian codes, established circa 1860 B.C., punishment for wrongdoing is based on vengeance and includes mutilation, flogging, and execution, sometimes personally administered by the victim. Both the Sumerian and the Hammurabi codes predate the concept of imprisonment as a form of punishment.

621 B.C.

- Draco, ruler of Greece, implements a harsh set of laws under which citizens and slaves receive equal punishment. Under the Draconian code, any citizen can prosecute an offender in the name of the injured party for the protection of society, thus shifting the goal of punishment from personal vengeance to maintaining social order. Under the Draconian code, the burden of punishment shifts from the individual to the state.

circa 64 B.C.

- The Mamertine prison, the earliest known prison, is built in ancient Rome. Consisting of a series of underground dungeons, it is unclear if the Mamertine prison functioned in the manner of modern-day prisons by using incarceration as a form of punishment or if the dungeons at Mamertine were simply holding areas for lawbreakers awaiting other punishments.

529–535 A.D.

- The legal code *Corpus Juris Civilis* is compiled under Byzantine emperor Justinian I. The concept of proportionality, that the punishment should fit the crime, is established, and the scales of justice are first depicted in art from the Justinian period. The administration of punishment by the state, as set forth in the Draconian code, and proportionality in punishment established under Justinian form the basis of Western law and laid the foundation for the use of incarceration as a form of punishment.

1233

- The Inquisition is created by Pope Gregory IX to abolish heresy. As a result, prisons are built within monasteries to confine those accused of heresy against the church, and solitary confinement is sometimes utilized to create an atmosphere of atonement and penitence for prisoners.

1300s

- As gunpowder comes into wider use in Europe, fortresses previously built for defensive purposes become increasingly obsolete and are sometimes converted to places of confinement for prisoners. Fortress architecture later becomes a model for prison design.

1557

- The Bridewell workhouse is established in London to house undesirables, including the homeless, the unemployed, and some orphans. Residents are subjected to strict discipline and long work hours in harsh conditions. According to public perception, Bridewell is a success for keeping undesirables out of sight.

1576

- The English Parliament orders the construction of a workhouse in every county in England, and the workhouse concept begins to spread throughout Europe. Conditions inside workhouses are often deplorable, with no segregation of males and females or juveniles and adults. Violence and abuse among inmates and exploitation by jailers is common, and poor sanitation results in outbreaks of typhus that sometimes infect the surrounding communities.

1681

- William Penn founds a Quaker settlement in Pennsylvania in colonial America. A Quaker himself, Penn advocates for more humane treatment of lawbreakers, according to the Quakers' Great Law, which calls for the punishment of most offenses with hard labor in a house of correction. The Quakers' concept of confinement as a component of punishment, instead of a prelude to execution or corporal punishment, is unique in colonial America. Also unique under the Quaker code is that punishable offenses are secular in nature and do not include religious offenses as the English codes do.

1704

■ The Hospice of San Michele is built in Rome by Pope Clement XI and is one of the first correctional institutions designed exclusively for juvenile offenders. The design of separate cells for sleeping quarters and a large central hall for working is modeled after monasteries and becomes a model for U.S. penal institutions in the 19th century under the Auburn System. In *State of Prisons*, published in 1777, John Howard uses the Hospice of San Michele as an example of a model facility.

1764

■ Cesare Beccaria, one of the most influential thinkers on issues of crime and punishment, publishes his most widely known work, *An Essay on Crimes and Punishment*. The book is originally published anonymously because Beccaria fears retribution from the Italian government for his views; for example, the idea that the purpose of punishment is to deter crime and not to exact social revenge. For the most serious crimes, Beccaria advocates life imprisonment over the death penalty, which is irreparable and impossible to correct if mistakes are later discovered in the criminal justice process.

1773

■ The Maison de Force is built in Ghent, Belgium, under the direction of Belgian administrator Jean-Jacques Vilain, who follows the basic pattern of European workhouses in designing the facility. At the Maison de Force, Vilain segregates females and juveniles from serious offenders and utilizes a system of individual cells to house inmates. Although Vilain requires prisoners to work in silence, he opposes cruelty as a means of inmate control. In *State of Prisons*, published in 1777, John Howard uses Maison de Force as an example of a model facility.
■ A state prison for felons is established in Simsbury, Connecticut, on the site of an abandoned coppermine. One year later, in 1774, inmates at the prison riot over poor conditions of confinement.

1776

■ The deportation of English prisoners to the American colonies abruptly ends due to the American Revolution. English authorities use Australia as an alternative, but transportation is limited, and the voyage is arduous. To ease overcrowding in prisons, inmates are confined in old transport ships and obsolete war vessels, known as hulks. Conditions in the unventilated, vermin-infested hulks are worse than in jails and prisons. Although English officials view the use of hulks as temporary, their use persists for 80 years, until 1858.

1777

■ In England, John Howard publishes *State of Prisons*, in which he describes the best of the correctional facilities he visited during his tours of correctional facilities throughout Europe. Howard publishes the book in an effort to reform the deplorable conditions that he witnessed in prisons and jails. Among Howard's recommendations are regular inspections of correctional facilities to ensure compliance with basic standards of sanitation and living conditions and the implementation of work and educational programs designed to deter criminals from reoffending.

1779

■ The English Parliament passes the Penitentiary Act, which implements some of the reforms suggested by John Howard in *State of Prisons*. Due to rising urban crime rates, however, many prisons in England experience serious overcrowding, making it difficult to implement the reforms and muting the impact of the Penitentiary Act.

1790

■ The Pennsylvania legislature permits the Quakers to operate a wing of the Walnut Street jail in Philadelphia as a penitentiary for convicted felons, except those sentenced to death. The basic design consists of solitary cells. Reformers, including Benjamin Franklin and Benjamin Rush, both signers of the U.S. Declaration of Independence, and Revolutionary Army war hero William Bradford, help to develop a system of prison discipline at the Walnut Street Jail that borrows from the principles for the humane treatment of inmates advanced by Quaker William Penn and European reformers like Cesare Beccaria and John Howard. The system developed at the Walnut Street Jail becomes known as the Pennsylvania system.

1791

■ The Bill of Rights, comprising the first 10 Amendments to the U.S. Constitution, is ratified, establishing freedom of speech and religious expression under the First Amendment, the right to trial by jury under the Sixth Amendment, and the prohibition of cruel and unusual punishment under the Eighth Amendment.

1816

- A new prison is built at Auburn, New York. Unlike the system of single cells designed for solitary confinement under the Pennsylvania system, Auburn prison's design includes communal areas where inmates congregate for work and meals. Smaller cells designed as sleeping quarters are built vertically in tiers on five floors. Prisoners work and eat in silence together during the day and are separated only at night. Under the Auburn system, as it comes to be known, solitary confinement is used as a punishment for disobeying prison rules. The use of long-term solitary confinement is abandoned at Auburn in 1823, however, because of mental breakdowns suffered by inmates as a result of the unrelenting isolation.

1825

- Sing Sing prison is built in New York. It uses the Auburn system. By 1869, the Auburn system is implemented at some 35 U.S. prisons nationwide, including San Quentin state prison in California, built in 1852. The Auburn system's structural design of tiers of cells, also known as cell blocks, becomes the model for most prisons built in the United States for the next 150 years.

1840

- In England, Captain Alexander Maconochie is placed in charge of a British penal colony on Norfolk Island which houses some of England's worst offenders. Maconochie implements a series of reforms and a system of early release earned by good conduct and hard work. In 1870, the reform-minded principles advanced by the American Prison Congress are based, in part, on Maconochie's work.

1850

- In Ireland, Sir Walter Frederick Crofton develops a system of indeterminate sentencing, which becomes know as the Irish system. Crofton reasons that if penitentiaries are designed as places of repentance and personal reform, then there must be a mechanism in place for prisoners to benefit when they demonstrate their reform. In 1870, Crofton's work influences the members of the newly formed American Prison Congress, which advances principles that are based, in part, on Crofton's sentencing scheme.

1865

■ With the end of the Civil War and slavery, able-bodied male inmates begin to be exploited as laborers on a national scale. In the South, prisoners are used to replace the freed slaves. In the North, state prisons are commonly paid an annual fee by companies for the use of their inmates as workers.

1868

■ The Fourteenth Amendment to the U.S. Constitution is ratified, establishing due process guarantees and equal protection under the law.

1870

■ Prison administrators and reformers meet in Cincinnati, Ohio, at the American Prison Congress to discuss the future of corrections in the United States. They form the National Prison Association, renamed the American Correctional Association in 1954, and elect as their first president the governor of Ohio, Rutherford B. Hayes, who in 1877 becomes the 19th president of the United States. Principles advanced by the National Prison Association include establishing a three-stage system of punishment, reform, and probation in all prisons and using indeterminate sentencing as a way to reward inmates for good behavior and hard work. Other principles include educational and treatment programs for prisoners, minimizing the use of physical force against inmates, and segregating juveniles, females, and males in separate facilities.

■ The Justice Department is established and, in 1871, placed in charge of the growing number of federal prisoners in state and local correctional facilities. Due to prison overcrowding, some states only accept federal prisoners who are residents of that state.

1871

■ The U.S. Congress passes the Ku Klux Klan Act of 1871, codified in part in Title 42 of the U.S. Code, section 1983, which gives individuals the right to seek legal remedy in federal court if their constitutional rights are violated by state or local laws. Originally designed to protect the newly acquired constitutional rights of African Americans after the end of the Civil War in 1865, beginning in the 1960s, section 1983 is widely used by prisoners to bring causes of action in federal courts for alleged violations of their constitutional rights.

1876

■ The first reformatory in the United States is built in Elmira, New York, to house adult felons. Under the direction of Zebulon Brockway, the first superintendent at Elmira, however, the reformatory is used for first-time male offenders between the ages of 16 and 30, in the hope that they are more amenable to rehabilitation than hardened criminals. The programs at Elmira include educational and vocational training. A system of indeterminate sentencing is implemented, including a grading system that allows inmates to earn points for early release through good conduct and hard work. These reforms reflect the principles advanced in 1870 by the National Prison Association. By 1913, reformatories modeled after Elmira are built in 17 U.S. states.

1890

■ *August 6:* Convicted murderer William Kemmler is executed by electrocution at the Auburn penitentiary in New York. Kemmler becomes the first prisoner to be put to death in the electric chair.

1895

■ The U.S. War Department transfers prisoners at the military prison in Fort Leavenworth, Kansas, to alternate facilities in the United States. As a result, space becomes available at Leavenworth for federal prisoners. For the first time in U.S. history, some nonmilitary federal prisoners are housed in a federal penitentiary instead of state or local correctional facilities.

1896

■ Congress appropriates funds for the construction of a federal prison for 1,200 inmates at a site approximately three miles from the Leavenworth prison. Built by convict labor, the prison is not completed until 1928.

1899

■ The Illinois Juvenile Court Act creates a new judicial jurisdiction for juvenile delinquents that is separate from the adult criminal justice system. Among the most important provisions of the act is the strict segregation of juvenile and adult offenders in correctional settings.

Using the Illinois Juvenile Court Act as a model, juvenile courts are established in 1901 in New York and Wisconsin, and in 1902 in Maryland and Ohio. By 1928, only Maine and Wyoming do not have juvenile court systems in place.

1919

■ The Dyer Act criminalizing the interstate transportation of stolen vehicles becomes federal law. As a result of the Dyer Act, the White Slave Act of 1910, outlawing interstate commerce in prostitution, the Harrison Narcotic Act of 1914, establishing controlled substances, and the Volstead Act of 1918, prohibiting the sale and consumption of alcoholic beverages, more Americans are arrested for violations of federal law, creating a significant increase in the number of federal prisoners nationwide.

1924

■ *February 8:* Gee Jon is executed in Nevada and becomes the first U.S. prisoner to be put to death in the gas chamber.

1929

■ The Hawes-Cooper Act is passed by the U.S. Congress and becomes law. Under the act, interstate prison products become subject to the law of the state to which they are shipped, allowing states to limit market competition of out-of-state prison products with goods manufactured in-state.

1930

■ President Herbert Hoover signs into law the legislation that creates the Federal Bureau of Prisons (BOP) and appoints as its first director Sanford Bates, then president of the National Prison Association, renamed the American Correctional Association in 1954.

1934

■ Under its director Sanford Bates, the Bureau of Prisons (BOP) implements a classification system unique in U.S. penology. Under the system, each federal correctional facility is classified as a penitentiary, reformatory, prison camp, hospital, or drug addiction treatment facility. Federal prisoners are classified according to such factors as age, sex, and type of offense, with the goal of developing individualized programs for rehabilitation. The BOP also establishes five regional training centers for correctional staff, and by 1937, all federal correctional personnel are under the jurisdiction of the Civil Service Commission. In addition, federal parole is reorganized, and the supervision of parolees is transferred from the U.S. Marshall's Office to the probation offices of the federal courts in order to develop an after-care system that is more treatment-oriented and less punitive in its approach to ex-convicts.

■ The U.S. Congress establishes Federal Prison Industries (FPI) to provide vocational training and employment to federal inmates. The FPI is commonly referred to by its trade name, UNICOR, which is not an acronym. UNICOR manufactures products that are generally not available in the private sector, including signs. By fiscal year 2002, UNICOR generates $679 million in sales from operations at 111 factories nationwide and employs nearly 22,000 federal inmates, who earn from 23 cents to $1.15 per hour.

■ The U.S. military prison at Alcatraz Island in the San Francisco Bay is converted to the first federal super maximum prison in the United States. Known as the Rock, Alcatraz is designed to house the worst offenders and those who are the least controllable and the most disruptive in other federal prisons. The prison at Alcatraz closes in 1963 due to high operating costs. During its 29 years of operation, Alcatraz gains a reputation as the most repressive federal prison in the United States. In 1972, the Alcatraz prison becomes part of the Golden Gate National Recreational Area.

1935

■ The Amhurst-Sumners Act is passed by the U.S. Congress and becomes law. As later amended in 1940, the act permanently stops the transport of prison products shipped out-of-state. As a result, many state prison industries are either closed or downsized, severely restricting opportunities for vocational training for many state prisoners.

1949

■ The United States signs the four Geneva Conventions, which establish the rights and protections afforded to prisoners of war, including members of armed forces and civilians. On June 8, 1977, two protocols are added to the Geneva Conventions that give similar protections to other types of victims of war, including victims of wars against racist regimes.

1954

■ The first state super maximum security prison is opened in Mississippi.

Chronology

1963

- The federal prison at Marion, Illinois, goes into operation. The prison is designed to hold 500 male felons who are difficult to control. In 1973, a section of the Marion prison is designated as a control unit to house the most violent and disruptive inmates. The control unit model is adopted by other prisons.

1964

- In *Cooper v. Pate* (378 U.S. 546), the U.S. Supreme Court holds that prisoners have a legitimate right to be heard in federal courts. By so ruling, the Court departs from the *hands-off doctrine* used by previous courts to deny prisoners the right to litigate prison-related grievances. The *hands-off doctrine* is first articulated in 1866 by the U.S. Supreme Court in the case of *Pervear v. Massachusetts* (72 U.S. 678). As late as 1958, in the case of *Gore v. United States* (357 U.S. 386), the U.S. Supreme Court maintains its hands-off policy with regard to prisoners seeking redress for violations of their civil rights.

1968

- The American Correctional Association (ACA) establishes an accreditation process for correctional institutions and creates a standards committee composed of criminal justice professionals to administer the accreditation process. Through accreditation, the ACA establishes minimum standards on issues such as inmate health, institutional safety, and staff training.

1969

- In *Johnson v. Avery* (393 U.S. 483), the U.S. Supreme Court issues the first in a series of landmark rulings on prisoners' rights on issues including legal representation, cruel and unusual punishment, religious freedom, and medical care.

1970

- Three prisoners and a corrections officer are killed in a riot at the Soledad prison in Salinas, California. Inmate uprisings occur at other prisons nationwide, including the Holmesburg prison in Philadelphia, Pennsylvania, where 84 prisoners and 24 guards are injured, and at the Tombs prison in New York City, where prisoners take 26 hostages to protest overcrowded conditions of confinement.

1971

- *September:* Inmate rioting at the state prison at Attica, New York, results in 39 deaths. In reaction to this and other inmate uprisings and to the prisoners' rights movement, in 1975 the Bureau of Prisons begins to phase out the use of the rehabilitative medical model in favor of the correctional philosophies of deterrence and incapacitation, which are more in line with maintaining control over what is viewed as an increasingly vocal and sometimes violent prisoner population.

1972

- In *Morrissey v. Brewer* (408 U.S. 271), the U.S. Supreme Court rules that parolees have certain constitutional rights at parole revocation hearings, including written notification of the hearing and the alleged violations and the right to present and hear evidence against them.
- Executions are halted in the United States when the U.S. Supreme Court, in the case of *Furman v. Georgia*, rules that Georgia's death penalty law violates the Eighth Amendment's ban against cruel and unusual punishment. In 1976, however, the Court holds in *Gregg v. Georgia* that Georgia's revised guidelines for the application of the death penalty are constitutional, and executions resume throughout the United States.

1974

- The Office of Juvenile Justice and Delinquency Prevention (OJJDP) is created under the Juvenile Justice and Delinquency Prevention Act of 1974 to monitor and study all facets of juvenile justice in the United States. In 2000, the OJJDP conducts its first census of residential facilities for juvenile offenders in the United States.

1976

- In *Estelle v. Gamble* (429 U.S. 97), the U.S. Supreme Court establishes the "deliberate indifference" standard for lawsuits brought by prisoners alleging cruel and unusual punishment, in violation of the Eighth Amendment. Under this standard, inmates are required to prove that their rights are violated because of deliberate indifference by prison officials and not mere negligence or oversight.

1977

- Oklahoma becomes the first state to legalize execution by lethal injection, which is viewed as more humane than hanging, electrocution, or other legal methods of execution. On December 6, 1982, in Texas, convicted murderer Charles Brooks is the first person in the United States executed by lethal injection, which becomes the primary mode of execution in both the federal and state correctional systems.

1978

■ The U.S. Bureau of Prisons adds a level 6 to its inmate classification system for the most violent and disruptive federal prisoners. The federal prison at Marion, Illinois, is designated as the only level 6 correctional facility in the federal prison system. As such, the U.S. prison at Marion becomes a supermax facility.

1984

■ The first privately operated correctional facility is created when the Corrections Corporation of America (CCA) is awarded a contract to operate a correctional facility in Hamilton County, Tennessee. In 1985, CCA offers to take over the entire state prison system in Tennessee for $200 million, but the bid is rejected due to opposition from state employee unions and skepticism by state legislators. By 1988, however, with prisons and jails in 39 states and the District of Columbia under court order to improve conditions of confinement and reduce prison overcrowding, the trend toward prison privatization gains momentum. By 2002, some 94,000 prisoners in 31 states and the federal system are confined in private correctional facilities.

1985

■ The U.S. Sentencing Commission, established in 1984 by Congress as an independent agency within the judicial branch of the federal government, calls for strict federal sentencing guidelines and issues recommendations for federal courts that include increasing the length of prison terms for violent crimes and reducing the use of probation for crimes against persons and serious drug offenses.

1989

■ The Security Housing Unit, or SHU, for the most violent and disruptive prisoners is opened at the state prison in Pelican Bay, California. The SHU at Pelican Bay becomes the model for supermax prisons and control units in both the state and federal prison systems. Prisoners in the SHU in Pelican Bay are confined in cells measuring eight by 10 feet for all but 90 minutes each day, when they are allowed to go alone to an enclosed concrete exercise area. Cell doors are constructed of solid steel and are opened and closed by remote control.

1992

- In *Hudson v. McMillian* the U.S. Supreme Court rules that the use of physical force against a prisoner may constitute cruel and unusual punishment even when the prisoner does not suffer serious injury. The Court holds that the force must be administered maliciously or sadistically with intent to cause harm in order to trigger a violation of the Eighth Amendment and that force applied in a good faith effort to maintain or restore discipline does not rise to that level.

1993

- The U.S. Bureau of Prisons opens a new supermax facility in Florence, Colorado, designed to house 480 of the most dangerous and aggressive inmates in the federal prison system.

1995

- At the federal prison in Terre Haute, Indiana, a lethal injection facility is built at a cost of $300,000 and consists of an execution chamber surrounded by five viewing rooms. During federal executions, all procedures are monitored by the Justice Department in Washington, D.C., through an open telephone line with prison officials.

1996

- The U.S. Congress passes the Prison Litigation Reform Act of 1995 (PLRA), which places significant restrictions on the ability of prisoners to file civil rights claims in federal court. Under the PRLA, indigent prisoner litigants must post a filing fee, courts have broader discretion to dismiss prisoners' lawsuits as frivolous or malicious, and prisoners with three prior lawsuits dismissed as frivolous or malicious are disqualified from filing additional lawsuits unless they are in imminent danger of serious harm. Also, under the PRLA, prisoners must exhaust all administrative remedies before filing a lawsuit in federal court over prison conditions, and prisoners must show physical injury in order to claim mental or emotional injury. The aim of the PRLA is to reduce the caseload in federal courts and to encourage state and local correctional agencies to develop alternatives to litigation in the federal courts.

Chronology

2000

■ **December 13:** Seven inmates escape from the Connally Unit Prison, a maximum security facility in Karnes City, Texas. Known as the Texas Seven, prisoners George Rivas, Michael Anthony Rodriguez, Larry Harper, Joseph Garcia, Patrick Murphy, Jr., Donald Keith Newbury, and Randy Halprin remain at large for several weeks as they travel from Texas to Colorado. On January 22, four of the seven are captured at a trailer park in Woodland Park, Colorado. A fifth convict, Larry Harper, commits suicide rather than surrender to police. On January 24, the remaining two, Donald Keith Newbury and Patrick Murphy, Jr., are apprehended by federal agents at a Holiday Inn near Colorado Springs, Colorado. The six surviving members are charged with the murder of police officer Aubrey Hawkins during a robbery in Irving, Texas, on Christmas Eve. By 2004, George Rivas, Donald Newbury, Michael Rodriguez, and Joseph Garcia are convicted of the crime and sentenced to death.

2001

■ **June 11:** Timothy McVeigh becomes the first federal prisoner executed by lethal injection. McVeigh is executed for his part in killing 168 people and injuring some 850 others in the 1995 bombing of the Alfred P. Murrah Federal Building in Oklahoma City, Oklahoma.

■ **June 28:** Inmate-on-inmate rape is the most pervasive yet underreported form of violence in prisons nationwide, according to a report by Human Rights Watch. The underreporting of prison rape may occur for several reasons, including the reluctance of correctional officials to recognize the extent of the problem, according to the report.

2002

■ **June 24:** In *Ring v. Arizona*, the U.S. Supreme Court rules that the Sixth Amendment requires a jury, not a judge, to determine all of the facts, including aggravating circumstances, in order to impose the death penalty. In *Ring*, the Court overrules its 1990 ruling in *Walton v. Arizona* that a jury is not required to determine such facts in order to satisfy the Sixth Amendment. *Ring* establishes that the same constitutional protections under the Sixth Amendment must be afforded to all defendants, regardless of whether their crimes qualify for the death penalty.

■ **August 7:** A report by the National Commission on Correctional Health Care, submitted to the U.S. Congress, estimates that 2–4 percent of state prisoners are schizophrenic or psychotic. In addition, according to the report, some 13–18 percent of prisoners suffer from major depression, and between 22 and 30 percent of prison inmates have an anxiety disorder.

2003

■ The Bureau of Justice Statistics announces that some 1.2 million inmates are incarcerated in state prisons nationwide, and nearly 160,000 inmates are confined in U.S. federal prisons. As a result, 429 out of every 100,000 people in the United States were in prison or jail, the highest rate of incarceration in the world.

2004

■ *January 22:* A report commissioned by the California Attorney General's Office in response to a lawsuit filed by the Prison Law Office determines that nine juvenile facilities in the California Youth Authority are run more like adult prisons, with emphasis placed on incapacitation instead of rehabilitation. According to the report, CYA facilities are deficient in 21 out of 22 minimal standards established by experts in juvenile corrections. Violations documented in the report include the use of locked cages to confine some wards during school classes. Other violations include excessive use of psychotropic medications for behavior control and the overuse of chemical restraints, including pepper spray, by staff members with insufficient training in behavior management.

■ *February 1:* Ending a 15-day standoff, corrections officer Lois Fraley is released after she and another officer were held hostage by two prisoners in an observation tower at the Lewis state prison in Buckeye, Arizona. The other hostage, corrections officer Jason Auch, was released and hospitalized on January 24, 2004.

■ *February 5:* According to a report by the Sentencing Project, one out of every 21 African-American men in the United States are incarcerated on any given day. For African-American males in their late 20s, one out of eight is incarcerated on any given day in the United States.

■ *March 20:* Photographs are made public that show the alleged physical and sexual abuse of prisoners of war by U.S. soldiers at the Abu Ghraib prison in Iraq, in possible violation of the standards of international law governing the humane treatment of prisoners of war, as established under the Geneva Conventions. The U.S. Congress and the Defense Department later announce investigations into the alleged abuse of U.S. prisoners of war in Iraq and Afghanistan, including the deaths of some 40 prisoners of war.

■ *June 24:* In *Hamdi v. Rumsfeld* and *Rasul v. Bush*, the U.S. Supreme Court rules that prisoners detained at the U.S. Naval Base at Guantánamo Bay, Cuba, as the result of the U.S. war on terrorism have limited rights to contest their detention in courts of law.

- *June 24:* In *Blakely v. Washington* (124 S. Ct. 2531) the U.S. Supreme Court applies the rule in its holding in *Apprendi v. New Jersey* (530 U. S. 466) that "other than the fact of a prior conviction, any fact that increases the penalty for a crime beyond the prescribed statutory maximum must be submitted to a jury and proved beyond a reasonable doubt." The significance of *Blakely* is its potential impact on the constitutionality of state sentencing statutes, particularly sentencing enhancement statutes that allow courts to increase maximum terms of imprisonment on elements not found by a jury or facts not admitted by a defendant.
- *August 5:* The California Youth Authority bans the use of isolation as punishment for misbehavior by juvenile wards. The decision comes under mounting pressure from critics, including legislators and parents of incarcerated youths, who claim that the California Youth Authority fails to rehabilitate youths, provide them with basic medical care, or protect them from violence.
- *September 21:* A report by Earl Devaney, inspector general of the U.S. Interior Department, calls conditions at some 70 American Indian jails and detention centers a "national disgrace." The report documents 11 fatalities, 236 attempted suicides, and 632 escapes that occurred since 2001 at Indian detention facilities. Other serious problems reported include the failure to segregate juvenile and adult offenders, poorly trained correctional staff, and substandard facilities.
- *December 3:* A report by the U.S. Department of Defense discloses findings that military detention centers in Afghanistan and Iraq used interrogation techniques that included placing detainees in stressful positions for extended periods of time and depriving them of sleep and light. The interrogation techniques fall outside the guidelines approved by Defense Secretary Donald H. Rumsfeld.
- *December 7:* New York state legislators vote to reform mandatory prison sentences for drug offenders. Under the so-called Rockefeller Drug Laws, implemented in the 1970s, some first-time drug offenders were sentenced to as much as 15 years to life in prison. Under the revised guidelines, similar drug offenses carry a sentence of eight to 20 years in prison. In addition, the law includes a provision allowing offenders sentenced under the old law to apply for early release.

2005

- *January 15:* Correctional Officer Manuel A. Gonzalez becomes the first prison guard in 20 years to be killed while on active duty in a California state prison. Inmate Jon Christopher Blaylock is charged with Gonzalez's murder, which occurs at the California Institution for Men at Chino, California. On June 10, 2005, warden Lori DiCarlo and two of her deputies are formally removed from their positions at the Chino prison based on findings by the state inspector general that they failed to monitor safety procedures at the prison.

- *January 27:* The California Department of Corrections orders an end to its long-standing policy of allowing male corrections officers to perform searches of female prisoners. The change in policy is the result of pressure brought by Dignity for Women Prisoners, a coalition of advocacy groups dedicated to reforming conditions of confinement for female prisoners in the United States.
- *February 23:* The U.S. Supreme Court rules in *Johnson v. California* (No. 03-636) that the policy of racial segregation at the California Department of Corrections inmate classification center is unconstitutional. The 5 to 3 decision overturns a lower court ruling that upheld the policy, which was defended by California prison officials as necessary to curb inmate violence, especially gang-related violence.
- *March 1:* The U.S. Supreme Court rules in *Roper v. Simmons* (No. 03-633) that imposing the death penalty on individuals whose crimes were committed before the age of 18 is a violation of the Eighth Amendment's ban against cruel and unusual punishment. The 5 to 4 decision spares the lives of some 72 individuals on death row in 12 states.
- *April 15:* The British medical journal *Lancet* publishes a study on executions in the United States that reports that death by lethal injection may inflict unnecessary pain and suffering as the result of using an inadequate amount of anesthesia during the execution process. The report's findings, based on a study of some 49 autopsies of individuals executed in the United States, concludes that in 43 of the executed inmates the concentration of anesthesia was less than that required to numb a surgical patient prior to making an incision.

CHAPTER 4

BIOGRAPHICAL LISTING

John Augustus, shoemaker in Boston, Massachusetts, who in 1841 began the practice of bailing out convicted criminal offenders from court and assisting them in finding, among other things, housing and employment. Augustus later reported on each offender's progress to the court, and the judge customarily fined each offender court costs plus one cent instead of sentencing the offender to prison. The system devised by Augustus was the basis for the practice of probation.

Sanford Bates, the first director of the federal Bureau of Prisons, from 1930 to 1937. During his tenure, Bates implemented a classification system unique in U.S. penology that identified federal prisoners according to factors including age, sex, and type of offense, with the goal of developing individualized programs for rehabilitation. Bates established five regional training centers for correctional staff, and by 1937, all federal correctional personnel were under the jurisdiction of the Civil Service Commission. In addition, under Bates, federal parole was reorganized, and the supervision of parolees was transferred from the U.S. Marshall's Office to the probation offices of the federal courts in order to develop an after-care system that was more treatment-oriented and less punitive in its approach to ex-convicts.

Cesare Beccaria, Italian philosopher and author on issues of crime and punishment who in 1764 published his most widely known work, *An Essay on Crimes and Punishment.* Among the ideas advanced by Beccaria were that punishment should be humane and serve the purpose of deterring crime, not exacting social revenge. For the most serious crimes, Beccaria advocated life imprisonment over the death penalty, which he cautioned was impossible to correct if mistakes were later discovered in the criminal justice process.

James V. Bennett, director of the federal Bureau of Prisons (BOP) from 1937 to 1964 who succeeded Sanford Bates, the first director of the BOP. Under Bennett, rules against the mistreatment of federal prisoners were

strictly enforced, and the BOP expanded programs for psychiatric counseling and medical care for inmates. Bennett's commitment to the rehabilitation of prisoners fell out of favor with later directors of the BOP,
resulting in the demise of many programs developed and expanded by
Bennett during his tenure.

Jeremy Bentham, social philosopher born in London, England, in 1748
who was influenced by the writings of Cesare Beccaria. Bentham designed a prison that he called the *panopticon*, which was shaped like a half-
sphere with tiers of cells around a central area, where one guard could
conceivably keep all prisoners under surveillance. Although Bentham's
panopticon prison was never built, it served as a model for the Eastern
State Penitentiary in Philadelphia, Pennsylvania, which was built in 1835
around a central hub from which rows of cell blocks extended like the
spokes of a wheel.

George Beto, commissioner of the Texas Department of Corrections from
1962 to 1972. Known as a strict disciplinarian, Beto advocated the use of
hard labor and literacy training for all prisoners. Under Beto, some of the
most violent and brutal prisoners were enlisted to run cellblocks and
maintain order with an iron hand. This practice, known as the tender system, was harshly criticized in the U.S. Supreme Court's 1980 ruling in
Ruiz v. Estelle, a class action suit brought by Texas inmates in which the
Court held that conditions of confinement at Texas prisons were unconstitutional.

John Billington, a passenger on the *Mayflower* who landed at Plymouth
Rock in 1620 to help establish the American colonies. In 1630, Billington
killed one of his neighbors, John Newcomen, and was quickly tried and
put to death, thereby becoming the first person to be executed in colonial
America.

Zebulon Brockway, the first superintendent of the reformatory at Elmira,
New York, which in 1876 was the first reformatory built in the United
States. Originally designed to house adult felons, Brockway used the reformatory for first-time male offenders between the ages of 16 and 30, in
the hope that they were more amenable to rehabilitation than hardened
criminals. The programs implemented by Brockway at Elmira included
educational and vocational training and a system of indeterminate sentencing, including a grading system that allowed inmates to earn points
for early release through good conduct and hard work. Many of Brockway's reforms reflected the principles advanced in 1870 by the National
Prison Association. By 1913, reformatories modeled after Elmira were
built in 17 U.S. states.

Charles Brooks, convicted murderer who, on December 6, 1982, in
Texas, was the first person in the United States executed by lethal in-

jection, which became the primary mode of execution in both the federal and state correctional systems. In 1977, Oklahoma was the first state to legalize execution by lethal injection, which was viewed as more humane than hanging, electrocution, or other legal methods of execution at that time.

Clement XI, Roman Catholic pope, under whose papacy the Hospice of San Michele was built in Rome in 1704. The Hospice of San Michele was one of the first correctional institutions designed for juvenile offenders. The design of separate cells for sleeping quarters and a large central hall for working was modeled after monasteries and became a model for U.S. penal institutions built during the 19th century under the Auburn system.

Donald Clemmer, author of *The Prison Community* (Holt, Rinehart, and Winston, 1958), in which he drew national attention to the social codes and subculture of prisoners. Clemmer's book presented a detailed sociological study of life in a maximum security prison and included interviews with inmates and essays written by inmates. Among Clemmer's findings was the tendency of prisoners to form groups according to their offense history, political beliefs, and sexual preferences. Clemmer documented how heterosexual male prisoners sometimes engage in homosexual relationships in order to help alleviate the loneliness of prison life. Clemmer also identified the process of prisonization, which is the assimilation into a prison culture with its own code of behavior.

Rhoda M. Coffin, a Quaker and prison reformer who in 1870 helped to persuade the National Congress on Penitentiary and Reformatory Discipline to include among its principles the use of separate prisons for women. In 1873, Coffin helped to found the Indiana Reformatory Institution for Women and Girls in Indianapolis, Indiana, after investigations of the Indiana state prison revealed that women prisoners were sometimes whipped by male guards and forced to have sexual contact with male prisoners. The Indiana Reformatory Institution for Women and Girls was the first independent women's prison in the United States and was run entirely by female staff.

Sir Walter Frederick Crofton, Irish reformer who in 1850 developed a system of indeterminate sentencing that became know as the Irish system. Crofton reasoned that if penitentiaries were designed as places of repentance and personal reform, then there must be a mechanism in place for prisoners to benefit when they demonstrate their reform.

Katharine Bement Davis, social worker and superintendent of the State Reformatory for Women in Bedford Hills, New York, from 1901 to 1913. Davis pioneered the use of research studies on the characteristics of inmates and was one of the first penologists to segregate mentally impaired inmates from the general population. After her tenure at the Bedford Hills reformatory, Davis was appointed as New York City's first female commissioner of corrections and later as the chairperson of the New York City Board of Parole.

Eugene V. Debs, U.S. labor leader who in 1893 founded the American Railway Union. In 1918, Debs was arrested after giving a speech opposing World War I, for which he was convicted under the Espionage Law and sentenced to 10 years in prison. In 1920, while an inmate at the Moundsville prison in West Virginia, Debs ran for president of the United States and received more than 900,000 votes. In 1921, Debs received a pardon from President Warren G. Harding.

Dorothea Lynde Dix, teacher and prison reformer who in 1841 visited the House of Corrections in East Cambridge, Massachusetts, to teach Sunday school and witnessed deplorable conditions, including the confinement of female inmates in subzero temperatures without blankets or appropriate clothing. Dix began a personal crusade against inhumane conditions of confinement and toured correctional facilities throughout Massachusetts and the United States, pressing courts and legislators to institute reforms.

Draco, ruler of ancient Greece, who in 621 B.C. implemented a harsh set of laws under which any citizen could prosecute an offender in the name of the injured party for the protection of society, thus shifting the goal of punishment from personal vengeance to maintenance of social order.

Clinton T. Duffy, prison warden and advocate for the rehabilitation of prisoners who in 1949 was appointed as warden of San Quentin state prison in California. Duffy, the son of a corrections officer, ended the practice of corporal punishment for prisoners at San Quentin and implemented a disciplinary system that awarded privileges for good conduct and revoked privileges for violations of prison rules. Duffy also established a night school for inmates and permitted inmates to operate a prison radio station. After his 12-year tenure as warden, Duffy continued to advocate for prison reform and was credited with the abolition of hanging as a mode of execution in California.

Louis Dwight, ordained minister and director, from 1825 to 1854, of the Prison Discipline Society of Boston, Massachusetts. Dwight distributed Bibles to prisoners, and was an advocate of the Auburn system, which allowed prisoners to congregate during the day for work and meals.

Eliza Farnham, chief matron at the prison for women at Mount Pleasant, New York, from 1844 to 1847. Farnham's attempt to rehabilitate inmates through medical treatment was a precursor to the medical model later advanced by Sanford Bates, the director of the Bureau of Prisons from 1930 to 1937. Farnham broke from the tradition of requiring absolute silence from prisoners and allowed inmates to have 30 minutes of quiet conversation each day. Farnham's reforms were harshly criticized by officials at Sing Sing prison, which was located next door to the Mount Pleasant prison, and Farnham was ultimately pressured to resign.

Lois Fraley, corrections officer who, on January 18, 2004, was taken hostage along with officer Jason Auch and held by two prisoners in an observation tower at the Lewis state prison in Buckeye, Arizona. Auch was held until January 24, 2004. Fraley, however, was not released until February 1, 2004, ending the 15-day standoff.

Benjamin Franklin, inventor, social reformer, and signer of the U.S. Declaration of Independence who in 1790 was among prominent Quakers who received permission from the Pennsylvania legislature to open a wing of the Walnut Street jail in Philadelphia as a penitentiary for convicted felons. Franklin helped to develop a system of prison discipline at the jail that borrowed from the principles for the humane treatment of inmates advanced by Quaker William Penn and European reformers like Cesare Beccaria and John Howard. The system developed at the Walnut Street jail became known as the Pennsylvania system.

Erving Goffman, author of the classic work *Asylums,* published in 1961, in which prisons are described as *total institutions* in which similarly situated individuals are kept in social isolation, cut off from society, in regimented and dehumanizing conditions.

Gregory IX, Roman Catholic pope who began the Inquisition in 1233 to abolish heresy on matters of church teachings. As a result, prisons were built within monasteries to confine those accused of heresy against the church, and solitary confinement was sometimes utilized to create an atmosphere of atonement and penitence for prisoners.

Jean Struven Harris, educator who in 1981 was convicted of second-degree murder and sentenced to 15 years to life for the murder of Herman Tarnower, the author of *The Scarsdale Diet* (Rawson Wade, 1979). While incarcerated at the women's prison at Bedford Hills, New York, Harris taught parenting classes to inmate mothers and helped to establish the Children's Center in the prison, where children could visit with their inmate mothers. In 1993, Harris was released from prison and placed on parole.

John Haviland, British architect who in 1820 was commissioned to design the Eastern Penitentiary in Cherry Hill, Pennsylvania. Havilands design was based on the Pennsylvania system of individual cells for solitary confinement but included a walled yard that was adjacent to each cell for an hour of daily exercise. Under Haviland's design, rows of individual cells extended outward from a central hub, giving the appearance of a spoked wheel. Each cell had two opposing doors, one of solid steel and the other of metal lattice that was usually draped with a black curtain. Although somewhat popular in the United States, Haviland's prison design was widely copied abroad in Europe, Asia, and Africa.

Rutherford B. Hayes, 19th president of the United States who in 1870, as the governor of Ohio, became the first president of the National Prison Association, renamed the American Correctional Association in 1954. The principles advanced by the National Prison Association included establishing a three-stage system of punishment, reform, and probation in all prisons and using indeterminate sentencing as a way to reward inmates for good behavior and hard work. Other principles included educational and treatment programs for prisoners, minimizing the use of physical force against inmates, and segregating juveniles, females, and males in separate facilities.

Herbert Hoover, 31st president of the United States who in 1930 signed into law the legislation creating the Federal Bureau of Prisons (BOP) and appointed as its first director Sanford Bates, then president of the National Prison Association, renamed the American Correctional Association in 1954.

Willie Horton, convicted murderer and rapist who, while serving a life sentence in a Massachusetts state prison, was released on a work furlough and never returned to prison. Horton was later arrested and convicted for raping a woman and assaulting her fiancé while Horton was at large in Maryland. The Horton case was used in political ads in the 1988 presidential election by Republican George Bush as an example of the ineffective policies of his Democratic opponent, Massachusetts governor Michael Dukakis. As a result of the publicity, work furlough programs were restricted in many states.

John Howard, English reformer and writer who in 1777 published *State of Prisons*, in which he described the best of the correctional facilities he had visited during his tours of correctional facilities throughout Europe. The book was aimed at reforming the deplorable conditions that Howard witnessed in prisons and jails. Among his recommendations were regular inspections of correctional facilities to ensure compliance with basic standards of sanitation and living conditions and the implementation of work and educational programs designed to deter criminals from reoffending.

John Irwin, author who, with Donald Cressey, identified the importation model, which views violent prison culture as a reflection of the criminal culture in the outside world and, as such, is not developed in prison or unique to prison. Irwin and Cressey divided the society of prison inmates into three subgroups: The thief subculture, which comprised professional criminals who kept to themselves; the convict subculture, which consisted of inmates concerned with obtaining power in prison and controlling others for their own needs; and the conventional subculture, which comprised inmates trying to retain some of the values of the outside world in their daily lives.

James B. Jacobs, sociologist and author of *New Perspectives on Prisons and Imprisonment* (Cornell University Press, 1983), in which he concluded that the development of the Black Power movement in the 1960s significantly influenced prison life. As a result of the movement, African-American and Latino inmates became more cohesively organized than their white inmate counterparts, giving rise to the formation of inmate groups, such as the Black Muslims, and some street and prison gangs, including La Familia, the Blackstone Rangers, and the Crips in California.

George Jackson, inmate at Soledad state prison in California in 1969 when three African-American prisoners were shot to death by a white correctional officer, who was later beaten to death. Jackson, who along with two other inmates was charged with killing the officer, was transferred to San Quentin state prison, where he was killed in 1971. Jackson's death attracted national attention because of the success of his book, *Soledad Brother: The Prison Letters of George Jackson* (Coward-McCann, 1970). In 1971, after Jackson's death, Jackson's two codefendants were acquitted of all charges in connection with the 1969 killing of the correctional officer at Soledad.

Robert Johnson, author and critic of prisons, especially maximum security facilities, for their dehumanizing and stressful conditions of confinement. Johnson's works included *Culture and Crisis in Confinement* (Lexington Books, 1976) and *Hard Time: Understanding and Reforming the Prison* (Brooks Cole, 1987).

James A. Johnston, prison administrator who in 1934 was appointed the first warden at the maximum security federal prison at Alcatraz Island in San Francisco Bay in California. Previously, Johnson had served as warden at the Folsom and San Quentin state prisons in California, where he established a reputation as a reformer. At Alcatraz, however, Johnson imposed some of the most restrictive regulations in the federal prison system, including an enforced rule of silence for the first four years of his administration. In 1948, Johnson retired as the warden of Alcatraz.

Gee Jon, convicted murderer who, on February 8, 1924, in Carson City, Nevada, became the first U.S. prisoner to be put to death in the gas chamber.

Justinian I, Byzantine emperor, under whose rule the legal code *Corpus Juris Civilis* was compiled from 529 to 535 B.C. The concept of proportionality, that the punishment should fit the crime, was established under the Justinian code, and the scales of justice were first depicted in art from the Justinian period.

William Kemmler, convicted murderer who, on August 6, 1890, at the Auburn penitentiary in New York became the first prisoner executed in the electric chair.

Lewis Edward Lawes, prison administrator who began his career in 1905 as a corrections officer, like his father. In 1915, at the age of 32, Lawes became the superintendent of the New York City reformatory and was later appointed by New York governor Alfred E. Smith as the warden of Sing Sing prison. At Sing Sing, Lawes established a unique system of inmate self-governance that did not allow any inmate to have control over other inmates, unlike the tender system in Texas. Lawes also allowed inmates to leave the prison to attend family funerals or visit dying relatives. As warden at Sing Sing, Lawes presided over executions, although he was an outspoken critic of capital punishment and even toured the country in a campaign to abolish the death penalty.

Ralph Lobaugh, ex-convict who in 1977 was released from an Indiana state prison after serving 30 years. Two months after his release, Lobaugh returned to the prison and requested a cell where he could reside. Lobaugh is cited as a classic case of release-from-prison trauma, which is an inability of an ex-convict to adjust to life in society after years of incarceration.

Cesare Lombroso, 19th century Italian criminologist who classified criminals as atavistic, or throwbacks, to an earlier stage of human evolution. Lombroso cataloged what he believed were the physical traits that were unique to criminals, including an asymmetrical face, receding forehead, darker skin, and long hair. In the United States, Lambroso's theories made an impact in the emerging field of criminology, and studies were conducted in California's San Quentin state prison and other U.S. prisons documenting and cataloging the physical characteristics of prisoners.

Josephine Shaw Lowell, prison reformer who in 1876 was appointed as the first female commissioner of the New York State Board of Charities. In that capacity, Lowell observed the often dangerous conditions to which women inmates were subjected while with male inmates. As a result, Lowell founded several institutions for women, including the State Reformatory for Women at Bedford Hills, New York.

Elam Lynds, former army captain who in 1816 was appointed as the chief warden of the state prison at Auburn, New York. Under Lynds, prisoners were known only by their inmate number and were required to wear black-and-white striped uniforms to discourage individuality. Lynds did not believe in rewarding inmates for good behavior, and he used flogging to punish violations of prison rules. In 1825, Lynds was commissioned to build the new state prison at Ossining, New York, which became known as Sing Sing. Lynds served as the warden at Sing Sing until 1830, when he resigned after an investigation criticized his management methods.

Alexander Maconochie, English officer who in 1840 was placed in charge of a British penal colony on Norfolk Island that housed some of England's worst offenders. Maconochie implemented a series of reforms, including a system of early release earned by good conduct and hard work. In 1870, the reform-minded principles advanced by the American Prison Congress were based in part on Maconochie's work.

Edna Mahan, prison reformer and administrator who in 1928 became the superintendent of the Reformatory for Women in Clinton Farms, New Jersey, a position that she held for over 40 years. Under her administration, Mahan implemented reforms that encouraged the humane treatment of inmates, including the use of low levels of security and the removal of iron bars on windows. As a result of Mahan's reforms, the Clinton Farms reformatory became known as one of the most progressive penal institutions in the United States. In 1967, Mahan opened Carpenter House, the first halfway house for women in New Jersey. After Mahan's death in 1968, the Clinton Farms reformatory was renamed the Edna Mahan Correctional Facility for Women in honor of Mahan's contributions to prison reform.

Robert Martinson, sociologist who in 1974 published the report "What Works? Questions and Answers about Prison Reform," in which Martinson concluded that none of the 231 correctional treatment programs he had studied between 1945 and 1967 were effective in rehabilitating inmates. Martinson's conclusions were embraced by conservatives, who wanted to abolish rehabilitative programs in favor of determinate sentencing, and by liberals, who contended that poor treatment programs hampered the chances for inmates to succeed after their release from prison, causing higher rates of recidivism.

Marc Mauer, author and assistant director of the Sentencing Project, a nonprofit organization dedicated to advocacy and reform on issues of incarceration and criminal justice policies in the United States. Mauer coauthored with Ryan S. King the 2004 report by the Sentencing Project, "Schools and Prisons: 50 Years after *Brown v. Board of Education,*" which examined the rising trend of imprisonment of African Americans since the desegregation of education in the United States in 1954.

Timothy McVeigh, convicted murderer who, on June 11, 2001, became the first federal prisoner executed by lethal injection for his role in the deaths of 168 people in the 1995 bombing of the Alfred P. Murrah Federal

Prisons

Building in Oklahoma City, Oklahoma. McVeigh's execution was carried out at the federal prison in Terre Haute, Indiana, where in 1995 a lethal injection facility was built at a cost of $300,000.

The Mecklenburg Six, death row prisoners who, on May 31, 1984, escaped from the correctional center at Mecklenburg, Virginia. Linwood Briley, the leader of the group, was joined by his brother, James B. Briley, Earl Clanton, Willie Leroy Jones, Derick Peterson, and Lem Tuggle. Their escape, which was planned for months and originally included 12 death row inmates, was carried out when the Macklenburg Six surprised prison guards, put on the guards' uniforms, and forced one of the guards to supply a prison van for transportation. The inmates were eventually captured, although the Briley brothers remained at large the longest, for 19 days. All six prisoners were eventually executed by the state of Virginia.

Montesquieu, Charles-Louis de Secondat, baron de, 18th-century French historian and philosopher who advanced the idea that harsh punishment undermined social morality.

Thomas O. Murton, professor of criminal justice who in 1966 was appointed warden at Tucker Prison Farm, a 300-bed unit of the Arkansas state penitentiary. One year later in 1967, Murton became the warden at the Cummins Farm Unit, a 1,300-bed facility in the Arkansas state prison system. Murton was a strong advocate for prison reform, and he was forced to resign after only two years at Cummins Farm when his views embarrassed state prison officials. Based on his experiences at the Tucker and Cummins facilities, Murton published the book *Accomplices to the Crime: The Arkansas Prison Scandal* (Grove Press, 1970). Murton's efforts at reforming the Arkansas prison system were the basis of the 1980 movie *Brubaker,* starring Robert Redford.

George O. Osborne, prisoner reformer and warden at the state prison in Trenton, New Jersey, in the late 19th and early 20th centuries. As warden, Osborne instituted reforms that eliminated standard practices at most U.S. prisons, including striped uniforms for convicts, shaved heads, and requiring prisoners to be attached to a ball and chain. Osborne also established prison schools and implemented new parole procedures that facilitated the reintegration of inmates into society.

Thomas Mott Osborne, businessman turned prison reformer who in 1913 was appointed to the New York State Commission on Prison Reform. In 1914, Osborne became the warden at Sing Sing prison in New York, where he instituted a program that paid inmates for their work. After resigning as warden in 1917, Osborne wrote books based on his experiences at Sing Sing, including *Within Prison Walls, Society and Prisons,* and *Prisons and Common Sense.*

Biographical Listing

William Penn, a Quaker who in 1681 founded the Quaker settlement at Pennsylvania in colonial America. Penn advocated more humane treatment of lawbreakers, in accordance with the Quakers' Great Law, which called for hard labor in a house of correction as the punishment for most offenses. The Quakers' concept of confinement as a component of punishment, instead of a prelude to execution or corporal punishment, was unique in colonial America. Also, under the Quaker code, offenses were secular in nature and did not include religious offenses as the earlier English codes did.

Helen Prejean, Roman Catholic nun whose work as a spiritual adviser to death row inmates in Louisiana was the basis of her book *Dead Man Walking: An Eyewitness Account of the Death Penalty in the United States* (Vintage Books, 1994). In 1996, the book was adapted into the movie *Dead Man Walking*, starring Susan Sarandon as Prejean and Sean Penn as Patrick Sonnier, a death row inmate at the state penitentiary in Angola, Louisiana, who was counseled by Prejean.

Joseph E. Ragen, warden of the Statesville and Joliet state prisons in Illinois for 26 years who implemented paramilitary-like standards of discipline among both inmates and correctional officers. Based on his experience, Ragen cowrote the book, with Charles Finston, *Inside the World's Toughest Prisons* (Charles C. Thomas Publishers Limited, 1962).

Wilbert Rideau, prisoner serving a life sentence at the state penitentiary in Angola, Louisiana, for bank robbery and murder. Rideau confessed to his crimes. In 1975, Rideau became the editor of Angola prison's institutional journal the *Angolite*. Rideau also became a filmmaker in prison. In 1999, his movie, *The Farm*, about life at Angola prison, shared the Grand Prize Award at the Sundance Film Festival.

Sir Samuel Romilly, attorney and reformer of English criminal law in the 18th and early 19th centuries. In 1816, Romilly helped to spearhead efforts to build the first modern English prison, at Milbank.

Benjamin Rush, member of the Continental Congress and signer of the Declaration of Independence who advocated for the humane treatment of prisoners and helped found the Walnut Street jail in Philadelphia, Pennsylvania, in 1790.

Richard Speck, mass murderer who was sentenced to death for killing eight student nurses in Chicago in 1966. Speck's death sentence was commuted after the 1972 decision by the U.S. Supreme Court in *Furman v. Georgia*. In 1991, Speck died of a heart attack in prison. Following his death, a videotape was released showing Speck taking drugs in prison and in various sex acts with another prisoner. On the tape, Speck claimed that he was having fun in prison.

Prisons

Dennis J. Stevens, author of the study *Violence Begets Violence,* published in 1997, which correlated strict enforcement of disciplinary rules in prison with a higher incidence of disciplinary problems among inmates.

Robert Stroud, ornithologist and federal prisoner who was portrayed by Burt Lancaster in the 1962 film *Birdman of Alcatraz.* Stroud was convicted of murder at the age of 19 and spent the rest of his life as a federal prisoner after he was convicted of stabbing a guard to death in 1916. In 1920, President Woodrow Wilson commuted Stroud's death sentence, and Stroud was transferred to Alcatraz from the Leavenworth federal prison in Kansas. At Alcatraz, Stroud was not allowed to work with birds, and he spent his time writing about the prison system. In 1959, Stroud was transferred to the medical center for federal prisoners in Springfield, Missouri, where he died in 1963.

Gresham Sykes, sociologist who, building on the ideas of Donald Clemmer, explored the social roles of inmates in prison culture. Sykes identified a specific inmate social code that included rules against arguing or quarreling with other inmates, never taking the side of a member of the prison staff against another inmate, and being prepared to deal with conflict, including fighting, if necessary in order not to lose dignity.

The Texas Seven, prisoners who, on December 13, 2002, escaped from the Connally Unit Prison, a maximum security facility in Karnes City, Texas. Escapees George Rivas, Michael Anthony Rodriguez, Larry Harper, Joseph Garcia, Patrick Murphy, Jr., Donald Keith Newbury, and Randy Halprin remained at large for several weeks as they traveled from Texas to Colorado. On January 22, four of the seven were captured at a trailer park in Woodland Park, Colorado. A fifth convict, Larry Harper, committed suicide rather than surrender to police. On January 24, the remaining two, Donald Keith Newbury and Patrick Murphy, Jr., were apprehended by federal agents at a Holiday Inn near Colorado Springs, Colorado. The six surviving members were charged with the murder of police officer Aubrey Hawkins during a robbery in Irving, Texas, on Christmas Eve. By 2004, George Rivas, Donald Newbury, Michael Rodriguez, and Joseph Garcia were convicted of the crime and sentenced to death.

Hans Toch, author who examined the coping strategies used by prison inmates to adjust to their conditions of confinement in his book *Living in Prison* (Free Press, 1977).

Miriam Van Waters, psychologist and superintendent of the Massachusetts State Reformatory for Women from 1932 to 1957. In 1925, Van Waters published the book *Youth in Conflict* (AMS Press), based on her experiences as superintendent of the Los Angeles County Juvenile Hall. In

1929, Van Waters began work on a juvenile delinquency project at Harvard Law School and was appointed by President Herbert Hoover to serve on the Wickersham Commission and report on the treatment of juveniles in the federal prison system. Van Waters was a proponent of prisoner rehabilitation.

Jean-Jacques Vilain, Belgian government official who in 1773 became the administrator of the Maison de Force, a newly built workhouse in Ghent, Belgium. Vilain segregated females and juveniles from serious offenders and utilized a system of individual cells to house inmates. Although Vilain required prisoners to work in silence, he opposed cruelty as a means of inmate control.

Voltaire (François-Marie Arouet), 18th-century French philosopher who objected to the legally sanctioned practice of torture in France and believed that shame was an effective deterrent to crime.

Earl Warren, Chief Justice of the U.S. Supreme Court from 1953 to 1969. In 1942, as governor of California, Warren ordered an investigation into the California state prison system, which led to its reorganization around the principle of inmate rehabilitation.

Enoch Cobb Wines, professor of classical languages who in 1862 became secretary of the New York Prison Association and devoted the rest of his life to prison reform. In 1867, Wines and reformer Theodore Dwight authored *Report on the Prisons and Reformatories of the United States and Canada,* in which they concluded that inmates were released from prison in worse psychological condition than when they entered. In 1870, Wines was among the prison reformers who founded the American Prison Association in Cincinnati, Ohio, and he helped to formulate many of the principles advance by the organization.

Frederick Howard Wines, minister and prison reformer who opposed the classification of inmates according to their physical characteristics by adherents to the theories of Cesare Lombroso. Wines, who was the son of prison reformer Enoch Cobb Wines, also advocated for the segregation of mentally ill inmates. Wines's book *Punishment and Reformation* was published in 1919, seven years after his death in 1912.

Malcom C. Young, author and executive director of the Sentencing Project, a nonprofit organization dedicated to advocacy and reform on issues of incarceration and criminal justice policies in the United States. Young is coauthor, with Marc Mauer and Ryan S. King, of the report "The Meaning of Life: Long Prison Sentences in Context," released by the Sentencing Project in May 2004. The report examines the trend in sentencing to eliminate indeterminate life sentencing, such as 25 years to life, and to impose sentences without the possibility of parole.

Prisons

Philip Zimbardo, Stanford University professor who set up a mock prison to investigate the psychological impact of incarceration. In the experiment, called the Stanford Prison Experiment, Zimbardo videotaped students playing prisoners and corrections officers. The student guards became cruel to the student inmates, who began to experience psychological deterioration, and the experiment was called off by Zimbardo after only six days.

CHAPTER 5

GLOSSARY

This chapter presents a glossary of terms relevant to issues of incarceration and correctional institutions, with emphasis on prisons in the United States.

abscond   To leave the area of jurisdiction prescribed by prison rules or by conditions imposed under probation or parole.

alternative facility   A placement, such as a drug treatment center, that is used as an alternative to incarceration in a traditional correctional institution.

commitment   An action by a court ordering an adjudicated juvenile or a sentenced adult to be admitted to a correctional institution.

community facility   A correctional facility that allows residents unsupervised leave for proscribed periods of time to attend school, treatment or counseling programs, or to work.

community service   A period of service to the community that is commonly imposed by courts as a condition of probation in lieu of incarceration.

conditional diversion   Suspension of prosecution at the pretrial to allow the defendant to meet certain conditions over a specified period of time. If those conditions are met in a timely manner, the period of conditional diversion expires and the case is dismissed. If not, the case is referred for a continuation of prosecution.

conditional release   The release of a defendant who agrees to meet specified conditions imposed by the court that may include steady employment, avoiding contact with the victim or associates in the alleged crime, participating in treatment, and avoiding certain behaviors, such as consuming alcoholic beverages.

confinement facility   A correctional facility from which inmates may not depart without supervision.

convict   An adult convicted of a criminal offense who is incarcerated in a correctional institution in order to serve the sentence imposed by the court.

155

conviction   A judgment in court imposed by a jury or a judge, or on the basis of a guilty plea by the defendant, that the defendant is guilty of the criminal offense for which the defendant was charged.

correctional agency   A federal, state, or local criminal justice agency under a single administrative authority with the principle function of intake screening, supervision, custody, confinement, or treatment of adjudicated juvenile offenders or convicted adult criminal offenders.

correctional day program   A nonresidential educational, vocational, or treatment program in which participation is ordered by a court, commonly as a condition of probation, or required as a condition of parole.

correctional facility   A physical setting, such as a building, a part of a building, or a set of structures, operated and administered by a government or private agency for the custody or treatment of adjudicated juveniles and convicted or committed adults as the result of a juvenile or criminal justice proceeding.

correctional institution   A confinement facility commonly referred to as a prison or penitentiary that is administered by a state or federal agency for the incarceration of adults for a period of confinement of one year or more. In addition, the term *correctional institution* is sometimes used to describe facilities for juvenile offenders committed to a period of confinement of one year or more.

corrections   A term that includes all agencies, facilities, programs, procedures, personnel, and techniques concerned with the intake, custody, confinement, supervision, or treatment of convicted criminal offenders or adjudicated juvenile offenders.

count   In a correctional setting, an accounting of all inmates at an institution or confined to a part of an institution, such as a cell block. Prisoner counts are commonly performed at specific times of each day, usually more than once per day.

crimes of violence   The crimes of murder, voluntary manslaughter, forcible rape, robbery, and aggravated assault, according to the Uniform Crime Reports by the Federal Bureau of Investigation.

defendant   A person against whom a legal action is pending in a court of law. A criminal defendant is someone facing criminal charges.

de novo   Anew or fresh, commonly used as a judicial term meaning a new trial or a new review of the facts in a case by a trial court or an appellate court.

detention   The legally authorized confinement of a person who is subject to criminal or juvenile court proceedings from the time of arrest until release or incarceration.

detention center   A government facility for juveniles that provides temporary care and restriction pending court disposition.

Glossary

detention facility   A general term used to describe facilities that hold adults or juveniles in confinement pending trial or adjudication or adults for a period of confinement of one year or less. Detention facilities include jails, county farms, honor farms, work camps, road camps, detention centers, and juvenile halls.

detention hearing   In juvenile proceedings, a hearing by a judge or judicial officer to determine if a juvenile is to be detained or released while proceedings are pending in juvenile court.

diagnosis or classification center   A unit within a correctional institution, or a separate facility, where individuals sentenced to incarceration are held and evaluated to determine their appropriate placement in permanent correctional institutions or programs. For example, a diagnosis or classification center may determine if an inmate requires incarceration at an institution with mental health services.

diversion   The halting or suspension of formal criminal or juvenile justice proceedings against an alleged offender. Commonly, minor drug offenders are offered diversion in a treatment program as an alternative to incarceration. If, during the diversionary period, the individual successfully complies with all conditions imposed by the court, the criminal proceedings against the individual may be dismissed without any record of a conviction.

early release   Release from a confinement facility before the sentence imposed by the court is completed. Early release can be achieved by parole, by time off for good behavior while incarcerated, or by a modification in the original sentence by the court.

escape   The unlawful departure of a lawfully confined person from a confinement facility or from custody while being transported.

felony   A criminal offense punishable by death or by incarceration in a state or federal correctional facility for a period of time prescribed by law, usually one year or more.

fugitive   An individual attempting to avoid prosecution or confinement by fleeing from a jurisdiction or attempting concealment from authorities in some other way.

group home   In general, a residential facility for adults or juveniles subject to criminal or juvenile justice proceedings that provides community activities or resources in a homelike setting.

halfway house   In general, a residential facility for adjudicated juveniles or convicted adults that is an alternative to incarceration in a traditional correctional facility or is used in an after-care setting to house individuals released from prison who are on parole or require certain services for reintegration into the community.

hearing   A proceeding in which arguments, evidence, or witnesses are heard by a judicial officer or an administrative body. For example, in a

157

probable-cause hearing, arguments, evidence, and witnesses are presented to a court to determine if an individual accused of a crime should be prosecuted or released.

indeterminate sentence   A type of sentence to imprisonment in which the exact length of imprisonment and parole supervision is later determined by a parole authority, generally based on the criminal offender's conduct while in confinement and the degree to which the offender demonstrates rehabilitation.

indictment   A formal written accusation by a grand jury and filed in criminal court alleging that certain crimes were committed by certain individuals.

information   A formal written accusation filed in criminal court by a prosecutor that alleges that a certain person committed a specific offense.

infraction   An offense punishable by a fine or other penalty, such as community service, but not by incarceration.

inmate   A person in custody who is confined in a jail, prison, or other correctional institution.

institutional capacity   The maximum number of inmates or residents that a correctional facility is designed to house.

intake unit   A government agency or branch of an agency that receives juvenile referrals from police or other agencies and screens them for possible referral to the juvenile court or to a social service agency.

jail   A confinement facility intended for adults and administered by a local law enforcement agency, or by a city or county, that holds individuals pending trial or sentencing in criminal cases or persons convicted of crimes and sentenced to a brief period of incarceration, generally for one year or less.

judicial officer   Any person exercising judicial powers in a court of law. Judges are judicial officers, but they are not the only type of judicial officer. Court commissioners or administrators, for example, may also serve as judicial officers, depending upon the laws of a particular jurisdiction.

jurisdiction   A territory, subject matter, or person over which lawful authority may be exercised. For example, under Title 42 of the U.S. Code, section 1983, federal courts were given jurisdiction over state prisoners alleging violations of their civil rights under the Constitution of the United States of America.

jury   A statutorily defined number of persons selected according to law and sworn to determine matters of fact in criminal or civil matters and to render a verdict of guilty or not guilty. A grand jury is a body of persons who are selected and sworn to investigate criminal activity and the conduct of public officials and to hear evidence against those accused in order to determine if there is sufficient cause to file an indictment in criminal court.

Glossary

mandatory sentence   A statutory requirement of certain fixed penalties for certain criminal offenses.

misdemeanor   An offense punishable by incarceration in a local jail or confinement facility, usually for a period of one year or less.

monitored release   The release of a criminal defendant facing pending charges under conditions of supervision that may require the individual to be electronically monitored or confined to a residence except when going to and from court.

pardon   An act of executive clemency that absolves someone in part or in full from the legal consequences of a crime and conviction.

parole   The status of a criminal offender who is conditionally released from a correctional facility before the expiration of the offender's full sentence and placed under the supervision of a parole agency, which is commonly administered by a department of corrections.

parole authority   A person or correctional agency with the authority to release on parole adults or juveniles committed to confinement facilities, to revoke parole, and to discharge from parole.

parolee   A person who is conditionally released from a correctional institution before the expiration of his or her sentence and who is placed under the supervision of a parole agency and required to comply with all conditions imposed by that parole agency.

parole violation   An act by an individual who is on parole that does not conform with the conditions of parole imposed upon that individual. Parole violations include violations of the law and technical violations of conditions of parole, such as reporting to a parole agent on a regular basis. Although technical violations of parole do not rise to the level of a criminal offense, they can nonetheless result in the re-incarceration of the parole violator.

partial confinement   An alternative to a traditional jail sentence, such as a weekend sentence that permits a criminal offender to work during the week and live at home and to report to jail on weekends. Also, furlough programs that allow offenders to leave jail or prison for limited periods of time to work or visit family members are examples of partial confinement.

petition   In juvenile court, a document alleging that a juvenile has violated the law or a status offense and asking the court to assume jurisdiction over the juvenile pending adjudication of the allegations.

population movement   Entries and exits of individuals to and from correctional institutions or within correctional facilities or programs.

prison   A confinement facility with custodial authority over adults sentenced to incarceration of one year or more for criminal offenses.

prisoner   A person in custody in a confinement facility or in the personal custody of a criminal justice official while being transported between confinement facilities.

probable cause　A set of facts and circumstances that would cause a reasonably intelligent person to believe that a person has committed a crime of which he or she stands accused.

probation　The conditional freedom granted by a judge or other judicial official to an adult or juvenile offender on the condition that the offender complies with certain conditions imposed by the court. Probation may be imposed in lieu of incarceration or in addition to a limited period of incarceration, usually in a county jail.

probation agency　An agency with the principle functions of intake, supervision, and investigation of adults or juveniles placed on probation by the courts.

probationer　An individual placed on probation by a court who is required to comply with the conditions of probation for a designated period of time.

probation officer　An employee of a probation agency whose primary duties include enforcing the functions of a probation agency.

probation violation　An act, or failure to act, by a person on probation that does not conform to the conditions of probation imposed by the court. Probation violations include violations of the law as well as violations of conditions of probation that do not rise to the level of a criminal offense.

pro se　Acting as one's own defense attorney in a criminal proceeding. *In propia persona*, or *pro per*, is also a term that means representing oneself in a court of law.

recidivism　The repetition of criminal behavior by a previously incarcerated individual that commonly results in a new period of incarceration. Recidivism is measured by criminal acts that result in a conviction by a court, when committed by individuals who are under correctional supervision or who have been released from correctional supervision within the past three years. Recidivism is also measured by technical violations of probation or parole that result in an adverse change to the offender's legal status, such as conviction or incarceration.

release from prison　Any lawful exit from a federal or state confinement facility for adults who are generally serving sentences of one year or more. Releases may be discretionary, as determined by a parole authority, or they may be mandatory, as determined by statute. Release may also be accomplished by a transfer of the individual to another jurisdiction.

residential treatment center　A facility for juvenile offenders who do not require confinement in a secure facility. Residential treatment centers allow offenders to have greater contact with the community, thereby enhancing the prospects for reintegration into society.

restitution　Usually a cash payment by a criminal offender to the victim in an amount deemed appropriate, usually by a court or by statute, to offset the loss incurred by the victim. Restitution payments are commonly made in monthly installments that fit the offender's earning capacity.

revocation   An administrative act performed by a parole authority or by a court that removes an individual from parole or probation as a result of a violation of parole or probation by that individual.

revocation hearing   An administrative or judicial hearing on the question of whether to revoke an individual's probation or parole status as the result of an alleged violation of the conditions of parole or probation.

sentence   The penalty imposed by a court on a convicted person, which may include incarceration, payment of fines, or the imposition of a term of probation for a period of time.

suspended sentence   The decision by a court to postpone the setting of a penalty for a criminal offense, often by imposing probation for the period of the sentence in lieu of incarcerating the offender in prison or jail.

supervised release   A type of release requiring regular monitoring and contact with designated correctional officials.

third-party release   The release of a criminal offender or defendant to another person who assumes responsibility for the offender or defendant.

time served   The total time spent in confinement by a convicted adult before and after sentencing.

PART II

GUIDE TO FURTHER RESEARCH

CHAPTER 6

HOW TO RESEARCH PRISONS AND CORRECTIONAL ISSUES

The subject of prisons is a broad area of study within the field of corrections. Major areas of interest to the researcher include the history of punishment, the legal rights of prisoners, the prison population, and the administration of state, federal, and private correctional systems. Related topics include rates of incarceration, sentencing laws, parole, community corrections, the death penalty, corrections professionals, the treatment and rehabilitation of prisoners, inmate labor and vocational programs, and the demographics of those sentenced to prison in the United States. Fortunately, there are many resources available for both the general researcher and the specialist.

PRINT RESOURCES

The following books on prisons and corrections in the United States provide an overview of the topic and are a good starting point for the general researcher and an efficient way to identify specific areas of interest for further inquiry.

Corrections in America: An Introduction, 10th Edition (Prentice Hall, 2004), by Harry E. Allen, Clifford E. Simonsen, and Edward J. Latessa, provides a comprehensive overview of the prison system in the United States. Included are chapters on the history of punishment, state and federal correctional systems, correctional ideologies, prisoners' rights, prisoner populations, and parole and community corrections. Earlier editions of the textbook, written by Allen and Simonsen, are also useful. Although statistical information may be dated, and recent court decisions and legislation may not be included, earlier editions of the textbook remain largely unchanged on topics including prison history, the development and organization of state and federal correctional agencies, and landmark court cases on prisoners' rights.

Prisons

Criminal Justice Case Briefs: Significant Cases in Corrections (Roxbury Publishing Company, 2004), by Craig Hemmens, Barbara Belbot, and Katherine Bennett, provides thorough briefings on important Supreme Court cases on issues including sentencing, the death penalty, access to courts, conditions of confinement, inmate medical care, due process, parole, and the Prison Litigation Reform Act. A useful section on case holdings offers a short synopsis of one or two sentences for each case that is briefed in the book. Each chapter is devoted to a single issue, such as sentencing or due process, and includes a brief introduction that provides an overview of that issue. Following each introduction is a briefing of the cases on that issue, presented in chronological order and organized by facts, issue, holding, and rationale.

The Encyclopedia of American Prisons (Checkmark Books, 2004) by Carl Sifakis, is a good starting point for the researcher interested in identifying a specific area of study. Entries, arranged alphabetically, include listings for significant individuals in the history of corrections and notorious prisoners. There are also helpful expanded listings on certain topics, including execution methods and jails and prisons.

Encyclopedia of American Prisons (Garland Press, 1996), by Marilyn D. McShane and Franklin P. William, presents an overview of U.S. prisons through a collection of some 160 essays arranged alphabetically by topics, including prison history and administration, prisoners' rights, mental illness among the prison populations, and prison overcrowding. A companion book, *American Prisons: An Annotated Bibliography* (Greenwood Press, 1998), by Elizabeth Huffmaster and Laura J. Moriarty, provides brief summaries of all books and articles referenced in the encyclopedia.

Dictionary of American Penology (Greenwood Press, 1996), by Vergil L. Williams, offers cross-referenced entries on issues including state and federal prison systems, prison reform organizations, trends in prison management, and adult and juvenile institutional populations.

The Oxford History of the Prison: The Practice of Punishment in Western Society (Oxford University Press, 1995), edited by Norval Morris and David J. Rothman, traces the development of prisons and the idea of incarceration as a form of punishment from biblical times. In addition to essays on prison history, there are chapters on such topics as female prisoners, juvenile detention, and political prisoners, as well as an overview of correctional facilities in the United States and Europe.

PERIODICALS

The following periodicals are devoted to various topics of interest in corrections. They provide information that is generally more current than that found in books. Their availability at local or school libraries may vary. Some of the publications offer full-text articles or abstracts, which are brief summaries of articles, that are available for download from the publication's web site.

The Angolite, a monthly magazine published by inmates at the Louisiana state prison at Angola, presents articles on current issues in corrections and aspects of daily life in prison. Subscription information is available by writing to *The Angolite*, Louisiana State Penitentiary, Angola, LA 70712 or online at URL: http://www.corrections.state.la.us/LSP/angolite.htm.

Corrections Compendium is a research journal published six times a year by the American Correctional Association (ACA). Issues are commonly organized around a central topic, including health care, family visitation and reunification, and corrections staff training and education. Each issue also includes commentary and reviews of books on corrections-related areas of interest. Subscription information is available from the ACA, 4380 Forbes Boulevard, Lanham, MD 20706 or online at URL: http://www.aca.org/adaview.asp?pageid=480.

Corrections Today, also published by the ACA, is a magazine that covers topics of general interest in corrections. Articles from current and archived issues are available for download free of charge at URL: http://www.aca.org/publications/ctmagazine.asp.

Journal of Correctional Health Care is a quarterly research journal published by the National Commission on Correctional Health Care (NCCH) that addresses issues of medicine, law, and medical ethics in correctional settings. Abstracts of articles from current and past issues are available free of charge online at URL: http://www.ncchc.org/pubs/journal.html. Subscriptions are available online or by writing to the NCCH, 1145 West Diversey Parkway, Chicago, IL 60614.

Journal of Offender Rehabilitation is a professional journal that focuses on methods of treatment and rehabilitation of criminal offenders. Contributing writers are experts in various fields of study, including psychology, social work, penology, and administration of justice. A free sample issue and abstracts of articles from current and past issues are available online at URL: http://www.haworthpressinc.com/store/product.asp?sku=J076. Subscriptions are available online or by writing to The Haworth Press Inc., 10 Alice Street, Binghamton, NY 13904.

National Prison Project Journal, a quarterly newsletter published by the American Civil Liberties Union (ACLU), provides information on issues related to prisoners' rights, including recent court decisions and updates on ongoing litigation. Subscriptions are available by writing to the ACLU National Prison Project, 733 15th Street, NW, Suite 620, Washington, DC 20005.

The *Prison Journal* is the official publication of the Pennsylvania Prison Society, which was founded in 1787 and is the oldest prison reform organization in the United States. The journal, published quarterly, explores various issues in corrections and has special issues on current topics of interest, which have included women prisoners, inmates with substance abuse problems, and education in correctional settings. Subscription information is available by writing to *The Prison Journal*, Sage Publications, Inc., 2455 Teller Road, Thousand Oaks, CA 91320.

LIBRARY RESOURCES

Library catalogs allow the researcher to identify books, audiovisual materials, and other sources of information on prisons. The success of locating information depends on good searching techniques. For example, the Library of Congress, with the largest library catalog in the world (URL: http://catalog.loc.gov) allows the researcher to conduct a basic search by title, author, subject, call number, keywords, and by LCCN, ISSN, or ISBN publishing numbers. A more advanced guided search is also possible, and its search parameters are explained on the web page. A basic search using the keyword *prisons* might generate some 10,000 results, hardly a manageable number for most researchers. By clicking on *Set Search Limits*, however, and selecting the categories *Language: English, Type: Book, Location: General Collections*, and *Place of Publication: United States*, some 18 results were generated, a far more manageable number. Similarly, searches may be streamlined through manipulation of the search phrase. The keyword *prisoners* generated some 10,000 results. By comparison, the search phrase *prisoners + women*, generated some 97 results. Local libraries as well as university and law libraries offer similar electronic catalogs that can be efficiently searched by using the same techniques.

PERIODICAL INDEXES

Most libraries subscribe to online periodical indexes, which are searchable databases of articles from newspapers and magazines. Although libraries pay to subscribe to periodical indexes, registered library patrons are often given free access to the databases. One of the more popular periodical indexes is Info Trac, which provides coverage for about 1,000 general interest magazines. Depending on the publication, Info Trac allows the researcher to view abstracts or to view and download full-text articles. In addition, helpful tips are provided on how to efficiently search the Info Trac database.

The Internet Public Library (IPL), an online library service sponsored by the University of Michigan's School of Information and freely available to the general public (URL: http://www.ipl.org), provides a directory of periodical indexes. From the web site's main page, click on *Ready Reference* and follow the link *Periodical Directories* to a listing of periodical directories, including the Alternative Press Index (URL: http://www.altpress.org/index.html) and Ingenta (URL: http://www.ingenta.com).

FindArticles.com (http://www.findarticles.com) is a useful archive of some 300 magazine and journal articles from 1998 to the present. Access to FindArticles.com is free, and full-text articles may be downloaded and printed at no cost.

BOOKSELLER CATALOGS

Online booksellers like Amazon and Barnes and Noble provide a valuable bibliographic source that allows the researcher to easily identify other titles on corrections-related topics and issues. Conducting a simple keyword search of the bookseller's web site is one approach to finding books of interest. Another useful feature of many online booksellers, however, is their ability to identify books that are similar in theme or subject matter to a known book title. For example, selecting *Books* from the pull-down menu and entering the partial book title *Corrections in America* generated a list of other corrections-related books, including *Exploring Corrections in America* (Anderson Publishing Company, 2003), by John D. Whitehead, Joycelyn M. Pollack, Michael C. Braswell, and Kimberly Dodson; *Prison Nation: The Warehousing of America's Poor* (Routledge, 2003), by Tara Herivel and Paul Wright; and *The Perpetual Prison Machine: How America Profits from Crime* (Westview Press, 2001), by Joel Dyer.

Another benefit of online booksellers is their ability to connect the researcher with a nationwide network of reputable used booksellers. Used copies of current or previous editions of books of interest are often available for purchase at substantially discounted prices. This is especially helpful to the researcher with limited library resources.

INTERNET RESEARCH

Searching the Internet through the World Wide Web is an excellent way to conduct research on prisons. However, due to the vast amount of online information that is available on prisons and corrections in the United States, the large number of results generated by using a simple search engine may be overwhelming. Some commonly used Internet search engines available to the researcher include:

Prisons

- AltaVista (www.altavista.com)
- Excite (www.excite.com)
- Go (www.go.com)
- Google (www.google.com)
- Hotbot (www.hotbot.com)
- Northern Light (www.northernlight.com)
- WebCrawler (www.WebCrawler.com)
- Yahoo (www.yahoo.com)

Like periodical indexes and library catalogs, Internet search engines are used most effectively by developing a focused search phrase. For example, a Google search using the keyword *prisons* generated 4.3 million results, an unmanageable amount. By using the *Advanced Search* option, however, and entering *prisons*, and the exact search phrase *incarcerated parents* and limiting the search to English-language web pages updated within the past three months, some 609 results were generated—still a large number but more manageable than 4.3 million.

WEB DIRECTORIES

Web directories, or indexes, are another way of using search engines such as Yahoo! or Google. Web directories provide a structured listing of topics and issues within a given subject area. When researching a broad subject, such as prisons, web directories are especially helpful in narrowing a search and identifying useful search phrases for further research.

For example, clicking on yahoo.com from the main web page under *Yahoo! Web Directory*, following the links *Society* to *Crime* to *Corrections and Rehabilitation* generated a listing of links to subcategories, including *Inmates, Prison History, Prisoner Rape, Women,* and *Supermax Prisons.* Also, by entering *prisons* in the search window on the yahoo.com main page and selecting *in Directory* from the pull-down menu—some 437 results were generated, including *Federal Bureau of Prisons, Prisons and Prisoners's Rights,* and *Private Prisons.*

Cbel.com is another useful web directory. Selecting *Society* from the main web page and following the link *Crime and Justice Issues* generated an extensive listing of categorized links, including *Death Penalty: Death Row Prisoner Pages, Prisons, Prison Activism, Prison Articles and Publications, Prison Organizations, Prison Privatization,* and *Prison Research.*

Another helpful web directory is Prentice Hall's Cibrary: The World's Criminal Justice Directory (URL: http://www.talkjustice.com/cybrary.asp).

How to Research Prisons

Category links include *Community Corrections, Corrections, Prisons, Probation and Parole,* and *Sentencing.* Following the link *Prisons* generated an extensive listing of annotated web links to organizations and agencies with corrections-related information, including *Behind Bars: Substance Abuse and America's Prison Population, Control Unit Prisons, Correctional News Online, Corrections Connection, Family and Corrections Network, Federal Bureau of Prisons,* and the *National Institute of Corrections.*

The Librarians Index to the Internet (URL: http://www.lii.org) is also a useful resource for the researcher that generates annotated links to subjects of interest. Entering *prisons* in the search window generated some 62 annotated links, including *A Prisoner's Dictionary, Writers in Prison, Escapes from Alcatraz, Geneva Convention Relative to the Treatment of Prisoners of War, Debt to Society: The Real Price of Prisons, World Prison Population List,* and *Prison Abuse: Patterns from the Past.*

NEWS ON PRISON ISSUES

Many popular Internet search engines, including Google and Yahoo!, allow the researcher to investigate current news and feature articles on prison-related issues. For example, on yahoo.com, following the links *News Front Page, Full Coverage, U.S.,* and *Prisons* generated a listing of current news stories, including reports on the rising number of women in U.S. prisons, the rising rate of imprisonment in the United States despite declining rates of crime, and recent court decisions on prison-related issues. There were also sections with links to *Featured Articles, Opinions & Editorials,* other *News Sources,* and annotated links to *Related Web Sites* on corrections-related topics. Similarly, on Google, following the link *News* from the main page, entering the search term *prisons* on the *Google News* page, and clicking on *U.S.* generated a listing of links to prison-related news articles on topics including the effects of incarceration in adult prisons on juvenile offenders, prison overcrowding, and the rising operating costs for California state prisons.

ONLINE RESOURCES FOR LAW AND LEGISLATION

The Legal Information Institute (LII) is an online research service by Cornell Law School that is available free of charge to the Internet user at URL: http://www.law.cornell.edu. Information available from the LII web site includes:

- U.S. Supreme Court decisions since 1990 and selected historic decisions by the Supreme Court

171

Prisons

- The United States Constitution, with linked court decisions of significance
- Decisions of the U.S. Courts of Appeal
- The U.S. Code, which is a compilation of all federal legislation enacted into law

As discussed in Chapter 2, there are a significant number of U.S. Supreme Court decisions on issues relating to imprisonment. LII makes it relatively easy for the researcher to identify significant court decisions on constitutional issues. For example, entering *due process* in the search window on the LII main web page and following the link *Law About . . . Prisons and Prisoners* generated a page that contained an overview of prisoners' rights on the issue of due process as guaranteed by the Fourteenth Amendment to the U.S. Constitution. Adjacent to the overview is a *menu of sources*, including links to the *Eighth Amendment* of the U.S. Constitution, which forbids cruel and unusual punishment, *U.S. Supreme Court Historic Decisions Dealing with Prisoners*, and *Recent Prison Decisions*. Other links included state *Appellate Decisions* on prisoners' rights, *Commentary, Human Rights Treaties*, and other online sources for information on prisons and the law. Selecting *U.S. Supreme Court Historic Decisions Dealing with Prisoners* generated a page with the search options *All decisions, Only decisions since 1991, Only summaries of decisions,* and *Only historic decisions.* Entering *prisoners & "due process"* in the search window generated links to landmark Supreme Court rulings, including *Estelle v. Gamble* (1976), *Hudson v. Palmer* (1984), *Sandin v. Connor* (1995), and *Lewis v. Casey* (1996).

It is also possible to find U.S. Supreme Court cases by case name on the LII web site. For example, entering *"Estelle v. Gamble"* on the search page for the U.S. Supreme Court (URL: http://supct.law.cornell.edu/supct/search) generated links to a *syllabus* of the Supreme Court's decision and the Court's full *opinion.*

FindLaw.com (URL: http://www.findlaw.com) is another excellent source of online legal and legislative information that is freely available to the researcher. Selecting the link *U.S. Law Cases and Codes: Federal* from the main web page generated a page with links including *U.S. Constitution, U.S. Code,* and *U.S. Supreme Court.* Selecting *U.S. Supreme Court* generated a page that was searchable by year, case citation, and party name. The case citation number for *Estelle v. Gamble* is 429 U.S. 97, meaning that the decision can be found in volume 429 of the U.S. *Supreme Court Reports* at page 97. The *Supreme Court Reports* is the official record of all U.S. Supreme Court decisions. Thus, entering the case citation number *429 U.S. 97* in the search windows generated the full-text opinion of the U.S. Supreme Court in *Estelle v. Gamble.*

FindLaw.com also provides a user-friendly search engine for the U.S. Code, which contains all laws enacted by the U.S. Congress. From the FindLaw.com search page for the U.S. Code (URL: http://www.findlaw.com/casecode/uscodes), the U.S. Code may be searched by title and section number or by entering a keyword. For example, entering *prisons* in the search window generated a page of links to sections of the U.S. Code that relate to prisons and prisoners, including section 1997e *Suits by Prisoners* and section 4122 *Administration of the Federal Prison Industries.*

Another useful feature of the FindLaw.com search page for the U.S. Code allows the researcher to search for federal legislation by popular name. For example, following the link *Popular Name* and entering *Prison Litigation Reform Act* in the search window generated a page of links to the full text of the act and commentary on the legislation. Similarly, following the same steps and entering *Prison Rape Elimination Act* in the search window generated a page with the full text of the act and commentary.

STATISTICS ON PRISONS AND PRISONERS

The Bureau of Justice Statistics (BJS) provides comprehensive statistical information on the criminal justice system in the United States. The BJS is a division of the Office of Justice Programs in the U.S. Department of Justice. The BJS web page (URL: http://www.ojp.usdoj.gov/bjs) contains links to corrections-related publications and statistical surveys. For example, following the link *Corrections* from the main web page generated links to statistical reports on a range of topics, including *capital punishment, prisons,* and *probation and parole.* Following the link *Corrections facts at a glance* generated links to graphical representations of statistics on the number of adults in the correctional population, increases in the prison population over time, and the number of prisoners under sentence of death.

The BJS publishes a number of annual reports on corrections-related areas of interest, including *Prison and Jail Inmates at Midyear, State Prison Expenditures, Census of State and Federal Correctional Facilities,* and *Prisoners*—all available by download. Links are also provided to current statistical information on the criminal justice system in the United States. Topics include criminal offenders, courts and sentencing, and special topics including prisoner reentry trends and drugs and crime.

OTHER USEFUL WEB SITES

The following selected web sites provide information on myriad corrections-related issues and valuable links for further research.

Prisons

American Correctional Association (ACA) (URL: http://www. aca.org.), founded in 1870 as the National Prison Association, is the oldest professional association in the field of corrections, with a membership that includes researchers, policymakers, and correctional agency staff in federal, state, and local corrections. The ACA publishes *Corrections Today*, a monthly magazine which is linked from the main web page and is helpful in identifying current issues of interest in the field of corrections. The *Corrections Today* web page offers links to downloadable articles from the current issue and two years of archived issues. Each issue is devoted to a corrections-related topic. For example, one recent issue was devoted to community corrections. Archived issues covered topics including probation and parole, juvenile corrections, military corrections, correctional health care, the correctional workforce, and inmate reentry and reintegration.

American Federation of State, County and Municipal Employees (AFSCME) is the largest labor union of public service employees in the United States. The AFSCME provides a comprehensive listing of corrections-related links on their AFSCME Corrections United (ACU) web page at URL: http://www.afscme.org/acu/aculink2.htm. Especially helpful are the links to issues related to U.S. corrections officers, including a feature that allows the researcher to conduct a state-by-state search on the salaries and employment trends for state corrections officers. Links on the ACU web page are arranged by topic, including *Inmates and Gangs* and *Prison Disturbances/Hostage Situations.*

American Probation and Parole Association (APPA) (URL: http:// www.appa-net.org.) is a professional association with membership throughout the United States and Canada. The APPA web site provides a helpful link to *Free Publications*, which offers annotated links to articles and research reports on issues relating to parole and offender reentry. For example, there were downloadable reports on topics including sex-offender registration, the victim's role in offender reentry, and new programs in probation and parole.

The **Association of State Correctional Administrators** (ASCA) (URL: www.asca.net) is a professional association established in 1970 to promote training, education, and the exchange of information on prison administration and management. The ASCA web site offers a helpful link to *Publications*, where articles and reports on issues of prison administration are available by download. Although sometimes technical in nature, the publications offer insight into the challenges of managing correctional facilities. For example, there are links to articles on assessing the performance of correctional institutions, financing prisons and correctional programs, and the outsourcing of prison services, such as food service and health care.

174

How to Research Prisons

The **Center for Community Corrections** (URL: http://www. communitycorrectionsworks.org) was established in 1987 to conduct research and disseminate information to corrections professionals, researchers, and academics. The center's web site offers a number of helpful resources to researchers, including links to how community corrections works, a national directory of organizations in the field of community corrections, state laws and legislation governing community corrections programs, and a glossary of commonly used terms in the field of community corrections. The web site also provides a link to recent publications on community corrections topics that are available by download. For example, there are publications on topics including halfway houses, special populations in community corrections, and balancing public safety and the interests of community corrections programs.

The **Centers for Disease Control and Prevention Correctional Health** (URL: http://www.cdc.gov/nchstp/od/cccwg) was created by the Centers for Disease Control and Prevention (CDC) to encourage collaboration between public health organizations and the correctional agencies. The CDC Correctional Health web page provides links to information and publications on correctional health that are useful to both beginning and advanced researchers. Among the web site's offerings are links to a primer on correctional health care, government agencies in correctional health care, and special health issues, including health-care issues for females and juveniles in correctional institutions, chronic and infectious diseases, health-care delivery in correctional settings, and mental health.

The **Corrections Connection** (URL: http://www.corrections.com) was established in 1996 to create a forum for the exchange of information and ideas by corrections professionals. The Corrections Connection web page offers an extensive database on corrections-related news, information, and downloadable publications available to the general public. From the web site's main page, the link *This Just In* provides links to news about prisons and corrections from newspapers and periodicals nationwide. There are also links to corrections-related topics including education, health care, juvenile detention, and prison privatization. Each of these web links offers links to information on that topic of interest and organizations within that field. For example, the web link for *Health Care* provides links to the American Correctional Health Services Association, the National Commission on Correctional Health Care, Brown University's HIV Education in Prison Project, and the Institute for Criminal Justice Healthcare.

Criminal Justice Links (URL: http://www.criminology.fsu.edu/cjlinks), sponsored by the Florida State University School of Criminology and Criminal Justice, provides links to online information in all areas of the U.S. criminal justice system. The web site's main page offers links to some 17

175

Prisons

Major Web Pages, one of which is *Community Corrections, Restorative Justice, Prisons and the Death Penalty*, which offers numerous links to corrections-related web sites and online information.

Criminal Justice Resources: Periodicals Available on the Web (URL: http://www.lib.msu.edu/harris23/crimjust/per.htm) offers an extensive listing of annotated web links to periodicals in all areas of criminal justice, including corrections, some of which offer full text articles online. Sponsored by Michigan State University, the web page also offers links to electronic journals in criminal justice and the law, with links to descriptions of the periodicals listed and links to each periodical's web page.

The **Federal Bureau of Prisons** (BOP) (URL: http://www.bop.gov) is a federal agency within the U.S. Department of Justice created in 1930 to administer the federal prison system in the United States. The BOP web site provides an extensive database of information on the federal prison system, including a federal inmate locator and links to current facts and statistics on inmate populations at BOP facilities nationwide. Among downloadable publications are the *State of the Bureau*, which provides an annual summary of statistical data on all phases of the BOP, and the *Federal Prisons Journal*, a quarterly professional journal that offers coverage of BOP correctional programs. There are also links to special reports. For example, there are special reports on the history of federal prison industries and on the final year of operation of the federal prison at Alcatraz Island in California.

FirstGov.gov (URL: http://www.firstgov.gov) is the U.S. government's clearinghouse for information from the executive, legislative, and judicial branches of the federal government and from state, local, and tribal governments. From the main web page, the link *Public Safety and Law* provides a gateway to online information in all areas of the U.S. criminal justice system, including prisons, correctional agencies, inmates, and parole.

The **National Archive of Criminal Justice Data** (NACJD) (URL: http://www.icpsr.umich.edu/ NACJD), established in 1978 as an interuniversity consortium for political and social research, provides an extensive online database of publications from federal and state agencies in criminal justice, including corrections. The NACJD web site offers a user-friendly search engine to access downloadable publications in specific areas of interest. Search results are displayed with links to a description of the publication and links to related literature in that field of study.

The **National Criminal Justice Reference Service** (NCJRS) (URL: http://www.ncjrs.org) is a federally sponsored database of publications in all areas of criminal justice. The NCJRS web site's main page offers a link to *Corrections*, where linked subcategories are listed that allow the researcher to easily narrow a search. In addition, the *Corrections* page lists corrections-related publications available by download that can be sorted by title, date, or document number. Also linked is a searchable database of library abstracts and full-text articles from some 600 periodicals. A helpful online research tutorial includes a *thesaurus term search* feature that helps the researcher narrow a search by generating a list of subcategories for a general search term. For example, the general search term *corrections* generated over 50 links to subcategories, including *assaults on corrections officers, correctional agencies, correctional costs, corrections research,* and *juvenile corrections.* The NCJRS *thesaurus term search* (URL: http://abstractsdb.ncjrs.org/content/Thesaurus/ Thesaurus_Search.asp) can be accessed from the main page by clicking on the *Help* link, then clicking on the *How do I search the NCJRS web site* link, then clicking on *What is the Advanced Thesaurus Search?*

The **National Institute of Corrections** (NIC) (URL: http://www.nicic.org) is an agency within the Federal Bureau of Prisons, U.S. Department of Justice, that provides training and correctional program development assistance and funding to federal, state, and local corrections agencies. The NIC web site offers an extensive collection of information and downloadable publications on corrections-related topics available through the *Resource Library Database,* which is linked from the web site's main page. The database provides a search engine that allows the researcher to narrow the search by the type of publication and the search phrase. The *Research Library Database* offers links to recent publications and to broader areas of interest, such as prisons and community corrections. There is also a *Research Assistance* link which allows the researcher to contact the NIC and request information on special areas of interest on corrections-related topics. Also helpful is the link on the web site's main page to *Web Links,* which provides a listing of linked web sites for corrections-related organizations and information clearinghouses. The listing is subdivided by categories, including *Federal Corrections-Related Agencies, Corrections-Related Associations and Organizations, Research Resources,* and *Inmate/Offender Services.* In addition, from the main page, the link *Resources for Students* directs the researcher to a page with links to explore selected topics for further research. Linked topics include *Mentally Ill Persons in Correctional Settings, The Prison Rape Elimination Act, Staff Sexual Misconduct, Women Offender Issues, Youthful Offenders in Adult Correctional Systems,* and *Transition from Prison to Community.*

The **Prison Policy Initiative** (PPI) (URL: http://www.prisonpolicy.org) is a prisoners' rights advocacy organization. The PPI web site provides numerous links to news articles, reports, and other publications on a range of corrections-related social issues including conditions of confinement, racial disparity in incarceration rates, and felony disenfranchisement laws. Among the links available from the main web page is *Research Index,* which provides an extensive listing of Web-based information on felony disenfranchisement, immigration detainees, incarceration rates, prison privatization, recidivism, and special inmate populations including females, juveniles, and the mentally ill, and many other issues. The PPI also operates two other web sites. Prisoners of the Census (URL: http://www.prisonersofthecensus.org) provides links to information on the counting of prison inmates and its impact on issues such as federal funding and congressional redistricting. PrisonSucks.com (URL: http://www.prisonsucks.com) offers links to information on prison-related issues including the death penalty, families of prisoners, mandatory minimum sentences, and the impact of prisons on state economies.

The **World Criminal Justice Library Network** (WCJLN) (URL: http://newark.rutgers.edu/~wcjlen/WCJ) was established at a meeting of librarians and criminal justice information specialists in 1991 at the Rutgers University School of Criminal Justice with the mission of sharing criminal justice information worldwide. As such, the WCJLN provides a clearinghouse for information on criminal justice systems in the United States and some 70 other countries. The WCJLN web page offers links to statistical resources, general reference sources, and online periodicals, some of which are corrections-related.

The **United States Parole Commission** (USPC) (URL: http://www.usdoj.gov/uspc) is an agency within the U.S. Department of Justice with jurisdiction over the parole of federal prisoners, military prisoners, and state parolees in the federal Witness Protection Program. The USPC web site provides links to the rules and procedures of federal parole, statutes governing parole, and statistics on the federal parole system.

CHAPTER 7

ANNOTATED BIBLIOGRAPHY

The following annotated bibliography focuses on prisons and corrections-related issues in the United States. Entries are grouped in the following three categories:

Correctional Systems, Facilities, and Staff
Classification, Treatment, and Parole
Prisoners, Inmates' Rights, and Sentencing

Each category is subdivided into three sections: *Books, Articles and Papers,* and *Web Documents.*

Correctional Systems, Facilities, and Staff

BOOKS

Allen, Harry E., et al. *Corrections in America: An Introduction, 10th Edition.* Upper Saddle River, N.J.: Prentice Hall, 2004. Presents a comprehensive overview of the prison system in the United States. Included are chapters on the history of punishment and prison development, state and federal correctional systems, correctional ideologies, prisoners' rights, prisoner populations, parole, and community corrections.

American Correctional Association. *The American Prison: From the Beginning—A Pictorial History.* Laurel, Md.: American Correctional Association, 1983. Presents a photographic review of prisons in the United States, with brief narrative descriptions for each photograph.

Ayers, E. L. *Vengeance and Justice: Crime and Punishment in the 19th Century in the American South.* New York: Oxford University Press, 1984. Presents a historical overview of crime and punishment in the South, with emphasis on the period between the Civil War and 1900. Includes a discussion of the plantation model for leasing prisoners for their labor that was widely adopted in southern prisons.

Badillo, Herman, and Milton Haynes. *A Bill of NO Rights: Attica and the American Prison System.* New York: Outerbridge and Lazard, 1972. Examines prison conditions that led to the 1971 riot at the New York state prison at Attica and presents a daily chronology of events that occurred during the siege and its immediate aftermath.

Baker, J. E. *The Right to Participate: Inmate Involvement in Prison Administration.* Metuchen, N.J.: Scarecrow Press, 1974. Presents a historical overview of inmate participatory management in U.S. prisons from 1793 to 1973.

Barnes, Harry Elmer. *The Evolution of Penology in Pennsylvania: A Study in American Social History.* Indianapolis, Ind.: Bobbs-Merrill, 1927. Presents a historical overview of the development of the Pennsylvania system, including an analysis of the system and its impact on the development of correctional institutions in the United States.

Bates, Sanford. *Prisons and Beyond.* New York: Macmillan, 1971. An analysis of the structure and administration of the federal prison system by the first director of the Federal Bureau of Prisons. Originally published in 1936, the book includes a discussion of the medical model of inmate classification and rehabilitation.

Bayse, Daniel J. *Working in Jails and Prisons: Becoming Part of the Team.* Lanham, Md.: American Correctional Association, 1995. Basic primer presents models for effective interaction between prison staff and inmates. Includes a brief history of corrections, discusses the differences between jail and prison, and provides a reference list and a glossary of terms of prison-related issues.

Beaumont, Gustave de, and Alexis de Tocqueville. *On the Penitentiary System in the United States and Its Application in France.* Carbondale: Southern Illinois University Press. Reprint, originally published in 1833. Presents an assessment of the prison system in the United States in the early 19th century, based upon visits to American prisons by the authors. Includes a proposal to establish a model prison in France based upon the Pennsylvania system.

Bennett, James V. *I Chose Prison.* New York: Alfred A. Knopf, 1970. A history of corrections in the United States by the former director of the Federal Bureau of Prisons from 1937 to 1964.

Braswell, Michael, et al. *Prison Violence in America.* Cincinnati: Anderson, 1994. Presents an overview of the types and causes of violence in U.S. prisons and discusses strategies for minimizing violence and its effects on inmates and correctional staff.

Annotated Bibliography

Butler, Ann, and C. Murray Henderson. *Angola: Louisiana State Penitentiary, A Half-Century of Rage and Reform.* Lafayette: Center for Louisiana Studies, University of Southwestern Louisiana, 1990. Examines the case histories of some inmates at the Louisiana State Prison at Angola, including their personal accounts of prison life and profiles of the victims of their crimes.

Carleton, Mark T. *Politics and Punishment: The History of the Louisiana State Penal System.* Baton Rouge: Louisiana State University Press, 1971. Provides a historical analysis of the political evolution and development of the state prison system in Louisiana.

Carlson, Bonnie E., and Neil J. Cervera. *Inmates and Their Wives: Incarceration and Family Life.* Westport, Conn.: Greenwood Press, 1992. Presents findings of a study of the New York Family Reunion Program for inmates, including an overview of the program and its possible application to corrections officers and their families.

Carroll, Leo. *Hacks, Blacks and Cons: Race Relations in a Maximum Security Prison.* Prospect Heights, Ill.: Waveland Press, 1988. Examines race relations among inmates and correctional staff at an Illinois state prison.

Cheek, F. E. *Stress Management for Correctional Officers and Their Families.* Laurel, Md.: American Correctional Association, 1984. Examines the consequences of occupational stress on corrections officers and the impact of such stress on the home life of correctional officers. Discusses coping strategies to alleviate workplace stress in correctional settings.

Chilton, Bradley Stewart. *Prisons under the Gavel: The Federal Court Takeover of Georgia Prisons.* Columbus: Ohio State University Press, 1991. Presents a case study of the Georgia state prison system and the causes for periodic court monitoring of the system.

Clear, Todd R., and George F. Cole. *American Corrections.* Belmont, Calif.: Wadsworth, 1994. Textbook that presents a comprehensive overview of corrections in the United States, including the evolution of prisons in America.

Clements, C. B. *Offender Needs Assessment.* Laurel, Md.: American Correctional Association, 1986. Presents an overview of inmate assessment under various correctional classification systems and the use of classification in diagnosis and treatment of mental illness and behavior disorders in prisoners.

Clemmer, Donald. *The Prison Community.* New York: Holt, Rhinehart, and Winston, 1940. Presents findings of a classic sociological study of imprisonment that examined prison subculture, language, and norms in U.S. state prisons with inmate populations of 2,300 or more.

Colvin, Mark. *Penitentiary in Crisis: From Accommodation to Riot in New Mexico.* New York: State University of New York Press, 1992. Presents a historical overview of inmate control strategies used at the New Mexico penitentiary.

Conrad, John P. *Justice and Consequences*. Lexington, Mass.: Lexington Books, 1981. Discusses the philosophy and goals of imprisonment and recommends improvement to institutional life in correctional settings.

Conte, William R. *Is Prison Reform Possible? The Washington State Experience in the Sixties*. Tacoma, Wash.: Unique Press, 1990. A discussion of the history of reforms in penal systems and an analysis of reforms implemented in the 1960s at prisons in Washington State that focused on identifying the causes of certain types of behavior among inmate populations.

Cordozo-Freeman, Inez, and Eugene P. Delorme. *The Joint: Language and Culture in a Maximum Security Prison*. Springfield, Ill.: Charles C. Thomas, 1984. An analysis of prison life based on taped interviews with inmates at the Washington state prison at Walla Walla, based upon the authors' theory that language is central to the shaping of culture.

Crawford, William. *Report on the Penitentiaries of the United States*. Montclair, N.J.: Patterson Smith, 1969. Presents findings of a classic study by the author, who was commissioned by the British government to study correctional systems and the architectural design of prisons in the United States.

Crouch, Ben M., and James W. Marquart. *An Appeal to Justice: Litigated Reform in Texas Prisons*. Austin: University of Texas Press, 1989. A discussion of the impact on the Texas Department of Corrections made by the decision in *Ruiz v. Estelle* (1980) 503 F. Supp. 1265, which found in favor of the plaintiff, a Texas state inmate who alleged that unsafe and overcrowded conditions in Texas prisons were unconstitutional, as was the use of the tender system, in which stronger and sometimes more violent inmates were given authority over other prisoners.

Currie, Elliott. *Crime and Punishment in America*. New York: Henry Holt, 1998. Examines the growth of prisons in the United States, including supermax prisons, and presents alternatives to incarceration, including social programs for individuals at high risk for criminal conduct.

Delucia, Robert C., and Thomas J. Doyle. *Career Planning in Criminal Justice*. Cincinnati: Anderson Publishing Company, 1990. Examines a range of employment opportunities in the field of criminal justice, including the requisite qualifications and job descriptions for careers in corrections.

DiIulio, John J. *Governing Prisons: A Comparative Study of Correctional Management*. New York: Macmillan, 1987. Comparative analysis of prison management in state correctional systems in California, Michigan, and Texas.

———. *No Escape: The Future of American Corrections*. New York: Basic Books, 1991. Examines correctional policies in the United States and offers recommendations for improvements based on a 10-year study of personnel at federal, state, and local correctional agencies.

————, ed. *Courts, Corrections, and the Constitution: The Impact of Judicial Intervention on Prisons and Jails.* New York: Oxford University Press, 1990. Presents case studies on judicial intervention in the administration of correctional facilities in Texas, Georgia, West Virginia, New Jersey, and New York City.

Duffy, Clinton T. *The San Quentin Story.* Garden City, N.J.: Doubleday, 1950. Firsthand account of a former warden at the state prison at San Quentin, California.

Earley, Pete. *The Hot House: Life Inside Leavenworth Prison.* New York: Bantam Books, 1992. Presents the day-to-day life of inmates and correctional staff inside the federal prison at Fort Leavenworth, Kansas, the oldest federal penitentiary in the United States.

Eriksson, Torsten. *The Reformers: An Historical Survey of Pioneer Experiments in the Treatment of Criminals.* New York: Elsevier North-Holland, 1976. Presents a historical overview of the reform of treatment efforts in correctional settings in the United States and Europe from the 16th through the 20th centuries.

Forer, Lois G. *Rage to Punish: The Unintended Consequences of Mandatory Sentencing.* New York: W. W. Norton, 1994. A former judge advocates for the abolition of capital punishment, sentencing guidelines, and mandatory sentencing rules because of their alleged failure to reduce the rate of crime in the United States and their cost to taxpayers by increasing the rate of incarceration nationwide.

Fortunate Eagle, Adam. *Alcatraz! Alcatraz! The Indian Occupation of 1969–1971.* New York: Heyday Books, 1992. Personal account of the Native American occupation of Alcatraz Island after the closing of the prison there in 1963 by the Bureau of Prisons. Includes a historical overview of Alcatraz when it was a maximum security prison.

Foster, Burk, et al., eds. *The Wall Is Strong: Corrections in Louisiana.* Lafayette: Center for Criminal Justice Research, University of Southwestern Louisiana, 1989. Includes chapters by various authors, with the focus on the history of the Louisiana state prison at Angola, including the administration of the facility and prison life there. Other state correctional facilities in Louisiana are also examined.

Fox, James G. *Organizational and Racial Conflict in Maximum Security Prisons.* Lexington, Mass.: Lexington Books, 1982. Presents findings of a study on racial conflicts in five state maximum security prisons, based on interviews with inmates, prison administrators, and corrections officers.

Fox, Vernon B., and Jeanne B. Stinchcomb. *Introduction to Corrections, Fifth Edition.* Englewood Cliffs, N.J.: Prentice Hall, 1999. Textbook presents an overview of corrections in the United States, including trends in correctional administration.

Friedman, Lawrence. *Crime and Punishment in American History*. New York: Basic Books, 1993. Discusses the development of the U.S. criminal justice system beginning in the colonial era in three major areas: law enforcement, the courts, and prisons.

Funke, Gail S., et al. *Assets and Liabilities of Correctional Industries*. Lexington, Mass.: D.C. Heath and Company, 1982. Presents an overview of prison industries and the advantages and disadvantages of prison industry programs.

Garland, David. *Punishment in Modern Society: A Study in Social Theory*. Chicago: University of Chicago Press, 1990. An analysis of how criminal offenders are punished in the United States and why punishment does not always address the goals of society.

Gildemeister, Glen A. *Prison Labor and Convict Competition with Free Workers in Industrialized America, 1840–1890*. New York: Garland Press, 1987. Historical analysis of the prison labor movement in the United States, including discussions of how prison-made goods competed with goods manufactured in the private sector.

Gottfredson, Don, et al. *Guidelines for Parole and Sentencing*. Lexington, Mass.: Lexington Books, 1978. Includes a comprehensive overview of the evolution of parole and sentencing in the United States.

Griset, Pamela L. *Determinate Sentencing: The Promise and the Reality of Retributive Justice*. Albany: State University of New York Press, 1991. Discusses determinate sentencing and the impact of determinate sentencing laws that remove or reduce the authority of sentencing decision makers, such as judges.

Hall, Basil. *Travels in North America in the Years 1827 and 1828, Volumes I and II*. Reprint, New York: Arno Press, 1974. Includes a firsthand report on a tour of New York's Sing Sing prison and a discussion of the Auburn system.

Hall, Henry. *The History of Auburn*. Auburn, N.Y.: Dennis Brothers and Company, 1869. A history of the town of Auburn, New York, including a discussion of the Auburn prison system and its development.

Hawkins, Richard, and Geoffrey P. Alpert. *American Prison Systems: Punishment and Justice*. Englewood Cliffs, N.J.: Prentice Hall, 1989. Presents a historical overview of the origins and objectives of imprisonment in the United States.

Hirsch, Adam Jay. *The Rise of the Penitentiary: Prisons and Punishment in Early America*. New Haven, Conn.: Yale University Press, 1992. Historical analysis of the development of penitentiaries in the United States and the use of corporal punishment for inmate control.

Hurley, Dennis James. *Alcatraz Island Memories.* Petaluma, Calif.: Barlow Printing, 1987. Account of the son of a former federal corrections officer of his life on Alcatraz Island from the age of seven to 18, including a historical overview with emphasis on the period when Alcatraz was a federal prison from 1934 to 1963.

———. *Alcatraz Island Maximum Security.* Petaluma, Calif.: Barlow Printing, 1989. Presents biographical sketches of the most famous inmates housed at Alcatraz federal prison and includes a discussion of the attempted escapes from the maximum security facility from its opening in 1934 to its closure in 1963.

Irwin, John. *Prisons in Turmoil.* Boston: Little, Brown, 1980. Presents a historical overview of violence in U.S. prisons, including violence arising from racial tensions among inmate groups.

Irwin, John, and James Austin. *It's about Time: America's Imprisonment Binge.* Belmont, Calif.: Wadsworth Corporation, 1994. A discussion of sentencing and imprisonment in the United States and possible alternatives.

Jacobs, James B. *Stateville: The Penitentiary in Mass Society.* Chicago: University of Chicago Press, 1977. Presents a historical overview of the Stateville maximum security penitentiary in Chicago, Illinois, which was built in 1925. Discusses prison life at Stateville from the viewpoints of inmates and correctional staff.

James, Adrian A., et al. *Privatizing Prisons: Rhetoric and Reality.* Thousand Oaks, Calif.: Sage Publications, 1997. Examines practical and ethical issues related to the privatization of correctional facilities and compares U.S. private prisons to privatized correctional institutions in Europe and Australia.

Johnson, Robert. *Hard Time: Understanding and Reforming the Prison.* Pacific Grove, Calif.: Brooks/Cole Publishing Company, 1987. Examines the life of male inmates in maximum security confinement and discusses coping mechanisms utilized by male prisoners who are confined for extended periods of time.

Johnston, Norman. *A Brief History of Prison Architecture.* New York: Walker and Company, 1973. Presents a historical analysis of the architecture of U.S. prisons, beginning with the design of the Walnut Street jail in Philadelphia, Pennsylvania.

Kalinich, David B., and Terry Pitcher. *Surviving in Corrections: A Guide for Corrections Professionals.* Springfield, Ill.: Charles C. Thomas, 1984. Discusses stress-inducing factors in the working environment of correctional staff.

Keve, Paul W. *The History of Corrections in Virginia.* Charlottesville: University Press of Virginia, 1986. Historical analysis of corrections in Virginia from the colonial period to the modern era, including a discussion of the political and social forces that shaped the style of management in Virginia prisons.

————. *Prisons and the American Conscience: A History of U.S. Federal Corrections.* Carbondale: Southern Illinois University Press, 1991. Historical analysis of federal imprisonment from the colonial era to 1987, including a discussion of the contributions to American corrections made by James Bennett during his tenure from 1937 to 1964 as director of the Federal Bureau of Prisons.

LaFave, Wayne R. *Search and Seizure: A Treatise on the Fourth Amendment.* St. Paul, Minn.: West Publishing, 1987. Presents a comprehensive discussion of the protection against unreasonable search and seizure guaranteed by the Fourth Amendment, including the legal precedents for search and seizure without consent in correctional settings.

Lamott, Kenneth. *Chronicles of San Quentin: The Biography of a Prison.* New York: David McKay Company, 1961. Presents a historical overview of the state prison at San Quentin, California.

Latessa, Edward J., et al. *Correctional Contexts: Contemporary and Classical Readings, Second Edition.* Los Angeles: Roxbury Publishing Company, 2001. Previously published articles and papers by authors in various disciplines, including penology, psychology, and sociology, are organized into seven parts: History of Punishment and Origins of Imprisonment, Living in Prison, Working in Prison, Prison Litigation and Inmate's Rights, Institutional Programming and Treatment, Release from Prison and Parole, and New Directions.

Lewis, Orlando Faulkland. *The Development of American Prisons and Prison Customs, 1776–1845.* Montclair, N.J.: Patterson Smith, 1965. Historical analysis of the development of the American prison system from the colonial period to 1845, including discussions on architectural design and the operation of penal institutions.

Lewis, W. David. *From Newgate to Dannemora: The Rise of the Penitentiary in New York, 1796–1848.* Ithaca, N.Y.: Cornell University Press, 1965. An analysis of the historical development of the prison system in New York State, including a discussion of correctional practices and the trend of the increasingly repressive management of inmates.

Lockwood, Daniel. *Prison Sexual Violence.* New York: Elsevier North/Holland, 1980. Discusses the causes and effects of sexual violence among prisoners and the role of correctional staff in responding to reports of incidents of sexual violence.

Logan, Charles H. *Private Prisons: Cons and Pros.* New York: Oxford University Press, 1990. Discusses the advantages and disadvantages of privately operated correctional facilities and compares private and public prisons in terms of operating costs, accountability, corruption, and security.

Annotated Bibliography

Lombardo, Lucien X. *Guards Imprisoned: Correctional Officers at Work.* New York: Elsevier North-Holland, 1981. Presents findings of a research study based on extensive interviews of correctional officers at the Auburn correctional facility in New York.

Maltz, Michael D. *Recidivism.* Orlando, Fla.: Academic Press, 1984. Presents a comprehensive overview of the problem of recidivism among prisoners, including a discussion of the difficulty in using recidivism as a measure of success for correctional programs.

Marshall, H. E. *Dorothea Lynde Dix: Forgotten Samaritan.* Chapel Hill, N.C.: University of North Carolina Press, 1937. Biography of Dorothea Dix that focuses on her contributions to the field of corrections and the prison reforms that resulted from her work.

Martin, Steve J., and Sheldon Ekland-Olson. *Texas Prisons: The Walls Came Tumbling Down.* Austin: Texas Monthly Press, 1987. Analysis of the Texas state prison system from 1967 to 1987, including the use of the tender system, in which stronger and sometimes more violent inmates were given authority over other prisoners. Includes a discussion of the impact of *Ruiz v. Estelle* (1980) 503 F. Supp. 1265, which found in favor of a Texas state inmate who alleged that unsafe and overcrowded conditions in Texas prisons were unconstitutional.

Mcgee, Richard A. *Prisons and Politics.* Lexington, Mass.: Lexington Books, 1981. Presents a historical analysis of the influence of political objectives on the management of the California state prison system.

McKelvey, Blake. *American Prisons: A History of Good Intentions.* 1936. Reprint, Montclair, N.J.: Patterson-Smith, 1977. Historical primer on the state and federal prison systems in the United States from 1835 to 1977 that addresses such issues as changing standards of correctional administration, prison reform, criminological theories, and the impact of state and federal legislation on prison industries.

McShane, Marilyn D., and Franklin P. Williams. *Encyclopedia of American Prisons.* New York: Garland Press, 1996. Presents a collection of some 160 corrections-related essays arranged alphabetically by topics, including prison history and administration, prisoners' rights, mental illness among the prison populations, and prison overcrowding.

Melossi, Dario D., and Massimo Pavarina. *The Prison and the Factory: Origins of the Penitentiary System.* London: Macmillan, 1981. Historical analysis correlating the rise of capitalism and the expansion of prison systems throughout Europe and the United States.

Morris, Norval, and David J. Rothman, eds. *The Oxford History of the Prison: The Practice of Punishment in Western Society.* New York: Oxford University Press, 1995. Traces the development of prisons and the idea of incarceration as a form of punishment from biblical times. In addition to essays on prison history, there are chapters on such topics as female prisoners, juvenile detention, political prisoners, and an overview of correctional facilities in the United States and Europe.

Morris, Roger. *The Devil's Butcher Shop: The New Mexico Prison Uprising.* New York: Franklin Watts, 1983. Chronicles the inmate riot in 1980 at the New Mexico state penitentiary at Sante Fe using eyewitness statements and reports by the New Mexico attorney general and the prison intelligence office.

Murton, Thomas O. *The Dilemma of Prison Reform.* New York: Holt, Rinehart and Winston, 1976. Examines the failure of prison reform movements in the United States, including the author's own experiences with reform as a warden with the Arkansas Department of Corrections.

Murton, Thomas O., and Joe Hyams. *Accomplices to the Crime: The Arkansas Prison Scandal.* New York: Grove Press, 1969. Examines styles of management, including the use of corporal punishment, throughout the state prison system in Arkansas. Coauthor Murton was the former superintendent at the Arkansas Prison Farm.

Nagel, William G. *The New Red Barn: A Critical Look at the Modern American Prison.* New York: Walker, 1973. Presents an overview of the design of modern U.S. prisons and the impact of prison design on the security and treatment of prisoners.

Nelson, William Ray, et al. *New Generation Jails.* Boulder, Colo.: Library Information Specialists, 1983. Discusses the design and management of modern jails, as well as the potential effectiveness of these if implemented in U.S. prisons.

New York State Special Commission on Attica. *Attica: The Official Report of the New York State Special Commission on Attica.* New York: Bantam Books, 1972. Examines the prison uprising at Attica that began on September 9, 1971, including an overview of the New York state prison system at the time of the rioting and a summary of prison conditions and events that led to the siege. Includes a description of the riot and its aftermath and presents recommendations for the reform of the New York state prison system.

Osborne, Thomas Mott. *Society and Prisons.* New Haven, Conn.: Yale University Press, 1916. A classic analysis of inmate participatory management by the former warden of Sing Sing prison in New York and a discussion of the improvement in overall inmate behavior when prisoners participated in the management of the prison.

Oswald, Russell G. *My Story.* Garden City, N.Y.: Doubleday, 1972. Personal account of the inmate uprising at the New York state prison at Attica in 1971 by the then commissioner of the New York state prison system.

Annotated Bibliography

Owen, Barbara A. *The Reproduction of Social Control: A Study of Prison Workers at San Quentin.* New York: Praeger Publishers, 1988. Presents findings of a study of some 35 correctional staff members at California's San Quentin state prison.

Paulus, Paul B., et al. *Prison Crowding: A Psychological Perspective.* New York: Springer-Verlag, 1988. Presents findings of a 15-year study on prison crowding and compares those findings with various theories on the psychological effects of crowding on inmates.

Sellin, John Thorsten. *Slavery and the Penal System.* New York: Elsevier, 1976. Analysis of the impact of slavery on practices in correctional systems in Europe and the United States, including forced inmate labor.

Senna, Joseph P., and Larry G. Siegel. *Introduction to Criminal Justice.* Belmont, Calif.: Wadsworth Publishing Company, 1999. Presents an overview of the U.S. criminal justice system, including chapters on punishment and sentencing and corrections systems.

Shichor, David. *Punishment for Profit: Private Prisons/Public Concerns.* Thousand Oaks, Calif.: Sage Publishing, 1995. Discusses economic, legal, and managerial issues related to correctional facilities operated by private companies and compares the merits of private prisons and public correctional institutions.

Sifakis, Carl. *The Encyclopedia of American Prisons.* New York: Facts On File, 2003. Entries are arranged alphabetically and include listings for significant individuals in the history of corrections and notorious prisoners. There are also expanded listings on certain topics, including execution methods and jails and prisons.

Slate, Risdon N. *Stress Levels and Thoughts of Quitting of Correctional Personnel: Do Perceptions of Participatory Management Make a Difference?* Ann Arbor, Mich.: University Microfilms, 1993. Presents findings from a study in six state prisons and two private correctional facilities on the relationship between employee stress and the perceived level of decision making by correctional employees and discusses the impact of such perceptions on the attrition rate among prison staff.

Smykla, John Ortiz. *Coed Prison.* New York: Human Sciences Press, 1980. An analysis of issues relating to coed prisons, including administrative and interpersonal issues that arise at institutions that house both male and female offenders.

Stastny, Charles C., and Gabrielle Tyrnauer. *Who Rules the Joint? The Changing Political Culture of Maximum Security Prisons in America.* Lexington, Mass: Lexington Books, 1982. Analysis of the historical struggle for power in correctional facilities by competing groups, including prisoners, guards, and wardens. Presents findings of a research study at the Washington state penitentiary at Walla Walla on the nature of power in prison.

Prisons

Stone, W. G. *The Hate Factory.* Agoura, Calif.: Dell Publishing, 1982. First-hand account by an inmate of the 36-hour prisoner riot that began on February 2, 1980, at the New Mexico state penitentiary and resulted in 33 deaths.

Sullivan, Larry E. *The Prison Reform Movement: Forlorn Hope.* Boston: Twayne Publishers, 1990. Presents a historical overview of the prison reform movement, beginning with reform efforts in the 19th century. Includes a discussion of the decline of treatment programs in the modern era, combined with rising inmate violence and a repressive management model in many U.S. correctional facilities.

Sykes, Gresham M. *Society of Captives: A Study of a Maximum Security Prison.* Princeton, N.J.: Princeton University Press, 1958. Presents findings of a classic sociological study of maximum security prisons, including organizational dysfunction in prison administration and the norms and language of prison subculture.

Teeters, Negley K. *The Cradle of the Penitentiary: The Walnut Street Jail at Philadelphia, 1773–1835.* Philadelphia: Pennsylvania Prison Society, 1955. Presents a historical overview of the Walnut Street jail in Philadelphia, Pennsylvania, and the influence of Quakers in the development and operation of the facility.

———. *They Were in Prison: A History of the Pennsylvania Prison Society 1787–1937.* Chicago: John C. Winston, 1937. Chronicles the development of the Pennsylvania systems and compares the Pennsylvania and Auburn systems using excerpts from prison records.

Teeters, Negley K., and John D. Shearer. *The Prison at Philadelphia, Cherry Hill: The Separate and Solitary System of Penal Discipline, 1829–1913.* New York: Columbia University Press for Temple University Publications, 1957. Scholarly discussion of the effectiveness of the strict work program and the policy of solitary confinement utilized at the Cherry Hill prison in Philadelphia, Pennsylvania.

Unseem, Bert, and Peter Kimball. *State of Siege: U.S. Prison Riots, 1971–1986.* New York: Oxford University Press, 1989. Discusses five significant riots at U.S. prisons from 1971 to 1986, beginning with the inmate uprising at the New York state prison at Attica in 1971. Also discussed are prison riots in Illinois, Michigan, New Mexico, and West Virginia, including analyses of the causes of the riots.

Unseem, Bert, et al. *Resolution of Prison Riots: Strategies and Policies.* New York: Oxford University Press, 1996. Examines the causes of inmate uprisings in U.S. prisons nationwide and discusses managerial policies aimed at reducing the tensions that lead to prison riots.

Welch, Michael. *Corrections: A Critical Approach.* New York: McGraw-Hill, 1995. Presents an overview of corrections in the United States, including a social history of punishment and incarceration and a discussion of prison violence, the death penalty, and alternatives to imprisonment.

Wicker, Tom. *Time to Die*. New York: Times Books, 1975. Eyewitness account by reporter and writer Tom Wicker of the riot at the state prison at Attica, New York, including a discussion of the negotiations between inmates and prison officials during the siege.

Williamson, Harold E. *The Corrections Profession*. Newbury Park, Calif.: Sage Publications, 1990. Presents an overview of the professional roles in corrections and discusses career preparation, the tasks of various corrections professionals, and the working environment in correctional settings.

Wines, Frederick Howard. *Punishment and Reformation: A Study of the Penitentiary System*. New York: Thomas Y. Crowell Company, 1910. A discussion of the benefits of inmate reformation and rehabilitation, based on a series of lectures given by the author during the 1890s at the University of Wisconsin.

Yackle, Larry W. *Reform and Regret: The Story of Federal Judicial Involvement in the Alabama Prison System*. New York: Oxford University Press, 1989. Discusses prison reform in the Alabama state prison system as the result of the intervention of state and federal courts.

ARTICLES AND PAPERS

Alarcon, Francisco J. "Juvenile Corrections: Why Would Anyone Want to Work in This Business?" *Corrections Today* 66 (February 2004): 8. Presents an assessment of working conditions in juvenile corrections, including training to enhance career development and the rewards of working restorative justice-based programs with the goal of addressing the needs of juvenile offenders and their victims.

Anderson, James F., et al. "Alabama Prison Chain Gangs: Reverting to Archaic Punishment to Reduce Crime and Discipline Offenders." *Western Journal of Black Studies* 24 (Spring 2000): 9. Discusses the revival of the use of prison chain gangs by the Alabama Department of Corrections as a means to address inmate disciplinary problems and as a deterrent for future criminal behavior.

Blakely, Curtis R., and Vic W. Bumphus. "Private and Public Sector Prisons: A Comparison of Select Characteristics." *Federal Probation* 68 (June 2004): 27. Presents findings of a study that examined and compared the correctional ideologies of private and public prisons in their treatment of inmates. According to the article, private prisons had higher incidents of violence and a greater proportion of drug-involved inmates, despite the fact that more serious and dangerous offenders were housed in public prisons.

Prisons

Branson, Helen K. "Random Drug Testing of Staff." *Corrections Technology & Management* 4 (March/April 2000): 30. Describes drug testing policies and procedures in the Hawaii and Idaho state departments of corrections and discusses the issue of smuggling drugs into correctional settings by corrections staff.

Brown, Sammie. "Are Prison Classification Systems Addressing the Diverse Inmate Population?" *Corrections Today* 64 (June 2002): 104. Discusses the development of comprehensive objective inmate classification systems to allow correctional agencies to manage diverse inmate populations.

Caeti, Tory J. "Management of Juvenile Correctional Facilities." *Prison Journal* 83 (December 2003): 383. Presents findings of a survey of correctional facility directors on managerial issues in juvenile corrections, including the implementation of treatment and rehabilitation programs.

Carlson, Joseph R., et al. "Cross-Gender Perceptions of Corrections Officers in Gender-Segregated Prisons." *Journal of Offender Rehabilitation* 39 (2004): 83. Presents findings of a study that examined the perceptions of male and female correctional officers on the acceptance of officers of the opposite gender. According to the article, acceptance of female correctional officers was high among male officers working in male prisons, and female officers perceived their male counterparts as more competent at supervising and counseling both female and male prisoners.

Eigenberg, Helen M. "Correctional Officers' Definitions of Rape in Male Prisons." *Journal of Criminal Justice* 28 (September/October 2000): 435. Presents findings of a 1991 survey of corrections officers in which most officers reported that they believed claims of violent rape or sexual assault under threat of violence but tended to discount other forms of coercion that resulted in sexual assaults by prisoners.

Finn, Peter. "Addressing Correctional Officer Stress: Programs and Strategies." *Issues and Practices in Criminal Justice* 18 (December 2000): 11. Discusses widespread job-related stress reported by corrections officers nationwide and the sources and ill effects of such stress.

Freeman, Robert M. "Social Distance and Discretionary Rule Enforcement in a Women's Prison." *Prison Journal* 83 (June 2003): 191. Examines the attitudes of male and female corrections officers in women's prisons and presents findings that corrections officers tend to exert broader discretion in enforcing prison rules in women's prisons than they do in men's prisons.

Glick, Barry. "Revitalizing Louisiana's Juvenile Justice System." *Juvenile Justice Update* 10 (February/March 2004): 1. Assesses reforms within the juvenile correctional system in Louisiana that were instituted in 1999 to ensure that adequate institutional programs and services were provided to wards.

Annotated Bibliography

Hall, Daniel E., et al. "Suing Cops and Corrections Officers: Officer Attitudes and Experiences about Civil Liability." *Policing: An International Journal of Police Strategies & Management* 26 (2003): 529. Presents findings of a study to determine if experience, rank, and education were significant factors in the frequency and nature of employment-related lawsuits filed against police and corrections officers.

Hemmens, Craig, and Mary K. Stohr. "Correctional Staff Attitudes Regarding the Use of Force in Corrections." *Corrections Management Quarterly* 5 (Spring 2001): 27. Presents findings of a survey of corrections officers on how they view the use of force in correctional settings, including the tendency by younger corrections officers to favor the use of force more than corrections officers with moderate to extensive experience working in correctional settings.

Hensley, Christopher. "Possible Solutions for Preventing Inmate Sexual Assault: Examining Wardens' Beliefs." *American Journal of Criminal Justice* 27 (2002): 19–33. Presents findings of a survey of opinions by U.S. prison wardens about the effectiveness of correctional policies, staff training, and staff supervision on the incidence of sexual assaults among inmates. Includes statistics on male-to-male prisoner sexual assault from 1968 to 2002 and female-to-female prisoner sexual assault from 1995 to 2002.

Hensley, Christopher, et al. "The Evolving Nature of Prison Argot and Sexual Hierarchies." *Prison Journal* 83 (September 2003): 289. Presents findings of a survey of Oklahoma state prisoners on changes in the jargon and hierarchy related to sexual activity among inmates, with the focus of assisting prison staff in better understanding the prison subculture and discerning potential threats of sexual violence.

Hill, Cece. "Survey Summary: Correctional Officers." *Corrections Compendium* 29 (July/August 2004): 10. Presents the results of a national survey on correctional officers in the United States and Canada for 2003 on recruitment, staff retention, educational levels, wages, and benefits.

Kifer, Misty, et al. "Goals of Corrections: Perspectives from the Line." *Criminal Justice Review* 28 (Spring 2003): 47. Examines corrections officers' attitudes on four key issues: retribution, deterrence, incapacitation, and rehabilitation.

Man, Christopher D., and John P. Cronan. "Forecasting Sexual Abuse in Prison: The Prison Subculture of Masculinity as a Backdrop for Deliberate Indifference." *Journal of Criminal Law and Criminology* 44 (Fall/Winter 2002): 308. Presents findings of a review of legal actions against prisons by sexually assaulted inmates in which deliberate indifference was demonstrated by prison staff and correctional agencies who failed to protect inmates who were at risk for sexual assault or to thoroughly investigate incidents of sexual assault and punish the perpetrators.

Prisons

McCarthy, Bernard J., and Laurie A. Gould. "E-Government and Corrections: An Analysis of Correctional Web Sites." *Corrections Compendium* 28 (October 2003): 6. Presents findings of a 2002 survey of state and federal corrections agency web sites and offers recommendations for improving the web sites of corrections agencies.

Moore, Ernie. "Common Sense Approach to Staff Safety." *Corrections Today* 66 (July 2004): 72. Discusses issues of correctional staff safety, as identified by a staff analysis of safety issues in work areas of Ohio state prisons.

Myers, David L., and Randy Martin. "Community Member Reactions to Prison Siting: Perceptions of Prison Impact on Economic Factors." *Criminal Justice Review* 29 (Spring 2004): 115. Examines factors that could potentially have an impact on a community where a new prison is built, with a focus on property values, the local economy, and the cost of living.

National Institute of Corrections. "Corrections Employment Eligibility for Ex-Offenders." Report, September 2002. Presents findings of a survey of the federal Bureau of Prisons, state departments of corrections nationwide, and Canadian departments of corrections on the practice of hiring corrections staff members with criminal records and discusses the eligibility of ex-offenders in each jurisdiction.

New York State Department of Correctional Services. "Psychological Screening Program for Correction Officer Applicants, 2001." Report, 2001. Describes New York State's psychological screening program for applications for the position of corrections officer in 2001, including an overview of the screening process and a detailed description of the evaluation process.

O'Donnell, Ian. "Prison Rape in Context." *British Journal of Criminology* 44 (2004): 241. Explores possible reasons for the higher incidence of inmate-to-inmate prison rape in U.S. prisons than in prisons in the United Kingdom. Among factors discussed are the greater levels of violence in American society, racial tensions in prison, and correctional staff training and supervision.

Pizarro, Jesenia, and Vanja M. K. Stenius. "Supermax Prisons: Their Rise, Current Practices, and Effect on Inmates." *Prison Journal* 84 (June 2004): 248. Examines the development of the super maximum security prison, also known as the supermax, explains how supermax prisons differ from other prisons, and examines their potential impact on inmate populations confined in supermax prisons in the United States. According to the article, supermax prisons share certain defining features, including the confinement of inmates in their cells for 22 to 23 hours per day with limited human contact.

Potok, Mark. "Behind the Wire." *Intelligence Report* 100 (Fall 2000): 24. Examines documented cases and allegations of racism and violence directed at inmates by corrections officers in state departments of corrections nationwide.

Reynolds, Carl. "The Final Chapters of *Ruiz v. Estelle.*" *Corrections Today* 64 (June 2002): 108. Discusses how the handwritten lawsuit originally filed in 1972 by Texas state inmate David Ruiz against the Texas Department of Corrections turned into one of the most far-reaching cases on the reform of prison conditions nationwide.

Reza, J. D. "Do You Know Where Your Offenders Are?" *Law Enforcement Technology* 31 (June 2004): 118. Discusses the use of biometrics, radio frequency transmitters, and global positioning satellite technology to track offenders in correctional facilities and under community supervision.

Riley, Frank E., and Beverly A. Wilder. "Hiring Correctional Staff with the Right Stuff." *Corrections Today* 64 (June 2002): 88. Examines the characteristics of individuals who choose to work in corrections, including interpersonal communication skills, flexibility, and level of intelligence.

Scott, Mike. "Inmate Health Care." *Law and Order* 52 (August 2004): 116. Discusses possible reasons for the increase in inmate health-care costs and suggests cost-reducing strategies.

Sproule, Charles F., and Stephen Berkley. "Selection of Entry-Level Corrections Officers: Pennsylvania Research." *Public Personnel Management* 30 (Fall 2001): 377. Examines the evolution over a period of 20 years of procedures to assess candidates for positions as entry-level corrections officers in the Pennsylvania Department of Corrections.

Turner, Allan. "More Terrorists, Less Resources: Confronting One of the Most Critical Challenges in Corrections History." *Corrections Today* 66 (July 2004): 52. Discusses the need for corrections facilities to implement programs and policies aimed at countering the recruitment of terrorists inside prisons and to prevent terrorist attacks inside prisons.

Warren, Jenifer. "Prisons Promise a New Code for Guards." *L.A. Times* September 13, 2004, p. A1. Discusses efforts by the California Department of Corrections to overhaul its internal disciplinary system due to the failure of the system to curb corruption and misconduct among some corrections officers.

———. "Youth Prisons to Stop Use of Extended Isolation." *L.A. Times* 39 (August 5, 2004): 1A. Reports on the decision by the California Youth Authority, an agency of the California Department of Corrections, to discontinue the use of special housing units called SHU units, which were previously used to house disruptive juvenile offenders in total isolation for up to 23 hours a day.

Watson, Belinda. "Work Force Issues and Trends in Corrections." *Corrections Today* 66 (February 2004): 82. Describes programs by the National

Institute of Corrections to assist in the recruitment and retention of the corrections staff.

Wright, Lester N., and M. Kay Northrup. "Examining the Health Risks for Corrections Professionals." *Corrections Today* 63 (October 2001): 106. Describes health risks for corrections professionals and discusses how security precautions and protective equipment that are intended to protect corrections officers are sometimes undermined by poor eating habits, lack of physical exercise, and ineffective stress management.

WEB DOCUMENTS

Bauer, Lynn, and Steven D. Owens. "Justice Expenditures and Employment in the United States, 2001." *Bulletin*, Bureau of Justice Statistics, May 2004. Available online. URL: http://www.ojp.usdoj.gov/bjs/pub/pdf/jeeus01.pdf. Presents a statistical overview of state and federal justice-related expenditures in 2001, including corrections. Provides state-by-state data on the amount of expenditures and offers comparisons to expenditures in 2001 and in previous years.

Blumstein, James F., and Mark C. Cohen. "Interrelationship Between Public and Private Prisons: Does the Existence of Prisoners under Private Management Affect the Rate of Growth in Expenditures on Prisoners under Public Management?" Report, Association for Private Correctional and Treatment Organizations, April 2003. Available online. URL: http://www.apcto.org/logos/study.pdf. Examines the economic impact on public prisons that house some inmates in privately operated correctional facilities. Includes findings from a three-year study from 1999 to 2001 showing that states that housed less than 20 percent of prisoners in private facilities had a 12.5 percent growth in per capita prison costs, compared with a 5.9 percent growth in per capita prison costs in states that housed at least 20 percent of their prison population in private facilities.

Bureau of Justice Statistics (BJS). "The Prison Rape Elimination Act: A Status Report from BJS." *Justice Research and Statistics Association Forum* 22 (March 2004): 1. Available online. URL: http://www.jrsa.org/pubs/forum/forum_issues/for22_1.pdf. Discusses issues relating to the implementation of the 2003 Prison Rape Elimination Act, including the Bureau of Justice Statistics' mandate to collect and disseminate data on the incidence of rape and sexual assault in U.S. prisons.

Duff, Marc C. "Corrections Privatization Generates Savings and Better Service." *Wisconsin Interest* 12 (Winter 2003): 12. Available online. URL: http://www.wpri.org/wiinterest/vol12no1/duff12.1.pdf. Discusses the economic impact of the 254 percent increase in the number of Wisconsin state prisoners from 1992 to 2000 and corrections privatization as a possible way to ease the state's costs of incarceration.

GRACE Project. *End-of-Life Care in Corrections: A Handbook for Caregivers and Managers.* Alexandria, Va.: Volunteers of America, 2001. Available online. URL: http://www.graceprojects.org/graceprojects/resources.htm. Presents an overview of end-of-life care in prisons and jails and offers guidelines for establishing and improving programs in correctional settings for elderly and dying inmates.

———. "Incarceration of the Terminally Ill: Current Practices in the United States." Report, Volunteers of America, 2001. Available online. URL: http://www.graceprojects.org/graceprojects/resources.htm. Presents a brief overview on the rise in the prisoner population nationwide, with emphasis on the increase in older and terminally ill inmates who require palliative care in correctional settings.

———. "Standards of Practice for End-of-Life Care in Correctional Settings." Report, Volunteers of America, 2001. Available online. URL: http://www.graceprojects.org/graceprojects/resources.htm. Discusses the criteria and practices of comprehensive palliative care programs in correctional settings.

Hanser, Robert D. "Labeling Theory as a Paradigm for the Etiology of Prison Rape: Implications for Understanding and Intervention." *Professional Issues in Counseling: Online Journal* (Summer 2002): 11. Available online. URL: http://www.shsu.edu/~piic/summer2002/Hanser.htm. Discusses how prison rape differs from rape in society and examines techniques for therapists to assist victims of prison rape and sexual assault.

King, Ryan S., et al. "Big Prisons, Small Towns: Prison Economics in Rural America." Report, The Sentencing Project, February 2003. Available online. URL: http://www.soros.org/initiatives/justice/articles_publications/publications/bigprisons_20030201. Reports on the impact of prison construction in rural America as a result of the building boom in state and federal correctional facilities that began in the 1980s to cope with the rising prison population in the United States. The report provides statistical analysis of the impact of prison construction on small town and rural areas as measured by various factors, including job creation and property values. Also provided are accounts of enticements offered to corrections agencies by local municipalities in order to encourage prison construction in their areas.

Lawrence, Sarah, and Jeremy Travis. "The New Landscape of Imprisonment: Mapping America's Prison Expansion." Research Report, Urban Institute Justice Policy Center, April 2004. Available online. URL: http://www.urban.org. Presents an overview of the overall growth in the number of prisons between 1979 and 2000, including statistics on the state-by-state rate of growth in the number of new correctional facilities, and assesses the impact of newly built correctional facilities on local communities.

Linke, Larry. "Inmate Sexual Assault: An Overview of Selected Print and Electronic Resources." National Institute of Corrections, 2003. Available online. URL: http://www.nicic.org/pubs/2003/018794.pdf. Presents an overview of research on prison rape. Includes links to the Prison Rape Elimination Act of 2003 and summaries of research finding on the incidence of rape and sexual assault in U.S. prisons.

Mariner, Joanne. "No Escape: Male Rape in U.S. Prisons." Human Rights Watch, 2001. Available online. URL: http://www.hrw.org/reports/2001/prison/report.html. Extensive report on male inmate-on-inmate sexual abuse in U.S. prisons. Includes a summary of research findings, recommendations for reform, and firsthand accounts by sexually victimized prisoners.

McDonald, Douglas, and Carl Patten. "Governments' Management of Private Prisons." Report, National Institute of Justice, January 2004. Available online. URL: http://www.ncjrs.org/pdffiles1/nij/grants/203968.pdf. Examines the management of private prisons by state and federal governments in the United States and by private firms under contract to state and federal correctional agencies. Topics include the prevalence of contracting of private prisons, payment structures, performance standards, state and federal monitoring, and case studies of prison privatization in Florida, Oklahoma, and Texas.

Sarabi, Brigette, and Edwin Bender. "Prison Payoff: The Role of Politics and Private Prisons in the Incarceration Boom." Report, Western Prison Project, November 2000. Available online. URL: http://www.tgsrm.org/pdfdocs/privatization%20of%20prisons%20-%20profit.pdf. Discusses strategies by private corrections firms to promote their services, including the use of political campaign contributions to state legislators, by developing model legislation and publicity campaigns that promote prison construction as a cost-effective means of enhancing public safety.

Sickmund, Melissa. "Juvenile Residential Facility Census, 2000: Selecting Findings." National Report Series, Office of Juvenile Justice and Delinquency Prevention, December 2002. Available online. URL: http://www.ncjrs.org/html/ojjdp/nrs_bulletin/nrs_2002_12_1/contents.html. Reports on findings of the Juvenile Residential Facility Census, a biennial census instituted in 2000 by the Office of Juvenile Justice and Delinquency Prevention. Includes statistical overviews of juvenile facilities nationwide and offenders under 21 years of age confined in private and publicly operated residential facilities. Also reported are deaths of juveniles in custody during the 12 months prior to the census-taking.

Stephan, James J. "State Prison Expenditures, 2001." Report, Bureau of Justice Statistics, June 2004. Available online. URL: http://www.ojp.usdoj. gov/bjs/pub/pdf/spe01.pdf. Presents and analyzes comparative data on the cost of operating state prisons nationwide.

Stephan, James J., and Jennifer C. Karberg. "Census of State and Federal Correctional Facilities, 2000." Report, Bureau of Justice Statistics, October 15, 2003. Available online. URL: http://www.ojp.usdoj.gov/bjs/ abstract/csfcf00.htm. Five-year census provides information on facilities, inmates, programs, and staff of state and federal correctional facilities nationwide, including private correctional facilities housing state or federal inmates. Provides comparisons to statistics gathered in 1995 for the previous census-taking of correctional facilities in the United States.

Toone, Robert E. "Protecting Your Health and Safety: A Litigation Guide for Inmates." Southern Poverty Law Center, 2002. Available online. URL: http://www.splcenter.org/legal/publications/pub.jsp. Provides guidelines for inmates representing themselves in legal actions to address grievances including excessive force by correctional staff, deliberate indifference to protecting inmates from assault by other inmates, inadequate medical care, and substandard conditions of confinement.

U.S. Bureau of Prisons. "Prison Rape: A Selected Bibliography." Central Office Library, 2004. Available online. URL: http://www.nicic.org/pubs/ 2004/019587.pdf. Lists of videos, web sites, books, reports, and articles dealing with the issue of prisoner rape and sexual assault.

108th U.S. Congress. "Prison Rape Elimination Act of 2003." Available online. URL: http://frwebgate.access.gpo.gov/cgi-bin/getdoc.cgi?dbname= 108_cong_public_laws&docid=f:publ079.108.pdf" Presents the Prison Rape Elimination Act of 2003, as passed by the 108th U.S. Congress. The act, which provides for the analysis of the incidence and effects of prison rape in federal, state, and local correctional institutions and mandates federal funding to protect prisoners from the threat of rape, was signed into law on September 4, 2003, by President George W. Bush.

U.S. Department of the Interior. "Neither Safe Nor Secure: An Assessment of Indian Detention Facilities." Report, Office of the Inspector General, September 2004. Available online. URL: http://www.oig.doi.gov/ main.php?menuid=0&approve=Y. Reports on conditions in Indian jails and detention facilities in the United States, which in 2002 held some 2,080 inmates. Among myriad problems discussed in the report was the failure to segregate juveniles and adults in some detention centers.

Wool, Jon, and Don Stemen. "Changing Fortunes or Changing Attitudes? Sentencing and Corrections Reforms in 2003." Available online. URL:

http://www.vera.org/publication_pdf/226_431.pdf. Reviews changes in state sentencing and corrections policies in 2003 and discusses those changes that represent a shift in corrections ideology. The report focuses on the increase in support for early release programs and new approaches for sanctioning technical violators of parole probation, each of which represented a departure from the "get tough" policy that was prevalent in corrections prior to 2003.

Classification, Treatment, and Parole

BOOKS

Alexander, Jack A., and James Austin. *Handbook for Evaluating Objective Prison Classification*. Washington, D.C.: National Institute of Corrections, 1992. A discussion of inmate classification systems and recommendations for improvement.

American Correctional Association. *Classification: A Tool for Managing Today's Offenders*. Laurel, Md.: American Correctional Association, 1993. A collection of 10 articles on effective inmate classification programs.

Braithwaite, Ronald L., et al. *Prisons and AIDS: A Public Health Challenge*. San Francisco: Jossey-Bass, 1996. Discusses the prevalence of HIV and AIDS in the U.S. prison population from a public health perspective, including the implementation of education and AIDS-prevention correctional programs.

Cavender, Gary. *Parole: A Critical Analysis*. Port Washington, N.Y.: Kennikat Press, 1982. Presents a historical overview of the development of parole in U.S. correctional systems, with emphasis on the modern use of parole as a rehabilitative tool.

Champion, Dean J. *Probation, Parole, and Community Corrections, Fourth Edition*. Upper Saddle River, N.J.: Prentice Hall, 2002. Presents the roles of probation and parole in the U.S. criminal justice system and describes probation and parole agency personnel and operations in the adult and juvenile justice systems. Chapters address such topics as a description of the components of the U.S. criminal justice system, the role of community corrections, the distinction between probation and parole, the philosophy and functions of parole, the nature of parolees, prerelease programs, and parole revocation.

Earley, Kevin E., ed. *Drug Treatment Behind Bars: Prison-Based Strategies of Change*. Westport, Conn: Praeger, 1996. Presents essays by mental health practitioners in drug treatment and therapy programs in correctional settings and includes a discussion of the impact of substance abuse on recidivism.

Flanagan, Timothy J., et al., eds. *Incarcerating Criminals: Prisons and Jails in Social and Organizational Context.* New York: Oxford University Press, 1998. Presents essays on the environments within U.S. correctional facilities, including staffing and programming, classification, treatment, and social control.

Freedman, Estelle B. *Maternal Justice: Miriam Van Waters and the Female Reform Tradition.* Biography of Miriam Van Waters (1887–1974), whose efforts to reform women's prisons and the juvenile justice system resulted in her appointment in 1932 as the superintendent of the Massachusetts Reformatory for Women.

Gelsthorpe, Loraine, and Nicola Padfield, eds. *Exercising Discretion: Decisionmaking in the Criminal Justice System and Beyond.* Portland, Ore.: Willan Publishing, 2003. Presents essays on the exercise of discretion in the administration of the criminal justice system in the United States, including judicial discretion in sentencing, the use of discretion by corrections staff, and the discretionary release of certain types of inmates, including violent offenders and the mentally ill.

Glaser, Daniel. *Preparing Convicts for Law-Abiding Lives: The Pioneering Penology of Richard A. McGee.* Albany: State University of New York Press, 1995. Discusses the work of Richard McGee, former director of the California Department of Corrections who promoted the rehabilitation of inmates. During his tenure, McGee provided drug treatment services in correctional settings and instituted conjugal visits at California state prisons.

Harden, Judy, and Marcia Hills, eds. *Breaking the Rules: Women in Prison and Feminist Therapy.* Binghamton, N.Y.: Haworth Press, 1998. Presents essays by authors in the fields of psychology, criminology, sociology, and women's studies on services and treatment programs in correction settings for female inmates. Includes a discussion of the experiences of women prisoners, including childhood sexual abuse, and issues relating to motherhood during their incarceration.

Inciardi, James A., ed. *Drug Treatment and Criminal Justice.* Newbury Park, Calif.: Sage Publications, 1993. Anthology of 11 articles on drug treatment programs for criminal offenders, with emphasis on new approaches to drug treatment in criminal justice settings.

Kratcoski, Peter C., ed. *Correctional Counseling and Treatment.* Prospect Heights, Ill.: Waveland Press, 1994. Various contributors discuss treatment programs available in U.S. prisons and factors that contribute to the success of treatment, including the role of inmate classification in properly identifying the needs of inmates and the role of the prison environment and correctional officers' characteristics in facilitating effective treatment in correctional settings.

Kupers, Terry A. *Prison Madness: The Mental Health Crisis Behind Bars and What We Must Do about It.* San Francisco: Jossey-Bass Publishers, 1999. Analysis of the treatment of mentally ill inmates in which the author, a physician, argues that prisons are warehousing and mistreating large numbers of mentally ill inmates and that prison management policies are traumatizing formerly normal prisoners and making them angry, violent, and vulnerable to severe emotional problems.

Lester, David, et al. *Correctional Counseling.* Cincinnati: Anderson Publishing Company, 1992. Presents an overview of counseling in a correctional setting, including discussions of inmate classification systems, individual and group treatment methods, and the effectiveness of treatment in prison.

Leukefeld, Carl G., and Frank M. Tims, eds. *Drug Abuse Treatment in Prisons and Jails.* Rockville, Md.: National Institute on Drug Abuse, 1992. Presents an overview of drug abuse treatment programs in correctional settings, including evaluations on the efficacy of certain types of substance abuse treatment and recommendations for new approaches to drug abuse treatment in U.S. prisons and jails.

Maletzky, Barry. *Treating the Sexual Offender.* Newbury Park, Calif.: Sage Publications, 1991. Presents an overview of therapeutic techniques for the treatment of sexual offenders in correctional and non-correctional settings.

McShane, Marilyn D. *Community Corrections.* New York: Macmillan, 1993. Presents an overview of community corrections in the United States and discusses interstate compact agreements for criminal offenders who commit crimes outside of their state of origin.

Morris, Norval, and Michael Tonry. *Between Prison and Probation: Intermediate Punishments in a Rational Sentencing System.* New York: Oxford University Press, 1990. Discusses the current sentencing structure in the United States and the need to include other means of punishment in addition to the common alternatives of probation and prison.

Newman, Graeme. *Just and Painful: A Case for the Corporal Punishment of Criminals.* Riverside, N.J.: Macmillan, 1983. A discussion of the possible use of corporal punishment as an alternative to imprisonment for nonviolent criminal offenders and the selective use of incarceration for only violent or habitual offenders.

Pisciotta, Alexander W. *Benevolent Repression: Social Control and the American Reformatory-Prison Movement.* New York: New York University Press, 1994. Presents a historical analysis of the adult reformatory movement in the United States, with the focus on the reform efforts of Zebulon Brockway, the chief administrator at the Elmira reformatory in New York from 1876 to 1920.

Pollack, Jocelyn M. *Counseling Women in Prison.* Thousand Oaks, Calif.: Sage Publications, 1998. Discusses treatment and counseling in correctional settings for female inmates and the importance of addressing factors in the female inmate's background, including drug abuse and cultural issues.

Rafter, Nicole Hahn. *Creating Born Criminals.* Urbana: University of Illinois Press, 1997. Discusses the history of biological theories of crime and their impact on the U.S. prison system in terms of the classification and treatment of inmates. Includes a discussion of eugenics, a popular 19th-century theory that blamed criminal behavior on bad breeding and the commonly held belief in the mid-19th century that the mentally retarded were inherently prone to criminal behavior.

Rhine, Edward E., et al. *The Practice of Parole Boards.* Lexington, KY.: Association of Paroling Authorities International, 1994. Presents findings of a study of the function of parole boards in prisons nationwide, including the role of the victim in the parole process and issues concerning adequate parole supervision.

Scholoegel, Judith M., and Robert L. Kinast. *From Cell to Society.* Grand Rapids, Mich.: W. B. Eerdmans Publishing, 1988. Analysis of the Liberation of Ex-Offenders Through Employment Opportunities program (LEEO) in Washington, D.C., to facilitate the reintegration of criminal offenders in society.

Simon, Jonathan. *Poor Discipline: Parole and the Social Control of the Underclass, 1890–1990.* Chicago: University of Chicago Press, 1993. Presents a historical overview of the parole system in the United States and discusses the disciplinary, clinical, and managerial models for parole.

Toch, Hans, and Kenneth Adams. *The Disturbed Violent Offender.* New Haven, Conn.: Yale University Press, 1989. Discusses the connection between mental illness and criminal violence among inmates in the New York state prison system in 1985.

Travis, Jeremy, and Michelle Waul, eds. *Prisoners Once Removed: The Impact of Incarceration and Reentry on Children, Families, and Communities.* Washington, D.C.: Urban Institute Press, 2003. Each chapter addresses an issue related to the impact of imprisonment on families and communities, including the impact of imprisonment on larger social networks linked to families of prisoners, parenting while incarcerated, and the special problems of the adolescent children of prison inmates.

ARTICLES AND PAPERS

Austin, James, and Patricia L. Hardyman. "Risks and Needs of the Returning Prisoner Population." *Review of Policy Research* 21 (January 2004): 13.

Prisons

Presents a general discussion of the risks and needs of inmates who are reentering communities and focuses on the special challenges faced by inmates with children who attempted to maintain a parental relationship while incarcerated in prison.

Brown, Devon, et al. "Outcome Research as an Integral Component of Performance-Based Offender Treatment." *Corrections Compendium*, 29 (July/August 2004): 1. Presents findings of a study of prisoners in the New Jersey Department of Corrections on the usefulness of treatment in a correctional setting.

Chappell, Cathryn A. "Post-Secondary Correctional Education and Recidivism: A Meta-Analysis of Research Conducted 1990–1999." *Journal of Correctional Education* 55 (June 2004): 148. Presents findings of a study to gather evidence establishing a link, if any, between higher education programs in prison and recidivism. Among the findings: There was a 22 percent rate of recidivism among inmates who participated in postsecondary correctional education courses, compared to a 41 percent rate of recidivism among inmates who did not participate in postsecondary educational programs in prison.

Cheakalos, Christina. "New Leash on Life." *Smithsonian* 35 (August 2004): 62. Presents an overview of the program Puppies Behind Bars (PBB), in which selected state prison inmates in New York, New Jersey, and Connecticut train dogs to determine their potential to serve as seeing-eye dogs for the blind. PBB began in 1997 at the Bedford Hills Correctional Center, a maximum security prison for women in Westchester County, New York.

Clemetson, Lynette. "Links Between Prison and AIDS Affecting Blacks Inside and Out." *New York Times*, August 6, 2004, p. 6. Examines the impact of human immunodeficiency virus (HIV) infection of prison inmates and the impact on society when inmates are released from prison, with a focus on African Americans.

Duncombe, Betsy. "Compassion Is at the Core of Prison Program in Hawaii." *Offender Programs Report* 8 (May/June 2004): 1. Describes the Free Inside program, established in 2003 to provide weekly yoga and meditation exercises to prisoners and staff at the Maui Community Correctional Center, based on the success of a similar program in Indian prisons. The article discusses research evidence that supports the use of yoga and meditation to facilitate better physical health, reduce anxiety, and as an adjunct to successful substance-abuse treatment.

Fretz, Ralph, et al. "Outcome Research as an Integral Component of Performance-Based Offender Treatment." *Corrections Compendium* 29 (July/August 2004): 1. Presents findings of a study of New Jersey state inmates by the New Jersey Department of Corrections on the usefulness of correctional treatment. Among the findings: New Jersey state inmates who received treatment had a significantly lower recidivism rate than inmates who did not receive treatment. In addition, the rates of rearrest for the New Jersey state inmates who received corrections-based treatment were significantly lower than the national average of the rate of recidivism.

Garcia, Crystal A. "Realistic Expectations: Constructing a Mission-Based Evaluation Model for Community Corrections Programs." *Criminal Justice Policy Review* 15 (September 2004): 251. Discusses the need for a standardized mission-based evaluation model to test if programs achieve their goals in order to reduce recidivism and costs.

Gumz, Edward J. "American Social Work, Corrections and Restorative Justice: An Appraisal." *International Journal of Offender Therapy and Comparative Criminology* 48 (August 2004): 449. Presents an overview of the role of social work in U.S. corrections and discusses the recent decline of social work in correctional settings and its potential effectiveness in restorative justice models in the United States and Europe.

Hochstetler, Andy, et al. "Damaged Goods: Exploring Predictors of Distress in Prison Inmates." *Crime and Delinquency* 50 (July 2004): 436. Presents findings of a study on inmate victimization and discusses the economically and socially disadvantaged circumstances that are present in the backgrounds of many prison inmates, including violence, substance abuse, and mental illness.

Humphries, Kermit. "Transition from Prison to the Community." *Corrections Today* 66 (August 2004): 16. Provides an overview of the Transition From Prison to the Community Initiative (TPCI), which was developed in 2001 by the National Institute of Corrections as a model for inmate transition to the community.

Hynes, Charles J. "Prosecution Backs Alternative to Prison for Drug Addicts." *Criminal Justice* 19 (Summer 2004): 28. Presents an overview of the Drug Treatment Alternative-to-Prison (DTAP) program, a diversion treatment program targeting nonviolent, repeat felony offenders with serious drug addictions. According to the article, two key premises behind DTAP are that the criminal recidivism of addicts can be reduced if the addiction is treated, and legal coercion can be utilized to motivate addicts to succeed in treatment and rehabilitation.

Immarigeon, Russ. "Reexamining Public Opinion and Its Impact on Community Corrections." *Community Corrections Report* 11 (July/August 2004): 55. Examines the use and influence of opinion polls in measuring public attitudes on criminal justice issues, with emphasis on the issues of punishment and community corrections.

Kovandzic, Tomislav V., et al. "When Prisoners Get Out: The Impact of Prison Releases on Homicide Rates, 1975–1999." *Criminal Justice Policy*

Review 15 (June 2004): 212. Presents findings of a study on whether the release of prisoners has any impact on homicide rates in the United States, based on data from 46 state departments of corrections and the Federal Bureau of Investigation. According to the article, the study findings failed to establish a significant nexus between prisoner releases and homicide rates.

Lovell, David, et al. "Evaluating the Effectiveness of Residential Treatment for Prisoners with Mental Illness." *Criminal Justice and Behavior* 28 (February 2001): 83. Presents findings of a study of inmates in residential program for the mentally ill in Washington state prisons. According to the article, inmates in the program were placed on medication, had their medication monitored to ensure compliance, and received training to help cope with life in prison. Among the findings: Participants were significantly less symptomatic when they left the program than when they entered, there were significant reductions in staff assaults and infractions and higher rates of work and school participation.

McCollister, Kathryn E., et al. "Long-Term Cost Effectiveness of Addiction Treatment for Criminal Offenders." *Justice Quarterly* 21 (September 2004): 659. Reports on the findings of a study that evaluated the cost-effectiveness of two in-prison therapeutic after-care programs in southern California, as measured by the length of time inmates were reincarcerated for criminal offenses or technical parole violations arising out of substance abuse.

Metraux, Stephen, and Dennis P. Culhane. "Homeless Shelter Use and Reincarceration Following Prison Release." *Criminology and Public Policy* 3 (March 2004): 139. Reports on the findings of a study examining the links between homeless shelter use and reincarceration among some 48,424 former inmates released between 1995 and 1998 from New York state prisons to New York City. Among the findings: Within two years of release, some 11.4 percent of former inmates entered a New York City homeless shelter, and 32.8 percent of those were subsequently reincarcerated in state prison.

Mountjoy, John J. "Drug Courts: Making Prison Sentences a Thing of the Past?" *Spectrum: The Journal of State Government* 72 (Winter 1999): 2. Discusses the increasing use of drug courts as an alternative to prison for certain drug offenders in the United States.

Nolan, Pat. "Prepared to Reenter Society?" *Law and Order* 52 (May 2004): 90. Describes the features and evaluates the efficacy of the InnerChange Freedom Initiative, a faith-based corrections program introduced in Texas state prisons in 1997 and later in Kansas, Iowa, and Minnesota state correctional facilities. Participating inmates receive biblical-based education and are required to work. In the final six months of the program, inmates must perform community service outside of prison.

Annotated Bibliography

Osofsky, Michael J. "Revolutionizing the Prison Hospice: The Interdisciplinary Approach of the Louisiana State Penitentiary at Angola." *Corrections Compendium* 29 (July/August 2004): 5. Presents an overview of the prison hospice program in the Louisiana state penitentiary at Angola, where in 2004 some 5,100 inmates were incarcerated, 94 percent of whom were expected to die in prison as the result of the length of their sentences. According to the article, the hospice program's goals included providing quality end-of-life care that addresses the patient's needs holistically, including the physical, social, spiritual, and emotional aspects of illness and dying.

Prendergast, Michael L., et al. "Reducing Substance Use in Prison: The California Department of Corrections Drug Reduction Strategy Project." *Prison Journal* 84 (June 2004): 265. Reports on the management and efficacy of the California Department of Corrections' Drug Reduction Strategy Project, which included random urine testing and drug interdiction programs in California state prisons.

Richards, Stephen C., et al. "Kentucky's Perpetual Prisoner Machine: It's about Money." *Review of Policy Research* 21 (January 2004): 93. Presents findings on the effectiveness of the Kentucky parole system, based on interviews with parolees released. The interviews, conducted in May and September 2002, revealed a lack of effective prison programs, the release of inmates with little or no money, problems with finding employment upon release, mistrust of parole officers, the need for protection from petty parole violations, the loss of credit for good time served on parole, and a lack of economic resources.

Schram, Pamela J. "Management Strategies When Working with Female Prisoners." *Women & Criminal Justice* 15 (2004): 25. Presents findings of a national survey that identified how the needs of female prison inmates differed from those of male inmates, based on data from 96 correctional administrators in women's prisons nationwide.

Scott, Mike. "Inmate Health Care." *Law and Order* 52 (August 2004): 116. Discusses possible reasons for the increase in inmate health-care costs and suggests strategies for reducing such costs. According to the article, rising health-care costs among prison inmates are largely the result of the general aging of the inmate population, inflation in the medical services industry, and an increase in the number of inmates with drug-related conditions, including the human immunodeficiency virus (HIV), tuberculosis, and kidney disease. Suggested strategies to reduce health-care costs in prisons include privatizing health-care services and establishing medical facilities within prisons as an alternative to costly hospital visits.

Seager, James A. "Refusers, Dropouts, and Completers: Measuring Sex Offender Treatment Efficacy." *International Journal of Offender Therapy and Comparative Criminology* 48 (October 2004): 600. Reports on findings of

207

a study measuring the effectiveness of a corrections-based sex-offender treatment program by comparing the two-year recidivism rates of inmates who completed the program and those who did not complete the program. Among the findings: Inmates who did not complete the program reoffended after release from prison at a rate six times higher than inmates who completed the program.

Severance, Theresa A. "Concerns and Coping Strategies of Women Inmates Concerning Release: It's Going to Take Somebody in My Corner." *Journal of Offender Rehabilitation* 38 (2004): 73. Presents findings of a study of 40 adult female inmates in the Ohio Reformatory for Women on their concerns and plans after release from prison. Among the findings: Inmates were primarily concerned about their basic survival needs after release, including sources of income, employment, and housing. Other concerns were relapse and recidivism, relationships with children, and community acceptance.

U.S. Departments of Justice and Labor. "Report of the Reentry Policy Council: Charting the Safe and Successful Return of Prisoners to the Community." Report, National Institute of Justice, 2004. Describes the goals of the Reentry Policy Council (RPC), established by the Council of State Governments to develop programs that assist reentering prisoners with housing and employment opportunities while promoting public safety.

Welsh, Wayne N., and Gary Zajac. "Building an Effective Research Partnership Between a University and a State Correctional Agency: Assessment of Drug Treatment in Pennsylvania Prisons." *Prison Journal* 84 (June 2004): 143. Examines a project to develop a collaborative research partnership between the Center for Public Policy at Temple University and the Pennsylvania Department of Corrections to develop effective substance abuse treatment and drug intervention programs in correctional settings.

Williford, Miriam, ed. *Higher Education in Prison: A Contradiction in Terms?* Phoenix, Ariz.: Oryx Press, 1996. Presents findings of a survey of some 300 prison educational programs serving some 50,000 U.S. inmates nationwide and suggests reforms for educational programs in correctional settings.

Wright, Richard. *In Defense of Prisons.* Westport, Conn.: Greenwood Press, 1993. Defends the use of incarceration as punishment and an effective means of crime deterrence and presents research findings that prisons are at least moderately effective in deterring crime.

WEB DOCUMENTS

Anno, B. Jaye, et al. "Correctional Health Care: Addressing the Needs of Elderly, Chronically Ill, and Terminally Ill Inmates." Report, Criminal

Justice Institute, Inc., February 2004. Available online. URL: http://www. cji-inc.com. Presents an overview of effective correctional health-care programs and addresses corrections-related issues, including the management and housing of inmates with special needs, cost containment of health care for such inmates, and staff training to better respond to the needs of special populations in correctional settings.

Beck, Allen J., and Laura Maruschak. "Hepatitis Testing and Treatment in State Prisons." Special Report, Bureau of Justice Statistics, April 2004. Available online. URL: http://www.ojp.usdoj.gov/bjs/abstract/httsp.htm. Presents an overview of policies by state and federal correctional agencies for testing and treatment for hepatitis C and vaccinations for hepatitis B. This report includes statistical data on the number of hepatitis C tests conducted in U.S. prisons as of June 30, 2000, including confirmed positive results and the number of inmates infected with hepatitis C who were under treatment.

Bobbitt, Mike, and Marta Nelson. "Front Line: Building Programs That Recognize Families' Role in Reentry." Report, New York Division of Parole and the Vera Institute of Justice, September 2004. Available online. URL: http://www.vera.org/publication_pdf/249_476.pdf. Examines correctional programs nationwide aimed at facilitating the successful reentry of inmates in the community after release from prison through family involvement in the reentry process.

Caliber Associates. "Navigating a New Horizon: Promising Pathways to Prisoner Reintegration." Report, U.S. Department of Health and Human Services, 2004. Available online. URL: http://www.calib.com/ home/work_samples/files/kairosissuebriefii.pdf. Examines the Kairos Horizon faith-based residential rehabilitation program and its impact on successful prisoner reintegration into the community.

———. "Prisoner Reentry, Religion and Research." Report, U.S. Department of Health and Human Services, 2004. Available online. URL: http://www.calib.com/home/work_samples/files/kairosissuebriefi.pdf. Discusses the role of the faith-based prisoner reentry programs nationwide and cites empirical evidence suggesting that religious beliefs reduce reoffending and recidivism among released prisoners.

The Fortune Society, Inc. "The Fortune Academy: Housing for Homeless Ex-Prisoners from Dream to Reality." Report, 2002. Available online. URL: http://www.ojp.usdoj.gov/eows/pdftxt/facasestudy.pdf. Describes a residential facility in West Harlem, New York, for recently released inmates returning to the New York City area. In 2002 the facility housed 59 former prison inmates, with 18 beds designated for returning inmates who would otherwise be homeless upon release from prison and 41 beds reserved for longer-term housing of former inmates, generally from six to

18 months. The population was largely African American and Latino and included a high prevalence of HIV-infected inmates who reported high levels of substance abuse prior to incarceration.

Gagliardi, Barbara. "Corrections-Based Services for Victims of Crime." Report, National Institute of Corrections, August 2004. Available online. URL: http://www.nicic.org. Presents findings of a survey of state departments of corrections on services provided by departments of corrections to crime victims. Among the findings: Some 62 percent of correctional agencies participate in victim services initiatives, while 98 percent provide victim notification services, 80 percent offer programs for inmates on issues related to victims of crime, and 56 percent of corrections agencies received grant funding for the statewide victim services and support programs.

Glaze, Lauren E. "Probation and Parole in the United States, 2003." *Bulletin*, Bureau of Justice Statistics, August 2004. Available online. URL: http://www.ojp.usdoj.gov/bjs/abstract/ppus03.htm. Provides statistics on individuals on probation and parole in the United States at year-end 2003 and offers comparisons to the number of probationers and parolees in 1995 and 2002 at year's end. The report identifies states with the largest and smallest parole and probation populations, states with the largest and smallest rates of community supervision, and states with the largest increases. Demographic characteristics of probationers and parolees in 2003 is also provided, as are the rates of successful completion and violation of probation and parole in the United States.

Idaho State Legislative Office of Performance Evaluations. "Programs for Incarcerated Mothers." Report, February 2003. Available online. URL: http://www2.state.id.us/ope/reports/rept0301.pdf. Reviews corrections-based programs for incarcerated mothers and their children in the Idaho state prisons. According to the article, some 70 percent of females in Idaho state prisons are mothers.

La Vigne, Nancy G., et al. "Portrait of Prisoner Reentry in Ohio." Report, The Urban Institute, November 2003. Available online. URL: http://www.urban.org/uploadedpdf/410891_ohio_reentry.pdf. Presents findings on Ohio state prison inmates released in 2001, including their demographic characteristics, the nature of the offenses for which they were incarcerated, the length of time served in prison, and the economic and social conditions of neighborhoods that they returned to, with emphasis on areas in and around Cleveland, Ohio, which were the destinations of some 79 percent of Ohio state inmates released in 2001.

Lowden, Kerry, et al. "Evaluation of Colorado's Prison Therapeutic Community for Sex Offenders: A Report of Findings." Report, National Institute of Justice, July 2003. Available online. URL: http://dcj.state.

210

co.us/ors/pdf/docs/webtcpart1.pdf. Presents findings and recommendations from an evaluation of the Colorado Department of Corrections sex
offender therapeutic community and the sex offender treatment and
monitoring program. The therapeutic community (TC) was created in
1993 within the Colorado Department of Corrections to implement
promising emergent strategies and programs for the treatment and management of sex offenders and substance abusers. Inmates enrolled in TC,
who were first required to complete a minimum of six months of psycho-
educational group sessions in the sex offender treatment and monitoring
programs, were less likely to be rearrested than inmates who did not participate in the TC program, according to the article.

Maruschak, Laura M. "HIV in Prisons, 2001." *Bulletin*, Bureau of Justice
Statistics, January 2004. Available online. URL: http://www.ojp.usdoj.
gov/bjs/abstract/hivp01.htm. Provides a statistical overview of the number of U.S. prison inmates infected with the human immunodeficiency
virus (HIV) in 2001, including active AIDS cases among prisoners held in
each state and the federal prison system at year-end. The report includes
data on the number of AIDS-related deaths among prisoners, rates of infection among male and female inmates, and statistical comparisons to
the rates of HIV infection in the general population. Historical comparisons of AIDS cases among prison inmates in 1991 and 1995 are also provided in the report.

McKean, Lise, and Charles Ransford. "Current Strategies for Reducing Recidivism." Report, Developing Justice Coalition, August 2004. Available online. URL: http://www.impactresearch.org/documents/recidivismfullreport.
pdf. Examines programs in state departments of corrections nationwide that
were cited by multiple sources as being effective in reducing recidivism. The
article cited as among the most promising: Drug courts and mandatory substance-abuse treatment, educational programs, and job preparedness and career development programs in correctional settings.

Minnesota Department of Corrections. "Symposium on Offenders with
Mental Illness: Understanding and Hope." Report, 2002. Available online.
URL: http://www.doc.state.mn.us/publications/pdf/mhsproceedings.pdf.
Summarizes the proceedings of the Symposium on Offenders with Men-
tal Illness: Understanding and Hope, cosponsored on January 25, 2002, by
the Minnesota Department of Corrections and Human Services.

National Center on Addiction and Substance Abuse at Columbia University. "Crossing the Bridge: An Evaluation of the Drug Treatment Alternative-to-Prison (DTAP) Program." Report, March 2003. Available
online. URL: http://www.casacolumbia.org/pdshopprov/files/crossing_
the_bridge_march2003.pdf. Discusses the DTAP Program in Brooklyn,
New York, a residential treatment program that is available to drug

sellers, unlike many similar programs that are available only to drug users. According to the article, participants in the program receive 15 to 24 months of intensive drug counseling and vocational training, and approximately 52 percent graduate from the program. Among preliminary findings: DTAP graduates were more than three times more likely to be employed than they were before arrest and entrance into the program. The average cost for a participant in DTAP was $32,975, compared to an average cost of $64,338 for imprisonment, according to the article.

National Institute of Corrections. "Corrections Agency Collaborations with Public Health." Report, September 2003. Available online. URL: http://www.nicic.org/Downloads/pdf/2003/019101.pdf. Reports on findings of a survey conducted in 2003 by the National Institute of Corrections on the use of public health agencies by corrections agencies to assist in the diagnosis and treatment of medical and mental health problems among state and federal inmates.

———. "Transition from Prison to Community Initiative." Report, 2004. Available online. URL: http://www.nicic.org/pubs/2002/017520.pdf. Presents an overview of the Transition from Prison to Community Initiative (TPCI), developed by the National Institute of Corrections to assist states in facilitating successful transitions for offenders into the community.

Pelissier, Bernadette, and Gerry G. Gaes. "United States Federal Prisons: Drug Users, Drug Testing, and Drug Treatment." *Forum on Corrections Research* 1 (September 2001): 15. Available online. URL: http://www. csc-scc.gc.ca/text/pblct/forum/index_e.shtml. Discusses the extent of drug abuse among inmates in federal prisons administered by the Bureau of Prisons (BOP) between 1990 and 1999 and describes drug-testing procedures used by the BOP and drug treatment programs available to federal inmates.

Travis, Jeremy, et al. "Portrait of Prisoner Reentry in New Jersey." Report, The Urban Institute, November 2003. Available online. URL: http://www.urban.org/uploadedpdf/410899_nj_prisoner_reentry.pdf. Examines prisoner reentry in New Jersey, including the characteristics of returning inmates, their geographic distribution, and the social and economic climates of the communities of returning prisoners released from New Jersey state prisons in 2002. Findings were based on data from the Bureau of Justice Statistics, the New Jersey Department of Corrections, the New Jersey State Parole Board, the New Jersey State Police, the Juvenile Justice Commission, and the U.S. Census Bureau.

Trusty, Brittani, and Michael Eisenberg. "Initial Process and Outcome Evaluation of the InnerChange Freedom Initiative: The Faith-Based Prison Program in Texas Department of Criminal Justice." Report, Texas

Annotated Bibliography

Criminal Justice Policy Council, February 2003. Available online. URL: http://www.cjpc.state.tx.us/reports/adltrehab/ifiinitiative.pdf. Presents an overview of the InnerChange Freedom Initiative (IFI), a faith-based, pre-release program operated since 1997 by Prison Fellowship Ministries in the Carol Vance Unit of the Texas Department of Criminal Justice. According to the article, IFI consists of a three-phase program in which inmates participate for 16 to 24 months while incarcerated and continue for six to 12 months after release, focusing on biblical education, life skills, and community service.

Visher, Christy, et al. "Baltimore Prisoners' Experiences Returning Home." Report, The Urban Institute, March 2004. Available online. URL: http://www.urban.org/uploadedpdf/310946_baltimoreprisoners.pdf. Presents findings of a study based on interviews of some 324 family members of prison inmates returning to the area in and around Baltimore, Maryland. Among the study's findings: Returning inmates who found employment after release did so as the result of personal connections and were more likely to have participated in work-release jobs while incarcerated; most returning inmates were clustered in a few neighborhoods with high levels of social and economic disadvantage; younger returning inmates with substance abuse in their families and among their friends were more likely to use drugs after release; and returning inmates who participated in substance-abuse treatment while in prison were less likely to use drugs after release than those who did not participate in such corrections-based programs.

Watson, Jamie, et al. "Portrait of Prisoner Reentry in Texas." Report, The Urban Institute, March 2004. Available online. URL: http://www.urban.org/uploadedpdf/410972_tx_reentry.pdf. Discusses the process of prisoner reentry in Texas and presents the characteristics and demographic distribution of the inmates released from Texas state prisons in 2001, their preparation for release, post-release supervision, and the social and economic environments in the neighborhoods of returning prisoners.

Wilkinson, Reginald A., and Gregory A. "Prison Reform Through Offender Reentry: A Partnership Between Courts and Corrections." Report, Ohio Department of Rehabilitation and Correction, October 2003. Available online. URL: http://www.drc.state.oh.us/web/articles/article93.htm. Describes the Ohio Plan for Productive Offender Reentry and Recidivism Reduction, developed as a strategy of collaboration between courts, corrections, and community agencies to promote successful offender reentry into the community after imprisonment. The program identified several key factors related to the outcome of offender reentry, including psychological and educational assessment of the reentering offender, family involvement in the reentry process, and employment training and job search skills.

Wynn, Jennifer R., et al. "Mental Health in the House of Corrections: A Study of Mental Care in New York State Prisons." Report, Correctional Association of New York. Available online, June 2004. URL: http://www.correctionalassociation.org/mental-health.pdf. Presents findings of a study of mental health care in New York state prisons. Among the findings: From 1991 to 2004, there was a 71 percent increase in mentally ill inmates in New York state prisons, leaving many correctional facilities understaffed and unprepared to provide adequate treatment and housing to mentally ill offenders.

Prisoners, Inmates' Rights, and Sentencing

BOOKS

Abbott, Jack. *In the Belly of the Beast: Letters from Prison.* New York: Vintage Books/Random House, 1991. Chronicles the author's life in prison as culled from letters written by the author to writer Norman Mailer. The letters to Mailer include an account of Abbott's childhood, his experiences in juvenile correctional facilities from the age of 12, and the impact of imprisonment as an adult on Abbott.

American Correctional Association. *The Female Offender: What Does the Future Hold?* Washington, D.C.: St. Mary's Press, 1990. Presents findings of the Task Force Study of Female Offenders by the American Correctional Association to determine the correctional needs for the rising number of female prisoners nationwide.

Andrews, D. A., and James Bonta. *The Psychology of Criminal Conduct.* Cincinnati: Anderson Publishing Company, 1994. Presents a general theory of the psychological underpinnings of criminal conduct.

Baunach, Phyllis Jo. *Mothers in Prison.* New Brunswick, N.J.: Transaction Press, 1985. Examines correctional programs that allow inmate mothers to maintain contact with their children during incarceration. Includes a discussion of the effects of the separation on incarcerated mothers and their children.

Bedau, Hugo Adam. *The Death Penalty in America.* New York: Oxford University Press, 1982. Presents historical, sociological, psychological, legal, and political analysis of capital punishment in the United States, including a discussion of landmark rulings on the death penalty by the U.S. Supreme Court.

Bloom, Barbara E., and David Steinhart. *Why Punish the Children? A Reappraisal of the Children of Incarcerated Mothers in America.* San Francisco: National Council on Crime and Delinquency, 1993. Presents findings of research on the increasing trend of female incarceration and its impact on inmate mothers and their children.

Bowers, William J., et al. *Legal Homicide: Death as Punishment in America: 1864–1982.* Boston: Northeastern University Press, 1984. Historical overview of capital punishment in the United States from 1864 to 1982, including a detailed analysis of the 1972 decision by the U.S. Supreme Court in *Furman v. Georgia.*

Bowker, Lee H. *Prison Victimization.* New York: Elsevier North-Holland, 1980. Presents an overview of the victimization of inmates in prison, including the physical and psychological damage experienced by both inmates and staff as the result of such victimization.

Carlen, Pat, and Anne Worrall. *Analysing Women's Imprisonment.* Portland, Ore.: Willan Publishing, 2004. Introductory text for students analyzes key issues associated with increases in the number of women in prison in the United Kingdom and throughout the world, with the intent of exploring prison issues in general and the historical and contemporary politics of gender and penal justice.

Center for Constitutional Rights and the National Lawyers Guild. *The Jailhouse Lawyer's Handbook: How to Bring a Federal Lawsuit to Challenge Violations of Your Rights in Prison, Fourth Edition.* New York: Center for Constitutional Rights, 2003. Available online. URL: http://www. jailhouselaw.org. Handbook provides a primer on prisoners' rights and how to file a lawsuit. Chapters address topics including the Prison Litigation Reform Act, filing lawsuits in appropriate jurisdictions, how to conduct legal research, legal forms and motion writing, and significant case law and constitutional amendments.

Champion, Dean J., and G. Larry Mays. *Transferring Juveniles to Criminal Courts: Trends and Implications for Criminal Justice.* New York: Praeger, 1991. Presents a comprehensive overview of the legal mechanism by which juveniles are transferred to criminal court and tried as adults. Describes various types of transfers.

Chaneles, Sol, and Cathleen Burnett, eds. *Older Offenders: Current Trends.* New York: Haworth Press, 1989. Provides an overview of issues relating to older offenders in correctional settings, including a discussion of the common motivations for crimes by older offenders and factors to be considered in the treatment and housing of such offenders in prison.

Cummins, Eric. *The Rise and Fall of California's Radical Prison Movement.* Stanford, Calif.: Stanford University Press, 1994. Presents a history of the so-called radical prison movement in California and discusses the influences of groups, including the Black Panther Party and the Symbionese Liberation Army, and state inmates who were active in the movement, including Caryl Chessman, Eldridge Cleaver, and George Jackson.

Davidson, R. Theodore. *Chicano Prisoners: The Key to San Quentin.* New York: Holt, Rinehart and Winston, 1974. Presents findings of an anthropological study of prisoners at California's San Quentin state prison, with the focus on the subculture of Chicano inmates, including the violence suffered by Chicano inmates and their lack of participation in prison programs.

DeRosia, Victoria R. *Living Inside Prison Walls: Adjustment Behavior.* Westport, Conn.: Praeger, 1998. Presents findings of a study of New York state prisoners comparing the adjustment of inmates with low social status prior to incarceration to that of inmates who earned college degrees and were successfully employed prior to their imprisonment.

Earle, Wilton. *Final Truth: The Autobiography of Mass Murderer/Serial Killer Donald "Pee Wee" Gaskins.* Atlanta: Adept, 1992. Presents the life story of serial killer Donald Gaskins and his motives for his crimes, as told to the author.

Eisenberg, James R. *Law, Psychology, and Death Penalty Litigation.* Sarasota, Fla.: Professional Research Press, 2004. Examines the role of forensic psychology in death penalty trials. Includes a discussion on the historical and legal issues related to capital punishment in the United States.

Elias, Stephen, and Susan Levinkind. *Legal Research: How to Find and Understand the Law.* 4th ed. Berkeley, Calif.: Nolo Press, 1995. A study guide for the legal novice on how to conduct legal research. Includes photographs of legal texts to assist in locating them in a law library.

Fleisher, Mark S. *Beggars and Thieves: Lives of Urban Street Criminals.* Madison: University of Wisconsin Press, 1995. Examines the lives of criminal offenders before and after imprisonment. Includes a bibliography and a glossary of slang terms.

Fletcher, Beverly R., et al. *Women Prisoners: A Forgotten Population.* Westport, Conn.: Praeger, 1993. Presents findings of a longitudinal study of recidivism of female inmates at two correctional facilities in Oklahoma.

Fleury-Steiner, Benjamin. *Jurors' Stories of Death: How America's Death Penalty Invests in Inequality.* Ann Arbor: University of Michigan Press, 2004. Presents the views of jurors who served in death-penalty trials on the effect of race on the sentencing process. Among the author's findings are that jurors who view themselves as more moral than the defendant often have difficulty examining complex mitigating evidence for the defense

Freedman, Estelle B. *Their Sisters' Keepers: Women's Prison Reform in America: 1830–1930.* Ann Arbor: University of Michigan Press, 1981. Presents

findings of a study of female prisoners in the 19th century, including an
analysis of the first state prisons designed exclusively for women.

Gabel, Katherine, and Denise Johnston. *Children of Incarcerated Parents.* New
York: Free Press, 1997. Discusses the impact of incarceration on the children of prisoners, including children who are born in prison and separated
from their mothers or provided with long-term care in prison nurseries.

Giallombardo, Rose. *Society of Women: A Study of Women's Prison.* New York:
John Wiley and Sons, 1966. Discusses correctional institutions for
women from a sociological perspective, including the effects of prisonization on female inmates.

Girshick, Lori B. *Soledad Women: Wives of Prisoners Speak Out.* Westport,
Conn.: Praeger, 1996. Examines the impact of incarceration on the
spouses of inmates based on interviews with the wives of some 25 prisoners incarcerated at the California state prison at Soledad.

Harris, Jean. *They Always Call Us Ladies: Stories from Prison.* New York: Scrib-
ner, 1988. Firsthand account of an inmate's experience at the Bedford Hills
correctional facility in New York State, including a history of the prison.

Harris, Mary B. *I Knew Them in Prison.* New York: Viking Press, 1942. Autobiography that focuses on Harris's work in penology, including her
tenure as warden at the Federal Industrial Institution for Women in
Alderson, West Virginia.

Hassine, Victor. *Life Without Parole: Living in Prison Today.* Los Angeles:
Roxbury Publishing Company, 1996. Describes adapting to prison life,
prison subculture, living conditions, prison violence, and the underground prison economy. Written by an inmate at the state correctional
institution at Graterford, Pennsylvania, who in 1981 was convicted of
murder and sentenced to life in prison without the possibility of parole.

Head, Ian, and Rachel Meeropol. *The Jailhouse Lawyer's Handbook.* 4th ed.
Center for Constitutional Rights and the National Lawyers' Guild, 2003.
Presents an overview of inmate rights in the form of a manual designed
to assist prisoners in the filing of court actions. Includes guidelines on the
drafting of legal documents.

Hemmens, Craig, et al. *Criminal Justice Case Briefs: Significant Cases in Corrections.* Los Angeles: Roxbury Publishing Company, 2004. Presents
briefings on important Supreme Court cases on issues including sentencing, the death penalty, access to courts, conditions of confinement, inmate
medical care, due process, parole, and the Prison Litigation Reform Act.
A section on case holdings offers a short synopsis of one or two sentences
for each case that is briefed in the book. Each chapter is devoted to a single issue, such as sentencing or due process, and includes a brief introduction that provides an overview of that issue.

Hersokowitz, Suzan. *Legal Research Made Easy.* Clearwater, Fla.: Sphinx Publications, 1995. Straightforward and streamlined guide for the legal novice on how to conduct legal research and identify legal issues.

Howard, Clark. *American Saturday.* New York: Richard Marek Publisher, 1981. Presents a detailed account of events leading to the death of inmate George Jackson on August 21, 1971, at San Quentin state prison in California.

Jackson, Bruce, and Diane Christian. *Death Row.* Boston: Beacon Press, 1980. Presents interviews with 26 male inmates on death row in Texas and prison staff assigned to the death row unit. Discusses daily life on death row and the psychological impact of a death sentence on condemned prisoners and their families.

Jackson, George. *Soledad Brother.* New York: Coward McCann, 1979. A collection of letters written by inmate George Jackson while incarcerated in California state prisons. Initially sentenced to serve one year to life for stealing $70 from a gas station, Jackson was convicted of killing a correctional officer while in prison. In 1971 Jackson was killed at San Quentin state prison in what was considered to be an act of retaliation for the correctional officer's death.

Johnson, Robert. *Condemned to Die: Life under Sentence of Death.* Prospect Heights, Ill.: Waveland Press, 1989. Describes life on death row, based on interviews of some 35 death row inmates in Alabama.

———. *Death Work.* Pacific Grove, Calif.: Brooks/Cole Publishing Company, 1990. Provides an overview of capital punishment in the United States and discusses the impact of stress on death row inmates and corrections personnel who work on death row units.

Kalinich, David B. *The Inmate Economy.* Lexington, Mass.: Lexington Books, 1980. Analysis of the markets for contraband in prisons based on data from state prisons in Michigan.

McCarthy, Belinda Rodgers, and Robert Langworthy, eds. *Older Offenders: Perspectives in Criminology and Criminal Justice.* New York: Praeger, 1988. Presents articles by 12 researchers who have studied the effects of confinement on older prison inmates.

Moyer, Imogene. *The Changing Roles of Women in the Criminal Justice System.* Prospect Heights, Ill.: Waveland Press, 1992. Examines characteristics of female prisoners based on race and other factors.

Muraskin, Roslyn, and Ted Alleman. *Women and Justice.* Englewood Cliffs, N.J.: Prentice Hall, 1993. Presents an overview of females in the criminal justice system and discusses factors including abortion, drug abuse, AIDS, and violence on the rising number of female prisoners.

O'Shea, Kathleen. *Women and the Death Penalty in the United States, 1900–1998.* Westport, Conn.: Praeger, 1998. Discusses the legal history

218

of capital punishment in the United States and methods of execution and includes interviews of female death row inmates awaiting execution, some of whom were subsequently put to death.

Pollock-Byrne, Joycelyn M. *Women, Prison and Crime.* Pacific Grove, Calif.: Brooks/Cole Publishing Company, 1990. A discussion of issues relating to female prisoners, including female criminality, a history of women's prisons in the United States, rehabilitative approaches to female inmates, and legal issues faced by female inmates.

Rafter, Nicole Hahn. *Partial Justice: Women in State Prisons, 1888–1935.* Boston: Northeastern University Press, 1985. Examines the state of women's prisons in the United States during the late 19th and early 20th centuries, based on data from national surveys of correctional institutions for women only. Includes demographic characteristics and the criminal offense statistics for some 4,600 female inmates.

Rideau, Wilbert, and Ron Wikberg. *Life Sentences: Rage and Survival Behind Bars.* New York: Times Books, 1992. A discussion of criminal sentencing, with emphasis on capital punishment and life without possibility of parole, based on a review of the literature and interviews with inmates. Written by two inmates at the Louisiana state prison at Angola.

Seymour, Cynthia B., and Creasie Finney Hairston, eds. *Children with Parents in Prison: Child Welfare Policy, Program, and Practice Issues.* New Brunswick, N.J.: Transaction Publishers, 2001. Presents an overview and selected issues on the problems faced by the nearly two million children in the United States with an imprisoned mother or father.

Shakur, Sanyika. *The Autobiography of an L.A. Gang Member.* New York: Penguin, 1993. Firsthand account of a gang member who, while incarcerated in California state prisons, became a proponent of black nationalism.

Shook, Chadwick L., and Robert T. Sigler. *Constitutional Issues in Correctional Administration.* Durham, N.C.: Carolina Academic Press, 2000. Presents briefs of landmark Supreme Court cases on corrections-related issues and includes discussions of significant issues, including the evolution of prisoners' rights, the impact of the Prison Litigation Reform Act, constitutional issues related to private prisons, and the involuntary civil commitment of sex offenders.

Simon, Rita J., and Heather Heitfield. *Crimes Women Commit: The Punishments They Receive.* Lexington, Mass.: Lexington Books, 2004. Examines social, economic, and environmental factors in the lives of females who commit crimes, based on 25 years of demographic data on female prisoners nationwide.

Stanton, Ann M. *When Mothers Go to Jail.* Lexington, Mass: Lexington Books, 1980. Discussion of problems that arise when incarcerated mothers are separated from their children.

Thomas, Jim. *Prisoner Litigation: The Paradox of the Jailhouse Lawyer.* Totowa, N.J.: Rowman and Littlefield, 1988. Discusses the work of prisoners who serve as legal counsel to themselves and other inmates and their role in the rising number of lawsuits brought against prisons and correctional agencies.

Toch, Hans. *Living in Prison: The Ecology of Survival.* New York: Free Press, 1977. Classic examination of how male inmates adjust to the stresses of prison life, including firsthand accounts by prisoners.

Trombley, Stephen. *The Execution Protocol: Inside America's Capital Punishment Industry.* New York: Crown, 1992. Chronicles the life and death of an inmate at the Potosi Correctional Center in Missouri from his sentencing to his execution.

Walens, Susann. *War Stories: An Oral History of Life Behind Bars.* Westport, Conn.: Praeger, 1997. Profiles 15 inmates confined in U.S. maximum security prisons.

Watterson, Kathryn. *Women in Prison: Inside the Concrete Womb.* Boston: Northeastern University Press, 1996. Discusses personal experiences of women in prison, including the trauma of separation from their children, the process of developing relationships in a prison setting, and the stress caused by the prospect of returning to society after release from prison.

Wolfgang, Marvin E., et al. *Delinquency in a Birth Cohort.* Chicago: University of Chicago Press, 1972. Classic work presents findings of a longitudinal study of juvenile delinquency among a cohort of males born in 1945 in Philadelphia, Pennsylvania. Using data from school, police, and selective service records, the study found that some 35 percent of the cohort group were identified as being involved in some type of delinquent behavior and that 6 percent of the cohort group accounted for most of the delinquent behavior.

Zehr, Howard. *Doing Life: Reflections on Men and Women Serving Life Sentences.* Intercourse, Pa.: Good Books, 1996. A discussion of the effectiveness of victim-offender reconciliation programs by the director of the Mennonite Central Committee's U.S. Office on Crime and Justice. Includes some 60 interviews of male and female inmates who discuss the impact of their criminal offenses on victims, the community, and the families of prisoners.

ARTICLES AND PAPERS

Alexander, Rudolph, Jr. "The United States Supreme Court and the Civil Commitment of Sex Offenders." *Prison Journal* 84 (September 2004):

361. Presents analyses of four significant court cases from 1940 to 2002 in which the U.S. Supreme Court ruled on the constitutionality of civil commitment for sex offenders to mental institutions. The four cases examined are *Pearson v. Probate Court of Ramsey County* (1940), *Kansas v. Hendricks* (1997), *Seling v. Young* (2001), and the 2002 case *Kansas v. Crane.*

Allender, David M., and Frank Marcell. "Career Criminals, Security Threat Groups, and Prison Gangs: An Interrelated Threat." *FBI Law Enforcement Bulletin* 72 (June 2003): 8. Examines the threats to correctional security posed by career criminals and prison gangs, including the failure to respect personal boundaries, disdain for authority, and the use of physical and psychological coercion to gain power.

Ammar, Nawal H., et al. "Muslims in Prison: A Case Study from Ohio State Prisons." *International Journal of Offender Therapy and Comparative Criminology* 48 (August 2004): 414. Presents findings of a study of Muslim male inmates in 30 Ohio state prisons between 1999 and 2000 to determine their characteristics, patterns of identification with Islam, religious behavior inside the prisons, and the relationship, if any, between their conversion to Islam and the crime for which they were sent to prison.

Beck, Allen J., et al. "Implementing the 2003 Prison Rape Elimination Act in Juvenile Residential Facilities." *Corrections Today* 66 (July 2004): 26. Reports on measures undertaken by the U.S. Justice Department's Bureau of Justice Statistics (BJS) to implement the provisions of the 2003 Prison Rape Elimination Act (PREA) in juvenile residential facilities. Under PREA, the BJS was mandated to institute a new national data collection system on the incidence and prevalence of rapes and sexual assault within all correctional facilities nationwide.

Belbot, Barbara. "Report on the Prison Litigation Reform Act: What Have the Courts Decided So Far?" *Prison Journal* 84 (September 2004): 290. Reviews significant court cases addressing the provisions of the Prison Litigation Reform Act (PRLA), which was enacted in 1996 by the U.S. Congress in response to concerns over the amount of prisoner litigation, and the involvement of the federal courts in the operations of state prison systems. The article is divided into two sections. Part one discusses court cases that have interpreted those parts of the PRLA aimed at reducing the amount of prisoner litigation, while part two reviews court cases that have interpreted the intent of the PRLA to curtail federal court intervention in state prisons.

Buell, Maureen. "Children of Inmates: An Issue for Criminal Justice." *Corrections Today* 66 (June 2004): 12. Discusses the Children of Prisoners initiative by the National Institute of Corrections to utilize private sector or nonprofit organizations to administer programs to assist the minor children of prisoners.

Bushfield, Suzanne. "Fathers in Prison: Impact of Parenting Education." *Journal of Correctional Education* 55 (June 2004): 104. Presents findings of a study on the short-term impact of parenting education on fathers in prison who were enrolled in a 30-day parenting class. Among the findings: While prisoners who attended parenting classes expressed that they were motivated to be good fathers to their children, most reported difficulty in maintaining contact with their children while in prison.

Center for Effective Public Policy. "The Prison Rape Elimination Act of 2003: Summary of Focus Group Discussion Points." Report, Bureau of Justice Assistance, March 25, 2004. Discusses key points developed by a focus group of researchers, correctional administrators, and mental health experts that was formed to advise the Bureau of Justice Statistics on effective data gathering on prison rape and sexual abuse, as mandated under the Prison Rape Elimination Act of 2003.

Devanney, Joe, and Diane Devanney. "Keeping Kosher." *Law and Order* 9 (May 2004): 96. Discusses the ruling in April 2002 by the 10th Circuit Court of Appeals that the Colorado Department of Corrections must provide kosher meals to inmates who adhere to the dietary commandments followed by orthodox Jews, without any co-payment from the Jewish inmates. The article analyzes the ruling, which was based on the U.S. Supreme Court decision in *Turner v. Safley* (1987), in which the Court set forth the following four-pronged criteria for deciding such issues: whether a rational basis exists between the policy and a governmental interest, whether alternative ways of enforcing the policy exist, what would be the effect on the prison of allowing a prisoner to exercise the right at issue, and whether there are alternatives that accommodate the inmate's right.

Fortune, Sandra H. "Prison Gang Leadership: Traits Identified by Prison Gangsters." *Journal of Gang Research* 11 (Summer 2004): 25. Discusses the traits characteristic of prison gang leaders, based on data from interviews with prison gang leaders in the Northeast Correctional Complex in Johnson County, Tennessee. According to the article, gang leaders serve as a role model of commitment to gang rules and gang life and use coercion and their status to impose their will on the gang's rank and file members.

Goodrum, Sarah, et al. "Urban and Rural Differences in the Relationship Between Substance Use and Violence." *International Journal of Offender Therapy and Comparative Criminology* 48 (October 2004): 613. Reports on findings of a study of 637 male inmates in Kentucky state prisons with a history of substance abuse and violence, grouped into two categories:

those from rural Appalachian regions and those from non-rural localities with populations of 50,000 or more.

Greene, Judith A. "Positive Trends in State-Level Sentencing and Corrections Policy." Report, Families Against Mandatory Minimums, November 2003. Reviews sentencing laws nationwide and examines trends in reforming so-called tough-on-crime sentencing laws, including eliminating mandatory sentencing laws, returning discretion in sentencing to judges, rolling back habitual offender statutes, diverting nonviolent drug offenders to treatment, increasing earned-time credits for prison inmates who participate in corrections-based programs, revising parole standards, and instituting alternatives to imprisonment for technical parole violations.

Gross, Samuel R., and Phoebe C. Ellsworth. "Second Thoughts: Americans' Views on the Death Penalty at the Turn of the Century." Report, Committee on Law and Justice Death Penalty Seminar, July 2004. Examines changing views on capital punishment, including findings that suggest a decline of support for the death penalty in the United States since 1996.

Haapasalo, Jaana, and Juha Moilanen. "Official and Self-Reported Childhood Abuse and Adult Crime of Young Offenders." *Criminal Justice and Behavior* 31 (April 2004): 127. Reports on the findings of a research study to determine the link, if any, between adult criminal behavior of young male prison inmates and childhood mistreatment, based on self-reporting and corresponding official records. Among the findings: Inmates whose self-reported childhood maltreatment corresponded to official documentation of the maltreatment offended at a higher rate than other inmates.

Hensley, Christopher, and Richard Tewksbury. "Inmate-to-Inmate Prison Sexuality: A Review of Empirical Studies." *Trauma, Violence, & Abuse* (July 2002): 226. Reviews research on inmate sexual behavior and sexual dynamics in correctional institutions and presents findings on the incidence of consensual sex and sexual assault among prisoners.

Hensley, Christopher, et al. "Characteristics of Prison Sexual Assault Targets in Male Oklahoma Correctional Facilities." *Journal of Interpersonal Violence* 18 (June 2003): 595. Presents findings of a survey of some 174 Oklahoma state prison inmates, 14 percent of whom reported begin sexually targeted by other prisoners.

———. "Inmate-to-Inmate Sexual Coercion in a Prison for Women." *Journal of Offender Rehabilitation* 37 (2003): 77. Reports findings of a study in 2000 on the low incidence of female sexual coercion among women and examines characteristics of victims and perpetrators of sexual aggression.

Lindquist, Christine, et al. "Reentry Court Initiative: Court-Based Strategies for Managing Released Prisoners." Report, National Institute of

Prisons

Justice, 2004. Describes nine Reentry Court Initiative (RCI) programs, sponsored by the U.S. Office of Justice Programs, designed to develop strategies to improve the tracking and supervision of criminal offenders after their release from prison and to provide services to assist offenders with family and community reintegration.

Liptak, Adam. "On Death Row, a Battle over the Fatal Cocktail." *New York Times*, September 16, 2004, p. A16. Discusses efforts in Kentucky and other states to change the three-chemical combination used for executions by lethal injection because of claims by some medical experts that the drug combination causes death by suffocation, in violation of the Eighth Amendment's ban against cruel and unusual punishment.

Loper, Ann Booker, and Jennifer Whitney Gildea. "Social Support and Anger Expression among Incarcerated Women." *Journal of Offender Rehabilitation* 38 (2004): 27. Reports on the findings of a study of some 216 female inmates at a maximum security state prison on the women's perceived social support within the prison and the relationship of these perceptions to manifestations of anger. Among the findings: Female inmates who perceived higher levels of social support from fellow inmates tended to express higher levels of anger than female inmates who perceived higher levels of social support from vocational, educational, and recreational activities.

Mathews, Ann H. "The Inapplicability of the Prison Litigation Reform Act to Prisoner Claims of Excessive Force." *New York University Law Review* 77 (May 2002): 536. Analyzes the Prison Litigation Reform Act (PRLA) of 1996 and argues that the PRLA should be interpreted narrowly to exempt prisoners' claims of excessive force used against them in correctional settings.

Mullings, Janet L., et al. "Exploring the Relationship Between Alcohol Use, Childhood Maltreatment, and Treatment Needs among Female Prisoners." *Substance Use & Misuse* 39 (January 2004): 277. Presents findings of a study on the relationship between childhood maltreatment and adult alcohol dependency among some 1,377 recently incarcerated female inmates admitted from May 1998 to March 1999 to Texas state correctional facilities. Data was based on interviews of the inmates, with the following six criteria: the prevalence of illicit substance use, criminal history, physical and mental health, high-risk sexual behaviors, prior physical and sexual abuse, including neglect, and demographics. Among the findings: Female inmates who suffered neglect as children were more likely to exhibit alcohol-related problems as adults, while those who suffered childhood sexual or physical abuse as children were no more likely to abuse alcohol as adults than those were did not suffer such abuse.

Annotated Bibliography

National Institute of Corrections. "Sexual Misconduct in Prisons: Law, Remedies, and Incidence." Report, May 2000. Presents a statistical overview of the incidence and outcomes of reported cases of sexual misconduct by prison staff against inmates in correctional settings nationwide and proposes prevention strategies, including better training of staff and the full prosecution of staff offenders.

O'Donnell, Ian. "Prison Rape in Context." *British Journal of Criminology* 44 (March 2004): 241. Examines the etiology of prison rape in the United States and suggests that sexual violence in U.S. prisons is rooted in the violent history of race relations in the United States.

Petersilia, J. "Unequal Justice? Offenders with Mental Retardation in Prison." *Corrections Management Quarterly* 1 (Fall 1997): 36. Discusses the custodial problems posed by offenders with mental retardation to state and federal corrections agencies.

Spohn, Cassia C. "Thirty Years of Sentencing Reform: The Quest for a Racially Neutral Sentencing Process." *Criminal Justice 2000* 3 (2000): 40. Reviews some 40 studies investigating the link between race and the severity of sentencing in state and federal courts. The article discusses how certain types of minority offenders, perhaps because they are perceived as being more dangerous, are sometimes singled out for harsher treatment, including black and Hispanic young males who are unemployed. The article also suggests that there is evidence that minorities convicted of drug offenses, those with longer prior criminal records, those who victimize whites, and those who refuse to plead guilty or are unable to secure pretrial release are punished more severely than similarly situated whites.

Tobolowsky, Peggy M. "Capital Punishment and the Mentally Retarded Offender." *Prison Journal* 84 (September 2004): 340. Presents analyses of two significant U.S. Supreme Court cases on the constitutionality of the execution of mentally retarded criminal offenders. In *Penry v. Lynaugh* (1989), the U.S. Supreme Court held that the Eighth Amendment's ban on cruel and unusual punishment did not categorically bar the execution of mentally retarded offenders. In *Atkins v. Virginia* (2002), the Court revisited the issue and held that the execution of mentally retarded offenders is categorically barred by the Eighth Amendment.

Vollum, Scott, et al. "Should Jurors Be Informed about Parole Eligibility in Death Penalty Cases? An Analysis of *Kelly vs. South Carolina.*" *Prison Journal* 84 (September 2004): 395. Analyzes the implications of the U.S. Supreme Court decision in *Kelly v. South Carolina* (2002) entitling a defendant to a jury instruction regarding parole eligibility when the only alternative to a death sentence is life without parole. The article examines potential legal issues raised in *Kelly,* including the contention that the *Kelly* decisions did not go far enough by guaranteeing that all criminal defendants in death penalty cases be allowed a jury instruction that the only alternative to a death sentence is life without parole.

Wacquant, Loïc. "Deadly Symbiosis: When Ghetto and Prison Meet and Mesh." *Punishment and Society* 19 (Fall 2000): 11. Presents a historical overview of the link between imprisonment and low socioeconomic status among black criminal defendants.

Warren, Janet I., et al. "Exploring Prison Adjustment among Female Inmates: Issues of Measurement and Prediction." *Criminal Justice and Behavior* 31 (October 2004): 624. Examines methods of determining the level of adjustment to prison by female state prison inmates.

Weidner, Robert R. "Explaining Sentence Severity in Large Urban Counties: A Multilevel Analysis of Contextual and Case-Level Factors." *Prison Journal* 84 (June 2004): 184. Examines the impact of legal and other variables on the decision to sentence felons to prison in a 1996 sampling of large urban counties in the United States. Using data from the Bureau of Justice Statistics' State Court Processing Statistics, sentencing was assessed using the following four contextual factors: level of crime, level of unemployment, racial composition, and the geographical region of the sentencing. According to the article, the data suggested that sentencing decisions were based primarily on case-level factors and not on the four contextual factors examined in this research.

Wilson, Franklin T. "Out of Sight, Out of Mind: An Analysis of *Kansas vs. Crane* and the Fine Line Between Civil and Criminal Sanctions." *Prison Journal* 84 (September 2004): 379. Presents an analysis of the impact of the U.S. Supreme decision *Kansas v. Crane* (2002) on the constitutionality of legislation that permitted the indefinite civil commitment of registered sex offenders after the completion of their prison sentence.

Wright, Randall. "Care as the Heart of Prison Teaching." *Journal of Correctional Education* 55 (September 2004): 191. Presents findings of a study that attempted to correlate the extent of a correctional teacher's interest in inmate students with inmates' successful completion of educational programs.

WEB DOCUMENTS

Bellatty, Paul, and Don Grossnickle. "Survey of High Risk Inmate Behaviors in the Oregon Prison System." Report, Oregon Department of Corrections, June 2004. Available online. URL: http://www.doc.state.or. us/publicaffairs/2004news/highrisk5-20-04.doc. Presents findings of a study of 236 male inmates and 97 female inmates in Oregon state prisons who were randomly selected to participate in a survey on high-risk inmate behaviors. The data were then extrapolated to the male and female prison populations for the entire Oregon prison system. Among the findings: Male inmates were far more likely to engage in high-risk behaviors, including getting tattoos and body piercings and using intravenous drugs. In addition, of the estimated 400 to 550 male inmates who were sexually active, about 150 were subjected to nonconsensual sexual acts. Female inmates were less likely to receive tattoos and body piercings or to use intravenous drugs, according to the report, which estimated that of the estimated 50 to 70 female inmates who were sexually involved with other inmates, all reported that the sexual activity was consensual.

Bonczar, Thomas. "Prevalence of Imprisonment in the U.S. Population, 1974–2001." Special Report, Bureau of Justice Statistics, August 2003. Presents estimates of the number of U.S. residents who were ever incarcerated in state or federal prison, including prison inmates, parolees, and all living individuals who are no longer incarcerated or under parole supervision. The report provides estimates of the lifetime chances of going to prison using demographic variables, including age, gender, and race.

Bonczar, Thomas P., and Tracy L. Snell. "Capital Punishment, 2003." *Bulletin*, Bureau of Justice Statistics, November 2004. Available online. URL: http://www.ojp.usdoj.gov/bjs/abstract/cp03.htm. Presents characteristics of inmates under sentence of death in state and federal prisons as of December 31, 2003, including those executed in 2003, and includes preliminary data on executions in 2004 in the United States. Statistical tables present data on the inmates under sentence of death and those executed, including sex, race, education, marital status, age at the time of arrest for the capital offense, methods of execution, and the length of time between imposition of death sentence and execution.

Durose, Matthew R., and Christopher J. Mumola. "Profile of Nonviolent Offenders Exiting State Prisons." Fact Sheet, Bureau of Justice Statistics, October 2004. Available online. URL: http://www.ojp.usdoj.gov/bjs/abstract/pnoesp.htm. Provides a description of the general characteristics of individuals who served time for nonviolent crimes at the time of their release from state prisons. The report defined nonviolent crimes as property, drug, and public order offenses that do not involve a threat of harm or an attack upon a victim.

Fortune, Sandra H. "Inmate and Prison Gang Leadership." Dissertation, East Tennessee State University, December 2003. Available online. URL: http://etd-submit.etsu.edu/etd/theses/available/etd-1103103-220112/unrestricted/fortunes112503f.pdf. Presents findings of a study identifying the characteristics of gang and non-gang inmate leaders based on interviews with 20 inmates in the Northeast Correctional Complex in Mountain City, Tennessee.

Harrison, Paige M., and Allen J. Beck. "Prisoners in 2003." *Bulletin,* Bureau of Justice Statistics, November 2004. Available online. URL: http://www. ojp.usdoj.gov/bjs/abstract/p03.htm. Presents statistics on state and federal inmates in 2003, including the increase in the prison population from 2002 to 2003 and the growth rate since 1995 of male and female inmates in U.S. prisons. The report also includes state incarceration rates and tabular data on prison capacities and the use of local jails and privately operated prisons. Estimates are provided on the number of sentenced prisoners by sex, gender, and race.

Harrison, Paige M., and Jennifer C. Karberg. "Prison and Jail Inmates at Midyear 2003." Report, Bureau of Justice Statistics, May 2004. Available online. URL: http://www.ojp.usdoj.gov/bjs/pub/pdf/pjim03.pdf. Presents data on prison and jail inmates nationwide, as collected by the National Prisoner Statistics survey and the Annual Survey of Jails in 2003. Includes statistics on the number and rate of incarceration of all adult prisoners in state and federal correctional facilities and those in private correctional facilities. The annual survey also includes data on inmates under 18 years of age held by state correctional facilities.

Hsia, Heidi M., et al. "Disproportionate Minority Confinement: 2002 Update." Report, Office of Juvenile Justice and Delinquency Prevention, September 2004. Available online. URL: http://ojjdp.ncjrs.org/dmc. Presents statistical data on the disproportionate confinement of minority youth in 2002 in detention and correctional facilities in the United States.

Human Rights Watch. "Ill-Equipped: U.S. Prisoners and Offenders with Mental Illness." Report, 2003. Available online. URL: http://www. hrw.org. Provides a historical overview of the causes of the influx of mentally ill individuals into the criminal justice system, presents statistics and empirical data on the rise in the mentally ill prison population, and argues that prisons and the criminal justice system are ill-equipped to deal with the mentally ill.

———. "No Escape: Male Rape in U.S. Prisons." Report, 2001. Available online. URL: http://www.hrw.org/reports/2001/prison. Provides a statistical overview of the prevalence of inmate-on-inmate rape and sexual assault in U.S. prisons, despite the lack of a nationwide database at the time of the report's publication. Includes firsthand accounts by prison inmates who were victims of rape and sexual assault while incarcerated in state or federal prisons.

King, Ryan S., and Marc Mauer. "State Sentencing and Corrections Policy in an Era of Fiscal Restraint." Report, The Sentencing Project, 2002.

Available online. URL: http://www.sentencingproject.org/pdfs/9091.pdf. Provides an overview of state legislative initiatives that have changed the direction of state sentencing and corrections policy and discusses the impact of fiscal concerns on sentencing and corrections-related legislation.

Mauer, Marc, and Ryan Scott King. "Schools and Prisons: Fifty Years after *Brown v. Board of Education.*" Report, The Sentencing Project, March 2004. Available online. URL: www.sentencingproject.org/pdfs/brownvboard.pdf. Reports on the disproportionate rates of imprisonment among African Americans in the United States during the 50 years following the U.S. Supreme Court decision in *Brown v. Board of Education* (1954), which resulted in the desegregation of public schools in the United States and is commonly perceived as the beginning of the civil rights movement in America. Includes a statistical overview of rates of incarceration among African Americans from 1954 to 2002 and offers causal factors for the rise in such rates, including crime rates, crack cocaine sentencing laws, and habitual offender mandatory sentencing statutes.

Mauer, Marc, et al. "The Meaning of Life: Long Prison Sentences in Context." Report, The Sentencing Project, May 2004. Available online. URL: http://www.soros.org/initiatives/justice/articles_publications/publications/lifers_20040511/lifers.pdf. Examines the sharp rise in the imposition of life sentences and discusses the issues of incapacitation, public safety issues, costs of incarceration, and the goal of punishment. The report also presents survey data from 2002 to 2003 on U.S. prison inmates serving life sentences in state and federal correctional facilities. Among the findings: Nearly 10 percent of state and federal prisoners were serving life sentences, an increase of 83 percent between 1992 and 2003. Of those serving a life sentence, some 26.3 percent of inmates had no possibility of parole.

Merritt, Nancy, et al. "Oregon's Measure 11 Sentencing Reform: Implementation and System Impact." Report, Rand Corporation, December 2003. Available online. URL: http:// www.ncjrs.org/pdffiles1/nij/grants/205507.pdf. Presents the findings of a study examining the implementation and impact of Oregon's Measure 11, which was approved by voters in 1994 and imposed long, mandatory prison terms for 16 designated violent and sex-related offenses, prohibited earned credit time in prison, and provided for mandatory waiver of youthful offenders to criminal court. According to the report, although the findings were consistent with the possibility that Measure 11 was partly responsible for a decrease in Oregon's crime rates after 1995, particularly violent crime, there was no clear evidence of a causal link.

Mumola, Christopher J. "Incarcerated Parents and Their Children." Special Report, Bureau of Justice Statistics, August 2000. Available online at http://www.ojp.usdoj.gov/bjs/abstract/iptc.htm. Presents findings of a 1999 survey of state and federal prisoners in the United States with minor children under 18 years of age.

National Institute of Justice. "The Health Status of Soon-to-Be-Released Inmates: A Report to Congress, Volumes 1 and 2." Report, September 2004. Available online. URL: http://virlib.ncjrs.org/Corrections.asp. Provides detailed statistical analysis of the health status of state and federal prison inmates in the United States who were within six months of their expected release.

Oregon Department of Corrections. "Survey of High-Risk Inmate Behaviors in the Oregon Prison System." Report, 2004. Available online. URL: http://www.doc.state.or.us/publicaffairs/2004news/highrisk5–20–04. doc. Presents findings on the incidence of high-risk behaviors by Oregon state inmates, including tattooing, body piercing, intravenous drug use, and sexual activity, and discusses the issue of sexual coercion in prison.

The Sentencing Project. Briefing Sheets, November 28, 2004. Available online. URL: http://www.sentencingproject.org/pubs_02.cfm. Provides brief statistical overviews on issues relating to sentencing and imprisonment in the United States, including "Facts about Prisons and Prisoners," "Factsheet: Women in Prison," "Hispanic Prisoners in the United States," "Prison Privatization and the Use of Incarceration," "The Expanding Federal Prison Population," "Truth-in-Sentencing and the Federal Prison System," "Prisoners Re-entering the Community," "Recidivism of State Prisoners: Implications for Sentencing," "Felony Disenfranchisement Laws in the United States," and "U.S. Prison Populations: New Prison Figures Demonstrate Need for Comprehensive Reform."

Sickmund, Melissa. "Juveniles in Corrections." Report, Office of Juvenile Justice and Delinquency Prevention, June 2004. Available online. URL: http://www.ncjrs.org/pdffiles1/ojjdp/202885.pdf. Presents federal and state data from the biennial Census of Juveniles in Residential Placement as of October 27, 1999. Public and private juvenile residential placement facilities in every state were surveyed on the number and characteristics of juvenile offenders in residential placement, including gender, age, race, and most serious offense charged.

Stop Prison Rape. "Academic Articles on Law, Corrections Policy, and Social Science and Psychology." 2003. Available online. URL: http://www.spr.org/en/publications/pub_academic.html. Provides links to more than 40 articles on rape and sexual assault in correctional settings.

Struckman-Johnson, Cindy, and David Struckman-Johnson. "Sexual Coercion Reported by Women in Three Midwestern Prisons." *Journal of Sex Research* 39 (August 2002): 217. Presents findings of self-reported data inmate-on-inmate sexual aggression among female prisoners and the incidence of staff-on-inmate sexual exploitation.

U.S. Department of Health and Human Services. "Prisoner Reentry, Religion and Research." Report, 2004. Available online. URL: http://www.calib.com/home/work_samples/files/kairosissuebriefi.pdf. Discusses faith-based prisoner reentry programs, focusing on the Kairos Prison Ministry's residential rehabilitation program for prisoners and their families.

CHAPTER 8

ORGANIZATIONS AND AGENCIES

A wide variety of information is available from the following organizations, including statistical data on prisons and inmates, reports on prison conditions, and links to prison-related issues, such as prisoners' rights and the death penalty. Also provided is a listing of state correctional agencies, whose web sites offer state-specific information on prison facilities, inmate populations, treatment programs, and correctional administration. Many state corrections agency web sites also provide links to local, state, and national organizations in the field of corrections.

360 Degrees: Perspectives on the U.S. Criminal Justice System
URL:
http://www.360degrees.org
176 Grand Street
3rd Floor
New York, NY 10013
Phone: (212) 226-3099
A joint venture by National Public Radio (NPR) and Picture Projects, a producer of online documentaries, to examine the criminal justice system in the United States. Included in the 360 Degrees web site are links to online audio diaries by prisoners and corrections officers and online documentaries on

issues related to corrections and prisoners' rights.

American Bar Association (ABA)
URL: http://www.abanet.org
321 North Clark Street
Chicago, IL 60610
Phone: (312) 988-5000
Professional association of attorneys and legal professionals that sponsors research and training on a wide range of law-related issues, including the criminal justice system. Publishers of *Criminal Justice* magazine, the web site for the ABA provides a link to articles from the magazine (URL:

http://www.abanet.org/crimjust/
raeder.html) on topics including female criminal offenders, sentencing
issues, and juvenile detention.

**American Civil Liberties Union
(ACLU)**
URL: http://www.aclu.org
125 Broad Street
18th Floor
New York, NY 10004
Phone: (212) 344-3005
Founded in 1920 and privately
funded, the ACLU offers legal support in defense of the constitutional rights of federal and state
prisoners through its National
Prison Project. The ACLU's web
site offers links to in-depth coverage of issues relating to prisoners'
rights, including conditions of confinement, medical care, and the
right to privacy.

**American Correctional
Association (ACA)**
URL: http://www.aca.org
4380 Forbes Boulevard
Lanham, MD 20706
Phone: (800) 222-5646
Founded in 1870 as the National
Prison Association, the ACA is
the oldest professional association
in the field of corrections, with a
membership that includes researchers, policymakers, and correctional agency staff. The ACA
publishes *Corrections Today* magazine
and the research journal *Corrections
Compendium*, as well as books, articles, and manuals on correctional

standards, many of which are linked
on their web site and available to the
general public.

**American Friends Service
Committee**
URL: http://www.afsc.org
1501 Cherry Street
Philadelphia, PA 19102
Phone: (215) 241-7000
A Quaker organization with members of various religious faiths
working for social reform in a variety of areas, including prisoners'
rights and the death penalty. The
committee's web site includes links
to numerous reports and articles on
prison-related issues.

**Association for the Treatment
of Sexual Abusers (ATSA)**
URL: http://www.atsa.com
4900 S.W. Griffith Drive
Suite 274
Beaverton, OR 97005
Phone: (503) 643-1023
Nonprofit organization established
in 1984 to sponsor research on the
treatment of sexual abusers. Publishers of the *ATSA Journal*, which
features scholarly articles on topics
including the treatment of sexual
abusers in correctional settings and
aftercare for sexual abusers after release from prison.

**Association of State Correctional
Administrators (ASCA)**
URL: http://www.asca.net
213 Court Street
6th Floor

Prisons

Middletown, CT 06457
Phone: (860) 704-6410
Established in 1970 with the goal of improving services and standards in state correctional facilities, the ASCA funds research and disseminates information on prisons and prison administration.

Bureau of Justice Statistics (BJS)
URL: http://www.ojp.usdoj.gov/ bjs
U.S. Department of Justice
810 7th Street, NW
Washington, DC 20531
Phone: (203) 307-0765
Advances research and disseminates information on a wide variety of criminal justice issues, including corrections. BJS publications on issues related to prisons include special reports and annual surveys of inmates and correctional facilities nationwide, all available to the general public free of charge by mail or by downloading from the BJS web site. The BJS also conducts and disseminates data from the National Victim Crime Survey, an annual survey that measures the incidence of violent and property offenses based on reports by victims.

California Prison Focus
URL: http://www.prisons.org
2940 16th Street
#B-5
San Francisco, CA 94103
Phone: (415) 252-9211
Advocates for prisoners' rights, California Prison Focus disseminates information on a range of prison-

related issues, including the use of special housing units to isolate inmates and medical care for prisoners with serious illnesses. Although the focus is on California state prisons, many issues have a broader application to prisons nationwide.

Center for Community Alternatives (CCA)
URL: http://www. communityalternatives.org
39 West 19th Street
10th Floor
New York, NY 10011
Phone: (212) 691-1911
Private, nonprofit agency founded in 1981 with the goal of advancing the use of community-based alternatives to incarceration in New York State, the CCA offers publications on a range of topics in the field of community corrections, including issues related to female and juvenile offenders and the restoration of rights for former inmates.

Center for the Children of Incarcerated Parents
URL: http://www.e-ccip.org
P.O. Box 41-286
Eagle Rock, CA 90041
Phone: (626) 449-2470
Founded in 1989 with the goal of advancing the development of model services for the children and families of incarcerated parents in the areas of education, family reunification, therapeutic services, and the dissemination of information to the general public.

234

Centurion Ministries
URL: http://www.
centurionministries.org
221 Witherspoon Street
Princeton, NJ 08542
Phone: (609) 921-0334
Nonprofit organization that works with a national network of attorneys and forensic experts to advocate for wrongly convicted prisoners in the United States and Canada and to assist with the social reintegration of exonerated inmates after their release from prison.

Citizens United
for Rehabilitation
of Errants (CURE)
URL: http://www.
curenational.org
P.O. Box 2310
National Capital Station
Washington, DC 20013-2310
Phone: (202) 789-2126
National organization established in 1972 that promotes reform in the U.S. criminal justice system. Among the main issues supported by CURE are prison labor and educational reform, prison rape prevention, private prison accountability, and alternatives to incarceration, including community corrections programs and post-release rehabilitation and vocational placement services.

Correctional Education
Association (CEA)
URL: http://www.ceanational.org
4380 Forbes Boulevard
Lanham, MD 20706
Phone: (301) 918-1915

An affiliate of the American Correctional Association, the CEA is a nonprofit professional association for educators and educational administrators in correctional settings that conducts research and publishes papers on issues related to education in prisons. Publications are available on the CEA web site, as are links to other organizations in the field of corrections.

The Corrections Connection
URL: http://www. corrections.
com
159 Burgin Parkway
Quincy, MA 02169
Phone: (617) 471-4445
An association for professionals in corrections that provides information and publications on all facets of corrections, including juvenile corrections and prison privatization. The Corrections Connection web site provides links to a wide range of national and state organizations with information on prisons and prison management.

The Edna McConnell Clark
Foundation
URL: http://www.emcf.org
415 Madison Avenue
10th Floor
New York, NY 10177
Phone: (212) 551-9100
Sponsor of the Program for Justice, which sponsors research on reforming the U.S. criminal justice system, with focus on issues of sentencing reform, prison overcrowding, conditions of confinement, and prisoners'

Prisons

rights. The foundation's web site offers links to publications and news articles on issues of interest.

Families Against Mandatory Minimums (FAMM)
URL: http://www.famm.org
1612 K Street, NW
Suite 700
Washington, DC 20006
Phone: (202) 822-6700
National nonprofit organization founded in 1991 to challenge mandatory sentencing laws and to promote more equitable sentencing polices at the state and federal levels. The FAMM website offers links to news articles and publications available by download on issues relating to sentencing and corrections.

Family & Corrections Network (FCN)
URL: http://www.fcnetwork.org
32 Oak Grove Road
Palmyra, VA 22963
Phone: (804) 589-3036
Established in 1983 as a resource for families of prisoners, the FCN facilitates communication between families of prisoners on their web site, which offers links to publications available by download on the issues of incarcerated parents and family members.

Federal Bureau of Prisons (BOP)
URL: http://www.bop.gov
320 First Street NW
Washington, DC 20534
Phone: (202) 307-3198

Federal agency within the U.S. Department of Justice that was created in 1930 to administer federal prisons in the United States. In addition to the central office in Washington, D.C., the BOP maintains six regional offices in Atlanta; Dallas; Philadelphia; Burlingame, California; Annapolis, Maryland; and Kansas City, Kansas. The BOP provides a wide range of publications on corrections-related issues. Among the services offered by the BOP is the federal inmate locator (URL: http://inmateloc.bop.gov/locator/ FindInmateHttpServlet), with a database that is updated daily on all federal prisoners who are incarcerated and those who have been released since 1982.

Federal Prison Industries, Inc. (UNICOR)
URL: http://www.unicor.gov
320 First Street
Washington, DC 20534
Phone: (800) 827-3168
Government corporation established by Congress in 1934 with the mandate to provide vocational training to federal inmates. Commonly referred to by its trade name, UNICOR, Federal Prison Industries is a self-sustaining organization funded by the profits from goods manufactured by federal prisoners.

Florida State University Criminal Justice Links
URL: http://www.criminology. fsu.edu/cjlinks
Florida State University

236

School of Criminology and Criminal Justice
Hecht House
634 West Call Street
Tallahassee, FL 32306-1127
Phone: (850) 644-4050
Clearinghouse for information on a wide range of criminal justice issues, including corrections, with links to information on prisons, community corrections, restorative justice, and the death penalty.

Human Rights Watch
URL: http://www.hrw.org
350 Fifth Avenue
34th Floor
New York, NY 10118
Phone: (212) 290-4700
Private, nonprofit group advocating for human rights worldwide that offers in-depth reports on prison-related issues, including prison rape, and offers links to information on prisoners' rights and conditions of confinement in correctional facilities nationwide.

Innocence Project
URL: http://www.innocenceproject.org
100 Fifth Avenue
3rd Floor
New York, NY 10011
Phone: (212) 364-5340
Nonprofit legal clinic founded in 1992 by attorneys Barry Scheck and Peter Neufeld to provide legal assistance in cases where post-conviction DNA testing of evidence may result in proof of innocence.

Legal Services for Prisoners with Children
URL: http://prisonerswithchildren.org
1540 Market Street
Suite 490
San Francisco, CA 94102
Phone: (415) 255-7036
Advocacy group founded in 1978 to provide legal assistance to incarcerated parents and to promote reform on legal and policy issues related to sentencing and imprisonment. The organization's web site offers links to articles, self-help manuals, and other publications on issues of interest.

National Commission on Correctional Health Care (NCCHC)
URL: http://www.ncchc.org
1145 West Diversey Parkway
Chicago, IL 60614
Phone: (773) 880-1460
Established in 1981 by the American Medical Association to promote reform in correctional health care, the NCCHC collaborates with other national organizations in the field of corrections to improve the quality of medical care in prisons, jails, and juvenile detention facilities. The NCCHC publishes the annual report *Standards for Health Services in Prisons*.

National Correctional Industries Association (NCIA)
URL: http://www.nationalcia.org
1202 North Charles Street
Baltimore, MD 21201
Phone: (410) 230-3972

Nonprofit association of state and federal correctional industries professionals, founded in 1941 as the Penal Industries Association. The NCIA web site provides links to information on correctional industries in prisons nationwide and products manufactured in state and federal correctional industry programs.

National Criminal Justice Reference Service (NCJRS)
URL: http://www.ncjrs.org
P.O. Box 6000
Rockville, MD 20849-6000
Phone: (800) 851-3420
Clearinghouse for publications produced by the U.S. government on a wide range of criminal justice issues, including corrections. The NCJRS web site provides a corrections page (URL: http://virlib. ncjrs.org/Corrections.asp) with links to topics including inmate characteristics, mentally ill offenders, sex offenders, parole, recidivism, community-based corrections, corrections technology, correctional personnel, and death row. The NCJRS web site also provides links to articles and abstracts on criminal justice issues culled from some 600 publications.

National GAINS Center
  for People with Co-Occurring
  Disorders in the Justice
  System
URL: http://www.gainsctr.com
Policy Research Associates, Inc.
345 Delaware Avenue

Delmar, NY 12054
Phone: (800) 311-4246
Established in 1995 as a national center for the collection and dissemination of information on the treatment of individuals with co-occurring mental health and substance abuse issues in the criminal justice system. Offers an online clearinghouse which includes publications on issues of mental health and substance abuse treatment in correctional settings.

National Institute
  of Corrections (NIC)
URL: http://www.nicic.org
320 First Street, NW
Washington, DC 20534
Phone: (800) 995-6423 or (202)
  307-3106
Government agency within the Federal Bureau of Prisons that provides training, technical assistance, and information to federal, state, and local corrections agencies. The NIC web site provides links to NIC publications and to corrections-related web sites with information on a range of prison-related issues.

National Juvenile Detention
  Association (NJDA)
URL: http://www.njda.com
Eastern Kentucky University
521 Lancaster Avenue
301 Perkins Building
Richmond, KY 40475
Phone: (859) 622-6259
Promotes the improvement of juvenile detention programs through

research funded by state and federal agencies, including the Office of Juvenile Justice and Delinquency Prevention. The NJDA web site offers links to publications and information on issues related to juvenile detention and the incarceration of minors in adult correctional facilities.

The National Lawyers Guild
URL: http://www.nlg.org
143 Madison Avenue
4th Floor
New York, NY 10016
Phone: (212) 679-5100
Professional association of attorneys, law students, and other legal professionals that promotes reform in corrections and other social issues. Publishes *The Jailhouse Lawyer Handbook*, a primer on prisoners' rights and a reference guide for inmates seeking legal remedy for violations of their civil rights while in prison or jail.

Office of National Drug Control Policy (ONDCP)
URL: http://www. whitehousedrugpolicy.gov
Drug Policy Information Clearinghouse
P.O. Box 6000
Rockville, MD 20849-6000
Phone: (800) 666-3332
Established by the Anti-Abuse Drug Act of 1988, the legislative mandate of the ONDCP is to implement a national drug policy program and disseminate information

on drug abuse and its impact on society, including the criminal justice system. The web site of the ONDCP provides a link to federal drug data sources (URL: http:// www.whitehousedrugpolicy.gov/ drugfact/sources.html), which references publications available by download on the interface between drug abuse and corrections.

Prison Activist Resource Center (PARC)
URL: http://www. prisonactivist.org
P.O. BOX 339
Berkley, CA 94701
Phone: (510) 893-4648
Provides information on prisoners' rights and other issues related to the mistreatment of prisoners in U.S. prisons.

Prison Law Office
URL: http://www.prisonlaw.com
Prison Law Office
General Delivery
San Quentin, CA 94964
Phone: (415) 457-9144
Provides free legal services to California state prisoners and parolees seeking legal recourse on issues relating to conditions of confinement in prison. The Prison Law Office web site offers links to publications on corrections-related topics.

Prison Policy Initiative
URL: http://www. prisonpolicy.org

Prisons

P.O. Box 127
Northampton, MA 01061
Phone: (413) 586-4985
Prisoners' rights advocacy organization that conducts research and provides information on a range of corrections-related social issues including conditions of confinement, racial disparity in incarceration rates, and felony disenfranchisement laws.

PrisonsandJails.com
URL: http://www.
prisonsandjails.com
Corrections Information, LLC
P.O. Box 8
Lewisburg, WV 24901
Phone: (304) 645-7277
Offers Web-based links to news articles and publications on corrections-related issues, including inmate health care and institutional security.

The Sentencing Project
URL: http://www.
sentencingproject.org
514 Tenth Street, NW
Suite 1000
Washington, DC 20004
Phone: (202) 628-0871
Established in 1986 to develop alternative sentencing programs and conduct research on criminal justice policy in the United States. The Sentencing Project web site offers links to publications on issues including the U.S. rate of incarceration, racial disparities among the prison population, and felony disenfranchisement.

Stop Prisoner Rape (SPR)
URL: http://www.spr.org
3325 Wilshire Boulevard
Suite 340
Los Angeles, CA 90010
Phone: (213) 384-1400
Nonprofit group that seeks to end sexual violence against incarcerated individuals by advocating for legislation and disseminating information on the issue of sexual violence in prison. The SPR offers resources for survivors of sexual assault in prisons.

U.S. Sentencing Commission
URL: http://www.ussc.gov
One Columbus Circle, NE
Washington, DC 20002
Phone: (202) 502-4500
Independent agency within the judicial branch of the federal government that establishes sentencing policies for the federal courts and monitors their implementation. The commission's web site offers links to articles and publications on the issues of federal sentencing, including significant court decisions on issues related to sentencing.

Volunteers of America
URL: http://www.voa.org
1660 Duke Street
Alexandria, VA 22314
Phone: (800) 899-0089
National nonprofit organization that advocates for the humane treatment of prisoners and programs aimed at the successful rein-

tegration of former inmates into society. Sponsors the Guiding Responsive Action in Corrections at End-of-Life Project (GRACE), a collaboration of organizations dedicated to the development of hospice and palliative care programs for prison and jail inmates.

STATE DEPARTMENTS OF CORRECTION

The following state departments of corrections provide state-specific information on prison facilities, inmate populations, treatment program, and correctional administration. In many cases, the information is Web-based and can be downloaded from the department of corrections' web site. Many state correctional agency web sites also provide links to local, state, and national organizations in the field of corrections.

Alabama Department of Correction
URL: http://www.doc.state.al.us
P.O. Box 301501
Montgomery, AL 36130-1501
Phone: (334) 353-3883

Alaska Department of Correction
URL: http://www.correct.state.ak.us
802 3rd Street
Douglas, AK 99824
Phone: (907) 465-4652

Arizona Department of Correction
URL: http://www.adcprisoninfo.az.gov
1601 West Jefferson Street
Phoenix, AZ 85007
Phone: (602) 542-3133

Arkansas Department of Correction
URL: http://www.state.ar.us/doc
P.O. Box 8707
Pine Bluff, AR 71611-8707
Phone: (870) 267-6999

California Department of Corrections
URL: http://www.corr.ca.gov
P.O. Box 942883
Sacramento, CA 94283-0001
Phone: (888) 562-5874
  or (916) 445-7682

Colorado Department of Corrections
URL: http://www.doc.state.co.us
2862 South Circle Drive
Colorado Springs, CO 80906-4195
Phone: (719) 579-9580

Prisons

Connecticut Department
of Correction
URL: http://www.ct.gov/doc
24 Wolcott Hill Road
Wethersfield, CT 06109
Phone: (860) 692-7780

Delaware Department
of Correction
URL: http://www.state.de.us/
correct
245 McKee Road
Dover, DE 19904
Phone: (302) 739-5601

Florida Department
of Corrections
URL: http://www.dc.state.fl.us
1126 East Park Ave
Tallahassee, FL 32301
Phone: (850) 222-4761

Georgia Department
of Corrections
URL: http://www.dcor.state.ga.us
2 Martin Luther King, Jr. Drive
NE
Atlanta, GA 30334
Phone: (888) 656-7660
or (404) 656-7660

Hawaii Department of Public
Safety
URL: http://www.hawaii.gov/psd
Department of Public Safety
919 Ala Moana Boulevard
Honolulu, HI 96814
Phone: (808) 587-1340

Idaho Department
of Correction
URL: http://www.corr.state.id.us

1299 North Orchard Street
Suite 110
Boise, ID 83706
Phone: (208) 658-2000

Illinois Department
of Corrections
URL: http://www.idoc.state.il.us
1301 Concordia Court
P.O. Box 19277
Springfield, IL 62794-9277
Phone: (217) 522-2666

Indiana Department
of Correction
URL: http://www.ai.org/
indcorrection
302 West Washington Street
Indianapolis, IN 46222
Phone: (317) 232-5715

Iowa Department of Correction
URL: http://www.doc.state.ia.us
420 Watson Powell, Jr. Way
Des Moines, IA 50309
Phone: (515) 242-5702

Kansas Department
of Corrections
URL: http://www.dc.state.ks.us
Landon State Office Building
900 SW Jackson
4th Floor
Topeka, KS 66612-1284
Phone: (888) 317-8204
or (785) 296-3317

Kentucky Department
of Corrections
URL: http://www.corrections.
ky.gov
State Offices

Frankfort, KY 40601
Phone: (502) 564-4734

Louisiana Department of Public
  Safety and Corrections
  Services
URL: http://www.doc.louisiana.
  gov
P.O. Box 94304
Baton Rouge, LA 70804-9304
Phone: (225) 342-9711

Maine Department
  of Corrections
URL: http://www.state.me.us/
  corrections
Tyson Building
Tyson Drive
AMHI Campus, SHS #111
Augusta, ME 04333
Phone: (207) 287-2711

Maryland Department
  of Correction
URL: http://www.dpscs.state.
  md.us/doc
300 East Joppa Road
Suite 1000
Towson, MD 21286-3020
Phone: (410) 339-5081

Massachusetts Department
  of Correction
URL: http://www.mass.gov/doc
50 Maple Street
Suite 3
Milford, MA 01757
Phone: (508) 422-3300

Michigan Department
  of Corrections
URL: http://www.michigan.gov/
  corrections

Grandview Plaza
206 East Michigan Avenue
P.O. Box 30003
Lansing, MI 48909
Phone: (517) 335-1426

Minnesota Department
  of Corrections
URL: http://www.corr.state.
  mn.us
1450 Energy Park Drive
Suite 200
St. Paul, MN 55108-5219
Phone: (651) 642-0200

Mississippi Department
  of Corrections
URL: http://www.mdoc.state.
  ms.us
723 North President Street
Jackson, MS 39202
Phone: (601) 359-5600

Missouri Department
  of Corrections
URL: http://www.corrections.
  state.mo.us
2729 Plaza Drive
Jefferson City, MO 65109
Phone: (573) 751-2389

Montana Department
  of Corrections
URL: http://www.cor.state.mt.us
1539 11th Avenue
Helena, MT 59620-1301
Phone: (888) 223-6332
  or (406) 444-7461

Nebraska Department
  of Correctional Services
URL: http://www.corrections.
  state.ne.us

243

P.O. Box 94661
Lincoln, NE 68509-4661
Phone: (402) 471-2654

Nevada Department
  of Corrections
URL: http://www.doc.nv.gov
P.O. Box 7011
Carson City, NV 89702
Phone: (775) 887-3285

New Hampshire Department
  of Corrections
URL: http://www.state.nh.us/doc
State Office Park South
P.O. Box 1806
Concord, NH 03302-1806
Phone: (603) 271-5600

New Jersey Department
  of Corrections
URL: http://www.state.nj.us/
  corrections
Whittlesey Road
P.O. Box 863
Trenton, NJ 08625
Phone: (609) 292-4036

New Mexico Corrections
  Department
URL: http://corrections.state.
  nm.us
4337 NM 14
Santa Fe, NM 87508
Phone: (505) 827-8660

New York State Department
  of Correctional Services
URL: http://www.docs.state.
  ny.us
1220 Washington Avenue
Building 2

Albany, NY 12226-2050
Phone: (518) 457-8126

North Carolina Department
  of Correction
URL: http://www.doc.state.nc.us
4202 Mail Service Center
Raleigh, NC 27699-4202
Phone: (919) 716-3700

North Dakota Department
  of Corrections
  and Rehabilitation
URL: http://www.state.nd.us/
  docr
3100 Railroad Avenue
Bismarck, ND 58501
Phone: (701) 328-6390

Ohio Department
  of Rehabilitation
  and Correction
URL: http://www.drc.state.oh.us
1050 Freeway Drive North
Columbus, OH 43229
Phone: (614) 752-1159

Oklahoma Department
  of Corrections
URL: http://www.doc.state.ok.us
3400 Martin Luther King
  Avenue
Oklahoma City, OK 73111
Phone: (405) 425-2500

Oregon Department
  of Corrections
URL: http://www.oregon.gov/
  DOC
2575 Center Street NE
Salem, OR 97301-4667
Phone: (503) 945-9090

Pennsylvania Department
of Corrections
URL: http://www.cor.state.pa.us
2520 Lisburn Road
P.O. Box 598
Camp Hill, PA 17001-0598
Phone: (717) 975-4862

Rhode Island Department
of Corrections
URL: http://www.doc.state.ri.us
40 Howard Avenue
Cranston, RI 02920
Phone: (401) 462-2611

South Carolina Department
of Corrections
URL: http://www.state.sc.us/
scdc
4444 Broad River Road
P.O. Box 21787
Columbia, SC 29210

South Dakota Department
of Corrections
URL: http://www.state.sd.us/
corrections/corrections.html
3200 East Highway 34
c/o 500 East Capitol Avenue
Pierre, SD 57501
Phone: (605)773-3478

Tennessee Department
of Correction
URL: http://www.state.tn.us/
correction
Rachel Jackson Building
320 6th Avenue North
4th Floor
Nashville, TN 37243-0465
Phone: (615) 741-1000

Texas Department of Criminal
Justice
URL: http://www.tdcj.state.
tx.us
Capitol Station
P.O. Box 13084
Austin, TX 78711-3084
Phone: (512) 463-9988

Utah Department
of Corrections
URL: http://www.cr.ex.state.
ut.us
14717 South Minuteman
Drive
Draper, UT 84020
Phone: (801) 545-5500

Vermont Department
of Corrections
URL: http://www.doc.state.
vt.us
103 South Main Street
Waterbury, VT 05671-1101
Phone: (802)241-2276

Virginia Department
of Corrections
URL: http://www.vadoc.state.
va.us
P.O. Box 26963
Richmond, VA 23261-6963
Phone: (804) 674-3000

Washington State Department
of Corrections
URL: http://www.doc.wa.gov/
home.asp
637 Woodland Square Loop
Olympia, WA 98504
Phone: (360) 753-1573

West Virginia Division
of Corrections
URL: http://www.wvf.state.wv.
us/wvdoc
State Capitol Complex
112 California Avenue
Building 4, Room 300
Charleston, WV 25305
Phone: (304) 558-2036

Wisconsin Department
of Corrections
URL: http://www.wi-doc.com

3099 East Washington Avenue
P.O. Box 7925
Madison, WI 53707-7925
Phone: (608) 240-5000

Wyoming Department
of Corrections
URL: http://doc.state.wy.us/
corrections.asp
700 West 21st Street
Cheyenne, WY 82002
Phone: (307) 777-7208

PART III

APPENDICES

APPENDIX A

STATISTICS ON STATE AND FEDERAL PRISONERS

STATE AND FEDERAL PRISONERS, 2000 TO 2003

Year	Total Jail and Prison Inmates	Federal Inmates	State Inmates	Incarceration Rate per 100,000 U.S. Population
2000	1,937,482	133,921	1,176,269	601
2001	1,961,247	143,337	1,180,155	685
2002	2,033,022	151,618	1,209,331	701
2003	2,085,620	161,673	1,226,175	714
Increase 2002–2003	2.6 percent	6.6 percent	1.4 percent	1.9 percent

MALE AND FEMALE INMATES IN STATE AND FEDERAL PRISONS

Year	Male Prisoners	Female Prisoners
2002	1,342,513	97,631
2003	1,368,866	101,179
Increase, 2002–2003	2.0 percent	3.6 percent
Average Annual Increase, 1995–2003	3.3 percent	5.0 percent

PERCENTAGE OF STATE AND FEDERAL PRISONERS BY ETHNIC ORIGIN, 2003

Race	Percent
White	35.0
Black	44.1
Hispanic	44.1
Other	1.9

Source: Harrison, Paige M., and Allen J. Beck, "Prisoners in 2003." *Bulletin,* Bureau of Justice Statistics, November 2004, pp. 2–9.

GROWTH IN U.S. CORRECTIONAL POPULATIONS

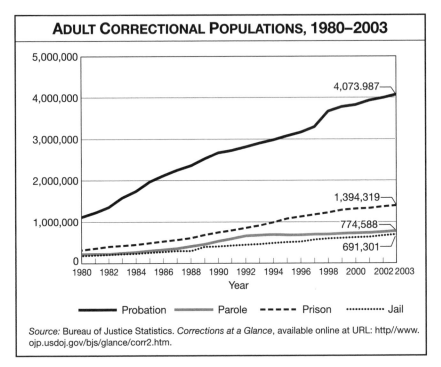

ADULT CORRECTIONAL POPULATIONS, 1980–2003

Source: Bureau of Justice Statistics. *Corrections at a Glance*, available online at URL: http//www. ojp.usdoj.gov/bjs/glance/corr2.htm.

APPENDIX B

THE PRISON LITIGATION REFORM ACT

Enacted on April 26, 1996,
by the 104th Congress of the United States

SEC. 801. SHORT TITLE.
This title may be cited as the PRISON LITIGATION REFORM ACT of 1995.
SEC. 802. APPROPRIATE REMEDIES FOR PRISON CONDITIONS.
(a) IN GENERAL.—Section 3626 of title 18, United States Code, is amended to read as follows:
Section 3626. Appropriate remedies with respect to prison conditions
(a) REQUIREMENTS FOR RELIEF. —
(1) PROSPECTIVE RELIEF.—(A) Prospective relief in any civil action with respect to prison conditions shall extend no further than necessary to correct the violation of the Federal right of a particular plaintiff or plaintiffs. The court shall not grant or approve any prospective relief unless the court finds that such relief is narrowly drawn, extends no further than necessary to correct the violation of the Federal right, and is the least intrusive means necessary to correct the violation of the Federal right. The court shall give substantial weight to any adverse impact on public safety or the operation of a criminal justice system caused by the relief.
(B) The court shall not order any prospective relief that requires or permits a government official to exceed his or her authority under State or local law or otherwise violates State or local law, unless —
(i) Federal law permits such relief to be ordered in violation of State or local law;
(ii) the relief is necessary to correct the violation of a Federal right; and
(iii) no other relief will correct the violation of the Federal right.
(C) Nothing in this section shall be construed to authorize the courts, in exercising their remedial powers, to order the construction of prisons or the

raising of taxes, or to repeal or detract from otherwise applicable limitations on the remedial powers of the courts.

(2) PRELIMINARY INJUNCTIVE RELIEF.—In any civil action with respect to prison conditions, to the extent otherwise authorized by law, the court may enter a temporary restraining order or an order for preliminary injunctive relief. Preliminary injunctive relief must be narrowly drawn, extend no further than necessary to correct the harm the court finds requires preliminary relief, and be the least intrusive means necessary to correct that harm. The court shall give substantial weight to any adverse impact on public safety or the operation of a criminal justice system caused by the preliminary relief and shall respect the principles of comity set out in paragraph (1)(B) in tailoring any preliminary relief. Preliminary injunctive relief shall automatically expire on the date that is 90 days after its entry, unless the court makes the findings required under subsection (a)(1) for the entry of prospective relief and makes the order final before the expiration of the 90-day period.

(3) PRISONER RELEASE ORDER.—(A) In any civil action with respect to prison conditions, no prisoner release order shall be entered unless —

(i) a court has previously entered an order for less intrusive relief that has failed to remedy the deprivation of the Federal right sought to be remedied through the prisoner release order; and

(ii) the defendant has had a reasonable amount of time to comply with the previous court orders.

(B) In any civil action in Federal court with respect to prison conditions, a prisoner release order shall be entered only by a three-judge court in accordance with section 2284 of title 28, if the requirements of subparagraph (E) have been met.

(C) A party seeking a prisoner release order in Federal court shall file with any request for such relief, a request for a three-judge court and materials sufficient to demonstrate that the requirements of subparagraph (A) have been met.

(D) If the requirements under subparagraph (A) have been met, a Federal judge before whom a civil action with respect to prison conditions is pending who believes that a prison release order should be considered may *sua sponte* request the convening of a three-judge court to determine whether a prisoner release order should be entered.

(E) The three-judge court shall enter a prisoner release order only if the court finds by clear and convincing evidence that —

(i) crowding is the primary cause of the violation of a Federal right; and

(ii) no other relief will remedy the violation of the Federal right.

(F) Any State or local official or unit of government whose jurisdiction or function includes the appropriation of funds for the construction, operation,

252

or maintenance of program facilities, or the prosecution or custody of persons who may be released from, or not admitted to, a prison as a result of a prisoner release order shall have standing to oppose the imposition or continuation in effect of such relief and to seek termination of such relief, and shall have the right to intervene in any proceeding relating to such relief.

(b) TERMINATION OF RELIEF. —

(1) TERMINATION OF PROSPECTIVE RELIEF.—(A) In any civil action with respect to prison conditions in which prospective relief is ordered, such relief shall be terminable upon the motion of any party or intervener —

(i) 2 years after the date the court granted or approved the prospective relief;

(ii) 1 year after the date the court has entered an order denying termination of prospective relief under this paragraph; or

(iii) in the case of an order issued on or before the date of enactment of the PRISON LITIGATION REFORM ACT, 2 years after such date of enactment.

(B) Nothing in this section shall prevent the parties from agreeing to terminate or modify relief before the relief is terminated under subparagraph (A).

(2) IMMEDIATE TERMINATION OF PROSPECTIVE RELIEF.—In any civil action with respect to prison conditions, a defendant or intervener shall be entitled to the immediate termination of any prospective relief if the relief was approved or granted in the absence of a finding by the court that the relief is narrowly drawn, extends no further than necessary to correct the violation of the Federal right, and is the least intrusive means necessary to correct the violation of the Federal right.

(3) LIMITATION.—Prospective relief shall not terminate if the court makes written findings based on the record that prospective relief remains necessary to correct a current or ongoing violation of the Federal right, extends no further than necessary to correct the violation of the Federal right, and that the prospective relief is narrowly drawn and the least intrusive means to correct the violation.

(4) TERMINATION OR MODIFICATION OF RELIEF.—Nothing in this section shall prevent any party or intervener from seeking modification or termination before the relief is terminable under paragraph (1) or (2), to the extent that modification or termination would otherwise be legally permissible.

(c) SETTLEMENTS. —

(1) CONSENT DECREES.—In any civil action with respect to prison conditions, the court shall not enter or approve a consent decree unless it complies with the limitations on relief set forth in subsection (a).

(2) PRIVATE SETTLEMENT AGREEMENTS.—(A) Nothing in this section shall preclude parties from entering into a private settlement agreement that does not comply with the limitations on relief set forth in subsection (a), if the terms of that agreement are not subject to court enforcement other than the reinstatement of the civil proceeding that the agreement settled.

(B) Nothing in this section shall preclude any party claiming that a private settlement agreement has been breached from seeking in State court any remedy available under State law.

(d) STATE LAW REMEDIES.—The limitations on remedies in this section shall not apply to relief entered by a State court based solely upon claims arising under State law.

(e) PROCEDURE FOR MOTIONS AFFECTING PROSPECTIVE RELIEF. —

(1) GENERALLY.—The court shall promptly rule on any motion to modify or terminate prospective relief in a civil action with respect to prison conditions.

(2) AUTOMATIC STAY.—Any prospective relief subject to a pending motion shall be automatically stayed during the period —

(A)(i) beginning on the 30th day after such motion is filed, in the case of a motion made under paragraph (1) or (2) of subsection (b); or

(ii) beginning on the 180th day after such motion is filed, in the case of a motion made under any other law; and

(B) ending on the date the court enters a final order ruling on the motion.

(f) SPECIAL MASTERS. —

(1) IN GENERAL.—(A) In any civil action in a Federal court with respect to prison conditions, the court may appoint a special master who shall be disinterested and objective and who will give due regard to the public safety, to conduct hearings on the record and prepare proposed findings of fact.

(B) The court shall appoint a special master under this subsection during the remedial phase of the action only upon a finding that the remedial phase will be sufficiently complex to warrant the appointment.

(2) APPOINTMENT.—(A) If the court determines that the appointment of a special master is necessary, the court shall request that the defendant institution and the plaintiff each submit a list of not more than 5 persons to serve as a special master.

(B) Each party shall have the opportunity to remove up to 3 persons from the opposing party's list.

(C) The court shall select the master from the persons remaining on the list after the operation of subparagraph (B).

(3) INTERLOCUTORY APPEAL.—Any party shall have the right to an interlocutory appeal of the judge's selection of the special master under this subsection, on the ground of partiality.

Appendix B

(4) COMPENSATION.—The compensation to be allowed to a special master under this section shall be based on an hourly rate not greater than the hourly rate established under section 3006A for payment of court-appointed counsel, plus costs reasonably incurred by the special master. Such compensation and costs shall be paid with funds appropriated to the Judiciary.

(5) REGULAR REVIEW OF APPOINTMENT.—In any civil action with respect to prison conditions in which a special master is appointed under this subsection, the court shall review the appointment of the special master every 6 months to determine whether the services of the special master continue to be required under paragraph (1). In no event shall the appointment of a special master extend beyond the termination of the relief.

(6) LIMITATIONS ON POWERS AND DUTIES.—A special master appointed under this subsection —

(A) may be authorized by a court to conduct hearings and prepare proposed findings of fact, which shall be made on the record;

(B) shall not make any findings or communications ex parte;

(C) may be authorized by a court to assist in the development of remedial plans; and

(D) may be removed at any time, but shall be relieved of the appointment upon the termination of relief.

(g) DEFINITIONS.—As used in this section —

(1) the term 'consent decree' means any relief entered by the court that is based in whole or in part upon the consent or acquiescence of the parties but does not include private settlements;

(2) the term 'civil action with respect to prison conditions' means any civil proceeding arising under Federal law with respect to the conditions of confinement or the effects of actions by government officials on the lives of persons confined in prison, but does not include habeas corpus proceedings challenging the fact or duration of confinement in prison;

(3) the term 'prisoner' means any person subject to incarceration, detention, or admission to any facility who is accused of, convicted of, sentenced for, or adjudicated delinquent for, violations of criminal law or the terms and conditions of parole, probation, pretrial release, or diversionary program;

(4) the term 'prisoner release order' includes any order, including a temporary restraining order or preliminary injunctive relief, that has the purpose or effect of reducing or limiting the prison population, or that directs the release from or nonadmission of prisoners to a prison;

(5) the term 'prison' means any Federal, State, or local facility that incarcerates or detains juveniles or adults accused of, convicted of, sentenced for, or adjudicated delinquent for, violations of criminal law;

(6) the term 'private settlement agreement' means an agreement entered into among the parties that is not subject to judicial enforcement other than the reinstatement of the civil proceeding that the agreement settled;

(7) the term 'prospective relief' means all relief other than compensatory monetary damages;

(8) the term 'special master' means any person appointed by a Federal court pursuant to Rule 53 of the Federal Rules of Civil Procedure or pursuant to any inherent power of the court to exercise the powers of a master, regardless of the title or description given by the court; and

(9) the term 'relief' means all relief in any form that may be granted or approved by the court, and includes consent decrees but does not include private settlement agreements

(b) APPLICATION OF AMENDMENT. —

(1) IN GENERAL.—Section 3626 of title 18, United States Code, as amended by this section, shall apply with respect to all prospective relief whether such relief was originally granted or approved before, on, or after the date of the enactment of this title.

(2) TECHNICAL AMENDMENT.—Subsections (b) and (d) of section 20409 of the Violent Crime Control and Law Enforcement Act of 1994 are repealed.

(c) CLERICAL AMENDMENT.—The table of sections at the beginning of subchapter C of chapter 229 of title 18, United States Code, is amended to read as follows: 3626. Appropriate remedies with respect to prison conditions.

SEC. 803. AMENDMENTS TO CIVIL RIGHTS OF INSTITUTIONALIZED PERSONS ACT.

(a) INITIATION OF CIVIL ACTIONS.

— Section 3(c) of the Civil Rights of Institutionalized Persons Act (42 U.S.C. 1997a(c)) (referred to in this section as the Act) is amended to read as follows:

(c) The Attorney General shall personally sign any complaint filed pursuant to this section.

(b) CERTIFICATION REQUIREMENTS.

— Section 4 of the Act (42 U.S.C. 1997b) is amended —

(1) in subsection (a) —

(A) by striking he each place it appears and inserting the Attorney General; and

(B) by striking his and inserting the Attorney General's; and (2) by amending subsection (b) to read as follows:

(b) The Attorney General shall personally sign any certification made pursuant to this section.

(c) INTERVENTION IN ACTIONS.—Section 5 of the Act (42 U.S.C. 1997c) is amended —

(1) in subsection (b) —

(A) in paragraph (1), by striking he each place it appears and inserting the Attorney General; and

(B) by amending paragraph (2) to read as follows:

(2) The Attorney General shall personally sign any certification made pursuant to this section.; and

(2) by amending subsection (c) to read as follows:

(c) The Attorney General shall personally sign any motion to intervene made pursuant to this section.

(d) SUITS BY PRISONERS.—Section 7 of the Act (42 U.S.C. 1997e) is amended to read as follows:

SEC. 7. SUITS BY PRISONERS.

(a) APPLICABILITY OF ADMINISTRATIVE REMEDIES.—No action shall be brought with respect to prison conditions under section 1979 of the Revised Statutes of the United States (42 U.S.C. 1983), or any other Federal law, by a prisoner confined in any jail, prison, or other correctional facility until such administrative remedies as are available are exhausted.

(b) FAILURE OF STATE TO ADOPT OR ADHERE TO ADMINIS-TRATIVE GRIEVANCE PROCEDURE.—The failure of a State to adopt or adhere to an administrative grievance procedure shall not constitute the basis for an action under section 3 or 5 of this Act.

(c) DISMISSAL.—(1) The court shall on its own motion or on the motion of a party dismiss any action brought with respect to prison conditions under section 1979 of the Revised Statutes of the United States (42 U.S.C. 1983), or any other Federal law, by a prisoner confined in any jail, prison, or other correctional facility if the court is satisfied that the action is frivolous, malicious, fails to state a claim upon which relief can be granted, or seeks monetary relief from a defendant who is immune from such relief.

(2) In the event that a claim is, on its face, frivolous, malicious, fails to state a claim upon which relief can be granted, or seeks monetary relief from a defendant who is immune from such relief, the court may dismiss the underlying claim without first requiring the exhaustion of administrative remedies.

(d) ATTORNEY'S FEES.—(1) In any action brought by a prisoner who is confined to any jail, prison, or other correctional facility, in which attorney's fees are authorized under section 2 of the Revised Statutes of the United States (42 U.S.C. 1988), such fees shall not be awarded, except to the extent that —

(A) the fee was directly and reasonably incurred in proving an actual violation of the plaintiff's rights protected by a statute pursuant to which a fee may be awarded under section 2 of the Revised Statutes; and

Prisons

(B)(i) the amount of the fee is proportionately related to the court ordered relief for the violation; or (ii) the fee was directly and reasonably incurred in enforcing the relief ordered for the violation.

(2) Whenever a monetary judgment is awarded in an action described in paragraph (1), a portion of the judgment (not to exceed 25 percent) shall be applied to satisfy the amount of attorney's fees awarded against the defendant. If the award of attorney's fees is not greater than 150 percent of the judgment, the excess shall be paid by the defendant.

(3) No award of attorney's fees in an action described in paragraph (1) shall be based on an hourly rate greater than 150 percent of the hourly rate established under section 3006A of title 18, United States Code, for payment of court-appointed counsel.

(4) Nothing in this subsection shall prohibit a prisoner from entering into an agreement to pay an attorney's fee in an amount greater than the amount authorized under this subsection, if the fee is paid by the individual rather than by the defendant pursuant to section 2 of the Revised Statutes of the United States (42 U.S.C. 1988).

(e) LIMITATION ON RECOVERY.—No Federal civil action may be brought by a prisoner confined in a jail, prison, or other correctional facility, for mental or emotional injury suffered while in custody without a prior showing of physical injury.

(f) HEARINGS.—(1) To the extent practicable, in any action brought with respect to prison conditions in Federal court pursuant to section 1979 of the Revised Statutes of the United States (42 U.S.C. 1983), or any other Federal law, by a prisoner confined in any jail, prison, or other correctional facility, pretrial proceedings in which the prisoner's participation is required or permitted shall be conducted by telephone, video conference, or other telecommunications technology without removing the prisoner from the facility in which the prisoner is confined.

(2) Subject to the agreement of the official of the Federal, State, or local unit of government with custody over the prisoner, hearings may be conducted at the facility in which the prisoner is confined. To the extent practicable, the court shall allow counsel to participate by telephone, video conference, or other communications technology in any hearing held at the facility.

(g) WAIVER OF REPLY.—(1) Any defendant may waive the right to reply to any action brought by a prisoner confined in any jail, prison, or other correctional facility under section 1979 of the Revised Statutes of the United States (42 U.S.C. 1983) or any other Federal law. Notwithstanding any other law or rule of procedure, such waiver shall not constitute an admission of the allegations contained in the complaint. No relief shall be granted to the plaintiff unless a reply has been filed.

(2) The court may require any defendant to reply to a complaint brought under this section if it finds that the plaintiff has a reasonable opportunity to prevail on the merits.

(h) DEFINITION.—As used in this section, the term 'prisoner' means any person incarcerated or detained in any facility who is accused of, convicted of, sentenced for, or adjudicated delinquent for, violations of criminal law or the terms and conditions of parole, probation, pretrial release, or diversionary program.

(e) REPORT TO CONGRESS.—Section 8 of the Act (42 U.S.C. 1997 f) is amended by striking his report and inserting the report.

(f) NOTICE TO FEDERAL DEPARTMENTS.—Section 10 of the Act (42 U.S.C. 1997h) is amended —

(1) by striking his action and inserting the action; and

(2) by striking he is satisfied and inserting the Attorney General is satisfied.

SEC. 804. PROCEEDINGS IN FORMA PAUPERIS.

(a) FILING FEES.—Section 1915 of title 28, United States Code, is amended —

(1) in subsection (a) —

(A) by striking (a) Any and inserting (a)(1) Subject to subsection (b), any;

(B) by striking and costs;

(C) by striking makes affidavit and inserting submits an affidavit that includes a statement of all assets such prisoner possesses;

(D) by striking such costs and inserting such fees;

(E) by striking he each place it appears and inserting the person;

(F) by adding immediately after paragraph (1), the following new paragraph:

(2) A prisoner seeking to bring a civil action or appeal a judgment in a civil action or proceeding without prepayment of fees or security therefor, in addition to filing the affidavit filed under paragraph (1), shall submit a certified copy of the trust fund account statement (or institutional equivalent) for the prisoner for the 6-month period immediately preceding the filing of the complaint or notice of appeal, obtained from the appropriate official of each prison at which the prisoner is or was confined; and

(G) by striking An appeal and inserting (3) An appeal;

(2) by redesignating subsections (b), (c), (d), and (e) as subsections (c), (d), (e), and (f), respectively;

(3) by inserting after subsection (a) the following new subsection:

(b)(1) Notwithstanding subsection (a), if a prisoner brings a civil action or files an appeal in forma pauperis, the prisoner shall be required to pay the full amount of a filing fee. The court shall assess and, when funds exist, collect, as a partial payment of any court fees required by law, an initial partial filing fee of 20 percent of the greater of —

(A) the average monthly deposits to the prisoner's account; or

(B) the average monthly balance in the prisoner's account for the 6-month period immediately preceding the filing of the complaint or notice of appeal.

(2) After payment of the initial partial filing fee, the prisoner shall be required to make monthly payments of 20 percent of the preceding month's income credited to the prisoner's account. The agency having custody of the prisoner shall forward payments from the prisoner's account to the clerk of the court each time the amount in the account exceeds $10 until the filing fees are paid.

(3) In no event shall the filing fee collected exceed the amount of fees permitted by statute for the commencement of a civil action or an appeal of a civil action or criminal judgment.

(4) In no event shall a prisoner be prohibited from bringing a civil action or appealing a civil or criminal judgment for the reason that the prisoner has no assets and no means by which to pay the initial partial filing fee;

(4) in subsection (c), as redesignated by paragraph (2), by striking subsection (a) of this section and inserting subsections (a) and (b) and the prepayment of any partial filing fee as may be required under subsection (b); and

(5) by amending subsection (e), as redesignated by paragraph (2), to read as follows:

(e)(1) The court may request an attorney to represent any person unable to afford counsel.

(2) Notwithstanding any filing fee, or any portion thereof, that may have been paid, the court shall dismiss the case at any time if the court determines that —

(A) the allegation of poverty is untrue; or

(B) the action or appeal —

(i) is frivolous or malicious;

(ii) fails to state a claim on which relief may be granted; or

(iii) seeks monetary relief against a defendant who is immune from such relief.

(b) EXCEPTION TO DISCHARGE OF DEBT IN BANKRUPTCY PROCEEDING.—Section 523(a) of title 11, United States Code, is amended —

(1) in paragraph (16), by striking the period at the end and inserting; or; and

(2) by adding at the end the following new paragraph:

(17) for a fee imposed by a court for the filing of a case, motion, complaint, or appeal, or for other costs and expenses assessed with respect to such filing, regardless of an assertion of poverty by the debtor under section 1915(b) or (f) of title 28, or the debtor's status as a prisoner, as defined in section 1915(h) of title 28.

(c) COSTS.—Section 1915(f) of title 28, United States Code (as redesignated by subsection (a)(2)), is amended —
(1) by striking (f) Judgment and inserting (f)(1) Judgment;
(2) by striking cases and inserting proceedings; and
(3) by adding at the end the following new paragraph:
(2)(A) If the judgment against a prisoner includes the payment of costs under this subsection, the prisoner shall be required to pay the full amount of the costs ordered.
(B) The prisoner shall be required to make payments for costs under this subsection in the same manner as is provided for filing fees under subsection (a)(2).
(C) In no event shall the costs collected exceed the amount of the costs ordered by the court.
(d) SUCCESSIVE CLAIMS.—Section 1915 of title 28, United States Code, is amended by adding at the end the following new subsection: (g) In no event shall a prisoner bring a civil action or appeal a judgment in a civil action or proceeding under this section if the prisoner has, on 3 or more prior occasions, while incarcerated or detained in any facility, brought an action or appeal in a court of the United States that was dismissed on the grounds that it is frivolous, malicious, or fails to state a claim upon which relief may be granted, unless the prisoner is under imminent danger of serious physical injury —
(e) DEFINITION.—Section 1915 of title 28, United States Code, is amended by adding at the end the following new subsection:
(h) As used in this section, the term 'prisoner' means any person incarcerated or detained in any facility who is accused of, convicted of, sentenced for, or adjudicated delinquent for, violations of criminal law or the terms and conditions of parole, probation, pretrial release, or diversionary program.
SEC. 805. JUDICIAL SCREENING.
(a) IN GENERAL.—Chapter 123 of title 28, United States Code, is amended by inserting after section 1915 the following new section:
s 1915A. Screening
(a) SCREENING.—The court shall review, before docketing, if feasible or, in any event, as soon as practicable after docketing, a complaint in a civil action in which a prisoner seeks redress from a governmental entity or officer or employee of a governmental entity.
(b) GROUNDS FOR DISMISSAL.—On review, the court shall identify cognizable claims or dismiss the complaint, or any portion of the complaint, if the complaint —
(1) is frivolous, malicious, or fails to state a claim upon which relief may be granted; or
(2) seeks monetary relief from a defendant who is immune from such relief.

(c) DEFINITION.—As used in this section, the term 'prisoner' means any person incarcerated or detained in any facility who is accused of, convicted of, sentenced for, or adjudicated delinquent for, violations of criminal law or the terms and conditions of parole, probation, pretrial release, or diversionary program.

(b) TECHNICAL AMENDMENT.—The analysis for chapter 123 of title 28, United States Code, is amended by inserting after the item relating to section 1915 the following new item:

1915A. Screening.

SEC. 806. FEDERAL TORT CLAIMS.

Section 1346(b) of title 28, United States Code, is amended —

(1) by striking (b) and inserting (b)(1); and

(2) by adding at the end the following:

(2) No person convicted of a felony who is incarcerated while awaiting sentencing or while serving a sentence may bring a civil action against the United States or an agency, officer, or employee of the Government, for mental or emotional injury suffered while in custody without a prior showing of physical injury.

SEC. 807. PAYMENT OF DAMAGE AWARD IN SATISFACTION OF PENDING RESTITUTION ORDERS.

Any compensatory damages awarded to a prisoner in connection with a civil action brought against any Federal, State, or local jail, prison, or correctional facility or against any official or agent of such jail, prison, or correctional facility, shall be paid directly to satisfy any outstanding restitution orders pending against the prisoner. The remainder of any such award after full payment of all pending restitution orders shall be forwarded to the prisoner.

SEC. 808. NOTICE TO CRIME VICTIMS OF PENDING DAMAGE AWARD.

Prior to payment of any compensatory damages awarded to a prisoner in connection with a civil action brought against any Federal, State, or local jail, prison, or correctional facility or against any official or agent of such jail, prison, or correctional facility, reasonable efforts shall be made to notify the victims of the crime for which the prisoner was convicted and incarcerated concerning the pending payment of any such compensatory damages.

SEC. 809. EARNED RELEASE CREDIT OR GOOD TIME CREDIT REVOCATION.

(a) IN GENERAL.—Chapter 123 of title 28, United States Code, is amended by adding at the end the following new section:

s 1932. Revocation of earned release credit

In any civil action brought by an adult convicted of a crime and confined in a Federal correctional facility, the court may order the revocation of such

earned good time credit under section 3624(b) of title 18, United States Code, that has not yet vested, if, on its own motion or the motion of any party, the court finds that —
(1) the claim was filed for a malicious purpose;
(2) the claim was filed solely to harass the party against which it was filed; or
(3) the claimant testifies falsely or otherwise knowingly presents false evidence or information to the court.
(b) TECHNICAL AMENDMENT.—The analysis for chapter 123 of title 28, United States Code, is amended by inserting after the item relating to section 1931 the following:
1932. Revocation of earned release credit.
(c) AMENDMENT OF SECTION 3624 OF TITLE 18.—Section 3624(b) of title 18, United States Code, is amended —
(1) in paragraph (1) —
(A) by striking the first sentence;
(B) in the second sentence —
(i) by striking A prisoner and inserting Subject to paragraph (2), a prisoner;
(ii) by striking for a crime of violence; and
(iii) by striking such;
(C) in the third sentence, by striking If the Bureau and inserting Subject to paragraph (2), if the Bureau;
(D) by striking the fourth sentence and inserting the following: In awarding credit under this section, the Bureau shall consider whether the prisoner, during the relevant period, has earned, or is making satisfactory progress toward earning, a high school diploma or an equivalent degree; and
(E) in the sixth sentence, by striking Credit for the last and inserting Subject to paragraph (2), credit for the last; and
(2) by amending paragraph (2) to read as follows:
(2) Notwithstanding any other law, credit awarded under this subsection after the date of enactment of the PRISON LITIGATION REFORM ACT shall vest on the date the prisoner is released from custody.
SEC. 810. SEVERABILITY.
If any provision of this title, an amendment made by this title, or the application of such provision or amendment to any person or circumstance is held to be unconstitutional, the remainder of this title, the amendments made by this title, and the application of the provisions of such to any person or circumstance shall not be affected thereby.
This Act may be cited as the Department of Commerce, Justice, and State, the Judiciary, and Related Agencies Appropriations Act, 1996. (b) For programs, projects or activities in the District of Columbia Appropriations Act, 1996, provided as follows, to be effective as if it had been enacted into law

as the regular appropriations Act: An Act making appropriations for the government of the District of Columbia and other activities chargeable in whole or in part against the revenues of said District for the fiscal year ending September 30, 1996, and for other purposes.

APPENDIX C

THE PRISON RAPE ELIMINATION ACT

Enacted on January 7, 2003,
by the 108th Congress of the United States

An Act

To provide for the analysis of the incidence and effects of prison rape in Federal, State, and local institutions and to provide information, resources, recommendations, and funding to protect individuals from prison rape.

Be it enacted by the Senate and House of Representatives of the United States of America in Congress assembled,

SECTION 1. SHORT TITLE; TABLE OF CONTENTS.

(a) SHORT TITLE— This Act may be cited as the "Prison Rape Elimination Act of 2003."

(b) TABLE OF CONTENTS— The table of contents of this Act is as follows:

SECTION 2. FINDINGS.

Congress makes the following findings:

265

Prisons

(1) 2,100,146 persons were incarcerated in the United States at the end of 2001: 1,324,465 in Federal and State prisons and 631,240 in county and local jails. In 1999, there were more than 10,000,000 separate admissions to and discharges from prisons and jails.

(2) Insufficient research has been conducted and insufficient data reported on the extent of prison rape. However, experts have conservatively estimated that at least 13 percent of the inmates in the United States have been sexually assaulted in prison. Many inmates have suffered repeated assaults. Under this estimate, nearly 200,000 inmates now incarcerated have been or will be the victims of prison rape. The total number of inmates who have been sexually assaulted in the past 20 years likely exceeds 1,000,000.

(3) Inmates with mental illness are at increased risk of sexual victimization. America's jails and prisons house more mentally ill individuals than all of the Nation's psychiatric hospitals combined. As many as 16 percent of inmates in State prisons and jails, and 7 percent of Federal inmates, suffer from mental illness.

(4) Young first-time offenders are at increased risk of sexual victimization. Juveniles are 5 times more likely to be sexually assaulted in adult rather than juvenile facilities—often within the first 48 hours of incarceration.

(5) Most prison staff are not adequately trained or prepared to prevent, report, or treat inmate sexual assaults.

(6) Prison rape often goes unreported, and inmate victims often receive inadequate treatment for the severe physical and psychological effects of sexual assault—if they receive treatment at all.

(7) HIV and AIDS are major public health problems within America's correctional facilities. In 2000, 25,088 inmates in Federal and State prisons were known to be infected with HIV/AIDS. In 2000, HIV/AIDS accounted for more than 6 percent of all deaths in Federal and State prisons. Infection rates for other sexually transmitted diseases, tuberculosis, and hepatitis B and C are also far greater for prisoners than for the American population as a whole. Prison rape undermines the public health by contributing to the spread of these diseases, and often giving a potential death sentence to its victims.

(8) Prison rape endangers the public safety by making brutalized inmates more likely to commit crimes when they are released—as 600,000 inmates are each year.

(9) The frequently interracial character of prison sexual assaults significantly exacerbates interracial tensions, both within prison and, upon release of perpetrators and victims from prison, in the community at large.

(10) Prison rape increases the level of homicides and other violence against inmates and staff, and the risk of insurrections and riots.

266

Appendix C

(11) Victims of prison rape suffer severe physical and psychological effects that hinder their ability to integrate into the community and maintain stable employment upon their release from prison. They are thus more likely to become homeless and/or require government assistance.

(12) Members of the public and government officials are largely unaware of the epidemic character of prison rape and the day-to-day horror experienced by victimized inmates.

(13) The high incidence of sexual assault within prisons involves actual and potential violations of the United States Constitution. In Farmer v. Brennan, 511 U.S. 825 (1994), the Supreme Court ruled that deliberate indifference to the substantial risk of sexual assault violates prisoners' rights under the Cruel and Unusual Punishments Clause of the Eighth Amendment. The Eighth Amendment rights of State and local prisoners are protected through the Due Process Clause of the Fourteenth Amendment. Pursuant to the power of Congress under Section Five of the Fourteenth Amendment, Congress may take action to enforce those rights in States where officials have demonstrated such indifference. States that do not take basic steps to abate prison rape by adopting standards that do not generate significant additional expenditures demonstrate such indifference. Therefore, such States are not entitled to the same level of Federal benefits as other States.

(14) The high incidence of prison rape undermines the effectiveness and efficiency of United States Government expenditures through grant programs such as those dealing with health care; mental health care; disease prevention; crime prevention, investigation, and prosecution; prison construction, maintenance, and operation; race relations; poverty; unemployment and homelessness. The effectiveness and efficiency of these federally funded grant programs are compromised by the failure of State officials to adopt policies and procedures that reduce the incidence of prison rape in that the high incidence of prison rape —

(A) increases the costs incurred by Federal, State, and local jurisdictions to administer their prison systems;

(B) increases the levels of violence, directed at inmates and at staff, within prisons;

(C) increases health care expenditures, both inside and outside of prison systems, and reduces the effectiveness of disease prevention programs by substantially increasing the incidence and spread of HIV, AIDS, tuberculosis, hepatitis B and C, and other diseases;

(D) increases mental health care expenditures, both inside and outside of prison systems, by substantially increasing the rate of post-traumatic stress disorder, depression, suicide, and the exacerbation of existing mental illnesses among current and former inmates;

267

(E) increases the risks of recidivism, civil strife, and violent crime by individuals who have been brutalized by prison rape; and

(F) increases the level of interracial tensions and strife within prisons and, upon release of perpetrators and victims, in the community at large.

(15) The high incidence of prison rape has a significant effect on interstate commerce because it increases substantially —

(A) the costs incurred by Federal, State, and local jurisdictions to administer their prison systems;

(B) the incidence and spread of HIV, AIDS, tuberculosis, hepatitis B and C, and other diseases, contributing to increased health and medical expenditures throughout the Nation;

(C) the rate of post-traumatic stress disorder, depression, suicide, and the exacerbation of existing mental illnesses among current and former inmates, contributing to increased health and medical expenditures throughout the Nation; and

(D) the risk of recidivism, civil strife, and violent crime by individuals who have been brutalized by prison rape.

SECTION 3. PURPOSES.

The purposes of this Act are to —

(1) establish a zero-tolerance standard for the incidence of prison rape in prisons in the United States;

(2) make the prevention of prison rape a top priority in each prison system;

(3) develop and implement national standards for the detection, prevention, reduction, and punishment of prison rape;

(4) increase the available data and information on the incidence of prison rape, consequently improving the management and administration of correctional facilities;

(5) standardize the definitions used for collecting data on the incidence of prison rape;

(6) increase the accountability of prison officials who fail to detect, prevent, reduce, and punish prison rape;

(7) protect the Eighth Amendment rights of Federal, State, and local prisoners;

(8) increase the efficiency and effectiveness of Federal expenditures through grant programs such as those dealing with health care; mental health care; disease prevention; crime prevention, investigation, and prosecution; prison construction, maintenance, and operation; race relations; poverty; unemployment; and homelessness; and

(9) reduce the costs that prison rape imposes on interstate commerce.

SECTION 4. NATIONAL PRISON RAPE STATISTICS, DATA, AND RESEARCH.

(a) ANNUAL COMPREHENSIVE STATISTICAL REVIEW —

Appendix C

(1) IN GENERAL—The Bureau of Justice Statistics of the Department of Justice (in this section referred to as the 'Bureau') shall carry out, for each calendar year, a comprehensive statistical review and analysis of the incidence and effects of prison rape. The statistical review and analysis shall include, but not be limited to the identification of the common characteristics of —
(A) both victims and perpetrators of prison rape; and
(B) prisons and prison systems with a high incidence of prison rape.
(2) CONSIDERATIONS—In carrying out paragraph (1), the Bureau shall consider —
(A) how rape should be defined for the purposes of the statistical review and analysis;
(B) how the Bureau should collect information about staff-on-inmate sexual assault;
(C) how the Bureau should collect information beyond inmate self-reports of prison rape;
(D) how the Bureau should adjust the data in order to account for differences among prisons as required by subsection (c)(3);
(E) the categorization of prisons as required by subsection (c)(4); and
(F) whether a preliminary study of prison rape should be conducted to inform the methodology of the comprehensive statistical review.
(3) SOLICITATION OF VIEWS—The Bureau of Justice Statistics shall solicit views from representatives of the following: State departments of correction; county and municipal jails; juvenile correctional facilities; former inmates; victim advocates; researchers; and other experts in the area of sexual assault.
(4) SAMPLING TECHNIQUES—The review and analysis under paragraph (1) shall be based on a random sample, or other scientifically appropriate sample, of not less than 10 percent of all Federal, State, and county prisons, and a representative sample of municipal prisons. The selection shall include at least one prison from each State. The selection of facilities for sampling shall be made at the latest practicable date prior to conducting the surveys and shall not be disclosed to any facility or prison system official prior to the time period studied in the survey. Selection of a facility for sampling during any year shall not preclude its selection for sampling in any subsequent year.
(5) SURVEYS—In carrying out the review and analysis under paragraph (1), the Bureau shall, in addition to such other methods as the Bureau considers appropriate, use surveys and other statistical studies of current and former inmates from a sample of Federal, State, county, and municipal prisons. The Bureau shall ensure the confidentiality of each survey participant.

(6) PARTICIPATION IN SURVEY—Federal, State, or local officials or facility administrators that receive a request from the Bureau under subsection (a)(4) or (5) will be required to participate in the national survey and provide access to any inmates under their legal custody.

(b) REVIEW PANEL ON PRISON RAPE —

(1) ESTABLISHMENT—To assist the Bureau in carrying out the review and analysis under subsection (a), there is established, within the Department of Justice, the Review Panel on Prison Rape (in this section referred to as the 'Panel').

(2) MEMBERSHIP —

(A) COMPOSITION—The Panel shall be composed of 3 members, each of whom shall be appointed by the Attorney General, in consultation with the Secretary of Health and Human Services.

(B) QUALIFICATIONS—Members of the Panel shall be selected from among individuals with knowledge or expertise in matters to be studied by the Panel.

(3) PUBLIC HEARINGS —

(A) IN GENERAL—The duty of the Panel shall be to carry out, for each calendar year, public hearings concerning the operation of the three prisons with the highest incidence of prison rape and the two prisons with the lowest incidence of prison rape in each category of facilities identified under subsection (c)(4). The Panel shall hold a separate hearing regarding the three Federal or State prisons with the highest incidence of prison rape. The purpose of these hearings shall be to collect evidence to aid in the identification of common characteristics of both victims and perpetrators of prison rape, and the identification of common characteristics of prisons and prison systems with a high incidence of prison rape, and the identification of common characteristics of prisons and prison systems that appear to have been successful in deterring prison rape.

(B) TESTIMONY AT HEARINGS —

(i) PUBLIC OFFICIALS—In carrying out the hearings required under subparagraph (A), the Panel shall request the public testimony of Federal, State, and local officials (and organizations that represent such officials), including the warden or director of each prison, who bears responsibility for the prevention, detection, and punishment of prison rape at each entity, and the head of the prison system encompassing such prison.

(ii) VICTIMS—The Panel may request the testimony of prison rape victims, organizations representing such victims, and other appropriate individuals and organizations.

(C) SUBPOENAS —

(i) ISSUANCE—The Panel may issue subpoenas for the attendance of witnesses and the production of written or other matter.

270

(ii) ENFORCEMENT—In the case of contumacy or refusal to obey a sub-poena, the Attorney General may in a Federal court of appropriate jurisdiction obtain an appropriate order to enforce the subpoena.

(c) REPORTS —

(1) IN GENERAL—Not later than June 30 of each year, the Attorney General shall submit a report on the activities of the Bureau and the Review Panel, with respect to prison rape, for the preceding calendar year to —

(A) Congress; and

(B) the Secretary of Health and Human Services.

(2) CONTENTS—The report required under paragraph (1) shall include —

(A) with respect to the effects of prison rape, statistical, sociological, and psychological data;

(B) with respect to the incidence of prison rape —

(i) statistical data aggregated at the Federal, State, prison system, and prison levels;

(ii) a listing of those institutions in the representative sample, separated into each category identified under subsection (c)(4) and ranked according to the incidence of prison rape in each institution; and

(iii) an identification of those institutions in the representative sample that appear to have been successful in deterring prison rape; and

(C) a listing of any prisons in the representative sample that did not cooperate with the survey conducted pursuant to section 4.

(3) DATA ADJUSTMENTS—In preparing the information specified in paragraph (2), the Attorney General shall use established statistical methods to adjust the data as necessary to account for differences among institutions in the representative sample, which are not related to the detection, prevention, reduction and punishment of prison rape, or which are outside the control of the State, prison, or prison system, in order to provide an accurate comparison among prisons. Such differences may include the mission, security level, size, and jurisdiction under which the prison operates. For each such adjustment made, the Attorney General shall identify and explain such adjustment in the report.

(4) CATEGORIZATION OF PRISONS—The report shall divide the prisons surveyed into three categories. One category shall be composed of all Federal and State prisons. The other two categories shall be defined by the Attorney General in order to compare similar institutions.

(d) CONTRACTS AND GRANTS—In carrying out its duties under this section, the Attorney General may —

(1) provide grants for research through the National Institute of Justice; and

(2) contract with or provide grants to any other entity the Attorney General deems appropriate.

(e) AUTHORIZATION OF APPROPRIATIONS—There are authorized to be appropriated $15,000,000 for each of fiscal years 2004 through 2010 to carry out this section.

SECTION 5. PRISON RAPE PREVENTION AND PROSECUTION.

(a) INFORMATION AND ASSISTANCE —

(1) NATIONAL CLEARINGHOUSE—There is established within the National Institute of Corrections a national clearinghouse for the provision of information and assistance to Federal, State, and local authorities responsible for the prevention, investigation, and punishment of instances of prison rape.

(2) TRAINING AND EDUCATION—The National Institute of Corrections shall conduct periodic training and education programs for Federal, State, and local authorities responsible for the prevention, investigation, and punishment of instances of prison rape.

(b) REPORTS —

(1) IN GENERAL—Not later than September 30 of each year, the National Institute of Corrections shall submit a report to Congress and the Secretary of Health and Human Services. This report shall be available to the Director of the Bureau of Justice Statistics.

(2) CONTENTS—The report required under paragraph (1) shall summarize the activities of the Department of Justice regarding prison rape abatement for the preceding calendar year.

(c) AUTHORIZATION OF APPROPRIATIONS—There are authorized to be appropriated $5,000,000 for each of fiscal years 2004 through 2010 to carry out this section.

SECTION 6. GRANTS TO PROTECT INMATES AND SAFEGUARD COMMUNITIES.

(a) GRANTS AUTHORIZED—From amounts made available for grants under this section, the Attorney General shall make grants to States to assist those States in ensuring that budgetary circumstances (such as reduced State and local spending on prisons) do not compromise efforts to protect inmates (particularly from prison rape) and to safeguard the communities to which inmates return. The purpose of grants under this section shall be to provide funds for personnel, training, technical assistance, data collection, and equipment to prevent and prosecute prisoner rape.

(b) USE OF GRANT AMOUNTS—Amounts received by a grantee under this section may be used by the grantee, directly or through subgrants, only for one or more of the following activities:

(1) PROTECTING INMATES— Protecting inmates by —

(A) undertaking efforts to more effectively prevent prison rape;

(B) investigating incidents of prison rape; or

(C) prosecuting incidents of prison rape.

Appendix C

(2) SAFEGUARDING COMMUNITIES—Safeguarding communities by —

(A) making available, to officials of State and local governments who are considering reductions to prison budgets, training and technical assistance in successful methods for moderating the growth of prison populations without compromising public safety, including successful methods used by other jurisdictions;

(B) developing and utilizing analyses of prison populations and risk assessment instruments that will improve State and local governments' understanding of risks to the community regarding release of inmates in the prison population;

(C) preparing maps demonstrating the concentration, on a community-by-community basis, of inmates who have been released, to facilitate the efficient and effective —

(i) deployment of law enforcement resources (including probation and parole resources); and

(ii) delivery of services (such as job training and substance abuse treatment) to those released inmates;

(D) promoting collaborative efforts, among officials of State and local governments and leaders of appropriate communities, to understand and address the effects on a community of the presence of a disproportionate number of released inmates in that community; or

(E) developing policies and programs that reduce spending on prisons by effectively reducing rates of parole and probation revocation without compromising public safety.

(c) GRANT REQUIREMENTS —

(1) PERIOD—A grant under this section shall be made for a period of not more than 2 years.

(2) MAXIMUM—The amount of a grant under this section may not exceed $1,000,000.

(3) MATCHING—The Federal share of a grant under this section may not exceed 50 percent of the total costs of the project described in the application submitted under subsection (d) for the fiscal year for which the grant was made under this section.

(d) APPLICATIONS —

(1) IN GENERAL—To request a grant under this section, the chief executive of a State shall submit an application to the Attorney General at such time, in such manner, and accompanied by such information as the Attorney General may require.

(2) CONTENTS—Each application required by paragraph (1) shall —

(A) include the certification of the chief executive that the State receiving such grant —

(i) has adopted all national prison rape standards that, as of the date on which the application was submitted, have been promulgated under this Act; and

(ii) will consider adopting all national prison rape standards that are promulgated under this Act after such date;

(B) specify with particularity the preventative, prosecutorial, or administrative activities to be undertaken by the State with the amounts received under the grant; and

(C) in the case of an application for a grant for one or more activities specified in paragraph (2) of subsection (b) —

(i) review the extent of the budgetary circumstances affecting the State generally and describe how those circumstances relate to the State's prisons;

(ii) describe the rate of growth of the State's prison population over the preceding 10 years and explain why the State may have difficulty sustaining that rate of growth; and

(iii) explain the extent to which officials (including law enforcement officials) of State and local governments and victims of crime will be consulted regarding decisions whether, or how, to moderate the growth of the State's prison population.

(e) REPORTS BY GRANTEE —

(1) IN GENERAL—The Attorney General shall require each grantee to submit, not later than 90 days after the end of the period for which the grant was made under this section, a report on the activities carried out under the grant. The report shall identify and describe those activities and shall contain an evaluation of the effect of those activities on —

(A) the number of incidents of prison rape, and the grantee's response to such incidents; and

(B) the safety of the prisons, and the safety of the communities in which released inmates are present.

(2) DISSEMINATION—The Attorney General shall ensure that each report submitted under paragraph (1) is made available under the national clearinghouse established under section 5.

(f) STATE DEFINED—In this section, the term 'State' includes the District of Columbia, the Commonwealth of Puerto Rico, and any other territory or possession of the United States.

(g) AUTHORIZATION OF APPROPRIATIONS —

(1) IN GENERAL—There are authorized to be appropriated for grants under this section $40,000,000 for each of fiscal years 2004 through 2010.

(2) LIMITATION—Of amounts made available for grants under this section, not less than 50 percent shall be available only for activities specified in paragraph (1) of subsection (b).

Appendix C

SECTION 7. NATIONAL PRISON RAPE REDUCTION COMMISSION.

(a) ESTABLISHMENT—There is established a commission to be known as the National Prison Rape Reduction Commission (in this section referred to as the 'Commission').

(b) MEMBERS —

(1) IN GENERAL—The Commission shall be composed of 9 members, of whom —

(A) 3 shall be appointed by the President;

(B) 2 shall be appointed by the Speaker of the House of Representatives, unless the Speaker is of the same party as the President, in which case 1 shall be appointed by the Speaker of the House of Representatives and 1 shall be appointed by the minority leader of the House of Representatives;

(C) 1 shall be appointed by the minority leader of the House of Representatives (in addition to any appointment made under subparagraph (B));

(D) 2 shall be appointed by the majority leader of the Senate, unless the majority leader is of the same party as the President, in which case 1 shall be appointed by the majority leader of the Senate and 1 shall be appointed by the minority leader of the Senate; and

(E) 1 member appointed by the minority leader of the Senate (in addition to any appointment made under subparagraph (D)).

(2) PERSONS ELIGIBLE—Each member of the Commission shall be an individual who has knowledge or expertise in matters to be studied by the Commission.

(3) CONSULTATION REQUIRED—The President, the Speaker and minority leader of the House of Representatives, and the majority leader and minority leader of the Senate shall consult with one another prior to the appointment of the members of the Commission to achieve, to the maximum extent possible, fair and equitable representation of various points of view with respect to the matters to be studied by the Commission.

(4) TERM—Each member shall be appointed for the life of the Commission.

(5) TIME FOR INITIAL APPOINTMENTS—The appointment of the members shall be made not later than 60 days after the date of enactment of this Act.

(6) VACANCIES—A vacancy in the Commission shall be filled in the manner in which the original appointment was made, and shall be made not later than 60 days after the date on which the vacancy occurred.

(c) OPERATION —

(1) CHAIRPERSON—Not later than 15 days after appointments of all the members are made, the President shall appoint a chairperson for the Commission from among its members.

275

(2) MEETINGS—The Commission shall meet at the call of the chairperson. The initial meeting of the Commission shall take place not later than 30 days after the initial appointment of the members is completed.

(3) QUORUM—A majority of the members of the Commission shall constitute a quorum to conduct business, but the Commission may establish a lesser quorum for conducting hearings scheduled by the Commission.

(4) RULES—The Commission may establish by majority vote any other rules for the conduct of Commission business, if such rules are not inconsistent with this Act or other applicable law.

(d) COMPREHENSIVE STUDY OF THE IMPACTS OF PRISON RAPE —

(1) IN GENERAL—The Commission shall carry out a comprehensive legal and factual study of the penological, physical, mental, medical, social, and economic impacts of prison rape in the United States on —

(A) Federal, State, and local governments; and

(B) communities and social institutions generally, including individuals, families, and businesses within such communities and social institutions.

(2) MATTERS INCLUDED—The study under paragraph (1) shall include —

(A) a review of existing Federal, State, and local government policies and practices with respect to the prevention, detection, and punishment of prison rape;

(B) an assessment of the relationship between prison rape and prison conditions, and of existing monitoring, regulatory, and enforcement practices that are intended to address any such relationship;

(C) an assessment of pathological or social causes of prison rape;

(D) an assessment of the extent to which the incidence of prison rape contributes to the spread of sexually transmitted diseases and to the transmission of HIV;

(E) an assessment of the characteristics of inmates most likely to commit prison rape and the effectiveness of various types of treatment or programs to reduce such likelihood;

(F) an assessment of the characteristics of inmates most likely to be victims of prison rape and the effectiveness of various types of treatment or programs to reduce such likelihood;

(G) an assessment of the impacts of prison rape on individuals, families, social institutions and the economy generally, including an assessment of the extent to which the incidence of prison rape contributes to recidivism and to increased incidence of sexual assault;

(H) an examination of the feasibility and cost of conducting surveillance, undercover activities, or both, to reduce the incidence of prison rape;

(I) an assessment of the safety and security of prison facilities and the relationship of prison facility construction and design to the incidence of prison rape;

(J) an assessment of the feasibility and cost of any particular proposals for prison reform;

(K) an identification of the need for additional scientific and social science research on the prevalence of prison rape in Federal, State, and local prisons;

(L) an assessment of the general relationship between prison rape and prison violence;

(M) an assessment of the relationship between prison rape and levels of training, supervision, and discipline of prison staff; and

(N) an assessment of existing Federal and State systems for reporting incidents of prison rape, including an assessment of whether existing systems provide an adequate assurance of confidentiality, impartiality and the absence of reprisal.

(3) REPORT —

(A) DISTRIBUTION—Not later than 2 years after the date of the initial meeting of the Commission, the Commission shall submit a report on the study carried out under this subsection to —

(i) the President;

(ii) the Congress;

(iii) the Attorney General;

(iv) the Secretary of Health and Human Services;

(v) the Director of the Federal Bureau of Prisons;

(vi) the chief executive of each State; and

(vii) the head of the department of corrections of each State.

(B) CONTENTS—The report under subparagraph (A) shall include —

(i) the findings and conclusions of the Commission;

(ii) recommended national standards for reducing prison rape;

(iii) recommended protocols for preserving evidence and treating victims of prison rape; and

(iv) a summary of the materials relied on by the Commission in the preparation of the report.

(e) RECOMMENDATIONS —

(1) IN GENERAL—In conjunction with the report submitted under subsection (d)(3), the Commission shall provide the Attorney General and the Secretary of Health and Human Services with recommended national standards for enhancing the detection, prevention, reduction, and punishment of prison rape.

(2) MATTERS INCLUDED—The information provided under paragraph (1) shall include recommended national standards relating to —

(A) the classification and assignment of prisoners, using proven standardized instruments and protocols, in a manner that limits the occurrence of prison rape;

277

(B) the investigation and resolution of rape complaints by responsible prison authorities, local and State police, and Federal and State prosecution authorities;

(C) the preservation of physical and testimonial evidence for use in an investigation of the circumstances relating to the rape;

(D) acute-term trauma care for rape victims, including standards relating to —

(i) the manner and extent of physical examination and treatment to be provided to any rape victim; and

(ii) the manner and extent of any psychological examination, psychiatric care, medication, and mental health counseling to be provided to any rape victim;

(E) referrals for long-term continuity of care for rape victims;

(F) educational and medical testing measures for reducing the incidence of HIV transmission due to prison rape;

(G) post-rape prophylactic medical measures for reducing the incidence of transmission of sexual diseases;

(H) the training of correctional staff sufficient to ensure that they understand and appreciate the significance of prison rape and the necessity of its eradication;

(I) the timely and comprehensive investigation of staff sexual misconduct involving rape or other sexual assault on inmates;

(J) ensuring the confidentiality of prison rape complaints and protecting inmates who make complaints of prison rape;

(K) creating a system for reporting incidents of prison rape that will ensure the confidentiality of prison rape complaints, protect inmates who make prison rape complaints from retaliation, and assure the impartial resolution of prison rape complaints;

(L) data collection and reporting of —

(i) prison rape;

(ii) prison staff sexual misconduct; and

(iii) the resolution of prison rape complaints by prison officials and Federal, State, and local investigation and prosecution authorities; and

(M) such other matters as may reasonably be related to the detection, prevention, reduction, and punishment of prison rape.

(3) LIMITATION—The Commission shall not propose a recommended standard that would impose substantial additional costs compared to the costs presently expended by Federal, State, and local prison authorities.

(f) CONSULTATION WITH ACCREDITATION ORGANIZA-TIONS—In developing recommended national standards for enhancing the detection, prevention, reduction, and punishment of prison rape, the Commission shall consider any standards that have already been developed, or are being developed simultaneously to the deliberations of the Commission. The Commission shall consult with accreditation organizations responsible for the accreditation of Federal, State, local or private prisons, that have developed or are currently developing standards related to prison rape. The Commission will also consult with national associations representing the corrections profession that have developed or are currently developing standards related to prison rape.

(g) HEARINGS —

(1) IN GENERAL—The Commission shall hold public hearings. The Commission may hold such hearings, sit and act at such times and places, take such testimony, and receive such evidence as the Commission considers advisable to carry out its duties under this section.

(2) WITNESS EXPENSES—Witnesses requested to appear before the Commission shall be paid the same fees as are paid to witnesses under section 1821 of title 28, United States Code. The per diem and mileage allowances for witnesses shall be paid from funds appropriated to the Commission.

(h) INFORMATION FROM FEDERAL OR STATE AGENCIES—The Commission may secure directly from any Federal department or agency such information as the Commission considers necessary to carry out its duties under this section. The Commission may request the head of any State or local department or agency to furnish such information to the Commission.

(i) PERSONNEL MATTERS —

(1) TRAVEL EXPENSES—The members of the Commission shall be allowed travel expenses, including per diem in lieu of subsistence, at rates authorized for employees of agencies under subchapter I of chapter 57 of title 5, United States Code, while away from their homes or regular places of business in the performance of service for the Commission.

(2) DETAIL OF FEDERAL EMPLOYEES—With the affirmative vote of 2/3 of the Commission, any Federal Government employee, with the approval of the head of the appropriate Federal agency, may be detailed to the Commission without reimbursement, and such detail shall be without interruption or loss of civil service status, benefits, or privileges.

(3) PROCUREMENT OF TEMPORARY AND INTERMITTENT SERVICES—Upon the request of the Commission, the Attorney General shall provide reasonable and appropriate office space, supplies, and administrative assistance.

(j) CONTRACTS FOR RESEARCH —

(1) NATIONAL INSTITUTE OF JUSTICE—With a 2/3 affirmative vote, the Commission may select nongovernmental researchers and experts to assist the Commission in carrying out its duties under this Act. The National

Institute of Justice shall contract with the researchers and experts selected by the Commission to provide funding in exchange for their services.

(2) OTHER ORGANIZATIONS—Nothing in this subsection shall be construed to limit the ability of the Commission to enter into contracts with other entities or organizations for research necessary to carry out the duties of the Commission under this section.

(k) SUBPOENAS —

(1) ISSUANCE—The Commission may issue subpoenas for the attendance of witnesses and the production of written or other matter.

(2) ENFORCEMENT—In the case of contumacy or refusal to obey a subpoena, the Attorney General may in a Federal court of appropriate jurisdiction obtain an appropriate order to enforce the subpoena.

(3) CONFIDENTIALITY OF DOCUMENTARY EVIDENCE—Documents provided to the Commission pursuant to a subpoena issued under this subsection shall not be released publicly without the affirmative vote of 2/3 of the Commission.

(l) AUTHORIZATION OF APPROPRIATIONS—There are authorized to be appropriated such sums as may be necessary to carry out this section.

(m) TERMINATION—The Commission shall terminate on the date that is 60 days after the date on which the Commission submits the reports required by this section.

(n) EXEMPTION—The Commission shall be exempt from the Federal Advisory Committee Act.

SECTION 8. ADOPTION AND EFFECT OF NATIONAL STANDARDS.

(a) PUBLICATION OF PROPOSED STANDARDS —

(1) FINAL RULE—Not later than 1 year after receiving the report specified in section 7(d)(3), the Attorney General shall publish a final rule adopting national standards for the detection, prevention, reduction, and punishment of prison rape.

(2) INDEPENDENT JUDGMENT—The standards referred to in paragraph (1) shall be based upon the independent judgment of the Attorney General, after giving due consideration to the recommended national standards provided by the Commission under section 7(e), and being informed by such data, opinions, and proposals that the Attorney General determines to be appropriate to consider.

(3) LIMITATION—The Attorney General shall not establish a national standard under this section that would impose substantial additional costs compared to the costs presently expended by Federal, State, and local prison authorities. The Attorney General may, however, provide a list of improvements for consideration by correctional facilities.

Appendix C

(4) TRANSMISSION TO STATES—Within 90 days of publishing the final rule under paragraph (1), the Attorney General shall transmit the national standards adopted under such paragraph to the chief executive of each State, the head of the department of corrections of each State, and to the appropriate authorities in those units of local government who oversee operations in one or more prisons.

(b) APPLICABILITY TO FEDERAL BUREAU OF PRISONS—The national standards referred to in subsection (a) shall apply to the Federal Bureau of Prisons immediately upon adoption of the final rule under subsection (a)(4).

(c) ELIGIBILITY FOR FEDERAL FUNDS —

(1) COVERED PROGRAMS —

(A) IN GENERAL—For purposes of this subsection, a grant program is covered by this subsection if, and only if —

(i) the program is carried out by or under the authority of the Attorney General; and

(ii) the program may provide amounts to States for prison purposes.

(B) LIST—For each fiscal year, the Attorney General shall prepare a list identifying each program that meets the criteria of subparagraph (A) and provide that list to each State.

(2) ADOPTION OF NATIONAL STANDARDS—For each fiscal year, any amount that a State would otherwise receive for prison purposes for that fiscal year under a grant program covered by this subsection shall be reduced by 5 percent, unless the chief executive of the State submits to the Attorney General —

(A) a certification that the State has adopted, and is in full compliance with, the national standards described in section 8(a); or

(B) an assurance that not less than 5 percent of such amount shall be used only for the purpose of enabling the State to adopt, and achieve full compliance with, those national standards, so as to ensure that a certification under subparagraph (A) may be submitted in future years.

(3) REPORT ON NONCOMPLIANCE—Not later than September 30 of each year, the Attorney General shall publish a report listing each grantee that is not in compliance with the national standards adopted pursuant to section 8(a).

(4) COOPERATION WITH SURVEY—For each fiscal year, any amount that a State receives for that fiscal year under a grant program covered by this subsection shall not be used for prison purposes (and shall be returned to the grant program if no other authorized use is available), unless the chief executive of the State submits to the Attorney General a certification that neither the State, nor any political subdivision or unit of local government within the State, is listed in a report issued by the Attorney General pursuant to section 4(c)(2)(C).

Prisons

(5) REDISTRIBUTION OF AMOUNTS—Amounts under a grant program not granted by reason of a reduction under paragraph (2), or returned by reason of the prohibition in paragraph (4), shall be granted to one or more entities not subject to such reduction or such prohibition, subject to the other laws governing that program.

(6) IMPLEMENTATION—The Attorney General shall establish procedures to implement this subsection, including procedures for effectively applying this subsection to discretionary grant programs.

(7) EFFECTIVE DATE —

(A) REQUIREMENT OF ADOPTION OF STANDARDS—The first grants to which paragraph (2) applies are grants for the second fiscal year beginning after the date on which the national standards under section 8(a) are finalized.

(B) REQUIREMENT FOR COOPERATION—The first grants to which paragraph (4) applies are grants for the fiscal year beginning after the date of the enactment of this Act.

SECTION 9. REQUIREMENT THAT ACCREDITATION ORGANIZATIONS ADOPT ACCREDITATION STANDARDS.

(a) ELIGIBILITY FOR FEDERAL GRANTS—Notwithstanding any other provision of law, an organization responsible for the accreditation of Federal, State, local, or private prisons, jails, or other penal facilities may not receive any new Federal grants during any period in which such organization fails to meet any of the requirements of subsection (b).

(b) REQUIREMENTS—To be eligible to receive Federal grants, an accreditation organization referred to in subsection (a) must meet the following requirements:

(1) At all times after 90 days after the date of enactment of this Act, the organization shall have in effect, for each facility that it is responsible for accrediting, accreditation standards for the detection, prevention, reduction, and punishment of prison rape.

(2) At all times after 1 year after the date of the adoption of the final rule under section 8(a)(4), the organization shall, in addition to any other such standards that it may promulgate relevant to the detection, prevention, reduction, and punishment of prison rape, adopt accreditation standards consistent with the national standards adopted pursuant to such final rule.

SECTION 10. DEFINITIONS.

In this Act, the following definitions shall apply:

(1) CARNAL KNOWLEDGE— The term 'carnal knowledge' means contact between the penis and the vulva or the penis and the anus, including penetration of any sort, however slight.

(2) INMATE—The term 'inmate' means any person incarcerated or detained in any facility who is accused of, convicted of, sentenced for, or adju-

dicated delinquent for, violations of criminal law or the terms and conditions of parole, probation, pretrial release, or diversionary program.

(3) JAIL—The term 'jail' means a confinement facility of a Federal, State, or local law enforcement agency to hold —

(A) persons pending adjudication of criminal charges; or

(B) persons committed to confinement after adjudication of criminal charges for sentences of 1 year or less.

(4) HIV—The term 'HIV' means the human immunodeficiency virus.

(5) ORAL SODOMY—The term 'oral sodomy' means contact between the mouth and the penis, the mouth and the vulva, or the mouth and the anus.

(6) POLICE LOCKUP—The term 'police lockup' means a temporary holding facility of a Federal, State, or local law enforcement agency to hold —

(A) inmates pending bail or transport to jail;

(B) inebriates until ready for release; or

(C) juveniles pending parental custody or shelter placement.

(7) PRISON—The term 'prison' means any confinement facility of a Federal, State, or local government, whether administered by such government or by a private organization on behalf of such government, and includes —

(A) any local jail or police lockup; and

(B) any juvenile facility used for the custody or care of juvenile inmates.

(8) PRISON RAPE—The term 'prison rape' includes the rape of an inmate in the actual or constructive control of prison officials.

(9) RAPE—The term 'rape' means —

(A) the carnal knowledge, oral sodomy, sexual assault with an object, or sexual fondling of a person, forcibly or against that person's will;

(B) the carnal knowledge, oral sodomy, sexual assault with an object, or sexual fondling of a person not forcibly or against the person's will, where the victim is incapable of giving consent because of his or her youth or his or her temporary or permanent mental or physical incapacity; or

(C) the carnal knowledge, oral sodomy, sexual assault with an object, or sexual fondling of a person achieved through the exploitation of the fear or threat of physical violence or bodily injury.

(10) SEXUAL ASSAULT WITH AN OBJECT—The term 'sexual assault with an object' means the use of any hand, finger, object, or other instrument to penetrate, however slightly, the genital or anal opening of the body of another person.

(11) SEXUAL FONDLING—The term 'sexual fondling' means the touching of the private body parts of another person (including the genitalia, anus, groin, breast, inner thigh, or buttocks) for the purpose of sexual gratification.

(12) EXCLUSIONS—The terms and conditions described in paragraphs (9) and (10) shall not apply to —

(A) custodial or medical personnel gathering physical evidence, or engaged in other legitimate medical treatment, in the course of investigating prison rape;

(B) the use of a health care provider's hands or fingers or the use of medical devices in the course of appropriate medical treatment unrelated to prison rape; or

(C) the use of a health care provider's hands or fingers and the use of instruments to perform body cavity searches in order to maintain security and safety within the prison or detention facility, provided that the search is conducted in a manner consistent with constitutional requirements.

APPENDIX D

THE GENEVA CONVENTION ON PRISONERS OF WAR

There are four Geneva Conventions, signed on August 12, 1949, by the United States and other countries that are parties to the conventions. Convention I established the protections for members of armed forces who become wounded or sick. Convention II expanded those protections to wounded, sick, and shipwrecked members of naval forces. Convention III listed the rights of prisoners of war. Convention IV outlined the protections afforded to civilians during times of war. The following is an abridged version of Convention III, which governs the treatment of prisoners of war.

CONVENTION III

Relative to the Treatment of Prisoners of War, Geneva, 12 August 1949.

Preamble

The undersigned Plenipotentiaries of the Governments represented at the Diplomatic Conference held at Geneva from April 21 to August 12, 1949, for the purpose of revising the Convention concluded at Geneva on July 27, 1929, relative to the Treatment of Prisoners of War, have agreed as follows:

Part I. General Provisions

Article 1. The High Contracting Parties undertake to respect and to ensure respect for the present Convention in all circumstances.

Article 2. In addition to the provisions which shall be implemented in peace time, the present Convention shall apply to all cases of declared war or of any other armed conflict which may arise between two or more of the High Contracting Parties, even if the state of war is not recognized by one of them.

Prisons

The Convention shall also apply to all cases of partial or total occupation of the territory of a High Contracting Party, even if the said occupation meets with no armed resistance.

Although one of the Powers in conflict may not be a party to the present Convention, the Powers who are parties thereto shall remain bound by it in their mutual relations. They shall furthermore be bound by the Convention in relation to the said Power, if the latter accepts and applies the provisions thereof.

Article 3. In the case of armed conflict not of an international character occurring in the territory of one of the High Contracting Parties, each Party to the conflict shall be bound to apply, as a minimum, the following provisions: (1) Persons taking no active part in the hostilities, including members of armed forces who have laid down their arms and those placed hors de combat by sickness, wounds, detention, or any other cause, shall in all circumstances be treated humanely, without any adverse distinction founded on race, color, religion or faith, sex, birth or wealth, or any other similar criteria. To this end the following acts are and shall remain prohibited at any time and in any place whatsoever with respect to the above-mentioned persons: (a) violence to life and person, in particular murder of all kinds, mutilation, cruel treatment and torture; (b) taking of hostages; (c) outrages upon personal dignity, in particular, humiliating and degrading treatment; (d) the passing of sentences and the carrying out of executions without previous judgment pronounced by a regularly constituted court affording all the judicial guarantees which are recognized as indispensable by civilized peoples. (2) The wounded and sick shall be collected and cared for. An impartial humanitarian body, such as the International Committee of the Red Cross, may offer its services to the Parties to the conflict.

The Parties to the conflict should further endeavor to bring into force, by means of special agreements, all or part of the other provisions of the present Convention.

The application of the preceding provisions shall not affect the legal status of the Parties to the conflict.

Article 4. A. Prisoners of war, in the sense of the present Convention, are persons belonging to one of the following categories, who have fallen into the power of the enemy:

(1) Members of the armed forces of a Party to the conflict, as well as members of militias or volunteer corps forming part of such armed forces.

(2) Members of other militias and members of other volunteer corps, including those of organized resistance movements, belonging to a Party to the conflict and operating in or outside their own territory, even if this territory is occupied, provided that such militias or volunteer corps, including

such organized resistance movements, fulfil the following conditions: (a) that of being commanded by a person responsible for his subordinates; (b) that of having a fixed distinctive sign recognizable at a distance; (c) that of carrying arms openly; (d) that of conducting their operations in accordance with the laws and customs of war.

(3) Members of regular armed forces who profess allegiance to a government or an authority not recognized by the Detaining Power.

(4) Persons who accompany the armed forces without actually being members thereof, such as civilian members of military aircraft crews, war correspondents, supply contractors, members of labor units or of services responsible for the welfare of the armed forces, provided that they have received authorization, from the armed forces which they accompany, who shall provide them for that purpose with an identity card similar to the annexed model.

(5) Members of crews, including masters, pilots and apprentices, of the merchant marine and the crews of civil aircraft of the Parties to the conflict, who do not benefit by more favorable treatment under any other provisions of international law.

(6) Inhabitants of a non-occupied territory, who on the approach of the enemy spontaneously take up arms to resist the invading forces, without having had time to form themselves into regular armed units, provided they carry arms openly and respect the laws and customs of war.

B. The following shall likewise be treated as prisoners of war under the present Convention: (1) Persons belonging, or having belonged, to the armed forces of the occupied country, if the occupying Power considers it necessary by reason of such allegiance to intern them, even though it has originally liberated them while hostilities were going on outside the territory it occupies, in particular where such persons have made an unsuccessful attempt to rejoin the armed forces to which they belong and which are engaged in combat, or where they fail to comply with a summons made to them with a view to internment.

(2) The persons belonging to one of the categories enumerated in the present Article, who have been received by neutral or non-belligerent Powers on their territory and whom these Powers are required to intern under international law, without prejudice to any more favorable treatment which these Powers may choose to give and with the exception of Articles 8, 10, 15, 30, fifth paragraph, 58–67, 92, 126 and, where diplomatic relations exist between the Parties to the conflict and the neutral or non-belligerent Power concerned, those Articles concerning the Protecting Power. Where such diplomatic relations exist, the Parties to a conflict on whom these persons depend shall be allowed to perform towards them the functions of a Protecting Power as provided in the present Convention, without prejudice to

the functions which these Parties normally exercise in conformity with diplomatic and consular usage and treaties.

C. This Article shall in no way affect the status of medical personnel and chaplains as provided for in Article 33 of the present Convention.

Article 5. The present Convention shall apply to the persons referred to in Article 4 from the time they fall into the power of the enemy and until their final release and repatriation.

Should any doubt arise as to whether persons, having committed a belligerent act and having fallen into the hands of the enemy, belong to any of the categories enumerated in Article 4, such persons shall enjoy the protection of the present Convention until such time as their status has been determined by a competent tribunal.

Article 6. In addition to the agreements expressly provided for . . . the High Contracting Parties may conclude other special agreements for all matters concerning which they may deem it suitable to make separate provision. No special agreement shall adversely affect the situation of prisoners of war, as defined by the present Convention, nor restrict the rights which it confers upon them.

Prisoners of war shall continue to have the benefit of such agreements as long as the Convention is applicable to them, except where express provisions to the contrary are contained in the aforesaid or in subsequent agreements, or where more favorable measures have been taken with regard to them by one or other of the Parties to the conflict.

Article 7. Prisoners of war may in no circumstances renounce in part or in entirety the rights secured to them by the present Convention, and by the special agreements referred to in the foregoing Article, if such there be.

Article 8. The present Convention shall be applied with the cooperation and under the scrutiny of the Protecting Powers whose duty it is to safeguard the interests of the Parties to the conflict. For this purpose, the Protecting Powers may appoint, apart from their diplomatic or consular staff, delegates from amongst their own nationals or the nationals of other neutral Powers. The said delegates shall be subject to the approval of the Power with which they are to carry out their duties.

The Parties to the conflict shall facilitate to the greatest extent possible the task of the representatives or delegates of the Protecting Powers.

The representatives or delegates of the Protecting Powers shall not in any case exceed their mission under the present Convention. They shall, in particular, take account of the imperative necessities of security of the State wherein they carry out their duties.

Article 9. The provisions of the present Convention constitute no obstacle to the humanitarian activities which the International Committee of the Red Cross or any other impartial humanitarian organization may, subject to the consent of the Parties to the conflict concerned, undertake for the protection of prisoners of war and for their relief.

Article 10. The High Contracting Parties may at any time agree to entrust to an organization which offers all guarantees of impartiality and efficacy the duties incumbent on the Protecting Powers by virtue of the present Convention.

When prisoners of war do not benefit or cease to benefit, no matter for what reason, by the activities of a Protecting Power or of an organization provided for in the first paragraph above, the Detaining Power shall request a neutral State, or such an organization, to undertake the functions performed under the present Convention by a Protecting Power designated by the Parties to a conflict.

If protection cannot be arranged accordingly, the Detaining Power shall request or shall accept, subject to the provisions of this Article, the offer of the services of a humanitarian organization, such as the International Committee of the Red Cross to assume the humanitarian functions performed by Protecting Powers under the present Convention.

Any neutral Power or any organization invited by the Power concerned or offering itself for these purposes, shall be required to act with a sense of responsibility towards the Party to the conflict on which persons protected by the present Convention depend, and shall be required to furnish sufficient assurances that it is in a position to undertake the appropriate functions and to discharge them impartially.

No derogation from the preceding provisions shall be made by special agreements between Powers one of which is restricted, even temporarily, in its freedom to negotiate with the other Power or its allies by reason of military events, more particularly where the whole, or a substantial part, of the territory of the said Power is occupied.

Whenever in the present Convention mention is made of a Protecting Power, such mention applies to substitute organizations in the sense of the present Article.

Article 11. In cases where they deem it advisable in the interest of protected persons, particularly in cases of disagreement between the Parties to the conflict as to the application or interpretation of the provisions of the present Convention, the Protecting Powers shall lend their good offices with a view to settling the disagreement.

For this purpose, each of the Protecting Powers may, either at the invitation of one Party or on its own initiative, propose to the Parties to the conflict a meeting of their representatives, and in particular of the authorities responsible for prisoners of war, possibly on neutral territory suitably chosen. The Parties to the conflict shall be bound to give effect to the proposals made to them for this purpose. The Protecting Powers may, if necessary, propose for approval by the Parties to the conflict a person belonging to a neutral Power, or delegated by the International Committee of the Red Cross, who shall be invited to take part in such a meeting.

Part II. General Protection of Prisoners of War

Article 12. Prisoners of war are in the hands of the enemy Power, but not of the individuals or military units who have captured them. Irrespective of the individual responsibilities that may exist, the Detaining Power is responsible for the treatment given them.

Prisoners of war may only be transferred by the Detaining Power to a Power which is a party to the Convention and after the Detaining Power has satisfied itself of the willingness and ability of such transferee Power to apply the Convention. When prisoners of war are transferred under such circumstances, responsibility for the application of the Convention rests on the Power accepting them while they are in its custody.

Nevertheless, if that Power fails to carry out the provisions of the Convention in any important respect, the Power by whom the prisoners of war were transferred shall, upon being notified by the Protecting Power, take effective measures to correct the situation or shall request the return of the prisoners of war. Such requests must be complied with.

Article 13. Prisoners of war must at all times be humanely treated. Any unlawful act or omission by the Detaining Power causing death or seriously endangering the health of a prisoner of war in its custody is prohibited, and will be regarded as a serious breach of the present Convention. In particular, no prisoner of war may be subjected to physical mutilation or to medical or scientific experiments of any kind which are not justified by the medical, dental or hospital treatment of the prisoner concerned and carried out in his interest.

Likewise, prisoners of war must at all times be protected, particularly against acts of violence or intimidation and against insults and public curiosity.

Measures of reprisal against prisoners of war are prohibited.

Article 14. Prisoners of war are entitled in all circumstances to respect for their persons and their honor.

Women shall be treated with all the regard due to their sex and shall in all cases benefit by treatment as favorable as that granted to men.

Prisoners of war shall retain the full civil capacity which they enjoyed at the time of their capture. The Detaining Power may not restrict the exercise, either within or without its own territory, of the rights such capacity confers except in so far as the captivity requires.

Article 15. The Power detaining prisoners of war shall be bound to provide free of charge for their maintenance and for the medical attention required by their state of health.

Appendix D

Article 16. Taking into consideration the provisions of the present Convention relating to rank and sex, and subject to any privileged treatment which may be accorded to them by reason of their state of health, age or professional qualifications, all prisoners of war shall be treated alike by the Detaining Power, without any adverse distinction based on race, nationality, religious belief or political opinions, or any other distinction founded on similar criteria.

Part III. Captivity

Section 1. Beginning of Captivity

Article 17. Every prisoner of war, when questioned on the subject, is bound to give only his surname, first names and rank, date of birth, and army, regimental, personal or serial number, or failing this, equivalent information.

If he willfully infringes this rule, he may render himself liable to a restriction of the privileges accorded to his rank or status.

Each Party to a conflict is required to furnish the persons under its jurisdiction who are liable to become prisoners of war, with an identity card showing the owner's surname, first names, rank, army, regimental, personal or serial number or equivalent information, and date of birth. The identity card may, furthermore, bear the signature or the fingerprints, or both, of the owner, and may bear, as well, any other information the Party to the conflict may wish to add concerning persons belonging to its armed forces. As far as possible the card shall measure 6.5 × 10 cm. and shall be issued in duplicate. The identity card shall be shown by the prisoner of war upon demand, but may in no case be taken away from him.

No physical or mental torture, nor any other form of coercion, may be inflicted on prisoners of war to secure from them information of any kind whatever. Prisoners of war who refuse to answer may not be threatened, insulted, or exposed to unpleasant or disadvantageous treatment of any kind.

Prisoners of war who, owing to their physical or mental condition, are unable to state their identity, shall be handed over to the medical service. The identity of such prisoners shall be established by all possible means, subject to the provisions of the preceding paragraph.

The questioning of prisoners of war shall be carried out in a language which they understand.

Article 18. All effects and articles of personal use, except arms, horses, military equipment and military documents, shall remain in the possession of prisoners of war, likewise their metal helmets and gas masks and like articles issued for personal protection. Effects and articles used for their clothing or feeding shall likewise remain in their possession, even if such effects and articles belong to their regulation military equipment.

291

Prisons

At no time should prisoners of war be without identity documents. The Detaining Power shall supply such documents to prisoners of war who possess none.

Badges of rank and nationality, decorations and articles having above all a personal or sentimental value may not be taken from prisoners of war.

Sums of money carried by prisoners of war may not be taken away from them except by order of an officer, and after the amount and particulars of the owner have been recorded in a special register and an itemized receipt has been given, legibly inscribed with the name, rank and unit of the person issuing the said receipt. Sums in the currency of the Detaining Power, or which are changed into such currency at the prisoner's request, shall be placed to the credit of the prisoner's account as provided in Article 64.

The Detaining Power may withdraw articles of value from prisoners of war only for reasons of security; when such articles are withdrawn, the procedure laid down for sums of money impounded shall apply.

Such objects, likewise sums taken away in any currency other than that of the Detaining Power and the conversion of which has not been asked for by the owners, shall be kept in the custody of the Detaining Power and shall be returned in their initial shape to prisoners of war at the end of their captivity.

Article 19. Prisoners of war shall be evacuated, as soon as possible after their capture, to camps situated in an area far enough from the combat zone for them to be out of danger.

Only those prisoners of war who, owing to wounds or sickness, would run greater risks by being evacuated than by remaining where they are, may be temporarily kept back in a danger zone.

Prisoners of war shall not be unnecessarily exposed to danger while awaiting evacuation from a fighting zone.

Article 20. The evacuation of prisoners of war shall always be effected humanely and in conditions similar to those for the forces of the Detaining Power in their changes of station.

The Detaining Power shall supply prisoners of war who are being evacuated with sufficient food and potable water, and with the necessary clothing and medical attention. The Detaining Power shall take all suitable precautions to ensure their safety during evacuation, and shall establish as soon as possible a list of the prisoners of war who are evacuated.

If prisoners of war must, during evacuation, pass through transit camps, their stay in such camps shall be as brief as possible.

Section II. Internment of Prisoners of War

Chapter I. General Observations

Article 21. The Detaining Power may subject prisoners of war to internment. It may impose on them the obligation of not leaving, beyond certain limits, the camp where they are interned, or if the said camp is fenced in, of not going outside its perimeter. Subject to the provisions of the present Convention relative to penal and disciplinary sanctions, prisoners of war may not be held in close confinement except where necessary to safeguard their health and then only during the continuation of the circumstances which make such confinement necessary.

Prisoners of war may be partially or wholly released on parole or promise, in so far as is allowed by the laws of the Power on which they depend. Such measures shall be taken particularly in cases where this may contribute to the improvement of their state of health. No prisoner of war shall be compelled to accept liberty on parole or promise.

Upon the outbreak of hostilities, each Party to the conflict shall notify the adverse Party of the laws and regulations allowing or forbidding its own nationals to accept liberty on parole or promise. Prisoners of war who are paroled or who have given their promise in conformity with the laws and regulations so notified, are bound on their personal honor scrupulously to fulfil, both towards the Power on which they depend and towards the Power which has captured them, the engagements of their paroles or promises. In such cases, the Power on which they depend is bound neither to require nor to accept from them any service incompatible with the parole or promise given.

Article 22. Prisoners of war may be interned only in premises located on land and affording every guarantee of hygiene and healthfulness. Except in particular cases which are justified by the interest of the prisoners themselves, they shall not be interned in penitentiaries.

Prisoners of war interned in unhealthy areas, or where the climate is injurious for them, shall be removed as soon as possible to a more favorable climate.

The Detaining Power shall assemble prisoners of war in camps or camp compounds according to their nationality, language and customs, provided that such prisoners shall not be separated from prisoners of war belonging to the armed forces with which they were serving at the time of their capture, except with their consent.

Article 23. No prisoner of war may at any time be sent to, or detained in areas where he may be exposed to the fire of the combat zone, nor may his presence be used to render certain points or areas immune from military operations.

Prisoners of war shall have shelters against air bombardment and other hazards of war, to the same extent as the local civilian population. With the exception of those engaged in the protection of their quarters against the aforesaid hazards, they may enter such shelters as soon as possible after the giving of the alarm. Any other protective measure taken in favor of the population shall also apply to them.

Detaining Powers shall give the Powers concerned, through the intermediary of the Protecting Powers, all useful information regarding the geographical location of prisoner of war camps.

Whenever military considerations permit, prisoner of war camps shall be indicated in the day-time by the letters PW or PG, placed so as to be clearly visible from the air. The Powers concerned may, however, agree upon any other system of marking. Only prisoner of war camps shall be marked as such.

Article 24. Transit or screening camps of a permanent kind shall be fitted out under conditions similar to those described in the present Section, and the prisoners therein shall have the same treatment as in other camps.

Chapter II. Quarters, Food and Clothing of Prisoners of War

Article 25. Prisoners of war shall be quartered under conditions as favorable as those for the forces of the Detaining Power who are billeted in the same area. The said conditions shall make allowance for the habits and customs of the prisoners and shall in no case be prejudicial to their health.

The foregoing provisions shall apply in particular to the dormitories of prisoners of war as regards both total surface and minimum cubic space, and the general installations, bedding and blankets.

The premises provided for the use of prisoners of war individually or collectively, shall be entirely protected from dampness and adequately heated and lighted, in particular between dusk and lights out. All precautions must be taken against the danger of fire.

In any camps in which women prisoners of war, as well as men, are accommodated, separate dormitories shall be provided for them.

Article 26. The basic daily food rations shall be sufficient in quantity, quality and variety to keep prisoners of war in good health and to prevent loss of weight or the development of nutritional deficiencies. Account shall also be taken of the habitual diet of the prisoners.

The Detaining Power shall supply prisoners of war who work with such additional rations as are necessary for the labor on which they are employed.

Sufficient drinking water shall be supplied to prisoners of war. The use of tobacco shall be permitted.

Prisoners of war shall, as far as possible, be associated with the preparation of their meals; they may be employed for that purpose in the kitchens. Furthermore, they shall be given the means of preparing, themselves, the additional food in their possession.

Adequate premises shall be provided for messing.

Collective disciplinary measures affecting food are prohibited.

Article 27. Clothing, underwear and footwear shall be supplied to prisoners of war in sufficient quantities by the Detaining Power, which shall make allowance for the climate of the region where the prisoners are detained. Uniforms of enemy armed forces captured by the Detaining Power should, if suitable for the climate, be made available to clothe prisoners of war.

The regular replacement and repair of the above articles shall be assured by the Detaining Power. In addition, prisoners of war who work shall receive appropriate clothing, wherever the nature of the work demands.

Article 28. Canteens shall be installed in all camps, where prisoners of war may procure foodstuffs, soap and tobacco and ordinary articles in daily use. The tariff shall never be in excess of local market prices.

The profits made by camp canteens shall be used for the benefit of the prisoners; a special fund shall be created for this purpose. The prisoners' representative shall have the right to collaborate in the management of the canteen and of this fund.

When a camp is closed down, the credit balance of the special fund shall be handed to an international welfare organization, to be employed for the benefit of prisoners of war of the same nationality as those who have contributed to the fund. In case of a general repatriation, such profits shall be kept by the Detaining Power, subject to any agreement to the contrary between the Powers concerned.

Chapter III. Hygiene and Medical Attention

Article 29. The Detaining Power shall be bound to take all sanitary measures necessary to ensure the cleanliness and healthfulness of camps and to prevent epidemics.

Prisoners of war shall have for their use, day and night, conveniences which conform to the rules of hygiene and are maintained in a constant state of cleanliness. In any camps in which women prisoners of war are accommodated, separate conveniences shall be provided for them.

Also, apart from the baths and showers with which the camps shall be furnished prisoners of war shall be provided with sufficient water and soap for their personal toilet and for washing their personal laundry; the necessary installations, facilities and time shall be granted them for that purpose.

Article 30. Every camp shall have an adequate infirmary where prisoners of war may have the attention they require, as well as appropriate diet. Isolation wards shall, if necessary, be set aside for cases of contagious or mental disease.

Prisoners of war suffering from serious disease, or whose condition necessitates special treatment, a surgical operation or hospital care, must be admitted to any military or civilian medical unit where such treatment can be given, even if their repatriation is contemplated in the near future. Special facilities shall be afforded for the care to be given to the disabled, in particular to the blind, and for their. rehabilitation, pending repatriation.

Prisons

Prisoners of war shall have the attention, preferably, of medical personnel of the Power on which they depend and, if possible, of their nationality.

Prisoners of war may not be prevented from presenting themselves to the medical authorities for examination. The detaining authorities shall, upon request, issue to every prisoner who has undergone treatment, an official certificate indicating the nature of his illness or injury, and the duration and kind of treatment received. A duplicate of this certificate shall be forwarded to the Central Prisoners of War Agency.

The costs of treatment, including those of any apparatus necessary for the maintenance of prisoners of war in good health, particularly dentures and other artificial appliances, and spectacles, shall be borne by the Detaining Power.

Article 31. Medical inspections of prisoners of war shall be held at least once a month. They shall include the checking and the recording of the weight of each prisoner of war.

Their purpose shall be, in particular, to supervise the general state of health, nutrition and cleanliness of prisoners and to detect contagious diseases, especially tuberculosis, malaria and venereal disease. For this purpose the most efficient methods available shall be employed, e.g. periodic mass miniature radiography for the early detection of tuberculosis.

Article 32. Prisoners of war who, though not attached to the medical service of their armed forces, are physicians, surgeons, dentists, nurses or medical orderlies, may be required by the Detaining Power to exercise their medical functions in the interests of prisoners of war dependent on the same Power. In that case they shall continue to be prisoners of war, but shall receive the same treatment as corresponding medical personnel retained by the Detaining Power.

INDEX

Locators in **boldface** indicate main topics. Locators followed by *g* indicate glossary entries.
Locators followed by *b* indicate biographical entries. Locators followed
by *c* indicate chronology entries.

Index

Index

Prisons

Index

Index

Index

Prisons

Index

Prisons

Index

3/10 ③ 6/25/69

6/11 ⑥

1/14 ⑦ 12/12

6/17 ⑧ 10/16